Facilitator's Manual

On Course:
Strategies for Creating Success in College and in Life

EIGHTH EDITION

and

STUDY SKILLS PLUS, THIRD EDITION

Skip Downing

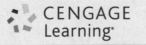

CENGAGE
Learning·

Australia • Brazil • Mexico • Singapore • United Kingdom • United States

ISBN-13: 978-1-305-64767-1

ISBN-10: 1-305-64767-X

Cengage Learning
20 Channel Center Street
Boston, MA 02210
USA

Cengage Learning is a leading provider of customized learning solutions with employees residing in nearly 40 different countries and sales in more than 125 countries around the world. Find your local representative at **www.cengage.com**

Cengage Learning products are represented in Canada by Nelson Education, Ltd.

To learn more about Cengage Learning Solutions, visit **www.cengage.com**

Purchase any of our products at your local college store or at our preferred online store **www.cengagebrain.com**

READ IMPORTANT LICENSE INFORMATION

Printed in the United States of America
Print Number: 02   Print Year: 2016

Contents

Introduction   1

Chapter 1: Getting On Course to Your Success   49

Chapter 2: Accepting Personal Responsibility   75

Chapter 3: Discovering Self-Motivation 99

Chapter 4: Mastering Self-Management 117

Chapter 5: Employing Interdependence 131

Chapter 8: Developing Emotional Intelligence   195

Introduction

Purpose of *On Course*

On Course offers students the opportunity to learn essential skills for creating success in college and in life. The central premise of this text is that **success occurs from the inside out.** Although providing students with information about study skills and campus resources is helpful (and presented extensively in *On Course*), in my experience, what most helps students achieve success (as they define it) is found at a deeper, more personal level that might best be called character.

The goal of *On Course*, then, is to empower students to develop inner qualities that will help them maximize their potential in college . . . and in life. At the center of the success skills addressed in *On Course* is the students' ability to make wise choices in every realm. *On Course* approaches the college experience as a laboratory where students practice making wise choices that support not only their academic success but their personal and professional success as well.

Teaching college students how to make wise choices is an extremely rewarding enterprise, one that generates benefits for all involved. Students benefit because they learn more effective ways to fashion the positive futures they have come to college to create. Colleges and universities benefit because retention, and therefore funding, improves. Instructors benefit because they have the gratifying experience of empowering students to live rich, personally fulfilling lives . . . and that, I suggest, is our greatest mission as educators, regardless of our specific discipline or job description.

Intended Courses for *On Course*

With its emphasis on making wise choices and on writing guided journals, *On Course* is appropriate for use in a variety of courses. It is ideal for use in student success or first-year experience (FYE) courses that seek to help students write more effectively. And *On Course* is perfect for writing courses that seek to help students achieve greater success in college and in life. Let's look more closely at how *On Course* supports the goals of both student success and writing courses.

STUDENT SUCCESS COURSES

On Course is designed for use in first-year seminars, student success courses, personal growth classes, leadership courses, self-awareness courses, college orientations, and all other courses intended to assist students with their personal, academic, and professional success. By reading and writing about proven success strategies, students discover many new options for improving all aspects of their lives. Specifically, *On Course* invites students to learn how they can . . .

- Accept greater personal responsibility
- Discover self-motivation
- Master self-management
- Employ interdependence
- Gain self-awareness
- Adopt lifelong learning
- Develop emotional intelligence
- Believe in themselves
- Learn effective study strategies*
- Develop critical and creative thinking skills*

On Course provides extensive instruction in **study skills**, introducing these skills as part of the CORE Learning System. This natural learning system empowers students to design their own effective approach to learning, one that is adaptable to any subject across the curriculum. In the Study Skills Plus edition of the text, students are exposed to even more learning strategies and additional examples to clarify their use.

WRITING COURSES

On Course is also intended for use in developmental writing courses, first-year composition courses, and courses in personal or journal writing. (This emphasis on writing will come as no surprise to those who know that I taught writing for more than three decades, as well as coordinating my college's student success program.) As students write the 32 guided journal entries in *On Course*, they get extensive practice in the same composition skills that accomplished writers use to create effective prose. The directions of the guided journals shepherd novice writers through three essential elements of the writing process:

1. **Prewriting strategies:** choices for focusing on a topic and generating ideas about it through various heuristic devices
2. **Drafting strategies:** choices for organizing, developing, and expressing the ideas gathered during the prewriting stage
3. **Revising strategies:** choices for improving the writing done during the drafting stage

By practicing this process in each journal entry, students are able to internalize the strategies and language skills necessary for college-level writing. In a community of fellow journal writers, students are motivated to write more effectively as they learn to live more effectively. Additionally, the journal entries in *On Course* give students compelling and motivating subject matter to explore in their formal writing assignments. The Study Skills section (Toolbox for Active Learners) contains instruction in the writing process as well as specific writing skills; thus, writing instructors may wish to assign this content early in their course. At the end of each chapter in this Facilitator's Manual, you'll find suggested writing assignments that will enable students to turn their private journal writing into engaging public writing. These formal writings typically constitute the major part of their course grade.

Unique Benefits of the Text

Regardless of the course in which it is used, *On Course* provides students with the skills to achieve . . .

- **greater success in college and in life.** The success strategies that students learn and apply will improve the outcomes and experiences they create in all areas of their lives. More than two dozen colleges and universities have documented evidence showing the improved retention and academic success of students who completed an *On Course* class. The "One Student's Story" essays in the text illustrate how individual student-authors used *On Course* skills to dramatically improve their lives.
- **increased motivation and class participation.** When students see improved results, they become more involved with their reading, writing, and classroom experiences. As students become personally engaged, they learn firsthand the value of an active learning style, a quality that is emphasized throughout the text and activities in this Facilitator's Manual.
- **improved written and oral communication skills.** Journal writing offers students extensive practice in effective writing skills. Class conversations and presentations stemming from activities in this Facilitator's Manual provide students with extensive practice in expressing their ideas orally to individuals, small groups, and the whole class.
- **stronger critical thinking and problem-solving skills.** Through reading about and practicing critical thinking skills, students become better at solving problems that interfere with their success, as well as constructing and deconstructing persuasive arguments.
- **a sense of empowerment.** By learning to make wise choices that can dramatically improve their lives, students learn to take control of their outcomes and experiences.

Changes in the Eighth Edition

The essence of the first seven editions has been maintained:

1. **Short articles about proven success strategies.** These strategies—from innovators in higher education, psychology, business, sports, personal effectiveness, and more—provide practical ways for students to achieve success in college . . . and beyond.
2. **Guided journal entries.** These writing activities encourage students to become active, responsible learners as they apply the success strategies to their own lives.

3. **Case studies in critical thinking.** Each case study offers students an opportunity to apply their understanding of key success principles (e.g., self-responsibility, self-motivation, and self-management) to real-life situations.

4. **CORE Learning System.** Students read about the latest understanding of how the human brain learns, including three principles that maximize learning. They use these principles and the four components of the CORE Learning System (**C**ollecting, **O**rganizing, **R**ehearsing, and **E**valuating) to design their own personalized learning system, one that will improve their learning in any subject across the curriculum.

5. **Strong coverage of study skills.** *On Course* is offered in two editions—regular and Study Skills Plus. Both options offer students instruction in the essential study skills of reading, note taking, studying, memorizing, test taking, and writing. The Study Skills Plus edition provides a greater number of learning strategies and practice activities than the regular edition.

6. ***On Course* at Work articles.** These articles show students how each *On Course* principle affects their success in the work world. Because many students come to higher education to improve their career opportunities, these articles can motivate them to higher levels of effort.

7. **Money management and stress management strategies.** These sections provide students with effective ways to overcome two obstacles that keep many students from achieving academic success.

8. **Self-Assessments.** A pre-course self-assessment helps students identify areas for improvement, and a post-course self-assessment provides evidence of their growth during the course. Another self-assessment (new to this edition) helps students identify how they prefer to learn, helping them decide which learning strategies will help them maximize their learning and course grades.

9. **College customs.** This feature, presented early in the text, helps first-year students learn and become comfortable with the unique customs and terminology of higher education.

10. **Articles about "Understanding the Culture of Higher Education" and "Respecting Cultural Differences" and accompanying journal entries.** Students are introduced to how culture influences the choices they make and therefore the outcomes and experiences they create. The introduction of culture is designed to help students understand how colleges in general and their college in particular are different from educational cultures they have experienced previously. With this knowledge, they will more quickly feel at home in their new culture. With this foundation about the nature of culture, students are introduced to the realities of a culturally diverse world and the importance of developing attitudes and skills to interact successfully with people who are different from themselves. The goal is to help students move from judging and fearing people who are different to respecting and interacting effectively with them. Throughout the text, students are presented with differing cultural perspectives on success principles and strategies.

11. **Growth and fixed mindsets.** In the chapter on Lifelong Learning, students are introduced to the work of psychologist Carol Dweck and her colleagues, who have documented the importance of developing a growth mindset for success in academia and beyond. Students both learn about the theory and about strategies for developing this important way of perceiving themselves as lifelong learners.

12. **Academic integrity.** Also in the chapter on Lifelong Learning are discussions of cheating and plagiarism, with a case made for both moral and pragmatic reasons to avoid such practices in the culture of higher education.

Enhancing this foundation from past editions are the following new or expanded features in the eighth edition:

1. **College Smart-Start Guide.** Many students get off course in their very first week of college. Author Skip Downing polled nearly 2,000 college and university educators, asking them, "What do you recommend that your students do in the first week of college to get off to a good start?" He then sent the top 20 suggestions back to these educators and asked them to vote for their top 10. The resulting Smart-Start Guide provides students with the top 13 actions recommended by the collective wisdom of this large group of educators. New activities in this Facilitator's Manual engage students in figuring out which of the 13 actions these instructors thought were the most important (versus which ones the students think are the most important). When students follow through on these actions, they will lay a quick and solid foundation for their academic success.

2. **Understanding the Expectations of College and University Educators.** This new essay and related journal entry help students better understand how to succeed in the culture of higher education. In this section, they learn "Eight Key Expectations" and "A Dozen Differences Between High School and College Culture." This information helps students quickly understand which behaviors they can continue doing and which they will need to modify or abandon. When students know what educators expect of them, they are much more likely to make wise choices.

3. **Seven new "One Student's Story" Essays.** A popular feature in earlier editions, these short essays—now numbering 28 in all—are authored by students who used *On Course* strategies to improve the quality of their outcomes and experiences in college. These personal stories show the positive and dramatic results possible when students apply what they learn in this course to overcome challenges that can sabotage success in college. Videos of many of the student-authors reading their essays may be viewed online in the MindTap College Success for *On Course*; some may also be viewed at oncourseworkshop.com (click on the Educator Resources tab). Hearing and seeing that their peers found great value in *On Course* strategies can motivate students to give them a try.

4. **Tech Tips.** Many websites and apps are available to help students achieve greater success. Each chapter now contains a Tech Tips section that provides suggestions for FREE websites and apps that can help students use the soft skills of personal responsibility, self-motivation, self-management, interdependence, self-awareness, lifelong learning, emotional intelligence, and believing in oneself, as well as hard skills related to effective studying.

5. **Discussion about Avoiding Procrastination.** Procrastination is the bane of many students' success. This discussion added to the chapter on self-management helps students understand why procrastination is so tempting and offers specific methods for not putting off until tomorrow what they would benefit from doing today. Included in the discussion is research from Dan Ariely, professor of psychology and behavioral economics at Duke University.

6. **A Sign of Maturity.** This discussion in the chapter about interdependence offers an explanation about the various kinds of relationships in which people engage: dependent, co-dependent, independent, and interdependent. Advantages and disadvantages of each are explained, and students are urged to use college not only to develop independence but also to recognize that there are many occasions when choosing interdependence is a true sign of maturity (as well as improving one's chances of achieving a goal or dream).

7. **Increasing Happiness.** This new article and accompanying journal entry explore the emotional intelligence skill of maximizing happiness. Drawn from the scientific research of positive psychologists, this information presents a number of choices students can make to increase their happiness. This topic has recently gained much interest on college campuses. For example, when a course in positive psychology was first offered at Harvard University, it immediately became the university's most popular course.

8. **Toolbox for Active Learners.** Many *On Course* instructors asked that the study skills be presented in one section (instead of being distributed throughout the book). Unlike texts that present a long menu of study options, *On Course* organizes study skills based on the logical learning steps as identified by research on the brain and effective methods for learning.

9. **Study Skills Self-Assessment.** This edition not only heeds the request of experienced *On Course* instructors to place all study skills in one section, but it also offers a new Study Skills Self-Assessment. Students can take this self-assessment before learning about study skills and discover areas in which they need to improve. At the end of the course, they can retake the test to see where they have grown as learners and where they may need to improve even more. Students have the option of completing the assessment either in the text or online in the MindTap College Success for *On Course*, where it appears in the context of the chapter reading. Students can complete this digital version and print or email their results upon completion.

10. **More Activities Added to This *On Course* Facilitator's Manual.** Additional classroom activities, especially for the new articles and discussions, have been added to help instructors facilitate active, learner-centered classrooms that engage and empower students to succeed.

11. **Conversation with the Author.** Since the first edition of *On Course* more than two decades ago, a number of students have contacted the author with thoughtful questions. This new section includes some of those questions and Skip Downing's answers.

12. **Short Videos to Enrich Classroom Activities and Discussions.** Different types of videos can be found in the MindTap College Success for *On Course* (accessible via login.cengage.com), at oncourseworkshop.com (see "Educator Resources" → Video Gallery), and on the *On Course* YouTube channel at www.youtube.com/user/DowningOnCourse.

Using *On Course*

On Course allows instructors maximum flexibility in its use. It stimulates lively class activities, including discussions of the success strategies articles in the text, in-class readings of students' journal entries, exploration of the writing process, and experiential exercises that actively engage students in processing the concepts they have read and written about. These exercises are described in detail later in this manual. For distance learning, *On Course* now provides all of the materials needed for a valuable online educational experience.

Naturally, you will want to adapt *On Course* to your own style of teaching. In the sections that follow, I offer my thoughts on some of the issues you will certainly consider as you design and deliver your course.

ASSIGNING READINGS, STUDENT JOURNALS, AND OTHER FEATURES

As a guideline, I recommend assigning one article and its companion journal entry for each hour of class time. For the Study Skills Plus edition of *On Course*, I recommend spending two to three hours of class time on each study skills section you choose to assign. For the regular edition of *On Course*, I recommend devoting one to two hours of class time to each study skills section you choose to cover, depending on the needs of your students. Thus, in a course with 45 or more class hours, you will be able to cover most, if not all of the book. Later in this Facilitator's Manual, I provide guidelines for how to adapt *On Course* for classes that meet for fewer than 45 hours.

READING STUDENT JOURNALS

I recommend collecting journals early and often, weekly if possible. I first thumb (or scroll) through students' journals to verify completion of each assigned journal entry and give credit for a job thoroughly done (I call this "Diving Deep"). I skim all journal entries and read thoroughly those entries that catch my interest. This reading gives me a sense of some of the academic and personal issues that each student is facing. In a writing course, I also look for the writing problems with which each student needs help.

Whatever you decide in regard to reading journals, I recommend letting students know your intentions at the outset of the course.

RESPONDING TO STUDENT JOURNALS

Some instructors believe they must comment on everything their students write. Others believe just as strongly that journal writing is a private act and they have no business intruding on this personal monologue.

I find myself falling somewhere in the middle of this debate. If I come across an idea that intrigues me, I write a response: encouragement, compliment, or question. The question I ask most often is: "Can you dive deeper here?" Then I write a couple of questions that would assist the student to do just that, asking for examples, experiences, further explanation, or evidence. I begin many of my questions and requests with "I": *I was wondering if . . . I would love to hear more about . . . I didn't understand . . . I wonder if this has gotten any better for you?* When reading an electronic journal (now my preference), I turn on the "tracking" feature and insert my comments in the margin. I invite students to add a comment or question to my comments, creating a dialogue that can be of great value to the students. This approach obviously is more time consuming and should be entered into with this knowledge.

HELPING STUDENTS WITH PERSONAL PROBLEMS

On rare occasions, a student will reveal in his or her journal a serious personal problem that is beyond my expertise. I refer this student to an appropriate resource for assistance.

However, I suggest that you first talk with the student privately. Express both your caring concern and your lack of training in the area of concern. Ask if the student would like you to connect him or her with someone who is trained to assist with the problem. I have never had a student refuse such a referral. I believe the keys to getting the student to agree to accept help are to (1) demonstrate a genuine caring for the student's welfare and a candid concern about the problem, (2) explain fully why you are recommending the person you want the student to see, and (3) offer to go with the student and introduce him or her to the person.

One last point: Some instructors with no training in counseling feel uncomfortable when encountering a student's personal problems. I felt this way in the past myself. I believed that students' personal lives were none of my business. Today I have a different view. I don't teach subjects; I teach students. I teach them strategies for living rich, personally fulfilling lives. Sometimes the strategies are how to write a compelling essay, and sometimes the strategies are how to be successful in college and in life. Anything that interferes with the success of my students is of concern to me. Some students won't be around to learn my academic subjects if I don't initiate an intervention into their personal problems. The problem will be there whether I read about it or not. But if I get to read about a problem in a student's journal, I have an opportunity to help that student transform a problem into an empowering learning experience.

GRADING

Without lowering my standards even an inch, my intention is to give students as much control over their final grade as possible. I want them to choose the grade they want and then perform the actions necessary to earn that grade. I believe this approach shows students that they are responsible both for what they learn and for the grades they earn. It is also consistent with theories of achievement motivation, which assert that students who expect to do well in a course and set personal goals to do so are more persistent in their academic efforts.

The sample syllabi that appear later in this Introduction offer specific examples of how you might put students in control of earning their grades. Meanwhile, here are some general suggestions for determining student grades:

Journal Entries

I don't believe that the spirit of writing a journal is compatible with grading students' ideas or writing styles, but I do believe in rewarding students for their efforts to explore a topic thoroughly. In my grading system (explained in greater detail later), I award up to 5 points for each journal entry. For entries that are lacking in completeness or quality of response, I award a score between 1 and 4. I award 5 points for each entry that is complete and that demonstrates a commendable effort to explore in depth the issues at hand. For an extraordinary effort that goes above and beyond the expected, I have been known to lose my head and award a 6. After I check journals the first time, I invite students to revise any entries for a higher score; this one-time offer allows them to discover and adjust to my evaluation standards without a penalty to their final grade. It also encourages them to improve the quality of later work.

Quizzes

Occasional quizzes on readings have at least four benefits: (1) They can motivate students to stay up to date on their assignments. (2) They give students immediate feedback about whether they understand a concept that is being explored. (3) They are great practice for what students will face in other classes. (4) Studies have shown that frequent quizzes help students learn some material more thoroughly than students not quizzed. Short-answer quiz questions (true/false, multiple choice, and fill in the blank) appear in this manual at the end of each chapter. Practice quizzes are available for students in each chapter of the MindTap College Success for *On Course*. To access the MindTap, go to login.cengage.com.

Essays

In both a student success course and a writing course, I ask students to transform their personal journal writings into formal public writings. Formal writing assignment topics appear in this manual at the end of each chapter discussion.

You may also want to be on the alert for formal writing assignments that could be motivating for an individual student. For example, during a discussion about preferred ways of learning (Journal Entry 25), one of my students stated that some of her high school teachers had "made" her dislike school. She expressed such outrage at her experience that I encouraged her to write a formal letter to the superintendent of her school district and express her experience, her anger, and her suggestions. (I accepted this assignment as a substitute for another class assignment.) She took me up on my offer and produced her best piece of formal writing for the entire semester. She also demonstrated effective critical thinking and strong emotional intelligence in her letter.

Chapter Tests

A Cognero test bank is available online via login.cengage.com, with LMS (e.g., Blackboard and Angel)-compatible files posted on the Instructor Companion Site (also available through login.cengage.com). There is a test bank for each chapter that allows you to choose from a menu of questions, including true/false, multiple-choice, fill-in-the-blank, matching, and essay. In my courses, I also consider both journals and essays to be take-home tests. I believe that the most valuable examinations are those that not only evaluate a student's knowledge but also give the student an opportunity to apply his or her knowledge in a real-life situation. Whether you prefer giving tests in class or as homework, I recommend using essay questions as well as short answer.

SAMPLE SYLLABI

What follows is my syllabus for a 45-hour student success course conducted over a 15-week semester using the Study Skills Plus (3rd) edition. For this syllabus, I offer two different schedules of assignment. The first is appropriate if you want to weave the soft skills and the hard (study) skills together over much of the semester. The second is appropriate if you want to present the hard (study skills) early in the course followed by the soft skills.

Following that is a syllabus for a 45-hour student success course that uses the regular 8th edition of *On Course*. Next is my syllabus for a 45-hour writing class using the regular 8th edition of *On Course*. Some instructors use my syllabi exactly as they are; others adapt them to their particular needs. Others totally create their own. If you are reading this Facilitator's Manual in book form, please note that these syllabi are available in electronic format within the online version of this Facilitator's Manual on the Instructor Companion Website.

SYLLABUS FOR A STUDENT SUCCESS COURSE:
STUDY SKILLS PLUS 3RD EDITION

Welcome! My goal in this course is to offer you one of the most valuable learning experiences of your entire life. And I need your full cooperation to make it work!

Course Purpose: This course is designed to help you create greater success in college and in life. In the coming weeks, you will learn many proven strategies for creating greater academic, professional, and personal success. We will use guided journal writings to explore these strategies, and as a bonus, you will learn to express yourself more effectively in writing. In addition, we will explore the strategies through classroom activities that are designed to be engaging and enlightening. You may never again have an opportunity quite like this one to discover how to create a rich, personally fulfilling life. I urge you to make the most of this extraordinary opportunity! If you do, you will dramatically change the outcome of your life—for the better!

Course Objectives: In this course, you will learn how to . . .

1. **Take charge of your life.** You will learn how to take greater personal responsibility, gaining more control over the outcomes and experiences that you create both in college and in life.
2. **Increase self-motivation.** You will learn to create greater inner motivation by, among other things, discovering your own personally meaningful goals and dreams.
3. **Improve personal self-management.** You will learn numerous strategies for taking control of your time and energy, allowing you to move more effectively and efficiently toward the accomplishment of your goals and dreams.
4. **Develop interdependence.** You will learn how to develop mutually supportive relationships with people who will help you achieve your goals and dreams as you assist them to achieve theirs.
5. **Increase self-awareness.** You will learn how to understand and revise your self-defeating patterns of behavior, thought, and emotion as well as your unconscious limiting beliefs.
6. **Maximize your learning.** You will learn key research on how the human brain learns. You will apply this knowledge to develop your own learning system, giving you the keys to learning important course content in college as well as becoming a more effective lifelong learner.
7. **Develop emotional intelligence.** You will learn effective strategies for managing your emotional life, decreasing stress while increasing your inner sense of well-being and happiness.
8. **Raise your self-esteem.** You will learn how to develop self-acceptance, self-confidence, self-respect, self-love, and unconditional self-worth.
9. **Write more effectively.** You will learn how to improve your writing skills through the extensive writing practice offered by your guided journal entries.
10. **Improve creative and critical thinking skills.** You will learn how to enhance the thinking skills essential for analyzing and solving problems in your academic, professional, and personal lives. You will also develop reasoning skills that will help you both construct persuasive arguments and deconstruct illogical arguments intended to persuade you to think or act against your own best interest.
11. **Master effective study skills.** You will learn how to raise your grades in college by improving essential skills such as reading, taking notes, studying, memorizing, taking tests and writing essays.
12. **Manage your money.** You will learn helpful techniques for increasing your income (including gaining more financial aid for college) and decreasing your expenses.

Course Supplies:

1. *On Course*, Study Skills Plus, 3rd edition, by Skip Downing
2. String-bound composition notebook or computer journal (with entries emailed to your instructor as attachments and then printed and stored in a three-ring binder)

Method: By reading *On Course* (our textbook), you'll learn empowering strategies that have helped others create great success. By keeping a guided journal, you'll discover how to apply these success strategies to achieve your own goals and dreams. By participating in class activities and focused conversations and by completing a course project, you will further improve your ability to stay on course to your success. When you make these new strategies your own through application, you'll have the ability to dramatically improve the outcome of your life—academically, professionally, and personally.

Course Grades:

	Points
A =	360–400
B =	320–359
C =	280–319
D =	240–279
E =	238 or below

Course Projects:

	Points
1. 15 Quizzes (5 points each)	75
2. 32 Success Journals (5 points each)	160
3. 6 Study Skills Activities: "Do One Different Thing This Week" (15 points each)	90
4. 1 Final Essay	75
Total Possible Points	400

Each of these four components of your grade is explained below.

1. Quizzes (75 Possible Points)

This is a course for students who choose to be successful in college and in life. One of the most important factors of success in any endeavor is consistent and active participation. To encourage and reward your preparation for active participation at every class, 15 unannounced quizzes on the readings will be given. If you have read the assignment and completed your journal entry, you should have no trouble earning the maximum points (5) for each quiz. **No quiz may be made up.**

Great success is created one small step at a time. Each time that you earn your quiz points you take an important step toward your success in this course . . . and in life!

2. Success Journals (160 Possible Points)

Your Success Journals provide an opportunity to explore your thoughts and feelings as you experiment with the success strategies presented in *On Course.* By carefully examining each strategy in your journal, you will discover which ones will assist you to create a rich, personally fulfilling life. Although I will be collecting your journals and looking through them, **write your journal for yourself,** not for me. Your journal entries may occasionally be read by your classmates.

Journal Writings: During this semester, you will write 32 numbered journal entries from our textbook. These entries will be written outside of class. Additionally, you will write occasional lettered journal entries based on class activities. These journal entries will be written in class. At various times, you may have an opportunity to read a journal entry to one or more classmates. **THEREFORE, PLEASE BRING YOUR TEXTBOOK AND JOURNAL TO EVERY CLASS.**

Note: If you wish, you may write the first draft of journal entries on loose sheets of paper, but all journal entries must be written in the composition notebook when it is handed in for evaluation. Or if you choose to write your journal on a computer, you will print hard copies of all entries and bring them to class neatly organized in a three-ring binder. This requirement will assure that none of your entries gets lost. At the end of this semester, you will have your entire journal to keep for years to come. Many students come to regard their personal journal as one of their most valued possessions.

Journal Evaluations: Journals are due weekly. It is not my intention to read every journal entry you write. Instead, I will look through your journal entries to verify the completion of each assignment and to give credit for a job well done. I read occasional journal entries to get a sense of the issues you are working on. With this knowledge, I can be of greater assistance to you this semester. If you want my comment on a specific journal entry, please let me know with a note in your journal.

Journal Points: Each journal entry will be awarded up to 5 points. Thus, all 32 journal entries will be worth a possible total of 160 points. A journal entry will be awarded the maximum of 5 points if it fulfills the following two criteria:

1. The entry is **complete** (all steps in the directions have been responded to), and
2. The entry is **written with high standards** (an obvious attempt has been made to **Dive Deep**).

Grammar, spelling, and punctuation will NOT be factors in awarding points in this journal. You are free to express yourself without concern for Standard English conventions.

3. Study Skills Activities: "Do One Different Thing This Week" (90 Possible Points)

You will complete a Study Skills Activity for the following six topics:

- Reading
- Taking Notes
- Organizing Study Materials
- Rehearsing and Memorizing Study Materials
- Taking Tests
- Writing

The creation of each Study Skills Activity will provide an opportunity to do one different thing for a week, something you have never done before. This experiment will help you determine the most effective way for you to deepen your learning in college and beyond, as well as raising your grades!

Each of your Study Skills Activities can earn up to 15 points; thus, all six plans will be worth a possible total of 90 points. To complete each plan, simply choose one new study skill with which you will experiment, track your choices for a week, and then answer the three questions provided, diving deep to squeeze the most value from your experience.

4. Final Essay (75 Possible Points)

As your final project, you will choose one of the two following topics and write an essay.

OPTION 1: ONE STUDENT'S STORY

In this essay, you will relate the story of how you used a specific *On Course* strategy to overcome an obstacle to your success in college or in life. Use the "One Student's Story" essays in our textbook as models of how to write your story. If your essay is done well, your instructor may submit it to the *On Course* Essay Contest. Winning entries will be published in the next edition of the *On Course* text to inspire future students. Winning entries will also be awarded a $100 prize. Full directions for writing this essay can be found at **oncourseworkshop.com/course-textbook/essay-contest.**

An "A" paper will . . .

1. Explain a specific obstacle the writer faced.
2. Describe the specific *On Course* strategy used to overcome the specific obstacle.
3. Present the outcome of using the specific *On Course* strategy to overcome the specific obstacle the writer faced.
4. Show a commitment to excellence in preparation, including professional appearance and a command of Standard English.

OPTION 2: PERSONAL PHILOSOPHY OF SUCCESS ESSAY

In this essay, you will present your own Personal Philosophy of Success, identifying the *On Course* success principles and strategies that you will use for years to come. This essay is your opportunity to write the script that will keep you on course to a rich, personally fulfilling life!

An "A" paper will . . .

1. Offer the writer's personal definition of success.
2. Demonstrate the writer's careful consideration of three or more *On Course* success principles and strategies that he or she will use to achieve success.
3. Contain extensive and specific support (examples, experiences, evidence, and explanation) for each strategy.
4. Show a commitment to excellence in preparation, including professional appearance and a command of Standard English.

Course Rules for Success

To create the very best environment for supporting your success and the success of your classmates, this course has three important rules. The more challenging these rules are for you, the more value you will experience by adopting them. By choosing to follow these three rules, you are choosing to be successful not only in this course but in your life. These rules will support your success in every goal you pursue!

1. **Show up!** To support my success, I choose to attend every scheduled class period in its entirety.
2. **Do the work!** To support my success, I choose to do my very best work in preparing all of my assignments and hand them in on time.
3. **Participate actively!** To support my success, I choose to stay focused and involved in every class session, offering my best comments, questions, and answers when appropriate.

Schedule #1 of Assignments (15-Week Course)

[NOTE TO INSTRUCTOR: **This Schedule #1 presents the study (hard) skills separately in weeks 1–5, with soft skills subsequently presented separately in Weeks 5–15. If you prefer to weave soft skills and study skills together, use Schedule #2 later in this section or modify the schedule as you prefer. If you use the MindTap College Success for *On Course*, you may present the online content in any order you choose.**]

REMINDER: Fifteen unannounced quizzes will be given. No quizzes may be made up.

The following assignments are due at the first class of the week in which they are due. Please bring your textbook and journal to every class.

Week 1:   **Read** "College Smart-Start Guide" and "Money Matters"

Read "Becoming An Active Learner" in *A Toolbox for Active Learners*. (including self-assessment)

Week 2:   **Read** "Reading" in *A Toolbox for Active Learners*

Do "Reading: Do One Different Thing This Week" Written report due next week

Read "Taking Notes" in *A Toolbox for Active Learners*

Do "Taking Notes: Do One Different Thing This Week" Written report due next week

Week 3:   **Turn in Written Report:** "Reading: Do One Different Thing This Week"

Turn in Written Report: "Taking Notes: Do One Different Thing This Week"

Read "Organizing Study Materials" in *A Toolbox for Active Learners*

Do "Organizing Study Materials: Do One Different Thing This Week" Written report due next week

Read "Rehearsing and Memorizing Study Materials" in *A Toolbox for Active Learners*

Do "Rehearsing and Memorizing Study Materials: Do One Different Thing This Week" Written report due next week

Week 4:   **Turn in Written Report:** "Organizing Study Material: Do One Different Thing This Week"

Turn in Written Report: "Rehearsing and Memorizing Study Material: Do One Different Thing This Week"

Read "Taking Tests" in *A Toolbox for Active Learners*

Do "Taking Tests: Do One Different Thing This Week" Written report due next week

Read "Writing" in *A Toolbox for Active Learners*

Do "Writing: Do One Different Thing This Week" Written report due next week

Week 5:   **Turn in Written Report:** "Taking Tests: Do One Different Thing This Week"

Week 6:   **Turn in Written Report:** "Writing: Do One Different Thing This Week"

Week 7:   **Read/Write** Journal 1: "Understanding the Culture of Higher Education"

Week 8:   **Read/Write** Journal 2: "Understanding the Expectations of College and University Educators"

Read/Write Journal 3: "Understanding Yourself" (including self-assessment)

Read "Soft Skills at Work"

Read/Write Journal 4: "Adopting a Creator Mindset"

Read/Write Journal 5: "Mastering Creator Language"

Read/Write Journal 6: "Making Wise Decisions"

Read "Personal Responsibility at Work"

Read/Write Journal 7: "Believing in Yourself—Change Your Inner Conversation"

Read/Write Journal 8: "Creating Inner Motivation"

Read/Write Journal 9: "Designing a Compelling Life Plan"

Read/Write Journal 10: "Committing to Your Goals and Dreams"

Read "Self-Motivation at Work"

Read/Write Journal 11: "Believing in Yourself—Write a Personal Affirmation"

Week 9:   **Read/Write** Journal 12: "Acting on Purpose"

Read/Write Journal 13: "Creating a Leak-Proof Self-Management System"

Read/Write Journal 14: "Developing Self-Discipline"

Read "Self-Management at Work"

Week 10:   **Read/Write** Journal 15: "Believing in Yourself—Develop Self-Confidence"

Read/Write Journal 16: "Creating a Support System"

Read/Write Journal 17: "Strengthening Relationships with Active Listening"

Week 11:	**Read/Write** Journal 18: "Respecting Cultural Differences"
	Read "Interdependence at Work"
	Read/Write Journal 19: "Believing in Yourself—Be Assertive"
	Read/Write Journal 20: "Recognizing When You Are Off Course"
Week 12:	**Read/Write** Journal 21: "Identifying Your Scripts"
	Read/Write Journal 22: "Rewriting Your Outdated Scripts"
	Read "Self-Awareness at Work"
	Read/Write Journal 23: "Believing in Yourself—Write Your Own Rules"
Week 13:	**Read/Write** Journal 24: "Developing a Learning Orientation to Life"
	Read/Write Journal 25: "Discovering Your Preferred Ways of Learning"
	Read/Write Journal 26: "Employing Critical Thinking"
	Read "Lifelong Learning at Work"
Week 14:	**Read/Write** Journal 27: "Believing in Yourself—Develop Self-Respect"
	Read/Write Journal 28: "Understanding Emotional Intelligence"
	Read/Write Journal 29: "Reducing Stress"
Week 15:	**Read/Write** Journal 30: "Increasing Happiness"
	Read "Emotional Intelligence at Work"
	Read/Write Journal 31: "Believing in Yourself—Develop Self-Acceptance"
	Read/Write Journal 32: "Planning Your Next Steps"
	Turn in Final Essay

Schedule #2 of Assignments (15-Week Course)

[NOTE TO INSTRUCTOR: **This Schedule #2 presents the study (hard) skills simultaneously with soft skills for the first nine weeks. The final six weeks focus exclusively on soft skills. If you prefer to present study skills first by themselves—followed by soft skills—use Schedule #1 above or modify the schedule as you prefer. If you use the MindTap College Success for *On Course*, you may present the online content in any order you choose.**]

REMINDER: Fifteen unannounced quizzes will be given. No quizzes may be made up.

The following assignments are due at the first class of the week in which they are due. Please bring your textbook and journal to every class.

Week 1:	**Read** "College Smart-Start Guide" and "Money Matters"
	Read/Write Journal 1: "Understanding the Culture of Higher Education"
Week 2:	**Read/Write** Journal 2: "Understanding the Expectations of College and University Educators"
	Read/Write Journal 3: "Understanding Yourself" (including self-assessment)
	Read "Soft Skills at Work"
	Read "Becoming An Active Learner" in *A Toolbox for Active Learners*. (including self-assessment)
Week 3:	**Read** "Reading" in *A Toolbox for Active Learners*
	Do "Reading: Do One Different Thing This Week" Written report due next week
	Read/Write Journal 4: "Adopting a Creator Mindset"
	Read/Write Journal 5: "Mastering Creator Language"

Week 4:	**Turn in Written Report:** "Reading: Do One Different Thing This Week"
	Read "Taking Notes" in *A Toolbox for Active Learners*
	Write "Taking Notes: Do One Different Thing This Week" Written report due next week
	Read/Write Journal 6: "Making Wise Decisions"
	Read "Personal Responsibility at Work"
	Read/Write Journal 7: "Believing in Yourself—Change Your Inner Conversation"
Week 5:	**Turn in Written Report:** "Taking Notes: Do One Different Thing This Week"
	Read "Organizing Study Materials" in *A Toolbox for Active Learners*
	Do "Organizing Study Materials: Do One Different Thing This Week" Written report due next week
	Read/Write Journal 8: "Creating Inner Motivation"
	Read/Write Journal 9: "Designing a Compelling Life Plan"
Week 6:	**Turn in Written Report:** "Organizing Study Material: Do One Different Thing This Week"
	Read "Rehearsing and Memorizing Study Materials" in *A Toolbox for Active Learners*
	Do "Rehearsing and Memorizing Study Materials: Do One Different Thing This Week" Written report due next week
	Read/Write Journal 10: "Committing to Your Goals and Dreams"
	Read "Self-Motivation at Work"
	Read/Write Journal 11: "Believing in Yourself—Write a Personal Affirmation"
Week 7:	**Turn in Written Report:** "Rehearsing and Memorizing Study Material: Do One Different Thing This Week"
	Read "Taking Tests" in *A Toolbox for Active Learners*
	Do "Taking Tests: Do One Different Thing This Week" Written report due next week
	Read/Write Journal 12: "Acting on Purpose"
	Read/Write Journal 13: "Creating a Leak-Proof Self-Management System"
Week 8:	**Turn in Written Report:** "Taking Tests: Do One Different Thing This Week"
	Read "Writing" in *A Toolbox for Active Learners*
	Do "Writing: Do One Different Thing This Week" Written report due next week
	Read/Write Journal 14: "Developing Self-Discipline"
	Read "Self-Management at Work"
	Read/Write Journal 15: "Believing in Yourself—Develop Self-Confidence"
Week 9:	**Turn in Written Report:** "Writing: Do One Different Thing This Week"
	Read/Write Journal 16: "Creating a Support System"
	Read/Write Journal 17: "Strengthening Relationships with Active Listening"
	Read/Write Journal 18: "Respecting Cultural Differences"
	Read "Interdependence at Work"
Week 10:	**Read/Write** Journal 19: "Believing in Yourself—Be Assertive"
	Read/Write Journal 20: "Recognizing When You Are Off Course"
	Read/Write Journal 21: "Identifying Your Scripts"
Week 11:	**Read/Write** Journal 22: "Rewriting Your Outdated Scripts"
	Read "Self-Awareness at Work"
	Read/Write Journal 23: "Believing in Yourself—Write Your Own Rules"
	Read/Write Journal 24: "Developing a Learning Orientation to Life"

Week 12:	**Read/Write** Journal 25: "Discovering Your Preferred Ways of Learning"
	Read/Write Journal 26: "Employing Critical Thinking"
	Read "Lifelong Learning at Work"
	Read/Write Journal 27: "Believing in Yourself—Develop Self-Respect"
Week 13:	**Read/Write** Journal 28: "Understanding Emotional Intelligence"
	Read/Write Journal 29: "Reducing Stress"
	Read/Write Journal 30: "Increasing Happiness"
	Read "Emotional Intelligence at Work"
Week 14:	**Read/Write** Journal 31: "Believing in Yourself—Develop Self-Acceptance"
	Read/Write Journal 32: "Planning Your Next Steps"
Week 15:	**Turn in** Final Essay

SYLLABUS FOR A STUDENT SUCCESS COURSE: REGULAR 8TH EDITION

Welcome! My goal in this course is to offer you one of the most valuable learning experiences of your entire life. And I need your full cooperation to make it work!

Course Purpose: This course is designed to help you create greater success in college and in life. In the coming weeks, you will learn many proven strategies for creating greater academic, professional, and personal success. We will use guided journal writings to explore these strategies, and as a bonus, you will learn to express yourself more effectively in writing. In addition, we will explore the strategies through classroom activities that are designed to be engaging and enlightening. You may never again have an opportunity quite like this one to discover how to create a rich, personally fulfilling life. I urge you to make the most of this extraordinary opportunity! If you do, you will dramatically change the outcome of your life—for the better!

Course Objectives: In this course, you will learn how to . . .

1. **Take charge of your life.** You will learn how to take greater personal responsibility, gaining more control over the outcomes and experiences that you create both in college and in life.
2. **Increase self-motivation.** You will learn to create greater inner motivation by, among other things, discovering your own personally meaningful goals and dreams.
3. **Improve personal self-management.** You will learn numerous strategies for taking control of your time and energy, allowing you to move more effectively and efficiently toward the accomplishment of your goals and dreams.
4. **Develop interdependence.** You will learn how to develop mutually supportive relationships with people who will help you achieve your goals and dreams as you assist them to achieve theirs.
5. **Increase self-awareness.** You will learn how to understand and revise your self-defeating patterns of behavior, thought, and emotion as well as your unconscious limiting beliefs.
6. **Maximize your learning.** You will learn key research on how the human brain learns. You will apply this knowledge to develop your own learning system, giving you the keys to learning important course content in college as well as becoming a more effective lifelong learner.
7. **Develop emotional intelligence.** You will learn effective strategies for managing your emotional life, decreasing stress while increasing your inner sense of well-being and happiness.
8. **Raise your self-esteem.** You will learn how to develop self-acceptance, self-confidence, self-respect, self-love, and unconditional self-worth.
9. **Write more effectively.** You will learn how to improve your writing skills through the extensive writing practice offered by your guided journal entries.
10. **Improve creative and critical thinking skills.** You will learn how to enhance the thinking skills essential for analyzing and solving problems in your academic, professional, and personal lives. You will also develop reasoning skills that will help you both construct persuasive arguments and deconstruct illogical arguments intended to persuade you to think or act against your own best interest.
11. **Master effective study skills.** You will learn how to raise your grades in college by improving essential skills such as reading, taking notes, studying, memorizing, taking tests and writing essays.
12. **Manage your money.** You will learn helpful techniques for increasing your income (including gaining more financial aid for college) and decreasing your expenses.

Course Supplies:

1. *On Course*, 8th edition, by Skip Downing
2. String-bound composition notebook or computer journal (with entries emailed to your instructor as attachments and then printed and stored in a three-ring binder)

Method: By reading *On Course* (our textbook), you'll learn empowering strategies that have helped others create great success. By keeping a guided journal, you'll discover how to apply these success strategies to achieve your own goals and dreams. By participating in class activities and focused conversations, and by completing a course project, you will further improve your ability to stay on course to your success. When you make these new strategies your own through application, you'll have the ability to dramatically improve the outcome of your life—academically, professionally, and personally.

Course Grades:

	Points
A =	270–300
B =	240–269
C =	210–239
D =	180–209
E =	179 or below

Course Projects:

	Points
1. 15 Quizzes (5 points each)	75
2. 32 Success Journals (5 points each)	160
3. 1 Final Essay	65
Total Possible Points	300

Each of these four components of your grade is explained below.

1. Quizzes (75 Possible Points)

This is a course for students who choose to be successful in college and in life. One of the most important factors of success in any endeavor is consistent and active participation. To encourage and reward your preparation for active participation at every class, 15 unannounced quizzes on the readings will be given. If you have read the assignment and completed your journal entry, you should have no trouble earning the maximum points (5) for each quiz. **No quiz may be made up.**

Great success is created one small step at a time. Each time that you earn your quiz points you take an important step toward your success in this course . . . and in life!

2. Success Journals (160 Possible Points)

Your Success Journal provides an opportunity to explore your thoughts and feelings as you experiment with the success strategies presented in *On Course*. By carefully examining each strategy in your journal, you will discover which ones will assist you to create a rich, personally fulfilling life. Although I will be collecting your journals and looking through them, **write your journal for yourself,** not for me. Your journal entries may occasionally be read by your classmates.

Journal Writings: During this semester, you will write 32 numbered journal entries from our textbook. These entries will be written outside of class. Additionally, you will write occasional lettered journal entries based on class exercises. These journal entries will be written in class. At various times, you may have an opportunity to read a journal entry to one or more classmates. **THEREFORE, PLEASE BRING YOUR TEXTBOOK AND JOURNAL TO EVERY CLASS.**

Note: If you wish, you may write the first draft of journal entries on loose sheets of paper, but all journal entries must be written in the composition notebook when it is handed in for evaluation. Or if you choose to write your journal on a computer, you will print hard copies of all entries and bring them to class neatly organized in a three-ring binder. This requirement will assure that none of your entries gets lost. At the end of this semester, you will have your entire journal to keep for years to come. Many students come to regard their personal journal as one of their most valued possessions.

Journal Evaluations: Journals are due weekly. It is not my intention to read every journal entry you write. Instead, I will look through your journal entries to verify the completion of each assignment and to give credit for a job well done. I read occasional journal entries to get a sense of the issues you are working on. With this knowledge I can be of greater assistance to you this semester. If you want my comment on a specific journal entry, please let me know with a note in your journal.

Journal Points: Each journal entry will be awarded up to 5 points. Thus, all 32 journal entries will be worth a possible total of 160 points. A journal entry will be awarded the maximum of 5 points if it fulfills the following two criteria:

1. The entry is **complete** (all steps in the directions have been responded to), and
2. The entry is **written with high standards** (an obvious attempt has been made to **Dive Deep**).

Grammar, spelling, and punctuation will NOT be factors in awarding points in this journal. You are free to express yourself without concern for Standard English conventions.

3. Final Essay (60 Possible Points)

As your final project, you will choose one of the two following topics and write an essay.

OPTION 1: ONE STUDENT'S STORY

In this essay, you will relate the story of how you used a specific *On Course* strategy to overcome an obstacle to your success in college or in life. Use the "One Student's Story" essays in our textbook as models of how to write your story. If your essay is done well, your instructor may submit it to the *On Course* Essay Contest. Winning entries will be published in the next edition of the *On Course* text to inspire future students. Winning entries will also be awarded a $100 prize. Full directions for writing this essay can be found at **oncourseworkshop.com/course-textbook/essay-contest.**

An "A" paper will . . .

1. Explain a specific obstacle the writer faced.
2. Describe the specific *On Course* strategy used to overcome the specific obstacle.
3. *Present* the outcome of using the specific *On Course* strategy to overcome the specific obstacle the writer faced.
4. Show a commitment to excellence in preparation, including professional appearance and a command of Standard English.

OPTION 2: PERSONAL PHILOSOPHY OF SUCCESS ESSAY

In this essay, you will present your own Personal Philosophy of Success, identifying the *On Course* success strategies that you will use for years to come. This essay is your opportunity to write the script that will keep you on course to a rich, personally fulfilling life!

An "A" paper will . . .

1. *Offer* the writer's personal definition of success.
2. *Demonstrate* the writer's careful consideration of three or more *On Course* success strategies that he or she will use to achieve success.
3. Contain extensive and specific support (examples, experiences, evidence, and explanation) for each strategy.
4. Show a commitment to excellence in preparation, including professional appearance and a command of Standard English.

Course Rules for Success

To create the very best environment for supporting your success and the success of your classmates, this course has three important rules. The more challenging these rules are for you, the more value you will experience by adopting them. By choosing to follow these three rules, you are choosing to be successful not only in this course but in your life. These rules will support your success in every goal you pursue!

1. **Show up!** To support my success, I choose to attend every scheduled class period in its entirety.
2. **Do the work!** To support my success, I choose to do my very best work in preparing all of my assignments and hand them in on time.
3. **Participate actively!** To support my success, I choose to stay focused and involved in every class session, offering my best comments, questions, and answers when appropriate.

Schedule of Assignments (15-Week Course)

REMINDER: Fifteen unannounced quizzes will be given. No quizzes may be made up.

The following assignments are due at the first class of the week in which they are due. Bring your textbook and journal to every class.

Week 1:	**Read** "College Smart-Start Guide" and "Money Matters"
	Read/Write Journal 1: "Understanding the Culture of Higher Education"
Week 2:	**Read/Write** Journal 2: "Understanding the Expectations of College and University Educators."
	Read/Write Journal 3: "Understanding Yourself" (including self-assessment)
	Read "Soft Skills at Work"
Week 3:	**Read/Write** Journal 4: "Adopting a Creator Mindset"
	Read/Write Journal 5: "Mastering Creator Language"
	Read/Write Journal 6: "Making Wise Decisions"
Week 4:	**Read/Write** Journal 7: "Believing in Yourself—Change Your Inner Conversation"
	Read "Personal Responsibility at Work"
	Read/Write Journal 8: "Creating Inner Motivation"
Week 5:	**Read/Write** Journal 9: "Designing a Compelling Life Plan"
	Read/Write Journal 10: "Committing to Your Goals and Dreams"
	Read "Self-Motivation at Work"
	Read/Write Journal 11: "Believing in Yourself—Write a Personal Affirmation"
Week 6:	**Read/Write** Journal 12: "Acting on Purpose"
	Read/Write Journal 13: "Creating a Self-Management System"
Week 7:	**Read/Write** Journal 14: "Developing Self-Discipline"
	Read "Self-Management at Work"
	Read/Write Journal 15: "Believing in Yourself—Develop Self-Confidence"
Week 8:	**Read/Write** Journal 16: "Creating a Support System"
	Read/Write Journal 17: "Strengthening Relationships with Active Listening"
	Read/Write Journal 18: "Respecting Cultural Differences"
Week 9:	**Read** "Interdependence at Work"
	Read/Write Journal 19: "Believing in Yourself—Be Assertive"
	Read/Write Journal 20: "Recognizing When You Are Off Course"

Week 10:	**Read/Write** Journal 21: "Identifying Your Scripts"
	Read/Write Journal 22: "Rewriting Your Outdated Scripts"
	Read "Self-Awareness at Work"
Week 11:	**Read/Write** Journal 23: "Believing in Yourself—Write Your Own Rules"
	Read/Write Journal 24: "Developing a Learning Orientation to Life"
	Read/Write Journal 25: "Discovering Your Preferred Ways of Learning"
Week 12:	**Read/Write** Journal 26: "Employing Critical Thinking"
	Read "Lifelong Learning at Work"
	Read/Write Journal 27: "Believing in Yourself—Develop Self-Respect"
Week 13:	**Read/Write** Journal 28: "Understanding Emotional Intelligence"
	Read/Write Journal 29: "Reducing Stress"
Week 14:	**Read/Write** Journal 30: "Increasing Happiness"
	Read "Emotional Intelligence at Work"
	Read/Write Journal 31: "Believing in Yourself—Develop Self-Acceptance"
Week 15:	**Read/Write** Journal 32: "Planning Your Next Steps"
	Turn in Final Essay

SYLLABUS FOR A WRITING COURSE

Welcome! My goal in this course is to offer you one of the most valuable learning experiences of your entire life. And I need your full cooperation to make it work!

Course Purpose: The purpose of this course is to offer you the opportunity to learn powerful writing strategies. The theme of our class is SUCCESS . . . what success is for you and how you can achieve it. In the coming weeks, you will learn many proven strategies for living a rich, personally fulfilling life. We will use writing to explore these strategies, and through this practice, you will learn to express yourself more effectively in writing.

Course Objectives: Specifically, by the end of this course, successful students (YOU!) will be able to write essays that

1. Are *controlled* by a clear **purpose**,
2. Develop that purpose with sufficient, well-organized **support**,
3. Adapt *the* purpose and support to a particular **audience**, and
4. Are *written* in a smooth, grammatically appropriate **style**.

Method: In this course, you will be reading, writing, and talking about how to create success (as you define it). You will keep a guided journal in which you will explore many strategies of success. Five times during the course, you will write a formal essay based on the ideas you have been developing in your journal.

When you make both these writing and success strategies your own, you will have the ability to dramatically improve the outcome of your life.

Course Supplies:

1. *On Course*, 8th *edition*, by Skip Downing
2. String-bound *composition* notebook or computer journal (with entries emailed to your instructor as attachments and then printed and stored in a three-ring binder)

Course Grades:

		Points
A	=	666–735
B	=	591–665
C	=	516–590
D	=	441–515
E	=	440 or below

Course Projects:

	Points
1. 15 Quizzes (5 points each)	75
2. 32 Success Journals entries (5 points each)	160
3. 5 Essays (100 points each)	500
Total Possible Points	735

Each of these three components of your grade is explained below.

1. Quizzes (75 Possible Points)

This is a course for students who choose to be successful in college and in life. One of the most important factors of success in any endeavor is consistent and active participation. To encourage and reward your preparation for active participation at every class, 15 unannounced quizzes on the readings will be given. If you have read the assignment and completed your journal entry, you should have no trouble earning the maximum points (5) for each quiz. **No quiz may be made up.**

   Great success is created one small step at a time. Each time that you earn your quiz points you take an important step toward your success in this course . . . and in life!

2. Success Journals (160 Possible Points)

Your Success Journal provides an opportunity to explore your thoughts and feelings as you experiment with the success strategies presented in *On Course*. By carefully examining each strategy in your journal, you will discover which ones will assist you to create a rich, personally fulfilling life. Although I will be collecting your journals and looking through them, **write your journal for yourself,** not for me. Your journal entries may occasionally be read by your classmates.

Journal Writings: During this semester, you will write 32 numbered journal entries from our textbook. These entries will be written outside of class. Additionally, you will occasionally write lettered journal entries based on class exercises. These journal entries will be written in class. At various times, you may have an opportunity to read a journal entry to one or more classmates. **THEREFORE, PLEASE BRING YOUR TEXTBOOK AND JOURNAL TO EVERY CLASS.**

Note: If you wish, you may write the first draft of journal entries on loose sheets of paper, but all journal entries must be written in the composition notebook when it is handed in for evaluation. Or if you choose to write your journal on a computer, you will print hard copies of all entries and bring them to class neatly organized in a three-ring binder. This requirement will ensure that none of your entries gets lost. At the end of this semester, you will have your entire journal to keep for years to come. Many students come to regard their personal journal as one of their most valued possessions.

Journal Evaluations: Journals are due weekly. It is not my intention to read every journal entry you write. Instead, I will look through your journal entries to verify the completion of each assignment and to give credit for a job well done. I read occasional journal entries to get a sense of the issues you are working on. With this knowledge I can be of greater assistance to you this semester. If you want my comment on a specific journal entry, please let me know with a note in your journal.

Journal Points: Each journal entry will be awarded up to 5 points. Thus, all 32 journal entries will be worth a possible total of 160 points. A journal entry will be awarded the maximum of 5 points if it fulfills the following two criteria:

   1. The *entry* is **complete** (all steps in the directions have been responded to), and
   2. The entry is **written with high standards** (an obvious attempt has been made to Dive Deep).

Grammar, spelling, and punctuation will NOT be factors in awarding points in this journal. You are free to express yourself without concern for Standard English conventions.

3. Formal Essays (500 Possible Points)

Purpose: Five times during the semester, you will turn in a formal essay. In these essays, you will take ideas explored in your private journal and write them for a public audience. In this manner, you will practice and demonstrate the essay-writing skills that we will be learning in this course. Topics will be provided, but you are invited to offer alternative topics that appeal to you. Alternative topics must be approved before you write the essay. The minimum length of each essay is 750 words, and it must be prepared on a word processor. Each essay will be awarded up to 100 points. An essay earning 100 points will:

1. Be controlled by a clear purpose,
2. *Develop* that purpose with sufficient, well-organized support,
3. *Adapt* the purpose and support to a particular audience, and
4. Show a commitment to excellence in preparation, including professional appearance and use of Standard English.

OPTIONAL ESSAY: ONE STUDENT'S STORY

In this essay, you will relate the story of how you used a specific *On Course* strategy to overcome an obstacle to your success in college or in life. Use the "One Student's Story" essays in our textbook as models of how to write your story. If your essay is done well, your instructor may submit it to the *On Course* Essay Contest. Winning entries will be published in the next edition of the *On Course* text to inspire future students. Winning entries will also be awarded a $100 prize. Full directions for writing this essay can be found at **oncourseworkshop.com/course-textbook/essay-contest.**

An "A" paper will . . .

1. Explain a *specific* obstacle the writer faced.
2. Describe the *specific On Course* strategy used to overcome the specific *obstacle*.
3. Present the outcome of using the specific *On Course* strategy to overcome the specific obstacle the writer faced.
4. Show a commitment to excellence in preparation, including professional appearance and a command of Standard English.

Essays will be penalized 5 points for each day late. You must complete all five essays to earn a passing grade in the course.

Course Rules for Success

To create the very best environment for supporting your success and the success of your classmates, this course has three important rules. The more challenging these rules are for you, the more value you will experience by adopting them. By choosing to follow these three rules, you are choosing to be successful not only in this course but in your life. These rules will support your success in every goal you pursue!

1. **Show up!** To support my success, I choose to attend every scheduled class period in its entirety.
2. **Do the work!** To support my success, I choose to do my very best work in preparing all of my assignments and hand them in on time.
3. **Participate actively!** To support my success, I choose to stay focused and involved in every class, offering my best comments, questions, and answers when appropriate.

Writing Course Schedule of Assignments (15-Week Course)

Note: Fifteen unannounced quizzes will be given. No quizzes may be made up. The following assignments are listed here on the day they are due in class. Please bring your textbook and journal to every class.

Week 1:   *On Course:* **Read** "College Smart-Start Guide"

On Course: **Read/Write** Journal 1

On Course: **Read** "Writing" in *A Toolbox for Active Learners*

Week 2:   *On Course:* **Read/Write** Journals 2 and 3

Week 3:	*On Course*: **Read/Write** Journals 4, 5, and 6	Essay 1 Due
Week 4:	*On Course*: **Read/Write** Journals 7, 8, and 9	
Week 5:	*On Course*: **Read/Write** Journals 10 and 11	
Week 6:	*On Course*: **Read/Write** Journals 12, 13, and 14	Essay 2 Due
Week 7:	*On Course*: **Read/Write** Journals 15, 16, and 17	
Week 8:	*On Course*: **Read/Write** Journals 18 and 19	
Week 9:	*On Course*: **Read/Write** Journals 20 and 21	Essay 3 Due
Week 10:	*On Course*: **Read/Write** Journals 22, 23, and 24	
Week 11:	*On Course*: **Read/Write** Journals 25 and 26	
Week 12:	*On Course*: **Read/Write** Journals 27, 28, and 29	Essay 4 Due
Week 13:	*On Course*: **Read/Write** Journals 30 and 31	
Week 14:	*On Course*: **Read/Write** Journal 32	
Week 15:		Essay 5 Due

[Reminder to writing instructors: Engaging topics for formal essays are offered in this manual at the end of every chapter.]

ADAPTING *ON COURSE* FOR CLASSES WITH FEWER THAN 45 CONTACT HOURS

Chapters 1 and 2 present concepts and vocabulary that are foundational for all subsequent chapters. Chapter 6 presents concepts and vocabulary that are fundamental for work in Chapters 7 and 8. Chapter 9 offers students a second opportunity to take the self-assessment questionnaire that they took in Chapter 1. By comparing the results of these two questionnaires, students can see evidence of the changes in their behaviors, thoughts, emotions, and beliefs.

As a guideline, I recommend assigning one article and its companion journal entry for each hour of class time. For the Study Skills Plus edition of *On Course*, I recommend spending two to three hours of class time on each study skills section you choose to assign. For the regular edition of *On Course*, I recommend devoting one to two hours of class time to each study skills section you choose to cover. With this guideline in mind, I suggest that you follow one of three plans if you assign students fewer than all 32 journal entries and six Academic Skills Plans to complete.

Plan 1: Start with Chapter 1 and go as far into the book as time allows. Then assign Journal 32 (with the post-course self-assessment) in the final week. For example, if you have a 15-week course that meets 1 hour per week (15 hours), you might assign the following 15 journals:

Journals 1–14 and 32

You can assign other features (e.g., Case Studies, Study Skills, On Course at Work, One Student's Story, Tech Tips) as you choose.

Plan 2: Assign foundational Chapters 1, 2, 3, and 6 and as many other chapters as time allows. For example, if you have a 15-week course that meets 2 hours per week (30 hours), you might assign the following 23 journals:

Chapters 1–4 (Journals 1–15)

Chapter 6 (Journals 20–23)

Chapter 7 (Journals 24–26)

Chapter 9 (Journal 32)

You can assign other features (e.g., Case Studies, Study Skills, On Course at Work, One Student's Story, Tech Tips) as you choose.

Plan 3: Assign foundational Chapters 1, 2, 3, and 6, and as many other individual journals as time allows. For example, if you have a 12-week course that meets 2.5 hours per week (30 hours), you might assign the following 28 journals:

Chapters 1–4 (Journals 1–15)

Chapter 6-9 (Journals 20–32)

You can assign other features (e.g., Case Studies, Study Skills, On Course at Work, One Student's Story, Tech Tips) as you choose.

Creating a Learner-Centered Classroom

Within every class hour, students will ideally experience three or more of the following activities:

1. A learner-centered activity from this *Facilitator's Manual* (or elsewhere) that reinforces the reading and journal writing in the text.
2. A Quick-Write activity in response to an in-class activity or prompt from the text (these Quick-Writes can be written in students' journals and lettered to contrast with the numbered journal entries from *On Course*).
3. A discussion (in pairs, trios, quartets, or with the entire class). For example, discussions could focus on one of the following features: "One Student's Story," "On Course at Work," or one of the case studies. See the suggestions below for specific ways to generate these discussions.
4. Lecture or instruction from the instructor, student(s), guest speaker(s), or a video.
5. Exploration of study skills strategies, especially the "Do One Different Thing This Week" activity in the Toolbox section of the Study Skills Plus edition.
6. A quiz.

Let's take a look at each of these six components:

1. **A Learner-Centered Activity:** I recommend engaging students in active learning exercises in every class period. The exercises in this Facilitator's Manual (supplemented by the many additional exercises found at **oncoursework-shop.com**) provide you with more activities than you could possibly use in one semester. Each exercise is designed to engage your students as active, responsible learners, deepening their understanding of the success strategies they have been reading about in the text and writing about in their journals.

   This Facilitator's Manual provides you with two broad categories of activities. First are the All-Purpose Exercises that utilize the features present in most chapters in the text. Second are the Chapter-Specific Exercises that are paired with—and meant to reinforce—specific success strategies your students will be learning in *On Course*. Let's look at the options within these two categories of exercises.

   All-Purpose Exercises: Numerous features appear in most chapters (e.g., case studies, Tech Tips, and One Student's Stories) of *On Course*. The eight all-purpose strategies—described directly below—provide you with options for turning these textbook features into active learning strategies. If you find a strategy here that you like, you can repeat it with multiple chapters because the new content will make it fresh each time.

   A. Journal Entries: Thirty-two journal entries are provided, one after each article about a success strategy. Have students sit in pairs with their journal entries in hand. (1) Student A reads a designated journal entry to Student B. (2) Student B responds to Student A, "What I hear you saying in this entry is . . . ." (3) Students now reverse roles and repeat Steps 1 and 2. (4) Students then take a few minutes to discuss or quick-write any thoughts or feelings that came up for them as they read or listened. (5) The whole class discusses what they experienced and learned during the process.

   This activity, as simple as it is, seldom fails to energize students' thinking, and it generates many benefits: (1) Readers hear their own ideas, often discovering how to take their thinking to deeper, more complex levels. (2) Readers hear their own voices, noting where their writing is clear and where it is muddy. As a result, they improve as both writers and editors of their writing. (3) Both readers and responders get to hear another person's thoughts on the same issue they have explored, an experience that often helps them develop critical and creative thinking (and makes them more aware of the importance of audience in communication). (4) Responders learn to practice active listening, which allows them to more effectively discover the heart of any communication. This is especially valuable for reinforcing the listening skills that students will learn in Journal Entry 17. (5) The sharing of ideas by readers and responders creates community among class members, which often raises their level of commitment to the activities and learning available in the course.

B. Case Studies: Chapters 2–8 open with a case study that focuses on the topic of that chapter (e.g., personal responsibility, self-motivation). The goal of each case study is to get students actively engaged in thinking about the topic and its impact on real-life situations. The collateral benefit of this active engagement is the development of critical thinking skills as students express or defend their own positions and analyze or dispute the positions of others. Here are three different ways to debrief case studies:

- After students score the case study, ask a volunteer to explain his or her score ("Who did you choose as Number 1 and why?"). Then invite others with different opinions to voice their positions and reasons. Without revealing your own viewpoint, pit ideas (not students) against one another: "Who has a different point of view? Why do you think that? What experience have you had that influenced this view?" More important than students' viewpoints, explore their reasons, urging them to support their opinions as concretely as possible. Instead of pointing out a weakness in an argument (and thus appearing to be taking sides), ask, "How would you respond to a person who says . . . ?" Guide the discussion to explore the topic of the chapter by simply spending more time with points of view that focus on that topic.

- After students score the case study, have them get in groups with others whose top choice is the same. Have the groups choose a spokesperson and arm their spokesperson with arguments that will change the mind of others. Invite each spokesperson to present his or her group's argument, allowing others to change groups if their minds have changed. (Ask anyone whose mind is changed to explain what changed it.) Again, avoid letting students know what you believe about the case study because they will often think that your opinion is the "correct" answer, and all critical thinking (and debate) will come to a screeching halt.

- After students read the case study, have them rewrite it so that the characters model the positive quality of the chapter. For example, in the chapter on emotional intelligence, students would rewrite the case study so that each character in the story speaks and acts with emotional intelligence (as opposed to the lack of emotional intelligence they display in the present version). You can have students either read or act out their revised case studies. Ask them to explain why they had their characters act and speak as they did (e.g., "How does that behavior illustrate emotional intelligence?")

C. One Student's Story: These brief essays, written by college students, explain how the authors applied *On Course* strategies to overcome an obstacle to their success in college or life. Following are three ways to debrief these essays. The goal is to get students to become more aware of (1) the many potential obstacles that can keep them from achieving success in college and (2) the importance of making wise choices to avoid or overcome these obstacles.

- Read the beginning of the essay to your students and stop after presenting the student's obstacle, problem, or challenge. Ask your students to identify any choices the student-author made that created the obstacle. Then discuss what they would do if they found themselves in the author's situation. Afterward, read the rest of the essay and have your students compare their options with what the student-author actually did.

- Have your students read the entire essay either in class or for homework. In class, ask them to discuss the choices that got the student into the predicament. Then have them propose additional ways the student-author could have overcome the obstacle.

- Ask students to identify a problem they are facing in college. Then ask them to read a "One Student's Story" and find a way that they can use the same strategy for solving their own problem that the author of the essay used to solve his or her problem. Obviously, sometimes the strategy will not work for their problem. But more times than they might expect, the "forced-fit" approach leads to creative solutions they might never have thought of otherwise.

D. On Course at Work: These articles explain how the soft skills explored in each chapter of *On Course* are beneficial to career success. The goal is to get students to be more motivated to learn these personal skills by seeing their practical value in future careers. Here are three ways to debrief these articles:

- Ask students to identify their present career goal and talk about situations in which the chapter's soft skill (e.g., personal responsibility) would be important in that career. For "undecided" students, ask them to imagine the importance of the soft skill in a particular career (perhaps their parents' careers).

- Ask students who have work experience to describe a time when someone at their workplace did or did not use the soft skill under examination (e.g., interdependence) and the consequence. As a variation, this story could be turned into a case study.

- Ask students to find and bring in employment ads that list soft skills required of applicants. Discuss the various terms used to ask for soft skills. For example, the employment ad may ask for a "self-starter who is organized and able to work without direct supervision." Translation: The employer wants someone who is self-motivated and self-managing.

E. Quotations: Quotations in the margins of the text express what others (famous and not so famous) have said about the success strategies being considered. The objective is to get students to realize that many people place great importance on the ideas and strategies they are learning in the course. Here are three ways to use these quotations:
  - Ask students to choose a quotation from the margins of *On Course* with which they strongly agree or disagree. Then they do a short (two- to four-minute) quick-write response to their chosen quote. Students then share their responses in pairs, in small groups, or with the entire class.
  - Have students identify a favorite quotation and do research to find out who the author is. They present their chosen quotation to the whole class, explain why they chose it, and share their findings about the author.
  - Ask students to find and bring in a quotation that could be placed in the margin of the chapter they are reading. Students present their quotation to the class and explain how it fits into the topic under discussion. Alternative: Ask students to find and bring in lyrics of a song that could be placed in the chapter. A number of Internet sites provide song lyrics (e.g., www.lyrics.com and www.songlyrics.com/)

F. Cartoons: The goal of this feature is to help students to see the humor in serious topics, as well as the seriousness of humorous topics. And they're fun!
  - Students read a cartoon and respond in a short writing to the question, "What does this cartoon say about being successful?" Or "Why is this cartoon funny . . . or not funny?" Students then share their responses in pairs (as in Exercise A), small groups, or with the entire class.
  - Have students find and bring in their own cartoons that illuminate one of the strategies of success being considered.
  - Provide students with a cartoon without any words. Have them add words to the cartoon to fit the topic they are studying (e.g., self-motivation). This is a fun activity that promotes creative thinking.

G. Focus Questions: One to three questions precede each of the 33 articles about success strategies. Discussing answers before they read the article enables students to preview the success strategies and discover what they already think and know about the topic. The point should also be made that reading the article through the filter of questions enables a reader to gain more valuable (usable) information. This exercise assists students to become better readers. It is wise to emphasize the focus questions early in the semester, so students get in the habit of thinking about them before beginning to read.
  - Before they read the chapter, have students read the focus questions and write their best present answers to the questions. Students then share their responses in pairs (as in Exercise A), in small groups, or with the entire class.
  - After they read the chapter, have students read the focus questions and write their best answers to the questions. Students then share their responses in pairs (as in Exercise A), in small groups, or with the entire class.
  - If students write both before and after they read the chapter, lead a discussion with questions such as "What did you know that was confirmed in the article? What did you learn in the article that you didn't know before? What else would you like to learn about this topic?"

H. Chapter-Opening Charts (Successful Students/Struggling Students): Each chapter begins with a graphic organizer comparing successful and struggling students. Again, make the point that previewing enables learners to gain more valuable (usable) information as they read.
  - Have students read the chapter-opening chart and respond in a short writing to the questions, "Which of these choices do you think will be easiest for you? The most difficult?" Then have students share their responses in pairs (as in Exercise A), in small groups, or with the entire class.

I. Tech Tips: Each chapter provides a short list of free websites and apps that students can use to apply the strategies being taught or deepen their understanding of the strategies.
  - Ask students to experiment with one of the websites or apps and report their findings to classmates. Their report about a Tech Tip can encourage other students to add helpful electronic resources to their growing repertoire of success tools and strategies.

- Have students find websites or apps not mentioned in the Tech Tips sections, write a review of their value, and present to their classmates. If your college has a student newspaper, encourage students to submit their reviews as articles.

Chapter-Specific Exercises: Most of the remainder of this Facilitator's Manual presents learner-centered exercises that are paired with the specific success strategies your students will be reading and writing about in *On Course*. You'll find more exercises here than you could possibly use in a semester or quarter, so choose the ones you believe will best help your students to understand the principles and strategies of success. Although each of these strategies is different, they all include the following six parts:

Purpose: Each exercise begins with a statement of the outcome(s) that the activity is intended to produce. This feature allows you to decide quickly whether or not a particular activity is appropriate for your course.

Supplies and Setup: This information tells you what supplies (if any) are needed for the exercise; most of the supplies are common items that you probably already own or to which you have easy access. Setup instructions indicate anything that needs to be arranged before the exercise begins.

Directions: *Words of direction that you speak to the students are italicized—like this.* Directions labeled "Optional" may be dropped to save time.

One essential point about directions: The success of an exercise depends on whether students fully understand the directions. I recommend confirming that every student is clear on the directions before starting them on the activity. One way to clarify directions (especially complex directions) is to provide them on a handout or project them on a PowerPoint slide. Also helpful is giving a demonstration (DEMO) of exactly what you are asking the students to do. *So, here's what this would look like . . .* [DEMO what the students are to do.] *What questions do you have? Okay, begin.*

Approximate Time: Each step in the directions has an approximate time indicated. These times are guidelines and can be adapted to your circumstances or time restraints. Most exercises have a step for conducting a class discussion. If the exercise is running long, you can shorten the discussion. If the exercise is running short, you can lengthen the discussion. In this way, you can always end right on time.

Instructor Notes: Sometimes there are special aspects of an exercise that are not part of the directions but that I have found make the activity more successful. I write these to myself after doing the activity so I'll remember them for next time. I have included my "Instructor Notes" here, and I suggest you add your own after you facilitate an exercise.

Source: Where appropriate, I have indicated my source for an exercise. In most cases, even if I have learned the idea from someone else, I have adapted it to my own style. I urge you to do the same. Make each exercise your own. Many exercises have been contributed by *On Course* instructors. Their names appear as the sources.

2. **Quick-Writes:** Class discussions are usually improved when students first write about the issue under consideration. That is why Quick-Writes appear in many of the classroom exercises. This brief writing gives reflective learners time to gather and organize their thoughts for discussion. Such in-class writings can be lettered in students' journals to distinguish them from the numbered journal entries in *On Course*. I recommend timing these writings, starting with short sessions (one or two minutes) early in the semester and lengthening them to perhaps five to eight minutes toward the end of the semester. Typical directions to the students are as follows: *When I say, "Go," begin writing about ___ until I say, "Stop." There is no right or wrong thing to write. Simply follow your thoughts and feelings about this issue, wherever they lead. If your mind goes blank at any time, write, "My mind is blank. . . . I can't think of anything to write . . . What am I going to do? My mind is still blank. . . . Let's see—what am I supposed to write about here? Oh, yes, . . ." Eventually, your mind will usually return to the task at hand. If not, whatever you write is fine. What questions do you have? Ready, begin.* Students soon learn that quick writings of this nature are a powerful pre-writing (or pre-discussion) strategy for generating ideas.

3. **Discussions:** Discussions (in pairs, trios, quartets, or with the entire class) are usually quite lively when preceded by a stimulating exercise or journal writing. Before entertaining a discussion by the entire class, you may wish to put the students in smaller groups (two, three, or four) for a warm-up discussion. Introverted, shy, and English as a second language (ESL) students are more likely to participate in these small groups and, after this dress rehearsal, may be ready and willing to express their ideas to the whole class. Each exercise in this manual offers suggested

debriefing questions for stimulating meaningful class discussions. However, one all-purpose discussion technique is the PMI, suggested by Edward de Bono in his book *De Bono's Thinking Course*. P stands for Plus (the good points of an idea), M stands for Minus (the bad points of an idea), and I stands for Interesting (the intriguing points of an idea). To do a PMI discussion, simply explore these three elements of any idea, one at a time. De Bono argues that a PMI forces learners out of thinking ruts and promotes critical thinking (although, to be accurate, he calls it *lateral* thinking).

4. **Lecture and instruction:** When students' mental juices are flowing (after an exercise, journal writing, or discussions), they are ripe for further instruction. For some topics, you can assign students the role of instructor and let them instruct the class themselves. This approach gives students ultimate responsibility for their own education. (It is usually wise to have students do a dress rehearsal with you before they present to the class. In this way, you can exert some quality control.) Guest speakers or videos also add a nice change of pace.

5. **Study Skills Strategies:**

    Regular 8th Edition: At the end of the study skills section (A Toolbox for Active Learners), you'll find an exercise that will help students practice the specific study skill they have been learning. You'll find additional strategies in this manual as well. Here, however, is a collaborative learning activity (a variation of a structure called the "Jigsaw") that can be used with any of the study skills.

    A. Put students into "home" groups of three. Ask students to open their *On Course* text to the study skill you are working on. You may have assigned the topic for homework (my preference), or you may have students seeing it for the first time.

    B. Point out to students that the menu of study skills strategies is divided into three sections: *Before*, *While*, and *After* (e.g., Before Reading, While Reading, and After Reading). Ask each student in a trio to choose one section.

    C. Say to students, "Take 10 minutes to learn the one or two strategies in your section (Before, While, or After) that you think are the most valuable."

    D. Have the students now move into three "expert" groups by the section they have chosen: Before, While, and After. Say to students, "You have 15 minutes to decide as a group which are the two most helpful strategies in your section and prepare to return to your home groups and teach these strategies to your two partners."

    E. Have the students return to their home groups. Say, "Now, going in order of Before, While, and After, teach your partners one strategy. After each of you has taught one strategy, continue going around, teaching additional strategies, until I call time. In this way, you will become familiar with six strategies."

    F. As a final step, you can ask students, "What new strategies will you commit to experimenting with?" Because each of us has preferences for the way we like to learn, encourage students to experiment with various strategies, making those that improve their results in college part of their repertoire of study skills.

    Study Skills Plus, 3rd Edition—Exercise in the Text: Each "Wise Choices in College" section in the Study Skills Plus edition ends with an activity called "Do One Different Thing This Week." This activity asks each student to choose one study strategy from the menu of options and experiment with it for one week. At the end of the week of experimentation, the student writes a simple report by answering three questions:

    1. During my seven-day experiment, what happened?

    2. As a result of what happened, what did I learn or relearn?

    3. As a result of what I learned or relearned, I will . . .

    I like having students present their reports to the class.

    Study Skills Plus, 3rd Edition—Exercise in the Facilitator's Manual: At the request of numerous instructors, the exercise of using the Wise Choice Process to have students design a personalized academic skills plan has been moved from the text to this Facilitator's Manual. It is described in detail in the section later on titled "Study Skills: A Toolbox for Active Learners." There is one set of directions for each of the six sections of the Toolbox.

    This exercise takes students through the six steps of the problem-solving method they encounter in Chapter 2: The Wise Choice Process. The goals of the activity are twofold. First, students develop a personalized academic skills plan that addresses their self-identified learning problems. Second, by using a problem-based learning approach, they practice the process of critically thinking through a problem and making wise choices based on that thinking. Here are some ways to engage students in this activity during class. (Please familiarize yourself first with the six steps of the Wise Choice Process in Chapter 2 so these directions will make sense):

- After students identify their "situation" (the study problem they identify in Step 1 of the Wise Choice Process), put students in pairs and facilitate an "Eagles and Hawks" activity. In each pair, one student designates him- or herself as an Eagle, and the other student becomes a Hawk. (This designation is to facilitate future movement of the students and has no other significance. If you live in Detroit and would prefer Fords and Chevys, that's fine.) One student in the pair shares his or her "situation" (study problem), and the other student offers suggestions for what that student could do about it. Then students switch roles, and they continue talking about the second student's "situation" and possible study options. After about four or five minutes, give a signal (e.g., ringing a chime) and announce either "Eagles Fly" or "Hawks Fly." The appropriate student in each pair flies off to find a new partner, and all of the new pairs immediately continue their sharing of study problems and possible solutions.
- After students have identified their situation (problem) and academic skills plan (solution), have them meet in trios. Provide each student with time to present his or her "situation" (study problem) and academic skills plan. The other two students critique the academic skills plan and offer kudos and alternatives.
- After students have carried out their academic skills plan (the study skills they determined would best help with their study problem), have students report on what they learned or relearned. This report can be made in pairs, trios, quartets, or with the whole class. I like the option of having the conversation begin in a pair and then inviting students to nominate their partners to share success stories or lessons learned with the entire group.

Quizzes: Frequent quizzes motivate some students to come to class prepared, and quizzes act as a great review of the reading. I recommend having students exchange and grade quizzes in class so they receive immediate feedback. Quiz questions for every journal topic appear later in this manual. Practice quizzes are available for students in each chapter of the MindTap College Success for *On Course*. To access the MindTap, go to **login.cengage.com**.

On Course Newsletter

Subscribe to the *On Course* Newsletter and receive FREE emails with helpful information and strategies for empowering your students to become active, responsible, and successful learners. This newsletter makes a great supplement to this Facilitator's Manual and is like a professional development workshop on your desktop. To subscribe, simply send an email request to workshop@oncourseworkshop.com.

On Course Website

For additional classroom activities and out-of-class assignments, visit the *On Course* website at **oncourseworkshop.com**. Under the tab titled "Educator Resources," you will find a large collection of student success activities that work extremely well in the *On Course* classroom. Additionally, you will find a video gallery with videos arranged by the topics in *On Course*. A popular option is the videos of student-authors reading their One Student's Story essays.

Other Resources for *On Course*

Support for Students

- **MindTap College Success for *On Course*.** MindTap is the digital learning solution that helps instructors engage and transform today's students into critical thinkers. Through paths of dynamic assignments and applications that you can personalize, real-time course analytics, and an accessible reader, MindTap helps you turn cookie cutter into cutting edge, apathy into engagement, and memorizers into higher level thinkers. Features of the MindTap College Success *of On Course* include the complete chapter readings from the printed text, digital versions of the self-assessments and journal entries, videos, and chapter homework assignments.
- **College Success Planner.** Package your *On Course* textbook with this 12-month, week-at-a-glance academic planner. The College Success Planner assists students in making the best use of their time both on and off campus and includes additional reading about key learning strategies and life skills for success in college. Ask your Cengage Learning Consultant for more details.

Support for Instructors

- **Annotated Instructor's Edition**. To help guide instructors to the many ideas found within this Facilitator's Manual, the Annotated Instructor's Edition provides specific cross-references in the margins of the text to ideas and activities available here.
- **Newly Revised Facilitator's Manual**. This Facilitator's Manual, also offered online on the Instructor Companion Site, offers educators specific suggestions for using *On Course* in various kinds of courses and endeavors to answer questions that educators might have about using the text. The Facilitator's Manual includes tried-and-true activities provided by *On Course* instructors from across the country, additional study skills and diversity activities, sample student journal entry responses, and suggestions for teaching in an online environment.
- **Updated Instructor Companion Site.** This website—free to adopters of *On Course*—provides educators with many resources to offer a course that empowers their students to become active, responsible, and successful learners. Read or download the Facilitator's Manual, download PowerPoint slides, and find a useful transition guide for educators who used previous editions of *On Course*.

To access instructor digital resources, such as the Instructor Companion Site and instructor access for the MindTap College Success for *On Course*, follow these steps:

1. Visit **login.cengage.com**.
2. If you have not previously created a faculty account, choose "Create a New Faculty Account" and follow the prompts.
3. If you have created a faculty account previously, log in with your email address or user name and password.
4. Search for *On Course* to add the available additional digital resources to your bookshelf.

You will always need to return to **login.cengage.com** and enter your email address and password to sign in to access these resources. You may wish to record your password in a safe place.

- **College Success Factors Index (CSFI)** is an online personal success indicator and reporting tool that assesses students' patterns of behavior and attitudes in 10 areas that research has shown to be key determinants of students' likelihood of succeeding in college: Responsibility/Control, Competition, Task Planning, Expectations, Wellness, Time Management, College Involvement, Family Involvement, Precision, and Persistence. The CSFI is a perfect means of tracking and demonstrating your students' success as a result of having taken the course. For more information about this resource, visit www.cengage.com/success/csfi2.
- ***On Course* Workshops and Annual Conference.** Skip Downing, author of *On Course*, offers faculty development workshops for all educators who seek innovative strategies for empowering students to become active, responsible, and successful learners. These highly regarded professional development workshops are offered at conference centers across North America, or you can host a one- to four-day event on your own campus. Additionally, you are invited to participate in the annual *On Course* National Conference, where hundreds of learner-centered educators gather to share their best practices. For information about the workshops and national conference (including testimonials galore), go to **oncourseworkshop.com**. Questions? Email workshop@oncourseworkshop.com.
- ***On Course* Newsletter.** All college educators are invited to subscribe to the free *On Course* e-Newsletter. More than 50,000 educator-subscribers worldwide receive these emails with innovative, learner-centered strategies for engaging students in deep and lasting learning. To subscribe, simply go to **oncourseworkshop.com** and follow the easy, one-click directions. Or you can email a request to workshop@oncourseworkshop.com.

Special note to instructors: If you have questions about or suggestions for improving either *On Course* or this manual, please email info@oncourseworkshop.com. I will be happy to acknowledge you as the source of any exercises or suggestions that are included in subsequent editions. For your students, I thank you for helping them live rich, personally fulfilling lives. May you experience the same.

Skip Downing

On Course Workshop

EMPOWER YOUR STUDENTS TO ACHIEVE THEIR GREATEST SUCCESS!

At this highly interactive professional development event, you'll learn practical strategies that engage your students to become active, responsible, and successful learners. Designed for educators across disciplines who want to help students achieve their greatest potential—academically, personally, and professionally—this workshop will inform and inspire you both professionally and personally.

You'll learn:

- How to use the seven domains available to educators to motivate and transform students.
- Best practices from innovators in education, psychology, business, sports, and personal effectiveness.
- New motivational strategies that appeal to a variety of learning preferences.
- How these strategies improve academic success and student retention.

These workshops are held at retreat centers in various parts of the United States and can be brought to your campus as well. Whether you use *On Course* as your course text or you simply want to revitalize your instruction techniques, this workshop is for you!

- Visit **oncourseworkshop.com** for workshop dates, locations, and registration information and to view a sampling of classroom strategies, or
- Email workshop@oncourseworkshop.com for more information.

BRING AN ON COURSE WORKSHOP TO YOUR CAMPUS

1. Meet with your Cengage Learning Learning Consultant.
2. Visit the On Course Workshop website to review options and costs.
3. Fill out the workshop information request form.
4. Work with your Learning Consultant to create your campus-specific edition of On Course that includes your original content, campus resources, event calendars, and more.
5. Receive royalties directly to your faculty development fund for each text sold.
6. Use your fund to bring 1, 2, 3, or 4 day On Course Workshop to your faculty and student support staff.
7. Watch your program and your students SOAR!

Find your Cengage Learning Learning Consultant to get started at http://sites.cengage.com/RepFinder/.

Getting Your Campus
On Course

The following three articles explain the creative ways that colleges are using the *On Course* principles to create a culture of success on their campus.

Creating an On Course Campus

More and more colleges are creating an "On Course Campus." Their goals are greater student retention, academic success, and completion of certificates and degrees. They do so by infusing *On Course* principles and practices into many aspects of college life. The following describes such an effort at Asheville-Buncombe Technical Community College in North Carolina.

1. To adopt an On Course Infusion at your college, first determine who the decision makers are for this initiative. Determine the goals and outcomes for college-wide adoption. Define the focus, either narrowly or broadly.
2. To create an On Course Campus, identify the "reach" or extent of involvement (e.g., faculty, staff, students, advisors or counselors, financial aid materials, policies, procedures, publicity).
3. Ensure that your college's executive leadership team or administration promotes an On Course Infusion. To do so:
   a. Facilitate a presentation to college administrators or the board of trustees that shares your own experiences with *On Course* along with data from *On Course* programs (http://oncourseworkshop.com/Data.htm).
   b. Encourage all administrators to attend an On Course I Workshop or the On Course National Conference.
   c. Make infusion of *On Course* principles a core component of the college's strategic plan.
4. Establish a taskforce or working group that reports to the chief academic officer and is charged with overseeing the implementation of an On Course Infusion.
5. Adopt the "best practices" of community colleges:
   a. Hold a mandatory New Student Orientation (NSO) session; infuse the language of *On Course* into the session and any printed materials and images.
   b. Do not allow late registration.
   c. Optional: Focus additional efforts on your underperforming student group (as identified by college data).
   d. Require mandatory first-semester registration for your First Year (FY) or Student Success course; require re-registration the following semester for a grade of F in the first semester. Consider adding an FY course into each academic program's core course requirements, including transfer and associate degrees.
6. Add the "Eight Choices of Successful Students" from *On Course* into your college's general education core competencies.
7. Use the "Eight Choices of Successful Students" as a component of your college's Quality Enhancement Plan (QEP), as part of the reaccreditation process.
8. If your college is a member of Achieving the Dream, choose the "Eight Choices of Successful Students" as an area of focus (initiative)—for example: "Infusing *On Course* into the Developmental Curriculum."
9. Seek funding to support your efforts, for example, the Perkins grant for infusing *On Course* into career/technical education (CTE) programs.

10. Hold "Lunch & Learn" sessions (for either faculty or On Course Ambassadors) around any of these topics:
    a. The "Eight Choices of Successful Students" throughout the academic year.
    b. *On Course* key topics such as the "Wise Choice Process," "Moving from Victim to Creator," "*On Course* Language for Frontline Staff," or an area particular to your college's needs or focus. Use the sessions as part of professional development.
    c. "Designing a Student Academic Skills Plan for ___ Using the Wise Choice Process" (e.g., reading, taking notes, taking tests). Note: See examples in *On Course, Study Skills Plus*.
11. Offer training to colleagues: On Course I Workshop, On Course II Workshop. Host training sessions on campus, provide lunch, and offer attendees professional development credits. As necessary, collaborate with area community colleges to share costs and benefits.
12. Offer training to frontline staff—from the offices of the registrar, bursar, financial aid, and admissions—on how to adopt practices consistent with *On Course* principles.
13. Fund attendance at On Course National Conferences.
14. Invite your college's president to speak in FY or College Success courses on an *On Course* topic. Consider capturing the session on video for use in online sections of your FY or College Success course.
15. Create *On Course* thematic posters, flyers, and so forth to display throughout your campus.
16. Add the "Eight Choices of Successful Students" to your college's student handbook or planner.
17. Mesh the "Eight Choices of Successful Students" with workplace readiness skills, activities, or initiatives.
18. Require mandatory completion of "Getting On Course to Academic Success," a one-hour session, for students receiving financial aid who are in jeopardy of losing aid because of academic warning or probation.
19. If your state is participating in the redesign of developmental math, reading, or writing, begin now to include the *On Course* "language of success" into the curriculum and materials.
20. Include the *On Course* "language of success" in materials used in your college's math lab, language lab, tutoring center, writing center, and so forth.
21. Use the *On Course* "language of success" with initiatives such as a Minority Male Leadership Academy.

Source: Submitted by Sue Heath Olesiuk, Dean, Division of Academic Success; Shelly Blackburn, Chair of Academic Related Instruction; and Barbara Brown-smith Campbell, Associate Director, Faculty Development and Assessment, Asheville-Buncombe Technical CC, North Carolina.

Building a Strong College Success Program

The key to a fruitful college success program is having faculty who are the right fit for the course, and in fact, having the wrong instructors can do more harm than good when it comes to fostering student success. However, nobody holds a degree in college success, so how do we determine which instructors are well suited for the endeavor? At our college, we found that the essential ingredients are recruiting, hiring, and training. We started by brainstorming a list of qualities needed to teach the course:

1. We look for great instructors who:
   - Hold a master's degree to qualify for teaching a 100-level course
   - Embrace the course objectives
   - Are both nurturing and empowering (helping to build student confidence while offering them the tools they need to succeed on their own)
   - Possess energy, creativity, and enthusiasm
   - Are willing to take an interactive, fun, and learner-centered approach in the classroom (as lecture is seldom used)
   - Are open to specific training to develop or strengthen this teaching style and to deliver the course objectives using *On Course*
   - Bring the qualities that make them good instructors in their discipline while being able to view and teach this course apart from that discipline
   - Have a passion for (and preferably experience with) teaching developmental students
   - Truly enjoy and care about students and their success

2. We conducted interviews of each candidate and selected those who met the criteria.
3. We then offered a full-day training session in which the faculty participated in the types of activities they would be using in the classroom. It was fun, festive, and well-received.
4. We also offered brown-bag lunch sessions to share best practices once a month throughout the semester and gave faculty access to a Blackboard site full of resources for grading, assignments, sample syllabi and schedules, multimedia, handy tips, and so forth.
5. Classroom observations of faculty hired and trained through this process have validated its effectiveness. It was well worth the time it took to lay a solid foundation to build the program.

The process for faculty development is ongoing, with a goal of continual improvement of instruction in the college success program.

Source: Submitted by Lisa Marks, Lead Instructor, Keys to College Success, Ozarks Technical Community College, Missouri.

On Course at Heartland Community College

When two colleagues and I attended an On Course I Workshop in June of 2009, we were hoping to learn some new ideas for helping support students who seemed to be struggling for non-academic reasons. My colleagues were Dr. Kim McHale, a professor of Mathematics, and Kim Kelley, who is now the Director of Student Success. We were cautiously optimistic but in no way prepared for the results we would come to realize six years later. I have included below a list of *On Course*–related accomplishments at Heartland Community College, but that list is not at all comprehensive. *On Course* has become a college-wide tool, and in talking with various teams about how they are using *On Course*, I quickly realized I could never capture everything. We set a goal in January of 2012 of becoming an On Course Campus, and I believe we have achieved that goal. Our campus was looking for a consistent and intentional way to support struggling students, and *On Course* has given us that intentional consistency. Beyond that scope, we have been able to introduce *On Course* to our high school partners, and we recently branched out into inviting some community members from the social services sector to an *On Course* event on our campus. The potential for collaboration among all these groups is exciting, and I look forward to seeing what happens next with these collaborative efforts!

One area of the college that has especially embraced *On Course* is our developmental reading program. That area has implemented *On Course* principles and active learning strategies at the core of the curriculum and infused the principles and strategies into the training for all faculty and staff. The On Course Ambassadors in that area consistently see the value of the common language afforded by cross-campus *On Course* training and were instrumental in supporting all the on-campus workshops we hosted by encouraging full and part-time faculty and staff to attend. Many other departments have implemented *On Course* in similar comprehensive ways, which has strengthened our ability to support students by developing a broad base of educators who are also excellent On Course Ambassadors. I encourage everyone who sees the value in what these principles can do for students to build their team and share *On Course* with anyone who will listen; there is nothing to lose, and our students stand to gain so much!

Hopefully, this list of what Heartland has done so far will offer insight into the many different ways a campus can implement *On Course* both within the curriculum and within the culture of the entire college:

- Brought three-day On Course I Workshop to campus three times
- Brought four-day On Course II Workshop to campus once
- More than 150 *On Course*–trained professionals on campus
- Dozens of faculty have received training and have implemented *On Course* into instructional design
- *On Course*–trained faculty and staff use active learning strategies in their interactions with students
- *On Course* strategies implemented into the student discipline processes
- *On Course* principles used as core of new student orientation
- *On Course* principles incorporated into the development of our new physical therapy assistant program, including policy and procedure language
- *On Course* active learning strategies have been implemented during employee development sessions for faculty, staff, and administrators

- *On Course* training incorporated into our NADE Certified Tutoring Services
- *On Course* training incorporated into our NADE Certified Reading Program
- Active learning strategies implemented in the required orientation for developmental math courses
- *On Course* Peer Mentor program developed in conjunction with the *On Course* Life Success course
- *On Course* "Buffet" developed by the Liberal Arts and Social Sciences Division for faculty needing quick, on-the-spot strategies
- Hosting of two regional conferences for educators to share and learn about *On Course* best practices
- Athletic program student success competition, Best in the Nest, built around the *On Course* principles
- On Course workshops required for all student athletes
- Guided Path to Success Workshops built around the eight principles offered free on campus and in area high schools for transferable credit
- Success workshops infused into the curriculum for upper-level English as a Second Language students and designed as transferable credit
- *On Course* training for district high school educators
- Active learning workshop for teachers in Uganda facilitated by two On Course Ambassadors

Source: Submitted by Amy Munson, Dean of Student Success, Heartland Community College, Illinois.

On Course: Online

Pratima Sampat-Mar, Online Education Coordinator, Prima Medical Institute

Purpose of This Guide

Most schools now offer online courses using software platforms such as Blackboard, Angel, and Moodle. Although many people are familiar with sending email, paying bills electronically, and shopping online, teaching and learning via web-based classes is often a new experience. Conveying information and assessing student understanding of it can be challenging for online instructors. Online students face their own set of challenges. For example, being able to learn on their own schedule may be convenient, but it also requires more self-discipline and motivation. Teaching study skills to students is one way to help them overcome potential problems they may face in college, but it does little to develop self-discipline, motivation, and many other critical inner qualities that lead to success. The *On Course* textbook goes beyond study skills by focusing on the students themselves, which helps make the course content much more personal and approachable. Your goal for your online course should be the same—to make the content learner focused and engaging.

This guide will help you, the online instructor, understand how to best use the information presented in *On Course*. I will provide suggestions for using the textbook and other resources and examples of assignments, activities, and grading rubrics.

Main Features of *On Course*

On Course is different from many student success books in that it focuses on students' inner qualities and resulting choices rather than just study skills. As in any class, the textbook is the main source of information for a student taking an online course. Using the online chapter readings in the MindTap digital product for this book is one way to link the online content with the book. The printed book or online readings can be used in much the same way as in a face-to-face setting, with students assigned a certain chapter or number of pages per week or class session, plus the associated journal entries. After students have read the book, present them with activities online. You can create activities, discussion board conversations, and assignments using the features within the printed or online chapters. These include the Soft Skills and Study Skills Self-Assessments, the success articles, the 32 Journal Entries, the Focus Questions at the start of each major section, the Case Studies in Critical Thinking, the "At Work" features, the Toolbox for Active Learners, and the 28 "One Student's Story" essays in which real students discuss how they successfully applied *On Course* strategies.

The self-assessment provided at the beginning of *On Course*, for example, can be completed online by accessing the MindTap. A good way to use the self-assessment is to have students review the introduction to the self-assessment in Chapter 1 of *On Course*, take the assessment, get their scores, and use the assessment as a discussion board topic. You can also use Journal Entry 1 in Chapter 1 of *On Course* to encourage students to reflect on their scores; this will help set the tone for the rest of the course. Have students consider whether their scores reflect the way they see themselves and whether they would like their scores to change. At the end of the course, have them return to this self-assessment to retake it. Students can send you their responses to Journal Entry 1, and if they feel comfortable, share their experiences with the self-assessment in a discussion board. Some students might not yet feel confident enough to share their initial experience with the self-assessment, but consider making a discussion board topic mandatory after students have taken the self-assessment at the end of the course. At this point, students should be confident of the progress they have made and more willing to share their journey from their initial score to their final score. (A similar self-reflection or discussion board activity could be created around the study skills self-assessment at the beginning and end of the Tool-box for Active Learners.)

The extensive journaling in *On Course* can be readily adapted to an online environment. Students can write online journal entries just as they would in a traditional classroom but submit them through the online course (or through the MindTap). As in a regular course, journal entries are used for reflection and to help students focus on and think through specific success strategies, such as the Wise Choice Process (Journal Entry 6) or active listening (Journal Entry 17), as well as inner qualities such as a Creator mindset (Journal Entry 5) and self-confidence (Journal Entry 15). Provide guidelines on length (this would vary depending upon the subject) and stress that the most important part of each entry is whether or not their writing is thoughtful and genuine—or in the author's words, are the students "Diving Deep"? Giving students a maximum of 5 points or so per entry provides motivation. I suggest you comment on at least some of the journals, not to point out errors but instead to give the students further questions to consider (based on what they write) and let them know how they're doing (e.g., "Your insights on success really show that you've changed the way you think about choices"). If you're assigning the journals online, you can put comments directly into the online platform. The important thing is to make sure students can see the comments. For detailed suggestions from the author, please see the section titled "Using *On Course*" in the introduction to this Facilitator's Manual. Topics covered there include "As-signing Reading," "Student Journals, and Other Feature," "Reading Student Journals," "Responding to Student Journals," "Helping Students with Personal Problems," and "Grading."

The Focus Questions throughout the book that help students prepare for the content that follows also make excellent questions for online discussions. You can have students answer several of the questions in the chapter or elaborate on just one. Make sure you provide guidelines for their responses. Here's a sample:

Focus Questions (from Chapter 1): What does "success" mean to you? What are the essential skills for creating that success? In which essential skills are you strong? In which are you weak?

Discussion: Post at least three times to this forum based on the following:
1. Respond to the Focus Questions. Also explain whether you agree with the ideas about success and choices from Chapter 1 of *On Course*.
2. How will you know you've been successful in this course? In your personal life? At your job? How will these suc-cesses affect you?
3. Respond to other students, critiquing their definitions of success, with the goal of coming up with a definition useful to you and others.

Let students know how you'll be grading them. Here's a simple 15-point grading rubric for an online discussion. You would award students 3 points per category if they meet the guidelines or 2, 1, or 0 depending on the degree to which they didn't.

Quality of Original Posts	Participation	Quality Replies to Classmates	Writing Mechanics	Timeliness
Posts demonstrate an understanding of course content and are supported by specific details, examples, and/or sources.	Responds to all questions. Exceeds requirement for minimum number of posts. Posts encourage further interaction within the group.	Replies to classmates' posts are relevant, offer constructive comments, and are respectful.	Posts are written in complete sentences and contain no spelling or grammatical errors.	First post written on or before required date; other posts done on separate days throughout the discussion period.

Online discussions should be graded to motivate students to participate. They are a good way for you and the students to get to know each other without face time, and they can help draw out students who might not speak up other-wise, especially in a regular face-to-face setting.

The Case Studies in Critical Thinking help relate the information in the book to real life. If you have the technology, you could get a group of people together to create video versions of the case studies for students to watch online. Giving students something other than written material is a great way to address different learning styles—those students who don't absorb information well through reading might prefer to watch the videos. The questions can then be presented on a document or in a discussion that students access online after watching the video. Even if you can't make videos, you can have students post short responses to the questions in a discussion board forum to get them thinking about the ideas in that chapter related to the case or even have students create their own video versions of the case studies.

To create a learner-centered environment, any presentations should address various learning styles. In addition to text, consider including videos (e.g., the videos in the MindTap for *On Course* of students reading their One Student's Story essays or the animations on key topics), audio clips, or visuals. By varying what you include in your online course, you have a greater chance of keeping students' interest while they are logged in. Written notes could expand on important points from the chapter, such as providing more information about reading techniques. Another technique I use is to apply the concepts by describing how they might fit into a student's life (*you* know your students and the challenges they may face, so be specific) and offering personal anecdotes, similar to how author Skip Downing provides stories from his own life to explain concepts in *On Course*. Finally, I sometimes create graphics to provide a visual version of some information (something simple like the word "choices" shown as a puzzle piece linked to the word "success") and put those on my notes and lecture pages.

Frequently Asked Questions

1. How do I know whether students are really reading the book and learning anything?

This is where your evaluations come in—make sure your assignments and discussions incorporate ideas from *On Course*. Give your students very specific questions and require them to provide details and examples in their answers. I always try to incorporate a requirement about a situation or example from their lives as part of each assignment or discussion because such personal details are more difficult to copy from one paper to another.

2. How can I prevent students from cheating in an online course?

If you have students take tests online, make sure you use a test bank whenever possible. A Cognero test bank is available online via login.cengage.com. There is a question set for each chapter that allows you to choose from a menu of questions, including true/false, multiple-choice, fill-in-the-blank, matching, and essay. Keep tests to a minimum, however, and require students to describe their own experiences whenever possible.

3. How can I successfully move my on-ground course online?

First, don't think of it as simply changing where the course material is presented but rather *how* it is presented. Remember that although your students may not see you and you won't be able to do some of the things you would in a face-to-face classroom, having a course online opens up a whole set of resources you might not otherwise use, such as videos and asynchronous discussions. Don't attempt to replicate your on-ground course exactly; instead, think of it as an opportunity to give students a different way to interact with the content. Investigate the available tools and offer your students as wide a variety as possible. Online courses give students (and instructors) a whole new way to engage with information and can be a great way to reach each student wherever he or she might be—literally and figuratively.

In short, *On Course* is well suited to an online student success course because it is much more learner centered than most titles for this course area. Keeping this spirit in mind and incorporating it into your online course is the best way to help students succeed. For more information about the online resources for *On Course*, including the MindTap, you can visit the Cengage Learning website at login.cengage.com or contact your local Learning Consultant.

MindTap College Success for *On Course*: Laying a Foundation for Success

Angela C. Thering, Ph.D., Instructor, Buffalo State College

Best practices in educational technology demand that we use technology to enhance our instruction only when it helps us meet our teaching objectives. MindTap is the ideal tool to help instructors meet their objectives while providing students with a framework for college and personal success. A positive experience with MindTap in an *On Course* program can help students build the confidence and skill set required for subsequent courses and beyond.

MindTap allows students to interact with the *On Course* text and features in a variety of ways. The various MindApps that may be accessed on the right side of the screen provide students with digital tools for effective studying and learning. With just the click of a button, students are able to highlight important parts of the text, review college terminology or develop their own flashcards, check on their grades and progress, look up new words in the dictionary, and even listen as the text is read aloud in one of several available voice options and reading speeds. Having the opportunity to use the MindTap features during class can help students figure out how they can best use the tools to enhance their learning during their own study time.

MindTap also helps students to develop and strengthen their skills of self-regulation as they prioritize their work and manage their time effectively to complete activities outside the classroom. As students explore the learning path, they are able to examine their performance, motivation, and approach to learning through a variety of study tools, including digital self-assessments, videos, chapter quizzes, and homework. Many of the activities, in particular the journals and self-assessments, provide students with the language and conceptual framework to help them to move beyond "talking the talk" and bring their ideas into action. Through a focus on critical self-reflection, including confronting their weaknesses and formulating strategies for improvement, students can work on developing the skills that are essential to college success and discover what sorts of learning activities are most useful to them personally.

Students especially appreciate the ease with which they can complete the self-assessment at the beginning of the semester and that their scores are instantly tallied for them to reflect on. For the first time, with this edition, students will be able to revisit their original pre-test scores at any point during the term and easily compare them with their post-test results at the end of the term to reflect on their personal growth as a result of having taken an *On Course* course. The addition of the study skills self-assessment, which functions similarly, gives them a context for engaging with the material in the new "Toolbox for Active Learners" section.

MindTap also allows for instruction (and instructor) time to be optimized. The MindTap quizzes and homework can be required as "open book" assignments as opposed to taking the time to administer them in class. There is also no need to grade these assignments the "old-fashioned way" and manually enter the grades in the gradebook: when a student completes a quiz or chapter homework set through MindTap, his or her grades are automatically entered into the gradebook for both the instructor and the student to see. The quizzes can be used with a mastery learning model in which students are allowed to take each one multiple times until they have earned a score of 100%, or the quizzes can be set to allow a fixed amount of time and a fixed amount of attempts.

As stated in the introduction to this manual (p. 1), "the goal of *On Course* . . is to empower students to develop inner qualities that will help them maximize their potential in college . . and in life." MindTap provides many opportunities for students to do just that in a digital format while beginning to build a structure for success within the college environment.

CSFI and *On Course*: A Successful Combination

Gary J. Williams, Ed.D., Crafton Hills College

As an instructor who has adopted *On Course*, you have chosen a learning system that incorporates the best concepts of student development and student achievement. However, one of the most critical elements of ensuring that students put the concepts into practice is early assessment. Helping students identify their strengths and needs at the earliest opportunity and connecting them to the best ideas and practices found in *On Course* is the focus and the advantage of using the College Success Factors Index (CSFI), version 2.0, an online survey assessment tool available through Cengage Learning.

The CSFI shares a close affinity with the instructional principles of *On Course*. The central premise of *On Course* is that success occurs from inside out, and the CSFI provides an effective means of facilitating that inner transformation. The CSFI measures 10 affective factors or themes that are common among successful college students. These factors are:

Responsibility & Control	Time Management
Competition	College Involvement
Task Planning	Family Involvement
Expectations	Precision
Wellness	Persistence

The purpose of administering the CSFI is to help students understand the skills and habits they possess that contribute to being successful in college and identify the areas where students can improve their chances for success. The goal is to empower students to become self-motivated, self-responsible, interdependent, and able to manage their own success in college. Students have the opportunity to link to transformative learning activities contained in *On Course*. Administering the CSFI and fully integrating the follow-up strategies will encourage your students to "Dive Deeper" into their lives and acquire new ways of being and doing that will propel them toward success.

What Is the CSFI? How Can It Help My *On Course* Students?

The CSFI is a 100-item assessment instrument that students take online. (For more details about how students can access the CSFI, contact your Cengage Learning Learning Consultant.) After it is completed, the results are instantly available online to both student and instructor in an easy-to-understand, color-coded visual format:

Student View Sample of CSFI Results

❶ Strongest/Weakest Factors

Strongest: College Involvement, Persistence, Responsibility & Control

Weakest: Precision, Task Planning, Family Involvement

The results for each of the 10 factors are arranged in a bar graph format, as displayed in the figure above. Three ranges of scores are identified for each factor—Good, Average, and the Watchline.

When shown in full color online, students can easily identify factors of strength (at or above the "Good" line and displayed in green), factors where they report an average awareness as compared with their peers (displayed in blue), and factors identified as area(s) of need (displayed in red). Clicking on the label below the bar graph of each factor provides the student with a detailed description of that particular factor, a list of strategies to build skills in that area, and bullet points that direct the student to specific readings in the *On Course* text.

The CSFI presents the instructor and institution with additional benefits as well. As colleges and universities seek to address the growing numbers of students who arrive at college underprepared for the challenges that await them, the CSFI provides a powerful means for collecting and aggregating student learning data that can help focus attention and resources where they are most needed. This comes in the form of an Early Alert report built into the instructor's account that displays the overall results of a cohort of students and identifies the factors where students scored the highest as well as the lowest.

CSFI Aggregated Class Results, and Early Alert

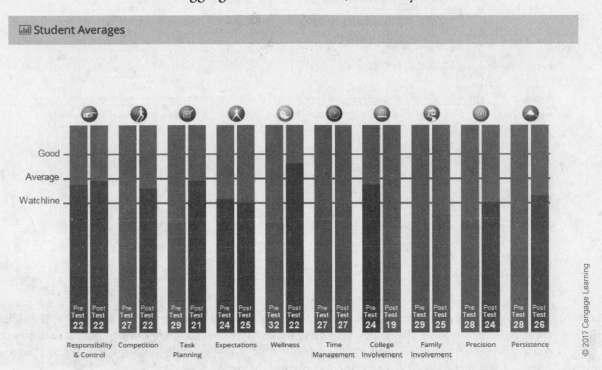

📊 Student Averages

The CSFI instantly organizes student results, which benefits instructors and programs. This sample CSFI report displays the aggregated (combined) student results that easily identify the strongest as well as weakest factors, allowing instructors to focus their energies on the factors of greatest need.

▼ Display Filtering

☑ Only Include Data from At-Risk Students (Early Alert Report)

☐ Only Show Rows with At Least One Take

Early Alert display filters allow you to refine results to show only at-risk students.

The CSFI's Early Alert function also provides the ability to identify specific students at high risk based on their CSFI results. Students whose CSFI scores identify four or more factors at risk are flagged in red online, as illustrated in italics in the following screenshot. This feature provides the opportunity for instructors and institutions to follow up immediately with high-risk students before they fall into difficulty.

CSFI Student Results

(Early Alert students are highlighted in red and italics.)

⊘ Student Score Detail

Student	Responsibility & Control		Competition		Task Planning		Expectations		Wellness		Time Management		College Involvement		Family Involvement		Precision		Persistence	
	Pre	Post	Pre	Post	Pre	Post	Pre	Post	Pre	Post	Pre	Post	Pre	Post	Pre	Post	Pre	Post	Pre	Post
☑ LCC, Student Demo	18	-	23	-	23	-	19	-	*30*	-	25	-	21	-	*28*	-	20	-	27	-
☑ Student, READ150	*27*	22	*32*	22	*35*	21	*30*	25	*35*	22	*28*	27	*28*	19	*30*	25	*37*	24	*28*	26
Averages:	22	22	*27*	22	*29*	21	24	25	*32*	22	27	27	24	19	*29*	25	*28*	24	*28*	26
% of National Averages:	90	88	114	91	120	87	98	100	116	78	103	103	90	70	131	113	118	100	103	96
National Averages:	25	25	24	24	24	24	25	25	28	28	26	26	27	27	22	22	24	24	27	27

Factor scores in red italic indicate that the score is below the watchline for that factor.

2 of 2 student(s) have taken the pre-test.
1 of 2 student(s) have taken the post-test.

Paired with the skills and strategies contained in *On Course*, the CSFI can direct struggling students to the skills and strategies that can help them overcome challenges, help them make wiser choices, and put them on the road to success.

The CSFI is entirely congruent with the goals of *On Course*. As the following table indicates, the 10 CSFI factors provide numerous points of connection with *On Course* concepts and themes.

College Success Factors Index and *On Course* Themes

CSFI Factor	*On Course* Concept(s)
Responsibility & Control: Students understand that they are responsible for their own success in college. They are in control of their education, make wise decisions, and take positive action to maintain a high academic standing.	What to do Before the End of your First Week in College (Ch. 1)
	Become an Active Learner (Ch. 1)
	Accept Personal Responsibility (Ch. 2)
	Adopting a Creator Mindset (Ch. 2)
	Mastering Creator Language (Ch. 2)
	Making Wise Decisions (Ch. 2)
	Designing a Compelling Life Plan (Ch. 3)
	Harness the Power of Quadrant II (Ch. 4)
	Being Assertive (Ch. 5)
	Gaining Self-Awareness (Ch. 6)
	Learning to Make Course Corrections (Ch. 7)
Competition: Students are motivated to perform at their highest level possible by setting high standards for achievement and by competing with themselves and/or their peers. They demonstrate a commitment to being successful in college.	Assess Your Soft Skills for College Success (Ch. 1)
	One Dozen College Customs (Ch. 1)
	Adopting a Creator Mindset (Ch. 2)
	Creating Inner Motivation (Ch. 3)
	Committing to Your Goals and Dreams (Ch. 3)
	Create a Success Identity (Ch. 4)
	Visualize Purposeful Actions (Ch. 4)
	Creating a Support System (Ch. 5)
	The Difference Between Heaven and Hell (Ch. 5)
	Write Your Own Rules (Ch. 6)
	How to Develop a Growth Mindset (Ch. 7)
	Employing Critical Thinking (Ch. 7)

College Success Factors Index and *On Course* Themes (*continued*)

CSFI Factor	*On Course* Concept(s)
Task Planning: Students are task oriented and can break larger projects and expectations into smaller, more manageable tasks. They meet deadlines and commitments and track progress toward completion of tasks.	What to do Before the End of your First Week in College (Ch. 1) Money Matters (Ch. 1) Acting on Purpose (Ch. 4) Harness the Power of Quadrant II (Ch. 4) Creating a Leak-Proof Self-Management System (Ch. 4) Visualize Purposeful Actions (Ch. 4) Creating a Support System (Ch. 5) Write Your Own Rules (Ch. 6)
Expectations: Students set high expectations for themselves through challenging goals that are meaningful to them. They seek out learning opportunities and new experiences, and they take risks. They articulate a strong desire for success in their chosen field or major. They demonstrate a high degree of commitment to their academic success.	Understanding the Expectations of College and University Educators (Ch. 1) A Dozen Differences Between High School and College Culture (Ch. 1) What Does Success Mean to You? (Ch. 1) Change Your Inner Conversation (Ch. 2) Designing a Compelling Life Plan (Ch. 3) Committing to Your Goals and Dreams (Ch. 3) Write a Personal Affirmation (Ch. 3) Discovering Your Preferred Learning Style (Ch. 7) Keep Commitments (Ch. 7) Increasing Happiness (Ch. 8)
Wellness: Students practice sound habits in personal health, nutrition, exercise, and stress management practices. They seek balance in their lives, their relationships, and the various roles they assume in addition to being a student. They understand what they need to perform at their best.	Mastering Creator Language (Ch. 2) Write a Personal Affirmation (Ch. 3) Developing Mutually Supportive Relationships (Ch. 5) Strengthening Relationships with Active Listening (Ch. 5) Rewriting Your Outdated Scripts (Ch. 6) How to Develop a Growth Mindset (Ch. 7) Developing Emotional Intelligence (Ch. 8) Reducing Stress (Ch. 8) Increasing Happiness (Ch. 8) Strawberry Moments (Ch. 8)
Time Management: Students practice sound skills in planning, calendaring, and prioritizing their tasks, commitments, and responsibilities. They exert control over the events in their lives and can manage interruptions without losing sight of what is most important to them. They use a planning system that helps them keep track of their assignments, tests, papers, projects, and deadlines.	Mastering Self-Management (Ch. 4) Creating a Leak-Proof Self-Management System (Ch. 4) Developing Self-Discipline (Ch. 4) Keep Commitments (Ch. 7) Reducing Stress (Ch. 8)
College Involvement: Students seek meaningful connections with the college through formal as well as informal means. They develop a circle of support on campus that can assist them through times of challenge. They articulate a sense of satisfaction with their college experience.	Understanding the Culture of Higher Education (Ch. 1) One Dozen College Customs (Ch. 1) Understanding the Expectations of College and University Educators (Ch. 1) A Dozen Differences Between High School and College Culture (Ch. 1) Value of College Experiences (Ch. 3) Employing Interdependence (Ch. 5) Creating a Support Network (Ch. 5) Believing in Yourself: Be Assertive (Ch. 5) Developing Emotional Intelligence (Ch. 8)
Family Involvement: Students have a circle of support that includes the people who are most important to them. Their circle of support provides advice and encouragement and has a positive involvement in their lives that enables them to succeed in college.	Developing Mutually Supportive Relationships (Ch. 5) Creating a Support Network (Ch. 5) Strengthening Relationships with Active Listening (Ch. 5) Developing Emotional Intelligence (Ch. 8)

College Success Factors Index and *On Course* Themes (*continued*)

CSFI Factor	*On Course* Concept(s)
Precision: Students operate with a sense of exactness in all they do. They listen carefully, express themselves clearly, and read and recall with exactness. They clarify details as needed and complete tasks with a high degree of precision.	What to do Before the End of your First Week in College (Ch. 1)
	Money Matters (Ch. 1)
	Designing a Compelling Life Plan (Ch. 3)
	Mastering Self-Management (Ch .4)
	Acting on Purpose (Ch. 4)
	Creating a Leak-Proof Self-Management System (Ch. 4)
	Developing Self-Discipline(Ch. 4)
	Active Listening (Ch. 5)
	Being Assertive (Ch. 5)
Persistence: Students understand that overcoming obstacles is the key to success in college and in life. They display a sense of determination and urgency when facing obstacles and challenges. They possess a high level of commitment, doing "whatever it takes" to succeed.	Mastering Creator Language (Ch. 2)
	Developing Self-Discipline (Ch. 4)
	Changing Your Inner Conversation (Ch. 2)
	Rewriting Your Outdated Scripts (Ch. 6)
	Designing a Compelling Life Plan (Ch. 3)
	Committing to Your Goals and Dreams (Ch. 3)
	Increasing Happiness (Ch. 8)
	Engagement (Ch. 8)

Incorporating the CSFI can help greatly in advancing the *On Course* goal of encouraging success from within by helping your students clarify their personal strengths and pinpoint the specific areas where they need the most help. It can be adapted to the demands of any course, orientation program, first-year experience, learning community, or other setting that is focused on student growth, development, and success. It can also provide a basis of documenting, measuring, and tracking the developmental learning outcomes of your course or program.

For more information about CSFI, visit our website at **www.cengage.com/success/csfi2** or contact your Cengage Learning Learning Consultant.

Getting On Course to Your Success

Concept

By offering students an opportunity to understand the culture of higher education, understand the expectations of college and university educators, and (perhaps most important) understand their strengths and weaknesses, we empower them with information that is essential to their success in higher education. Additionally, when we help students begin their academic journeys in an engaging and purposeful way, we motivate them to give their best effort. Students are more likely to commit to working hard in a course when they understand . . .

1. What actions they should take during their first week in college
2. What makes higher education unique and potentially challenging
3. What this course is about
4. Why this course is of personal value to them academically and personally
5. How they can do well in the course and in higher education
6. That they will enjoy the experience

It is as necessary for students to feel comfortable in this course as it is important for them to learn what this course is about and how it will benefit them. When students feel at ease in the classroom, they are more likely to stretch beyond their comfort zones and risk new behaviors, beliefs, and attitudes. As we begin our journey in this course, our first goal is to create a safe and motivating learning environment that encourages students to change.

EMPOWERS STUDENTS TO . . .

1. Understand the cultural norms of higher education.
2. Begin thinking about what it means to them to be successful in college and in life.
3. Understand the value they can create for themselves in the course.
4. Assess their strengths and weaknesses.

Remember also to use the all-purpose exercises mentioned in the introduction, actively engaging students in the exploration of JOURNAL ENTRIES, CASE STUDIES, ONE STUDENT'S STORY, ON COURSE AT WORK, QUOTATIONS, CARTOONS, FOCUS QUESTIONS, CHAPTER-OPENING CHARTS, and TECH TIPS. Remind students to use letters to label any in-class writing they do in their journals.

College Smart-Start Guide

EXERCISE 0-1: Travel with Me

Purpose

To give an overview of the *On Course* text. Also, to raise student awareness of the choices successful students make in college. When students are engaged in thinking about these choices, they become more motivated to value the course and have high expectations for being successful in college.

Supplies and Setup

Each student needs a copy of "Travel with Me," a message from author Skip Downing that appears at the end of the Preface to the *On Course* text (both editions). Post the following five questions at stations around the room:

Paragraph 1. What does being a successful college student mean to you?

Paragraph 2. List reasons why Downing always had some students who were successful and others who disappeared or failed.

Paragraph 3. Downing discusses struggling in his personal and professional life in his 20th year of teaching. He then chose to improve the quality of his life in various ways. Why do you think that Downing shared this information with us?

Paragraph 4. Why are successful people able to make wiser choices than people who struggle?

Paragraph 5. Discuss why Downing wrote this book and then answer the following question: Why is this book titled *On Course*?

At each station, place an easel and easel pad (or five large sheets of paper at least 11 × 14).

Directions

1. [Ask volunteers to stand and read one paragraph each of "Travel with Me." If you want to check students' comprehension, ask someone to explain the main idea of each paragraph.] [5 minutes]
2. [Have students form groups at each of the five stations.] *At your station, discuss the prompt and then write a response on the easel pad. You will have about 5 minutes at each station.* [5 minutes]
3. [Have students rotate to the other four stations and repeat what they did at the first station.] [20 minutes]
4. [Post all five sheets on the wall. Conduct a "gallery walk" in which students move to each sheet, reading what is posted on each.] [5–10 minutes]
5. [Class discussion] *What will you need to do to be successful this semester? What strategies will you need to learn about to become a successful student?* [List the strategies suggested on the board or easel pad. Discuss which ones they already use and which ones they will need to learn.] [5–15 minutes]

Approximate time: 40–50 minutes

Instructor Notes

1. My original purpose for this activity was to introduce *On Course* to the students at my community college. I wanted to find an activity that would not only motivate them but would also give them an overview and deeper understanding of the outcomes and experiences they could achieve in this course. However, I've also used this activity as part of faculty training. For the final discussion with faculty, you might ask questions such as: "What do you think are the reasons why students struggle in college? Does it appear that *On Course* will address these issues?"
2. "Travel with Me" does much more than summarize the book. It has given insight to both faculty and students on why *On Course* was written. Student engagement in this activity leads them into thinking about the strategies they can use to be successful. I find that their motivation increases as well as their participation in class.

Source: Submitted by June Pomann, Union County College, NJ

EXERCISE 0-2: College Smart-Start Guide (1)

Purpose

To have students identify actions they should take in their first week in college; to help students get off to a good start in college.

Supplies and Setup

Whiteboard (or other means of recording items that all can see); students in groups of three or four

Directions

1. *In your group, create a list of actions that new students should do in their first week in college to get on course to success.* [5 minutes]
2. *Okay, let's hear what you came up with.* [Record choices on the whiteboard, combining when identical or similar.] [5 minutes]
3. *Which of these choices do you think are the most essential for getting off to a good start in college? As I call off a choice, raise your hand to cast your vote. You may vote for three.* [Tally the votes each time and record them next to the item on the list.] [5 minutes]
4. [Identify the top 5–10 vote getters.] *Which of these choices are you willing to commit to so you can get off to a good start this semester? Make a list of them in your journal.* [5 minutes]
5. *Let's hear what you wrote.* [Invite students to stand and state the choices they committed to do.] [5 minutes]

Approximate time: 25 minutes

Instructor Notes

1. Consider following this activity immediately by Exercise 0-3.

EXERCISE 0-3: College Smart-Start Guide (2)

Purpose

To help students learn what actions college and university educators think are important for students to take in their first week in college; to help students get off to a good start in college.

Supplies and Setup

Whiteboard (or other means of recording items that all can see); students start working alone and then move into groups of three or four; each student needs a copy of the handout "What Educators Say Students Should Do in Their First Week in College."

Directions

1. *The author of our* On Course *text, Dr. Skip Downing, polled nearly 2000 college and university educators and asked them to list the actions they would advise first-year students to take in their first week in higher education. He then determined the top 20 suggestions, sent this list back to the educators, and asked them to vote for their top 10. On the handout are the 13 actions that received the most votes (but not in the order of the votes they received). Working alone, rank the actions from 1 to 13, seeing if you can duplicate the actual ranking by the educators. Place your scores in Column B, leaving the other columns blank for now.* [5 minutes]
2. [Form students into groups of four or five.] *In your group, discuss and refine the rankings based on the collective wisdom of your group. Record your group's consensus rankings in Column D.* [10 minutes]
3. [Provide the educator's rankings and have learners record them in Column C.] [5 minutes]
4. *First, see how well you did when working alone. For each of the 13 items, determine the number of points your individual answer (Column B) differed from the educators' answer (Column C) and write that difference in Column A. Then*

total all the numbers in Column A. The lower the total, the better you predicted the advice of the educators. [Ask students to reveal their total scores when working as an individual. Consider making a chart on the white board. Give kudos to the person who came closest to the educators' scores.] [10 minutes]

5. *Now, see how well you did when working with a group. For each of the 13 items, determine the number of points your group's answer (Column D) differed from the educators' answer (Column C) and write that difference in Column E. Then total all the numbers in Column E. The lower the total, the better your group predicted the advice of the educators.* [Ask students to reveal their group's total scores. Consider making a chart on the white board. Give kudos to the group that came closest to the educators' scores.] [10 minutes]

6. *Which total is lower, yours (Column A) or your team's (Column E)? What is your explanation for this outcome?* [Usually the group's score is lower, thus closer to the educator's score, suggesting the wisdom of interdependence, which will be explored further in Chapter 5.] [10 minutes]

7. [Discussion] *Which of the educators' top five choices have you already done? Which are you willing to commit to so you can get off to a good start this semester? Make a list of them in your journal.* [5 minutes]

Approximate time: 55 minutes

Instructor Notes

1. To reduce the time by 20–30 minutes, focus on individual scores only. Accomplish this by skipping Steps 2 and 3, modifying Step 4, and skipping Steps 5 and 6.
2. Here are the rankings of the educators:

A	B	C	D	E	
					GET FAMILIAR
		12			Learn your campus.
		6			Locate your classrooms.
		4			Learn your instructors' names, office locations, and office hours.
		3			Study—don't just skim—the first-day handout (syllabus) for each course.
					GET ORGANIZED
		5			Get all of your learning supplies.
		2			Create a schedule.
		10			Get comfortable with campus technology.
		13			Manage your money.
					GET SERIOUS
		9			Set goals for each course.
		1			Attend all classes and arrive on time.
		11			Participate in every class.
		8			Complete and hand in all assignments on time.
		7			Commit to your success.
					Total Columns A and E.

What Educators Say Students Should Do in Their First Week in College.

A	B	C	D	E	
					GET FAMILIAR
					Learn your campus.
					Locate your classrooms.
					Learn your instructors' names, office locations, and office hours.
					Study—don't just skim—the first-day handout (syllabus) for each course.
					GET ORGANIZED
					Get all of your learning supplies.
					Get comfortable with campus technology.
					Manage your money.
					GET SERIOUS
					Set goals for each course.
					Attend all classes and arrive on time.
					Participate in every class.
					Complete and hand in all assignments on time.
					Commit to your success.
					Total Columns A and E.

EXERCISE 0-4: The Importance of Names!

Purpose

To begin creating a learner-centered classroom community where classmates and instructor learn how to pronounce and know each others' names.

Supplies and Setup

Black markers, table tents—cardstock or file folders cut in half, a sample with instructor's name and phonetic spelling underneath

Directions

1. [As the first three to five students enter the classroom on the first day of class, greet the students.] *Please take a table tent and marker and then write your first and last name in large letters. Underneath write the phonetic spelling of your name.* [Display your table tent as a model for students. Then ask these three to five students to pass these same directions on to other classmates as they enter, using their own tents as a model. This allows you to focus your attention on welcoming students at they arrive.] [10 minutes]

> Gina Nguyen
>
> Geenuh Nu-when

[When everyone is in class and has completed their table tent.] *Welcome to the first day of class, I believe that learning each other's names is one of the most important things we can do to create a safe and welcoming classroom. We will now go around the room, and I would like you to stand up and state your name and one thing you like to do or you value.* [You can use any prompt you would like.] *I will go first, my name is . . . and I value. . . .* [10 minutes]

2. [Ask students to turn in the table tents at the end of class. Use the table tents to take attendance. Return the table tents at the beginning of the next class period. Have students use them until names are learned.]

Approximate time: 20 minutes

Instructor Notes

1. This activity ensures the correct pronunciation of everyone's name and makes known the names the students wish to be called by (i.e., this honors nicknames; speakers of other languages; and transgendered students, whose names may not be legally changed). Collecting the table tents allows instructors to practice pronouncing student names correctly before the next class.
2. One way to be green is to reuse file folders by cutting them on the fold. Then fold each side in half, top to bottom. You will have two table tents per file folder.
3. The website www.inogolo.com gives "English pronunciation to the names of people, places, and stuff."

Source: Submitted by Cris Davis and LuAnn Wood, Century College, MN; adapted from Dianne Del Giorno, Century College, MN

EXERCISE 0-5: Meet Your Classmates

Purpose

First- or second-day icebreaker to help the students and instructor to get to know each other.

Supplies and Setup

None

Directions

1. One activity I use on the first day of class is a combination of icebreakers I've heard of over the years. I have each student come up with a descriptive adjective starting with the letter of his or her first name (e.g., "Lucky Lisa"). I then pair them up and have them introduce themselves with that moniker and tell one interesting, unusual, or surprising fact about themselves.
2. After the pairs have had a few minutes to talk, we come back together as a large group. Partner A then introduces the rest of the class to Partner B, using the descriptive name and telling us the fact learned about the partner. Partner B then introduces Partner A in the same fashion. (The only caveat is to make sure students share only ONE fact about their partners, although they may learn more than one fact in getting to know each other.)
3. I challenge myself to go back to the beginning and repeat all the names each time a pair finishes. It works fabulously to help me remember their names early on in the semester, and it lets the students know that I care enough to learn them.
4. I don't require them to stand up when giving the introductions. Even the shyest students seem more comfortable introducing someone other than themselves, and it gives them a chance to get to know other people, find commonalities, and develop a sense of community.

Approximate time: Varies depending on class size

Source: Submitted by Lisa Marks, Ozarks Technical Community College, MO

Journal Entry 1 Understanding the Culture of Higher Education

EXERCISE 1-1: Get Connected!

Purpose

(1) To get students engaged in the college culture and (2) to encourage students to explore cultures different from their own.

Supplies and Setup

"Get Connected!" handout; list of current events at your campus

Directions

1. *Research shows that students who are involved in college events are more likely to feel connected to their campus culture; enjoy their college experience; and, as a result, persist in higher education. In this assignment, you will become aware of the many extracurricular activities our campus has to offer. "Extracurricular" activities are those that are not part of any courses you are taking. You will attend three different campus events over the course of the semester. One event must be multicultural; one must be a student success workshop; and one must be a club or organization meeting . . . no need to join but at least check one out.* [Adapt the three events to those available on your campus.] *After each visit, write a reflection for the event attended. Use the following questions to guide your reflection and dive deep! Answer in paragraph form and be specific.* [Review the reflection questions on the "Get Connected!" handout.]

Approximate time: 10 minutes to introduce assignment, brainstorm potential events, and answer student questions

Instructor Notes

1. Encourage students to attend events with a classmate, friend, or family member.
2. Scheduling due dates throughout the semester helps students get involved right away on campus as well as continue involvement throughout the semester.

Source: Submitted by LuAnn Wood based on a collaboration of many staff and faculty, Century College, MN

Get Connected!

1. Attend three different campus events or resources over the semester.

    Choose an event that fits each of the following categories.
    a. Multicultural Event (e.g., speakers and activities sponsored by the multicultural center, salsa dancing)
    b. Student Success Workshop
    c. Campus Club or Organization Meeting (you do not need to commit long term but at least check one out)

2. Write a reflection after each of the three campus events or resources attended. Use the following questions to guide your reflection of the activity or event attended—be specific and dive deep!

    a. List the event or resource; include the title (name of activity or event), location, and date.
    b. **Why?** Explain the reason you were interested in this event or resource.
    c. **What?** Describe the event and what you learned. Especially note any similarities or differences you notice when comparing this event with the culture of the most recent school you attended.
    d. **So What?** Describe how this event impacted you or others. (What difference did it make—did this event change your thinking, and was this event different than you expected?)
    e. **Now What?** Describe what you plan to do with the information learned. (How can you apply this new experience to your life, what would you like to learn more about, what follow-up is needed, and what information can you share with others?)

3. Turn in each reflection by each due date listed below.

    #1 Get Connected Reflection: due <u>by the end of Week 5</u>

    #2 Get Connected Reflection: due <u>by the end of Week 9</u>

    #3 Get Connected Reflection: due <u>by the end of Week 14</u>

EXERCISE 1-2: What's Going on Around Here?

Purpose

To help students understand how deep-culture rules create confusion and frustration for people new to the culture. (This activity can also be used with Journal Entry 18: Respecting Cultural Differences.)

Supplies and Setup

This activity can be done either before or after students read and write Journal Entry 2: Understanding the Culture of Higher Education.

Directions

1. [Ask for three volunteers to play a game. Ask them to leave the room for a few minutes.] [2 minutes]
2. [Ask the remaining students to stand and form groups of five to seven.] *Each culture creates rules by which it operates. Some of these rules are visible, such as the appropriate clothing that people wear. Other rules are invisible to people who are unfamiliar with the culture, such as the proper way to talk to others. For the next few minutes, imagine that everyone here is in a culture that believes that people should always touch their faces briefly before speaking. If someone does not do that, others will ignore that person.* [Demonstrate what that would look like.] *When I invite our three volunteers to return to the room, each group will hold a conversation about what you've been experiencing so far in college. Keep the conversation going and be sure you briefly touch your face each time before speaking. When the volunteers talk to you, unless they first touch their faces, ignore them. Keep talking to someone else . . . even turn your back to them. Of course, if they do briefly touch their faces, touch your own face and respond enthusiastically. However, if at any time they do not touch their faces before talking, go back to ignoring them. Do not explain the rule about touching your face before talking.* [5 minutes]
3. [Retrieve the three volunteers. Before they enter the room, tell them,] *"Your classmates are having a discussion. Please join in."* [3 minutes]
4. [Observe the efforts of the volunteers to interact with the group. Note any behaviors that might illustrate the difficulties of people trying to learn the rules of a new culture. Use these to help propel the later discussion.] [5–10 minutes]
5. [Discussion with volunteers] *What was your experience? Why do you think people were responding to you as they did? How did you feel? Can you recall any time in your life when you ever felt like that before? What happened? Did you ever figure out why people were responding to you as they were? If so, how did you figure it out? How did you feel after you figured it out? What did you do after you figured it out?* [5–10 minutes]
6. [Discussion with class members] *What was your experience? How do you think it made the volunteers feel? How did you feel? Can you recall any time in your life when you ever felt like that? What happened?* [If the volunteers did not figure out the rule about touching faces:] *Who would like to explain to the volunteers why you were behaving as you were?* [5–10 minutes]
7. *What you've just experienced is what can happen when different cultures meet. Each culture has rules that dictate the "right" way to do something. In the experience we just had, the right way to talk with someone was to touch your face first. If you don't know a different culture's rules, you can feel awkward, embarrassed, ineffective, or even angry. Higher education has a culture, too. The culture of higher education has rules that the natives know but the people new to college don't know. What have you noticed already that makes college culture different from other educational cultures you have been in?* [e.g., "In college, instructors expect students to have read assignments before coming to class. College students are expected to find out where to get help with problems." For other examples, see the chart "A Dozen Differences between High School and College Culture" in the section titled *Understanding the Expectations of College and University Educators* accompanying Journal Entry 2.] [5–10 minutes]
8. [Quick-Write and/or Class Discussion] *What's the life lesson here for you, and how will you apply it?* [e.g., "It's going to take a while for me to learn the culture of higher education. In the meanwhile when I don't understand something, I should ask questions."] [5–10 minutes]

Approximate time: 35–60 minutes

Source: Adapted from Leeva Chung, University of San Diego, CA

EXERCISE 1-3: Culture Shock

Purpose

To help students identify and become more comfortable with aspects of college culture that they find upsetting and stressful.

Supplies and Setup

Index cards, one for each student. Write on the white board or project on a PowerPoint slide the following: "Culture shock is the upset and stress we experience when confronted with behaviors and beliefs that differ significantly from our own."

Directions

1. *According to our* On Course *textbook, "Culture shock is the upset and stress we experience when confronted with behaviors and beliefs that differ significantly from our own." On your index card, write a brief description of something you've experienced here at [your college] that you have found to be confusing, upsetting, or stressful. For example, maybe an instructor used a word that you have never heard before and you didn't know what the instructor was talking about. Or maybe someone got upset with you because you didn't do something that you didn't even know you were supposed to do. Do not put your name on your card. As we read the cards later, no one will know who wrote it.* [5–10 minutes]

2. [Collect the cards and shuffle them. Ask students to form groups of four to six. Give a card to each student.] [5 minutes]

3. *In your group, decide which card expresses the best example of culture shock in college. Remember, "Culture shock is the upset and stress we experience when confronted with behaviors and beliefs that differ significantly from our own." If your group happens to get your own card, do not reveal that it is your card. Just treat it as if it is someone else's card.* [5–10 minutes]

4. [One at a time, ask each group to read the card it chose. After each card is read, lead a discussion of the experience that led to culture shock. Help students understand what occurred. Start by asking students if they can clarify what happened. As a last resort, offer a clarification yourself.] [15–25 minutes]

5. [Quick-Write and/or Class Discussion] *What's the life lesson here for you, and how will you apply it?* [e.g., "It's natural to experience upset and stress when we find ourselves in a new culture. I'm not going to pretend I'm in a foreign country and make it my goal to learn all of the customs."] [5–10 minutes]

Approximate time: 40–60 minutes

EXERCISE 1-4: Mattering and Marginalizing

Purpose

(1) To help students understand their role in creating a community of learners who value and support each other and (2) to help students identify actions they will commit to doing to show their classmates that they matter.

Supplies and Setup

Handout, "Mattering and Marginalizing" (copied back to back), one for each student; 4" × 6" index cards, one for each student; whiteboard or large white poster paper or marker

Directions

1. [Distribute the handout "Mattering and Marginalizing." Inform students that they should look at only side 1, which says MATTERING.] *Today you are going to do an exercise called Mattering and Marginalizing. I am not going to say much by way of introduction. Together we will read the directions, and then you will have time to answer the prompts. After each section, you will share your answers.*

2. [Read aloud the text following the title MATTERING, including the Cues, Feelings, and Actions statements. You may need to provide an example for each. For example, Cues—the person looked me in the eye; Feelings—that made me feel happy; Actions—I wanted to work harder for that person.] *I will give you five minutes to think of a time you felt valued by someone. After you have thought of the experience, please write down the cue(s), feeling(s), and action(s) related to the experience you are thinking of.* [5 minutes]

3. [Using the whiteboard or poster paper, write the word *Mattering* and then *Cues, Feelings,* and *Actions.* Ask the students to call out the cues they wrote down. Then repeat the process with feelings and actions.] [10 minutes]

4. [Next, have the students turn the handout over to side 2, which says MARGINALIZING. Repeat Steps 2 and 3 with the word *Marginalizing.*] [15 minutes]

5. [Have the students form small groups.] *On the bottom of your handout, you will find two questions. "What are some ways we (can) show our peers they matter or are valued?" and "What are ways we (can) show our peers they are being marginalized or are not valued?" In your small group, share your thoughts on these two questions with each other. One student from each group will need to write down your answers and then record those answers on the board.* [10 minutes]

6. [After having the students read the responses on the board, pass out one 5 × 7 index card to each student.] *You will be answering two more questions. What did you learn from this activity? and What one action will you commit to doing in this class or college to show your peers that they matter? After you are done writing, I will ask you to share your commitment with the large group. I will collect your index cards at the end of the activity.* [10 minutes]

Approximate time: 50 minutes

Instructor Notes

1. The Noel-Levitz Survey of Student Engagement has shown that students are more successful in their classes if they feel connected to part of a larger community. As student populations in colleges become increasingly diverse, educators need to find ways to ensure all students feel a sense of belonging.

2. Use this activity within the first six weeks of class to build a community of learners grounded in a mutual level of respect. When students believe that they matter to their classmates, they are more likely to stay in the course and participate with each other.

Source: Submitted by LuAnn Wood and Cris Davis, Century College, MN; adapted from Schlossberg, N. K. (1989). Marginality and mattering: Key issues in building community. In D. C. Roberts (Ed.), *Designing campus activities to foster a sense of community.* San Francisco: Jossey-Bass.

Mattering and Marginalizing

MATTERING

Please think of a time when you felt as if you really mattered, when who you are or what you did was valued. You do not need to disclose the circumstances of the particular event. Please write down the following:

Cues: What in the interaction let you know you were being valued?

Feelings: How did you feel as a result of this interaction?

Actions: What were your behaviors or actions that occurred as a result of this interaction?

CUES	FEELINGS	ACTIONS

MARGINALIZING

Please think of a time when you felt as if you did not really matter, when who you are or what you did was not valued. Sometimes marginalization in an interaction stems from identity characteristics, such as race, gender, perceived sexual orientation, ability status, age, and so on. Sometimes marginalization is influenced by our position within a group. Sometimes it is the result of an interpersonal dynamic in the absence of any other factor. You do not need to disclose the circumstances of the particular event. Please write down the following:

Cues: What in the interaction let you know you were not being valued?

Feelings: How did you feel as a result of this interaction?

Actions: What were your behaviors or actions that occurred as a result of this interaction?

CUES	FEELINGS	ACTIONS

What are some ways we (can) show our peers they matter or are valued? What are ways we (can) show our peers they are being marginalized or not valued?

Source: Schlossberg, N. K. (1989). Marginality and mattering: Key issues in building community. In D. C. Roberts (Ed.), *Designing campus activities to foster a sense of community*. San Francisco: Jossey-Bass.

EXERCISE 1-5: Cultural Crossword Puzzle

Purpose

Students become familiar with terms associated with surface and deep college culture.

Supplies and Setup

In the previous class, assign students to read the article in *On Course* titled "Understanding the Culture of Higher Education" and complete Journal 1.

Have students sit in groups of three or four; each group should have one easel pad page and three or four markers.

Directions

1. [Either prepare beforehand or ask students to create a crossword puzzle grid of 15 rows and 15 columns on their easel pad page.] [2 minutes]
2. *On your crossword puzzle, fill in as many terms or concepts as possible that are part of the surface or deep culture of higher education. For example, you could write the term "syllabus." Any new word you add must connect to a word already on your page, just as if you were completing a crossword puzzle.* [Optional: Announce that the team with the most correct words will be crowned the winner.] [15 minutes]
3. [Have students present their crossword puzzles to the class. Clarify any terms that others may not understand and correct any misunderstandings students may have about the culture of higher education.] [Optional: Announce the winning team and provide prizes.] [20 minutes]
4. [Have students write a brief reflection journal.] *A good way to begin the journal would be, "By completing the culture crossword puzzle, I learned that. . . ." Or, "By completing the culture crossword puzzle, I have a greater appreciation for . . . ." Or, "After completing the culture crossword puzzle, what surprised me is . . . . ."* [5 minutes]
5. [Invite students to share their reflection journal.] [5–10 minutes]

Approximate time: 45–50 minutes

Source: Submitted by Essie Childers, Blinn College, TX

Journal Entry 2 Understanding the Expectations of College and University Educators

EXERCISE 2-1: Cultural Values and Expectations

Purpose

(1) To develop a sense of what different cultural groups value in home, school, and work lives and (2) to understand the hidden rules or expectations that govern mainstream North American schools and workplaces.

Supplies and Setup

"Cultural Values and Expectations" handout

Directions

1. *People belong to many different cultural groups (e.g., race, ethnicity, gender, socioeconomic, religion, sexual orientation) and are shaped by the values, beliefs, and norms of those groups and thus engage in certain patterns of behavior. However, most schools and businesses in mainstream North America operate under their own set of hidden rules or expectations (values, beliefs, and norms) that we need to be aware of. This does not mean that you need to change your beliefs,*

views, and behaviors, but you need to know these hidden rules to be successful. To explore your multicultural self by identifying your cultural group and your group norms and values, you will have 10 minutes to complete the "Cultural Values and Expectations" handout. [This handout could also be given to the class beforehand as an exercise or homework assignment]. [10 minutes]

2. *Now form groups of four or five students. Going around your group one at a time, share one of your cultural groups that may have many of the* **same** *values as the mainstream North American academic and work culture. Then share one of your cultural groups that may have* **different** *values from those of the mainstream North American academic and work culture.* [15 minutes]

3. [Journal Quick-Write and/or Class Discussion] *What did you learn from this discussion about what different cultures value? What did you learn about mainstream North American academic and workplace values or expectations? What value, belief, or behavior did you realize you may need to adapt in a college or work environment to be successful? What is the life lesson here for you?* [e.g., "Sometimes I used to think people of a different culture than mine were doing things wrong. Now I understand that I need to learn the hidden rules or values of mainstream North American academic and workplace culture, and I need to learn these hidden rules to be successful in college and work. For example, in my culture, it is OK to be late. However, in college, being on time is expected and valued by instructors. I need to leave my house five minutes earlier than I have been to be on time and earn class participation points."] [10 minutes]

Approximate time: 50 minutes

Instructor Notes

It is important to remind students that these mainstream North American academic and cultural norms are generalizations and may change based on regions. Avoid using these generalizations to stereotype, "write off," or oversimplify your ideas about another person and his or her culture.

Source: Submitted by Cris Davis and LuAnn Wood, Century College, MN

CULTURAL VALUES AND EXPECTATIONS

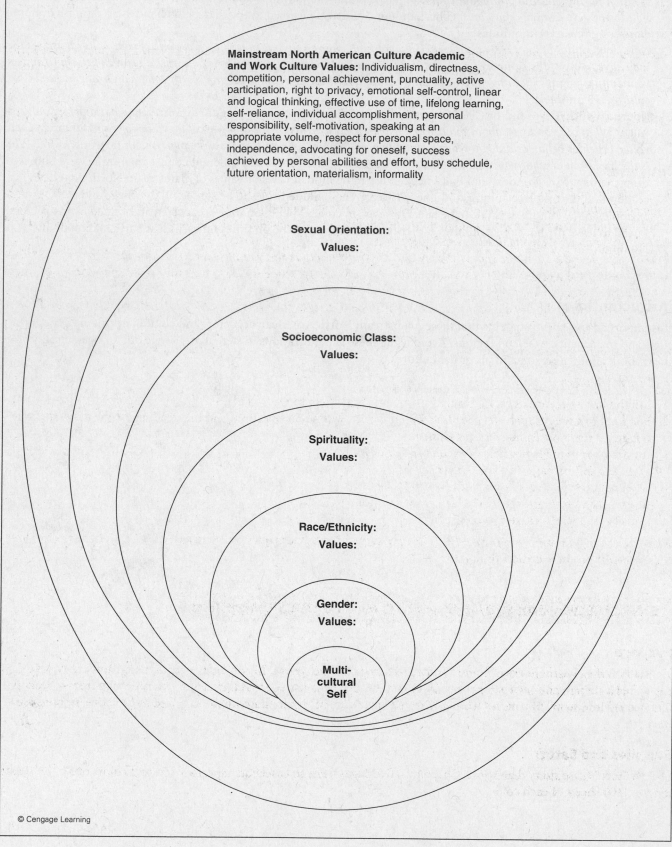

Mainstream North American Culture Academic and Work Culture Values: Individualism, directness, competition, personal achievement, punctuality, active participation, right to privacy, emotional self-control, linear and logical thinking, effective use of time, lifelong learning, self-reliance, individual accomplishment, personal responsibility, self-motivation, speaking at an appropriate volume, respect for personal space, independence, advocating for oneself, success achieved by personal abilities and effort, busy schedule, future orientation, materialism, informality

Sexual Orientation:

Values:

Socioeconomic Class:

Values:

Spirituality:

Values:

Race/Ethnicity:

Values:

Gender:

Values:

Multi-cultural Self

EXERCISE 2-2: Focus Questions

Purpose

To preview the course content and focus students' attention on finding answers to personally meaningful questions. Students also learn the power of using questions to find personally meaningful answers in readings, lectures, and class exercises or discussions.

Supplies and Setup

On Course, journal

Directions

1. *Thumb through* On Course. *Examine the table of contents. Check out the charts that precede each chapter. Look at the focus questions before each section of the text. Note the words in bold print in the text. Examine the diagrams, charts, and cartoons. Read some of the quotations in the margins. In your journal, jot down at least five questions that if you discovered answers during this class, it could improve your life.* [5–10 minutes]
2. *Now, let's hear the questions you want answered. If you hear a question you'd like an answer to, add it to your list.* [Call for questions and record them for all to see. This process allows students to see the range of questions to which they could be finding answers during this semester.] [5–10 minutes]
3. *Put a star next to the five questions in your list that you most want answered. Your job this semester is to discover the answers to at least these five questions.*

Approximate time: 10–20 minutes

Instructor Notes

1. I find it best to record questions exactly as students give them to me.
2. Point out to students that every reading section begins with focus questions and that reading for the answers is one way to get the most from every assignment.
3. An option is to publish a class question list. For example,
   a. How can I manage my time better?
   b. What can I do to feel less anxious when I take tests?
   c. How can I feel more confident about asking questions in class?
   d. Why do I have to take this course?

When discussing questions in Journal Entry 26, you can return to these questions and analyze which of them are *probing* questions that promote critical thinking.

EXERCISE 2-3: Using a Fish Story to Create Course Expectations

Purpose

To establish the classroom environment and expectations for the course. In conjunction with the syllabus, they have developed a student and instructor contract. Hopefully, they will also see that they will be transitioning from a "teacher-directed environment" to a more "learner-directed environment" where they will be expected to be active, responsible learners.

Supplies and Setup

"A Fish Story" (case study that begins Chapter 7), five pages from an easel pad, tape, two different colors of 3" × 3" Post-it notes (100 sheets of each color)

Directions

1. [Assign for homework "A Fish Story," the case study that begins Chapter 7. In the next class, read "A Fish Story" to the class, with emphasis on certain parts of the story, such as "_PLEASE OBSERVE THE FISH AND WRITE DOWN ALL YOUR OBSERVATIONS_." Then briefly discuss and assign questions pertaining to the story that students are to include in a one- or two-page reflective paper.]

   "A Fish Story"—questions to help you organize your essay:

   1. _Why do you think the professor did what he did in the story?_
   2. _Was the professor looking for something specific?_
   3. _In your opinion, what is the meaning behind this story?_
   4. _How would you feel if you were one of the students in this lab?_
   5. _What, if anything, did the students learn?_
   6. _Why did our instructor read us this story?_
   7. _What is our instructor's purpose? Is our instructor looking for something specific?_

2. [During the next class session, the students come into class and see five easel pad pages taped on the board in the front of the classroom. Each page has a line dotted vertically down the middle with "Student" on one side and "Instructor" on the other. Each of the five pieces of paper has one of the following headings on the top:
   - Preparation for Class
   - Attitude and Behaviors in Class
   - Written Assignments Will Be
   - Quiz and Exam Preparation Will Be
   - Earning an A =, Earning a B =, Earning a C =, Earning a D =, How You Could Earn an F in This Course =]

3. [Split the class into four or five groups depending on the size of the class. Hand out the Post-it notes (about 20 sheets of each color) to each group. Explain what each group will be doing—responding to what is written on each of the large papers hanging in the front of the classroom. For example:

   Preparation for Class—Student side = arrive on time, arrive with all your necessary materials, arrive to class prepared with assignments complete.

   Preparation for Class—Instructor side = have a lesson plan with established goals and objectives (active learning practices also), using multiple visual aids and techniques, focusing on student engagement and less on lecturing.]

4. [Each group must offer at least three ideas for each of the easel pad pages. You can also elaborate and add more during the discussion. Type these up and hand them back in the next class session. In the third class session, relate this activity to "A Fish Story." How does it relate? Why does it relate? See if they "GET IT."]

Instructor Notes

There are a lot of teachable concepts and lessons in "A Fish Story"—for example, motivation; locus of control; organization; neat written work; intellectual curiosity; and most of all, "initiative." This ties in nicely with Chapter 1 and the self-assessment that students complete.

Approximate time: Two 50-minute classes

Source: Submitted by Cynthia Thorp, Alfred State College—SUNY College of Technology, NY

Journal Entry 3 Understanding Yourself

EXERCISE 3-1: The Choices of Successful Students

Purpose

To identify the choices of successful students and have students see that they are capable of making these choices.

Supplies and Setup

Whiteboard; students in groups of four or five

Directions

1. *In your group, create a list of the choices of successful students. In other words, what choices do successful students make that struggling students don't? Think about the choices you can see (outer behaviors) and the choices you can't see (inner attitudes or beliefs).* [5 minutes]
2. *Okay, let's hear what you came up with for the choices of successful students.* [Record the choices on the whiteboard.] [5 minutes]
3. *Which of these choices do you think are the most essential for success in college? Vote for three. As I call off a choice, raise your hand to cast your vote.* [Tally the votes each time and record them next to the item on the list.] [5 minutes]
4. *Which of these choices are you willing to commit to so that you can be a successful student this semester? Make a list of them in your journal.* [5 minutes]
5. *Let's hear what you wrote.* [Invite students to stand and state the choices they commit to.] [5 minutes]

Approximate time: **25 minutes**

Instructor Notes

1. Encourage students to identify inner choices (attitudes or beliefs) as well as outer choices (behaviors). One way to distinguish them is to point out that behaviors are visible, so they can be recorded with a video camera. Attitudes or beliefs are invisible, so they cannot be recorded with a camera.
2. In faculty development workshops that I conduct, I've asked thousands of college instructors which behaviors and attitudes or beliefs they consistently see in their successful students. Here are the top vote getters for behaviors: (1) attend class regularly, (2) do all assigned work and turn it in on time, and (3) participate actively. Instructors say the three crucial attitudes or beliefs are to (1) take personal responsibility, (2) be goal directed, and (3) believe in yourself. Other attitudes and beliefs high on the educators' lists are to be self-disciplined, love learning, and have a positive attitude. You can inform students that all of these essential behaviors and attitudes are explored in *On Course*.
3. If there are any commitments that students choose unanimously, you could make them your course rules.

EXERCISE 3-2: Making Changes

Purpose

To identify specific changes students may wish to make in their lives.

Supplies and Setup

Students sitting in pairs (Student A and Student B). Students need their completed Journal Entry 3.

Directions

1. *Student A, read to your partner what you wrote for Step 2 in Journal Entry 3 about your highest scores. Student B, when your partner finishes, tell him or her what you heard. Say, "What I heard you say is. . . ." See how much you can*

remember. You'll have five minutes for reading and responding. Don't switch roles until I call time. If you finish early, take the time to get to know one another better. [5 minutes]

2. *Now switch roles. B reads Step 2 to A. Then A responds, "What I heard you say is. . . ." Again, you'll have five minutes for reading and responding.* [5 minutes]

3. *Student A, read to your partner what you wrote in Step 3 about your lowest scores. Student B, when your partner finishes, you'll say, "What I heard you say is. . . ." Again, see how much you can remember. You'll have five minutes for reading and responding. Don't switch roles until I call time.* [5 minutes]

4. *Now switch roles. B reads Step 3 to A. Then A responds, "What I heard you say is. . . ." Again, you'll have five minutes.* [5 minutes]

5. [Quick-Write and/or Class Discussion] *As a result of what you learned in the self-assessment, are there any changes you'd like to make in yourself? What's the life lesson here for you?* [e.g., "It's amazing how much more I hear when I make a conscious effort to really listen."] [5–10 minutes]

Approximate time: 30–50 minutes

Instructor Notes

1. This exercise is a powerful way to introduce the important issue of change. Points that might be made include: *If you keep doing what you've been doing, you'll keep getting what you've been getting . . . Improving our lives requires change . . . Change can be threatening . . . Change takes courage . . . One purpose of college is to help you change so you can improve your life.*

2. If time allows, you might introduce this question: *What might keep you from successfully making the changes you want to make?*

3. Many teachers report the value of having students complete the self-assessment during class time. In this way, you can better ensure that students understand the directions and complete the questionnaire with a serious and purposeful attitude.

Students can also take the self-assessment online in the MindTap College Success for *On Course*, where it appears in the context of the chapter reading. Students can complete this digital version and print or email their results upon completion.

EXERCISE 3-3: Notice of Vacancy

Purpose

To help students understand the importance of soft skills in the workplace.

Supplies and Setup

One "Notice of Vacancy" handout per student.

Directions

1. *I have exciting news for you! Just a few minutes ago, I found out that I have been given a grant that will allow each of you to hire someone to work for you for one year.* [Pause for a few seconds for effect while students look around at each other suspiciously.] *Okay, I was kidding about the grant, but I would like for you to pretend that I did receive a grant that will allow you to hire someone to work for you for one year. What kind of employee would make your life easier? Maybe a personal assistant, housekeeper, cleaning person, chef, gardener, tutor, driver, or nanny?*

2. *You are now going to fill out a Notice of Vacancy form that will describe the job you are hiring for. Please fill out the job title, write in your name as the supervisor, and then include a brief summary of the job under "Job Description."* [5 minutes]

3. *Next, you will list five required qualities or skills that your employee must have. These things are mandatory, and you would not hire someone who did not possess these qualities or skills.* [5 minutes]

4. *The next section asks for five desirable qualities and skills. These are things you would love for your employee to be good at, but they are not required.* [5 minutes]

5. *Finally list five "No need to apply if . . ." qualities. These are the deal breakers, the things that would keep you from hiring someone.* [5 minutes]

6. *Now we are going to compile your qualities on the board. Please start calling out to me your required qualities and skills, and I will write them on the board.* [5 minutes]

7. [*After they have exhausted the first list.*] *Now call out your desirable qualities and skills, and I will compile those.* [5 minutes]

8. *Do you understand the difference between soft skills and hard skills? Hard skills are the skills specific to one type of job, and soft skills are the skills that will benefit you in any job you have. A nurse, for instance, must have hard skills such as drawing blood, taking blood pressure, and administering medicine. A nurse also needs soft skills such as good communication abilities, friendliness, punctuality, problem-solving skills, and honesty. Let's go through our lists and circle the items that are soft skills.* [Sometimes there are some gray areas, but I talk through it if there is disagreement.] [5 minutes]

9. *Now let's count the soft skills and the hard skills that you said you wanted in your employees.* [Without fail, more soft than hard skills are listed on the board. Most students want the same qualities in their employees (e.g., ethical, hardworking, possessing a sense-of-humor, able to be taught or trained easily, positive).]

10. *So often in college, students focus on hard skills. Hopefully this activity will remind you that your hard skills might help you get a job, but your soft skills will help you keep it.*

11. *And now, just for fun, what kinds of employees were you hiring for? What were some of your "No need to apply if's . . ."?*

Approximate time: 35–45 minutes

Source: Submitted by Martha Crise, Ozarks Technical Community College, MO

Notice of Vacancy

Job Title: _____

Supervisor: _____

Job Description:

Required Qualities and Skills:
1.

2.

3.

4.

5.

Desirable Qualities and Skills:
1.

2.

3.

4.

5.

No need to apply if . . .
1.

2.

3.

4.

5.

Chapter 1: Quiz Questions

(The Answer Key to Chapter 1: Quiz Questions appears at the end of this Facilitator's Manual. Please visit the Instructor Companion Site for *On Course* at login.cengage.com for a digital version of this quiz and its answer key.)

Money Matters

1. Managing money is a skill as important and challenging as reading and writing.   TRUE   FALSE

2. According to a source at the University of Indiana, credit card debt can be more dangerous to your college success than academic failure.   TRUE   FALSE

3. The benefit of qualifying for grants and student loans is that you don't need to pay them back.   TRUE   FALSE

4. If you make poor choices with your credit card in college, what consequences could result?

    A. You could have trouble purchasing a home or a car.

    B. You could lose out on a job.

    C. You could be charged higher interest rates on future credit cards.

    D. All of the above.

5. Which of the following typically offers lower costs for financial services (checking accounts or loans, for example)?

    A. Banks

    B. Credit unions

Understanding the Culture of Higher Education

1. According to Geert Hofstede, a Danish psychologist and anthropologist, deep culture is

    A. the collective programming of the mind that distinguishes the members of one human group from another.

    B. a way of determining which group of people is more likely to be successful in college.

    C. the clothing and art that distinguish one group of people from another.

    D. a set of rules voted upon by a group of people, usually from the same country.

2. Surface culture (above the waterline in the picture of the iceberg) consists of the shared beliefs, attitudes, norms, rules, opinions, expectations, and taboos of a group of people.   TRUE   FALSE

3. In the culture of higher education, a "prerequisite" is a course that must be successfully completed before taking a more advanced course.   TRUE FALSE

4. If you stop attending a class, you _____ expect your instructor to drop you from the course.

    A. should

    B. should not

5. Five suggestions to help you create a meaningful journal are (1) be spontaneous, (2) write for yourself, (3) be honest, (4) be creative, and (5) dive _____.

Understanding the Expectations of College and University Educators

1. In the culture of higher education, students are expected to be mature and responsible for their choices. TRUE   FALSE

2. In the culture of higher education, students typically spend 30 or more hours in class each week, and teachers cover the majority of course content during class.   TRUE   FALSE

3. In the culture of higher education, educators expect students to be intellectually curious, pursuing knowledge rather than merely grades.   TRUE   FALSE

4. In the culture of higher education, educators realize that they are 100 percent responsible for motivating students. TRUE   FALSE

5. In the culture of higher education, educators expect students to collaborate with peers and make use of available help to achieve academic success.   TRUE   FALSE

Understanding Yourself

1. The author of *On Course* offers the following definition of success: "Success is staying on course to your desired outcomes and _____."

2. Doing taxes, taking people's blood pressure, and using video editing software are examples of _____ skills.

3. Persistence, self-confidence, and motivation are examples of _____ skills.

4. The skills you'll learn in the course are essential for making wise _____ and achieving great success in higher education . . . and beyond.

5. People who are strong in the eight qualities measured by the *On Course* self-assessment tend to make wiser choices at forks in the road than do people who are weak in these qualities.   TRUE   FALSE

On Course at Work: Soft Skills at Work

1. The *soft skills* you'll learn in *On Course* are ideal for succeeding in both college and your career.   TRUE   FALSE

2. *Soft skills* may be the skills that determine whether you will keep a job or lose it.   TRUE   FALSE

3. According to the SCANS report, *hard skills* are all you need to get, keep, and excel at the job of your dreams. TRUE   FALSE

4. One estimate suggests that only _____ percent of workers lose their jobs because they can't do the work; the others lose their jobs because they lack necessary soft skills.

   A. 5

   B. 15

   C. 30

   D. 50

5. According to the SCANS report, employers consider *soft skills*, such as those taught in *On Course,* to be

   A. essential for work-world success.

   B. unnecessary for continued job success.

   C. a thing of the past—no one worries about those any longer.

Chapter 1: Essay Topics

1. Many students come to college to be a "success," yet few have given great thought to what they mean by the term. In an essay written to your classmates in this course, offer your personal definition of success.

2. In a letter to a trusted friend, share with him or her what your self-assessment questionnaire revealed to be your greatest areas of strength and weakness.

3. Imagine that you have entered a writing contest for a college scholarship. The topic this year is to explain the changes that you want to make in yourself to be more successful in college and in life. Write this essay for the college scholarship committee.

4. Inform your teacher in this course about which of the Eight Choices of Successful Students will be the easiest for you to make and which will be the most difficult for you to make. Dive deep as you explain why.

5. Write an article for your college newspaper in which you describe the things you found most surprising, confusing, strange, or upsetting during your first week in your new college culture.

6. Using the "One Student's Story" essays in *On Course* as a model, write an essay about how you used a strategy from Chapter 1 to overcome a problem in your life—academic, personal, or even at work. First, explain the problem; then discuss the specific strategy you used and how you put it into action; finally, identify what happened. Your instructor may submit your essay for possible publication in the next edition of *On Course*. Additional directions for writing and submitting these essays can be found at http://oncourseworkshop.com/course-textbook/essay-contest/.

Accepting Personal Responsibility

Concept

There is great value in perceiving ourselves as the primary creators of the outcomes and experiences of our lives. At the very least, we are responsible for how we respond to any event, whether the event is of our creation or not. When academic outcomes and experiences are negative, many students blame others, often teachers. When academic outcomes and experiences are positive, many students credit others. Because the cause of their results is seen as existing outside of themselves, these students have no reason to evaluate and possibly change their own behaviors. Students like this typically wait for the world to change while they complain, blame, make excuses, and repeat ineffective behaviors. They may even blame themselves, all the while thinking there is nothing they can do to change their fate. By offering students the opportunity to see how their own choices contribute to their past, present, and future outcomes, we empower them to approach life with the beliefs and behaviors of a Creator mindset, thus giving up the passivity and bitterness of a Victim mindset.

EMPOWERS STUDENTS TO . . .

1. Adopt a Creator mindset, taking responsibility for creating the outcomes and experiences of their lives (including their education), *and* reject a Victim mindset, giving up complaining, blaming, excusing, and paralyzing self-judgment.
2. Master Creator language, understanding that Creators and Victims choose different ways of thinking and speaking about their experiences, consequently changing both their perceptions of reality and the outcomes that they create.
3. Live more consciously, becoming more aware of their inner aspects—Inner Critic, Inner Defender, and Inner Guide, among others—and the corresponding inner dialogue that dictates students' subsequent actions.
4. Make wise choices by consciously recognizing important decision points in their lives, identifying all possible options at this point, and making decisions with awareness of their future consequences.
5. Make mature decisions, choosing to make long-term gain more important than immediate pleasure or immediate escape from discomfort.
6. Replace outer authority with inner authority and resistance with cooperation.
7. Gain greater control over the outcomes of their lives.

Remember also to use the all-purpose exercises mentioned in the introduction, actively engaging students in the exploration of JOURNAL ENTRIES, CASE STUDIES, ONE STUDENT'S STORY, ON COURSE AT WORK, QUOTATIONS, CARTOONS, FOCUS QUESTIONS, CHAPTER-OPENING CHARTS, and TECH TIPS. Remind students to use letters to label any in-class writing they do in their journals.

Case Study in Critical Thinking: The Late Paper

Purpose

To develop critical thinking skills by exploring a real-life situation concerning personal responsibility and the power of choices.

Supplies and Setup

"The Late Paper" in *On Course*

Directions

1. [Have students read "The Late Paper." One way to be sure everyone has read the selection before taking the next step is "Popcorn Reading." Have one volunteer read the first paragraph aloud, another volunteer read the second, and so on until the reading is complete. Then have students record their scores for the six characters.] [5 minutes]

2. [Find out by a show of hands how many students have picked each character as number one—that is, most responsible for Kim's failing grade. If two or more characters are chosen as number one, move on to Step 3. In the unlikely event that everyone chooses the same character as number one (or there is otherwise little diversity in opinion), ask how many students have picked each character as number six—that is, *least* responsible for Kim's failing grade. Often there is more diversity of opinion here.] [5 minutes]

3. [Create groups of like-minded students.] *Because you agree in your group about which character is most (or least) responsible for Kim's failing grade, decide how you are going to persuade other groups to agree with you.* [5–10 minutes]

4. [Have a spokesperson from each group present the group's position; then lead a debate on the issue by moving the discussion from group to group, allowing students to explain their positions in more detail and to rebut opposing views. Invite students to demonstrate a change in their opinions by getting up and going to the group with which they now agree.] [5–20 minutes]

5. [Quick-Write and/or Class Discussion] *Did you change your mind? If so, why? What did you learn from this discussion about personal responsibility? What's the life lesson here for you?* [e.g., "Sometimes I used all of my energy blaming someone else for a problem rather than doing what I needed to do to reach my goal."] [5–10 minutes]

6. Additional debriefing questions:
   a. *Is there someone in the story who may also bear responsibility for Kim's failing grade?* [This is the Diving Deeper question.]
   b. *If Kim chose to strengthen the quality of personal responsibility, what different choices might she have made in this situation? How would those different choices have changed her outcomes and experiences?*
   c. *In what ways did Kim fail to understand the culture of Professor Freud's class?*

Approximate time: 25–50 minutes

Instructor Notes

1. So as not to stifle discussion, I don't reveal my own opinion.
2. This class discussion is an excellent prewriting activity to be followed by students writing a persuasion essay supporting their choices for most or least responsible. Because students are now sharply aware of opposing views, they often write much more thorough and persuasive essays (including rebuttals) than would be the case without the debate.
3. An optional step for this activity is to ask students to do a Quick-Write and then a discussion about the Diving Deeper question: Is there someone not mentioned in the story who may also bear responsibility for Kim's failing grade?
4. After students have read the case study, another option is to have them get in groups and see if they can come to consensus about which person is **second** most responsible for Kim's failing grade in Psychology 101.

Journal Entry **4** Adopting a Creator Mindset

EXERCISE 4-1: Responsibility Circle

Purpose

To become more aware of how we create or contribute to many of the outcomes and experiences in our lives.

Supplies and Setup

Groups of five or six students sitting in a circle. Each student needs a pen and paper.

Directions

1. *Write four statements that are true about you as a student (or other roles). Alternate between facts that you are happy with and facts that you are not happy with; for example: (1) I have a great schedule this semester (fact about which I'm happy), (2) my math teacher is boring (fact about which I'm unhappy), (3) my history teacher seems like a nice guy (fact about which I'm happy), or (4) I'm not very motivated this semester (fact about which I'm unhappy).* [5 minutes]

2. *Within each group, start with the person who lives farthest from this room. Go clockwise around your circle, with each person reading his or her first statement, then around the circle again with each person reading the second statement, then a third time around, and so forth, until everyone has read all four statements. As you read your statement, add the following words: "... and I am responsible." For example, "I have a great schedule this semester, and I am responsible." "My math teacher is boring, and I am responsible." Become aware of how it feels to say that you are responsible for the situation with which you are happy or unhappy. When you hear others, decide whether there is any truth in the statements that they are responsible.* [5 minutes]

3. *[Quick-Write and/or Class Discussion] Were there situations about which you said, "There's no way I'm responsible for this"? Were there situations about which you said, "Well, I guess I have to admit that I am at least partially responsible for that"? How do you decide what you are, in fact, responsible for in life? Would it be of any benefit to always assume that you are responsible for the results in your life? What's the life lesson here for you?* [e.g., "I have been blaming others for a situation in my life that I am actually more responsible for than I have wanted to admit. That awareness encourages me to make a number of changes, including...."] [10–20 minutes]

Approximate time: 20–30 minutes

Instructor Notes

1. Scott Peck, author of *The Road Less Traveled,* says that one of the most difficult things for human beings to decide is what they are and are not responsible for. Someone else (I don't recall who) has said that whereas people who are neurotic take too much responsibility for the results in their lives, people who are psychotic take too little responsibility. The challenge of being a Creator, then, is taking responsibility for the appropriate results in your life and not taking responsibility for the results that belong to others. Help students see that although they are certainly not responsible for all the outcomes and experiences in their lives, they are, however, 100 percent responsible for how they *respond* to these outcomes and experiences. If they always act *as if* they are responsible for the results in their lives, they will often discover life-improving choices for which they would not otherwise have even looked, let alone discovered.

2. In this activity (and all that deal with the Victim/Creator mindset), acknowledge that some people truly *are* victims. For example, they may be unjustly treated by others because of their race, gender, religion, or sexual preference. Or they may have terrible things happen to them that were out of their control (e.g., a flood). The distinction is in the mindset and the way one responds to injustice or hardships. Victims typically complain, blame, make excuses, and fail to take action to improve their situation. In contrast, Creators consistently look for ways to take action with the goal of creating the outcomes and experiences they want. Creators aren't always successful, but they persevere in the face of adversity with a clear intention of creating a better life for themselves and others.

EXERCISE 4-2: Victim/Creator Role-Play

Purpose

(1) To become familiar with the difference between how those with a Creator mindset and those with a Victim mindset respond to life's stimuli; (2) to see that we often have more options than we realize; (3) to understand that each person responds sometimes as a Creator, sometimes as a Victim; and (4) to see the value of responding as a Creator as often as possible.

Supplies and Setup

Two student volunteers (A and B). Role-playing is enhanced if students have already completed reading and writing Journal Entry 4.

Directions

1. [To Student A] *Imagine that you work for B* [student's name]. *You're often late or absent. Today you arrived 10 minutes late, and B confronts you. Because you're operating within a Victim mindset, whatever B says to you, respond by making excuses; blaming others; or complaining about something, such as the employer's "unfair" rules. Whatever you do, don't accept any responsibility for your absence or lateness and don't agree to try anything new.*
2. [To Student B] *You're the employer who has watched A often be late or absent. You're angry because A was 10 minutes late again today. Go ahead and role-play. As the angry employer, what would you say to A?*
3. *Let's repeat the same scene, except this time, A, you'll respond to your employer from a Creator instead of a Victim mindset.*
4. [Invite students to invent additional situations, especially in college, where some people respond as Victims. Repeat the role-play with as many situations as time allows.]
5. [Quick-Write and/or Class Discussion] *How do people with a Victim mindset typically respond to life? How about people with a Creator mindset? Can you think of a time when you responded as a Victim? A Creator? Can you imagine the same person acting like a Victim in one situation and a Creator in another situation? What's the life lesson here for you?* [e.g., "When I get upset, I tend to act more like a Victim than when I am feeling good."]

Approximate time: About 10–12 minutes for each role-play and discussion

Instructor Notes

1. An important point to bring out here is that a person is not solely a Victim or a Creator. We each have the capacity in any moment to respond as either. One key to success is to begin responding to life more often with a Creator mindset.
2. After each role-play, you might say to the class, "Any suggestions on how the worker could be an even better Victim? An even better Creator?" Other students often want to try the same roles. Sometimes the original pair wishes a second take on the scene.

EXERCISE 4-3: The Broken Escalator

Purpose

To show students that even when they think they are stuck, they often have options they don't see.

Supplies and Setup

Prepare to show the video "Stuck on an Escalator" (2:30) in class or assign for homework. The video can be found at OnCourseWorkshop.com → Educator Resources → Video Gallery → Self-Responsibility.

Directions

1. [Show the video.]
2. *A number of you laughed. What's funny about this video?* [It's so obvious what the people need to do that staying stuck is ridiculous.]
3. *If you were stuck on an escalator, what would you do?* [I would walk up the stairs.]
4. *Why do you think the people on the escalator don't do that?* [They don't see that as an option. They expect someone else to solve their problem. They are being Victims, not Creators.]
5. *Is there a time in your past where you got stuck and didn't see an option to solve your problem? Did someone else help you solve it? Did you ever find a solution? What did you do?*
6. *Is there any situation you are facing here in college where you feel stuck? Can you think of any options that would get you unstuck from your broken escalator?*

Approximate time: 10–15 minutes

Instructor Notes

After your students view and discuss this video, you have metaphorical language to use for the rest of the semester. When they talk about a problem that they should be able to solve, you can say, "Sounds like you're stuck on a broken escalator. What can you do to get off?"

EXERCISE 4-4: Excuses and Expectations

Purpose

To help students be more accountable for their actions and illustrate the importance of meeting with their academic advisors.

Supplies and Setup

Copies of the "Three Scenarios" Handout, one for each student

Directions

1. [After reading each scenario, have students choose a side on what should be done. Have students of like mind gather and discuss reasons for their position.]
2. [Have a spokesperson from each group present his or her group's position; then lead a debate, allowing students to explain their position and rebut opposing views.] [10–15 minutes for each scenario]
3. [Class Discussion] *What did you learn or relearn from this discussion? What choices will you make that perhaps you would not have before this discussion?* [5–10 minutes]

Approximate time: 35–55 minutes

Instructors Notes

1. This activity is great to do during the first few weeks of the course, especially before midterm exams.
2. Students must learn the importance of attending every class session and taking personal responsibility.

Source: Submitted by Annette D. Fields, University of Arkansas at Pine Bluff

Three Scenarios

Scenario #1

Jennifer is a freshman at Success University. She overslept and missed her midterm exam. She emailed the instructor and said, "Dear Mr. Thomas, I have been stressed out about my dad being sick, and I overslept. Can I please take the exam?"
Success University's attendance policy states

"When a student accumulates as many un-excused absences as the number of credit hours of the class, whether due to negligence or some other reason, the instructor will warn the student that additional absences will result in failure to pass the course. These absences will be excused only when the student presents official documentation of the situation to the teacher. All other absences are un-excused."

The course is one credit hour, and Jennifer has two unexcused absences. Mr. Thomas did warn Jennifer that additional absences would result in her failing the course. She presently has a D in the course. **Should Jennifer be allowed to take the exam? What choices could she have made earlier to avoid this situation?**

Scenario #2

Allen is a freshman at the University of Determination. He works part time on campus. His supervisor asked him to organize some files and record grades. One day while recording grades, he noticed that his girlfriend was missing two exam grades and had an F in the class. He texted his girlfriend and told her that the instructor was available and to come right away. When his girlfriend arrived, Allen explained to his supervisor that his girlfriend missed the two exams because she was feeling really homesick. He asked his supervisor, "Can she please take the exams she missed?" **Should the instructor allow Allen's girlfriend to take the exams she missed? What choices could she have made earlier to avoid this situation?**

Scenario #3

Mark is senior at the University of I Can. Mark has a 3.8 grade point average. Because he is a graduating senior, he did not meet with his academic advisor and self-registered online. Four weeks after the semester started, Mark met with his advisor and was informed that he was one credit hour short of graduating. Mark was missing a one-credit physical education hour, a university requirement. Mark has already accepted his dream job, which starts immediately upon his graduation. Without a degree, he will lose the job. Additionally, Mark's family lives 900 miles away and has already purchased nonrefundable airline tickets for his graduation. **Should Mark's advisor allow him to graduate? What choices could Mark have made earlier to avoid this situation?**

Journal Entry 5 Mastering Creator Language

EXERCISE 5-1: The Language of Responsibility

Purpose

To practice language that supports responsible choices and to have an opportunity to meet a classmate.

Supplies and Setup

"Language of Responsibility" handout (next page). It's best if students have completed Journal Entry 5 before doing this activity.

Directions

1. *Victims and Creators see the world very differently. As a result, they use different vocabularies to represent their respective realities. In other words, you can tell a Victim and a Creator by their choice of words. On the handout, translate the Victim language into Creator language. Keep in mind two qualities that characterize Creator Language. First, Creators accept ownership of their outcomes and experiences. Second, Creators plan and take specific actions to improve their outcomes and experiences. So, you can recognize Creators because they accept ownership and take action!* [5–10 minutes]

2. [Class Discussion] *Okay, let's see what you came up with. Read one of the Victim statements and give us your translation into Creator language. Are there any statements you had trouble translating and you'd like to hear what someone else wrote?* [5–10 minutes]

3. [Quick-Write and/or Class Discussion] *Based on their different vocabularies, what would you say are the differences in the beliefs that Victims and Creators have about themselves? About other people? About the world? What do you think is the difference in the results created by Victims and Creators? What's the life lesson here for you?* [e.g., "If I want to create my goals and dreams, I better learn to think and act more like a Creator and less like a Victim."] [5–10 minutes]

Approximate time: 15–30 minutes

Instructor Notes

1. Important concepts to come out in the discussion include the following: Victims believe that other people and bad luck are responsible for their problems. As a result, Victims seldom achieve their goals and dreams (although sometimes they get lucky and do). Creators often achieve their goals and dreams (although sometimes they get unlucky and don't). Acting from a Creator mindset is a way to improve the odds of being successful, but (alas) it isn't a guarantee.

2. As you lead the discussion of the students' translations, reinforce the two qualities that characterize Creator language: (1) ownership and (2) a plan of action.

3. If you have 45 or more minutes for this activity, you can put students into groups of four to six. After they write their translations individually (Step 1), have them discuss their translations in these small groups. Then move on to a class discussion (Step 2).

Language of Responsibility

Victim Talk	Creator Talk
1. I would be doing a lot better at this college if the teachers were any good.	
2. They ought to do something about the food around here.	
3. I couldn't come to class because I had to go to the dentist for a checkup.	
4. You just can't pass a course when it's that hard.	
5. My boss makes me so angry.	
6. I can't help talking in class.	
7. I couldn't get the assignment because I was absent.	
8. I couldn't keep my appointment with you yesterday because my math teacher made me take a makeup test.	
9. People always get angry when they work hard and still fail a course.	
10. I couldn't attend class because I had to drive my mother to work.	
11. I would have called you, but my daughter got sick.	
12. They don't know what they're doing around here.	
13. I couldn't get to class on time because my last teacher kept us late.	
14. I tried calling him, but he's never home.	
15. I didn't have time to do my homework.	

EXERCISE 5-2: Have to/Choose to

Purpose

To demonstrate how language choices affect our attitude and our energy levels; to meet and interact with classmates.

Supplies and Setup

Journal

Directions

1. *In your journal, draw a vertical line down the middle of a page. On the left side of the line, make a list of five things you "have to" do. Examples: "**I have to** go to college," "**I have to** call my mother on Sundays," or "**I have to** eat . . ."* [3 minutes]
2. *[Milling] Everyone stand and choose a partner. Each partner reads from his or her list three things that he or she "has to" do. If you hear a new "have to" that is true for you, add it to your list. Then move on to a new partner and repeat the exchange of "have to's." Keep going until I call stop. As you do this activity, be aware of how you are feeling.* [5 minutes]
3. *Now, on the right side of the line, rewrite each of your sentences. Change "have to" to "choose to" and add a "because . . ." or "so . . ." clause to the sentence, one that gives a positive reason for your choice. Examples: "**I choose to** go to college because my degree will qualify me for the job I want," "**I choose to** call my mother on Sundays so she will feel loved," or "**I choose to** eat because I want to be healthy."* [7 minutes]
4. *[Milling] Everyone stand and meet a partner as we did before. This time each of you read three things that you "choose to" do. After you both read, move on to another partner. Keep going until I call stop. Notice if you feel any different this time.* [5 minutes]
5. *[Quick-Write and/or Class Discussion] Did you feel any different when you said "choose to" rather than "have to"? What does this experience suggest about how your language choices affect you? What is the life lesson here for you?* [e.g., "I get myself upset by thinking I 'have to' do something when the truth is that I really *don't* have to do it. . . . I'm *choosing* to do it. Realizing this makes me feel a lot more calm and in control of my life."] [5–10 minutes]

Approximate time: About 20–30 minutes

Instructor Notes

1. A great way to clarify directions is to give a demonstration (DEMO). Steps 2 and 4 (above) will be most clear if you say, "So here's what that would look like . . ." and DEMO what you're asking for.
2. A point worth making in the discussion is that most people feel their energy level go up when they switch from "have to" to "choose to." That's because most people are depressed by Victim talk and energized by Creator talk.

EXERCISE 5-3: Choices and Ripples

Purpose

To explore how the choices students make now will have rippling effects in the near and distant future.

Supplies and Setup

Two student volunteers and one Slinky

Directions

1. Ask for two student volunteers. Each student takes an end of the Slinky and stretches it out. One student serves as the "choice" and the other as the "effect." Ask the student serving as the "choice" to shake the Slinky once. The class will see how by shaking the Slinky once, there are multiple and continuous effects on the other student. You could have the other students time how long it takes for the Slinky to stop having these "effects."
2. *On a sheet of paper, please state a choice you have made that had or continues to have rippling effects.*

3. *Now make a list of the effects that the choice had. Also, don't forget that sometimes our choices can have effects on those around us. Please don't forget those!*

4. *After looking over your choice and any negative rippling effects it had, reflect on how you could have prevented these rippling effects. What are some strategies from the* On Course *text that may have helped you prevent or minimize these negative effects?*

Approximate time: 25 minutes

Source: Submitted by Katy Goforth, Tri-County Technical College, SC

Journal Entry 6 Making Wise Decisions

EXERCISE 6-1: The Wise Choice Process

Purpose

To give students an opportunity to practice the Wise Choice Process, a powerful critical- and creative-thinking tool of Creators.

Supplies and Setup

Journal Entry 6 in *On Course* (students will need to refer to the six steps of the Wise Choice Process); students in pairs

Directions

1. *In your journal, briefly write about a current problem or difficulty in your life. It doesn't have to be a major problem. Choose a problem that you are comfortable talking about with your partner.*

2. *Decide which partner will present a problem and which will be the Guide. The Guide will use the Wise Choice Process to assist the other person to discover his or her best options.*

3. *Guide, ask your partner the six questions of the Wise Choice Process. Your role is to guide your partner to discover his or her best options without giving advice. If you come up with an option your partner doesn't think of, you can always tell him or her after class. For this dialogue, offer no advice. The easiest way to do this is simple: **Stick to the six steps of the Wise Choice Process.** Here's what that might look like. [DEMO the Wise Choice Process.] Any questions? When you're ready, begin.*

4. *[Optional: If time allows, have partners switch roles and repeat Step 3.]*

5. *[Quick-Write and/or Class Discussion] What was your experience as a Guide? How was it to avoid giving advice while helping your partner to solve his or her own problem? What was your experience as the person seeking a solution to a problem? Did you discover positive options for solving your problem? What's the life lesson here for you? [e.g., "By not giving advice to my partner, she came up with a solution I never would have suggested. By answering the questions of the Wise Choice Process, I came up with options that I had never thought of before."]*

Approximate time: 15 minutes for each time through the Wise Choice Process; 5–15 minutes for discussion

Instructor Notes

1. An alternative format is to put students in trios instead of pairs. The third student acts as a silent observer during the Wise Choice Process. Afterward, the observer's role is to give feedback to the Guide about how well he or she followed the six steps of the Process. The observer's presence often causes the other two participants to focus more consciously on their purpose—coming up with positive options—raising the quality of the results they create. If time allows, you can rotate the trio so each person has a chance to experience all three roles.

2. This process is very powerful. Students often say, "I didn't think this process would really work, but now that I've tried it, I see that it's a great tool for helping someone find positive options to solve a problem."

3. Later in the semester, if a student asks you for advice (either privately or in class), ask if he or she would be willing to choose a classmate to act as a Guide through the Wise Choice Process. The class can observe and see the power of this decision-making process in action.

EXERCISE 6-2: The Road Not Taken

Purpose

To offer students an opportunity to see how their choices make all the difference in the outcomes of their lives.

Supplies and Setup

"The Road Not Taken" by Robert Frost. (The text of this poem can be found in many literature books and on the Internet.) Project the poem on a PowerPoint slide or give it as a handout.

Directions

1. *I'd like a volunteer to read "The Road Not Taken" by Robert Frost.*
2. *The narrator of this poem came to a fork in the road: "Two roads diverged in a yellow wood." He had to take one road or the other, and he made a choice "that has made all the difference." In your journal, make a list of the major choice points you've faced in your life. For example, you might put "Attend college after high school or get a job," "Get married or stay single," or "Have a child or not." [5 minutes]*
3. *Let's hear some of your choice points. Just tell us your options, not what you chose. If you hear someone else mention a choice that reminds you of one you've made, add it to your list. [2–5 minutes, depending on the energy. A way to pick up the energy is to ask after a choice has been called out, "How many of you have also made a choice like this?"]*
4. *In the poem, Frost says, "Knowing how way leads on to way, I doubted if I should ever come back." Now pick one of your choices and go back to the moment of decision. In your journal, Quick-Write about what your life would be like today if you'd chosen the road not taken. For example, if one of your choice points was to marry or not, and you did marry, write what you imagine your life would be like today if you had not gotten married back then. [5 minutes]*
5. *Who'd be willing to read aloud what you wrote? How do you feel about that choice now that you've looked down the other road? Did you make a wise choice back then? Why do you think so? What's the life lesson here for you? [e.g., "After I've made a decision, it's going to affect my life for years to come, so I'd better think it through before I make an important choice."] [3–5 minutes for each volunteer]*

Approximate time: 15 minutes for Steps 1–4; 3–5 minutes for each volunteer in Step 5

Instructor Notes

1. The point here is threefold: to assist students to examine the wisdom of the previous choices they have made, to help them see that every choice they make impacts the quality of their future, and to show that all experiences contain life lessons if we look for them.
2. Listen for the Inner Critic badgering a student about a "bad choice." If a student is critical of his or her past choice, you might ask, "Is that your Inner Guide speaking or your Inner Critic?" If the student says, "That's my Inner Critic," you might respond, "Remember, your Inner Critic likes to wallow in what you did wrong, but your Inner Guide takes ownership and then creates a plan to make things better. Which voice would be more helpful to listen to?" Most of all, resist giving advice to the student. Merely be a questioner and an active listener.

EXERCISE 6-3: Excuses and Reasons

Purpose

To consider the difference between mature reasons and immature excuses.

Supplies and Setup

Copies of the "Excuses and Reasons" handout (next page)

Directions

1. *Rank the statements on the "Excuses and Reasons" handout as explained in the* **Directions.** [5 minutes]
2. *Which statement did you rank #1 . . . as a Victim's excuse? Why?* [5 minutes]
3. *Which statement did you rank #9 . . . as a Creator's reason? Why?* [5 minutes]
4. [Discuss the Diving Deeper questions on the handout.]
5. [Quick-Write and/or Class Discussion] *What differences do you see that distinguish Victims' excuses from Creators' reasons? What's the life lesson here for you?* [e.g., "People love to pretend that their excuses are actually reasons, but pretending doesn't make it so."] [5–10 minutes]

Approximate time: 20–25 minutes

Instructor Notes

1. Important points to make in the discussion:
   - Payoff of excuses for Victims: They minimize present discomfort or maximize present pleasure.
   - Price of excuses for Victims: They seldom achieve their desired outcomes and experiences.
   - Price of reasons for Creators: They sometimes experience present discomfort.
   - Payoff of reasons for Creators: They often achieve their desired future outcomes and experiences.
2. An alternative is to choose one statement and have students line up by the score they gave that statement from 1 to 9. This structure is called a "Value Line." (You may want to make a horseshoe so that the two ends of the line are closer to each other.) Going from one end of the line to the other, have students say their scores out loud to make sure everyone is in the right place. (In a large group, you may have students at every number.) Now ask students at each end of the line to explain their choices. A point that often arises is that we see "reasons" when we've had a similar experience and see "excuses" when we have not.

Excuses and Reasons

Here are some choices that students have made more important than turning in a college assignment on time. Rank them from 1 through 9. Put a *1* next to the decision you consider to be the weakest Victim's excuse. Put a *9* next to the decision you consider to be the strongest Creator's reason. Rank the other decisions in order from 2 through 8, giving a different number to each statement. You may assume that all nine students believe they are telling the truth (which is why this activity is not called "Lies and Reasons").

Victim's Excuse 1 2 3 4 5 6 7 8 9 Creator's Reason

I didn't turn in my assignment on time because . . .

_____ I helped my aunt move to a new apartment.

_____ I rushed my daughter to the hospital because she was having an asthma attack.

_____ I stayed home to wait for the television repair man.

_____ I visited my boyfriend because he's having problems at home, and I felt like he needed me.

_____ I didn't look at my schedule carefully, so I totally forgot when the assignment was due.

_____ I had a headache and stayed home.

_____ I decided I could improve the assignment if I worked on it for a few more days.

_____ I started the assignment last night, and I didn't have time to finish it.

_____ I went to an appointment with another teacher instead of coming to class.

Diving Deeper

What criteria do VICTIMS use to make their choices? What's the payoff? What's the price?

What criteria do CREATORS use to make their choices? What's the payoff? What's the price?

Educator John Holt wrote, "Caring teachers accept no excuses." What do you think of this belief?

EXERCISE 6-4: Counselor to a Celebrity

Purpose

To give students an opportunity to practice the Wise Choice Process, a powerful critical-thinking tool of Creators. This activity also helps deepen the camaraderie among students and is highly engaging.

Supplies and Setup

Students should have read "Making Wise Decisions" in the *On Course* textbook; students in groups of three or four; distribute "The Wise Choice Process" handout.

Directions

1. *The Wise Choice Process works best on complex problems that require a lot of thought, especially those that have significant consequences.* [Give a brief DEMO of how the Wise Choice Process can be used. Ask for student participation in steps of the process.] [10 minutes]
2. *Now that you know how to use the Wise Choice Process, each group will serve as advisors or counselors to a celebrity. Each group must select only one celebrity and one of the celebrity's problems, as sometimes there are many!*] [5 minutes]
3. [Give students several minutes to select a celebrity with a problem. Ask the groups to send a representative to the instructor to get approval for the celebrity and the problem they have chosen. Next, the student representatives from each group write the approved name and problem of their celebrity on the board. Having these names on the board prevents duplicates, gets students excited about the upcoming discussion, and helps serve as examples to any groups that having trouble with the selection process.] [5 minutes]
4. [Have students work together to complete the handout. Walk around and assist students with this part. Students have more difficulty with Wise Choice Process steps three and four, which motivated creation of the handout.] [10–15 minutes]
5. [When finished with the handout, each group chooses a spokesperson to read the completed handout to the class. Be sure to leave a few minutes after each reading to allow for an impromptu whole-class discussion about the celebrity!] [5 minutes per group]
6. [Quick-Write and/or Class Discussion] *Rate the difficulty of using the Wise Choice Process on a scale from one to ten, with 10 meaning very challenging to 1 meaning very simple. What is the reason for your rating? Will you use the Wise Choice Process personally in the near future? If so, could you share an example? Just describe the problem, in general. Specific details are not needed.* [5–15 minutes]

Approximate time: At least 35 minutes for #1 through #5 of the directions; the time for #6 depends on the number of groups; 5–15 minutes for discussion

Instructor Notes

1. When selecting the celebrity, I have found it best to avoid a celebrity/problem in the realm of politics or religion.
2. I encourage you to do directions #1 though #3 during the last part of a class, continuing with the next steps during the first part of the next class. This gives students time to research and become familiar with the celebrities on their own, before their groups complete the Wise Choice Process handout.
3. As you walk around the classroom checking on the groups' progression through the handout, you may enjoy chatting with students about the celebrities they have chosen. It may also help you learn a bit more about your students by knowing whose lives they choose to follow.

Source: Submitted by Debra Ford, Ph.D., Davidson County Community College, NC

The Wise Choice Process

Your group will act as an advisor or counselor to the celebrity. You will help the celebrity as he or she fills out this form.

1. "What's my present situation?" (Describe the main problem you will address.)

2. "How would I like my situation be?" (What is the ideal outcome after the problem has been solved?)

3. "What are the possible choices" that could help solve this problem? (List as many actions as you can.)

   A. _____

   B. _____

   C. _____

   D. _____

4. "What's the likely outcome of each possible choice?"

   A. Would choice "A" solve the problem?

       Circle one: Yes! Probably Probably Not No!

   B. Would choice "B" solve the problem?

       Circle one: Yes! Probably Probably Not No!

   C. Would choice "C" solve the problem?

       Circle one: Yes! Probably Probably Not No!

   D. Would choice "D" solve the problem?

       Circle one: Yes! Probably Probably Not No!

5. "Which choice(s) listed above will I commit to doing?"

6. "When and how will I evaluate my plan?" (Identify the specific date and criteria by which you will determine the success of your plan. This is when the celebrity will report back to you, his or her advisor or counselor.)

Journal Entry **7** Believing in Yourself: Change Your Inner Conversation

EXERCISE 7-1: Inner Dialogue Role-Play

Purpose

To dramatize the impact of the ongoing inner dialogue among the Inner Critic, Inner Defender, and Inner Guide.

Supplies and Setup

Four volunteers (A, B, C, and D) for a role-play. Have student A sit in a chair.

Directions

1. *Student A, you're going to speak to the class about your thoughts and feelings about college. There's no right or wrong thing to say, so just tell us whatever you want about your experience so far in college. After you speak, pause to hear what your inner voices have to say. When they are finished, make another statement about college.*

2. *Student B, you'll position yourself at Student A's right side and be his or her Inner Critic. This means that whatever Student A says, you'll find some way to criticize him or her for it. For example, if Student A says, "I like college," you might say, "You're a lousy math student; you can't even get to your classes on time . . . ."*

3. *Student C, you'll position yourself at Student A's left side and be his or her Inner Defender. This means that whatever the Inner Critic says, you'll find some way to defend against the accusations by blaming problems on other people or circumstances. For example, you might say, "No one could be a good math student with such a lousy teacher. And with the terrible parking around here, of course you're late to your classes . . . ."* [5–10 minutes for Steps 1–3]

4. *[After the scene has played out] So, Student A, what's on your mind right now? Did you recognize any of those voices? Do you think those voices have any effect on your success?* [Ask Inner Critic, Inner Defender, and class to add their observations.] [3–5 minutes]

5. *Now, Student D, you'll position yourself behind Student A and be his or her Inner Guide. Your job is to offer a more objective view on Student A's life. The key is "accountability and a plan." Help Student A own the problem and come up with a plan to solve it. For example, if the Inner Critic says, "You're a lousy math student," you might say, "You can improve your math skills by spending more time studying." If the Inner Defender says, "You have a lousy math teacher," you might say, "You can always go to the math lab to get additional help."* [3–5 minutes]

6. *[Quick-Write and/or Class Discussion] So, what did you learn from this role-play? What's the life lesson here for you?* [e.g., "I've got a lot of voices chattering in my head, and some of them won't help me achieve my goals. That's why it's really important that I am careful about which one I listen to."] [5–15 minutes]

Approximate time: 25–40 minutes

Instructor Notes

1. Let the role-play go for as long as it's entertaining and making a point. You'll probably have to slow down the dialogue, especially so the Inner Guide has time to respond to the comments of the Inner Critic and Inner Defender. An important point to make is that the Inner Critic and the Inner Defender are both inner voices of the Victim. The difference is whether the finger of judgment is pointed inward (Inner Critic) or outward (Inner Defender). The Inner Guide is the inner voice of the Creator. Our choice about which voices to listen to affects how we feel and what we do and therefore determines our results in life.

EXERCISE 7-2: Revising Stinkin' Thinkin'

Purpose

To practice identifying irrational beliefs that tear away at our self-esteem.

Supplies and Setup

Students should have completed Journal Entry 7. Copies of the "Revise Stinkin' Thinkin'" handout (next page).

Directions

1. *Fill in all the empty spaces in the A + B = C chart. Some items give you "A" (the Activating event) and "C" (the Consequence), and you must fill in "B" (the Belief). Others give you "A" and "B," and you must fill in "C." Still others give you only "A" and ask you to fill in both "B" and "C." Go ahead and do that now.* [10 minutes]
2. [Lead a discussion about the Beliefs and Consequences the students have filled in for each event. For each item, ask:] *Is this belief wise thinkin' or stinkin' thinkin'? Is this event likely to raise or lower the person's self-esteem? What is the life lesson here for you?* [e.g., "How I feel about myself depends more on what I think and believe than on what I accomplish."] [15–20 minutes]

Approximate time: 25–30 minutes

Instructor Notes

1. Remind students of psychologist Albert Ellis's belief that much of the world's emotional misery is caused by stinkin' thinkin' and that stinkin' thinkin' leads not only to poor outcomes and experiences but also to lowered self-esteem.
2. The important point to be made here is that any activating event allows for many possible responses. How we respond is a result of the core beliefs we hold about ourselves, other people, and the world, and these core beliefs powerfully affect our self-esteem.

Revising Stinkin' Thinkin'

Activating Event (What happened)	+	Belief(s) (What I think)	=	Consequence (Emotions and behaviors)
1. I fail a midterm test.		1.		1. I get depressed and stop attending the course.
2. A friend doesn't meet me at the time we agreed on.		2. My friend is usually very reliable and keeps his agreements.		2.
3. A speeding car cuts across two lanes of highway, just missing my car, and then rockets off the next exit ramp.		3.		3.
4. Shortly after I hand in an essay, my instructor tells me, "I need to see you right away."		4.		4. I get very nervous and put off making an appointment to see my instructor.
5. I get an application for financial aid.		5. This form is very Complicated, and I'm sure to make a mistake filling it out. I don't want anyone to know I'm confused.		5.
6. I'm going to be late for work for the third time this week. I've had one unexpected problem after another this week, but my employer doesn't know this, and she's bound to be furious when I get there.		6.		6.

EXERCISE 7-3: Recognizing Inner Voices

Purpose

To help students understand the differences between the Inner Critic, Inner Defender, and Inner Guide, and to recognize the ways in which the Inner Critic and Inner Defender undermine us.

Supplies

Three volunteers. Three printed signs to indicate the role each volunteer will play: Inner Critic, Inner Defender, and Inner Guide.

Directions

1. *Thank you for volunteering to be our inner voices. One of you will be the Inner Critic, another will be the Inner Defender, and a third will be the wise Inner Guide.* [Give one sign to each volunteer.]
2. *I am going to read a statement aloud; then you will respond in the voice of your assigned role: Inner Critic, Inner Defender, or Inner Guide. If you can't think of a good response, the rest of the class will help you:*
   a. *I have to give a speech in my communication class, and I HATE speaking in front of a group.*
   b. *My boyfriend/girlfriend was really quiet on the phone this morning.*
   c. *My job is so boring—I hate it!*
   d. *My boss was very short with me. She was almost rude when I asked her a question.*
   e. *I had plans to go out to eat with two of my friends, and they both cancelled at the last minute.*
   f. *I have so much homework. I'll never get it all done!*

   [The responses tend to go something like this: "I have to give a speech in my communication class, and I HATE speaking in front of a group."

   Inner Critic: "You are going to be horrible. You'll probably go blank and you'll start crying."

   Inner Defender: "Speeches are stupid. I'll never have to give a speech in my job. What's the point? My teacher is terrible."

   Inner Guide: "You can do this. Learning to give speeches will help you in your other classes. Everyone in the class is just as nervous as you. You are prepared."]
3. *I hope this activity helps you understand how our Inner Critic and Inner Defender can "mess" with us. These voices waste our energy on blaming, complaining, and making excuses. It is always better to listen to our Inner Guide. It's the only one of the three voices that uses our energy to seek a solution to a challenging situation.*

Approximate time: 15–20 minutes

Instructor Notes

1. Be prepared to prompt the "inner voices." Sometimes the Inner Defender will make an Inner Critic–type statement. Point out that what was said was a perfect Inner Critic response, but the job of the Inner Defender is to blame someone else. Remind them who they are blaming.
2. If one of the volunteers is struggling, open it up to the class. Someone else will usually jump in and offer a statement.

Source: Submitted by Martha Crise, Ozarks Technical Community College, MO

Chapter 2: Quiz Questions

(The Answer Key to Chapter 2: Quiz Questions appears at the end of this Facilitator's Manual. Please visit the Instructor Companion Site for *On Course* at login.cengage.com for a digital version of this quiz and its answer key.)

Adopting a Creator Mindset

1. When people create the best life possible given their circumstances, they are using _____.

   A. a Creator mindset

   B. a Victim mindset

   C. a student mindset

   D. all of the above

2. When people allow life to happen to them, they are using _____ .

   A. a Creator mindset

   B. a Victim mindset

   C. a student mindset

   D. none of the above

3. When we respond to a stimulus as a Creator we are most likely to

   A. seek solutions.

   B. take action.

   C. try something new.

   D. all of the above.

4. When we respond to a stimulus as a Victim, we are most likely to

   A. blame.

   B. complain.

   C. excuse.

   D. all of the above.

5. The key ingredient of personal responsibility is choice.   TRUE   FALSE

Mastering Creator Language

1. "I failed because my instructor is terrible" is something that would probably be said by your Inner

   A. Critic.

   B. Defender.

   C. Guide.

   D. Creator.

2. "I'm so stupid; it's no surprise I failed math" is something that would probably be said by your Inner

   A. Critic.

   B. Defender.

   C. Guide.

   D. Creator.

3. When you hear ownership and an action plan, you know you are talking to a Victim.   TRUE   FALSE

4. "I was late because I chose to sleep 30 minutes later this morning" is something that would probably be said by your Inner

   A. Critic.

   B. Defender.

   C. Guide.

   D. Victim.

5. "I don't think I'm smart enough to make it in college" is something that would probably be said by your Inner

   A. Critic.

   B. Defender.

   C. Guide.

   D. Creator.

Making Wise Decisions

1. What we will experience in 5 or 10 years is greatly affected by the choices we make from here on.   TRUE   FALSE

2. Your Inner Defender will be of great help as you take the first step of the Wise Choice Process, which is objectively identifying "What's my situation?"   TRUE   FALSE

3. In Step 4 of the Wise Choice Process, the ideal is to come up with how many possible choices?

   A. One

   B. Two

   C. Three

   D. As many as possible

4. If you can't predict the outcome of one of your possible choices, you should stop and gather more information before making any decisions.   TRUE   FALSE

5. After implementing your plan, the final step of the Wise Choice Process is to evaluate the success of your plan. One good way to do this is to compare your new situation (results of your plan) with how you would like your situation to be (as you defined it in Step 2).   TRUE   FALSE

On Course at Work: Personal Responsibility at Work

1. As long as I believe my career success belongs to someone else (such as "lousy" bosses), I'm being a Victim, and my success is unlikely.   TRUE   FALSE

2. Creators know that the foundation of success at work (as in college) is accepting this truth: By our choices, we are each the primary creators of the outcomes and experiences of our lives.   TRUE   FALSE

3. Victims usually don't explore their career options thoroughly or match career requirements with their own talents and interests, and they make uninformed choices.   TRUE   FALSE

4. What are the advantages of being a Creator in the workplace?

   A. Creators bring a positive and productive attitude to the workplace.

   B. Absenteeism and poor working habits are not problems for Creators.

   C. Creators get the job and then excel at the job.

   D. All of the above are advantages.

   E. None of the above are advantages.

5. Taking responsibility for your work life means

   A. planning your career path to keep your options open and your progress unobstructed.

   B. reacting emotionally to disappointments on the job.

   C. placing responsibility for obstacles on those who are creating them (bosses, coworkers, "the man").

   D. Acting immediately on any and every opportunity offered you, so you won't miss out on them.

Believing in Yourself: Change Your Inner Conversation

1. According to psychologist Albert Ellis, the following formula explains why people respond differently to the same event: A + B = C. In this formula, "A" stands for the activating event, and "C" stands for the consequence (how we feel about the activating event). What does "B" stand for?

   A. Behaviors

   B. Beliefs

   C. Brains

   D. Brawn

2. "I'm stupid" is a typical comment made by an Inner _____.

3. "He's stupid" is a typical comment made by an Inner _____.

4. Disputing irrational beliefs is best done by the

   A. Inner Critic.

   B. Inner Defender.

   C. Inner Guide.

   D. Inner Tube.

5. Being able to dispute irrational beliefs will strengthen your self-esteem.   TRUE   FALSE

Chapter 2: Essay Topics

1. Many people who commit crimes believe that they have been wronged by society and that this justifies their crimes. Write an essay to inform a group of prison inmates about the differences between a Creator and a Victim.

2. Some people have charged that North America has become a continent of Victims: Whenever North Americans don't like the way something is, the argument goes, they blame others instead of taking personal responsibility. Present an argument for a newspaper editorial supporting or contradicting this viewpoint.

3. Interview three or more instructors at your college and find out their opinions on how well students accept personal responsibility for their education. Write an editorial for your college newspaper explaining what you discover.

4. Do most people use Victim language or Creator language? Take on the role of one who studies the way people use language. Go to a public place and listen to people talk. Write an article for a local magazine detailing what your research uncovers.

5. Recall a time when you received extraordinarily good or bad service from someone at a business where you were a customer. If the service was extraordinarily good, write a letter to the owner of the business explaining how an employee went "above and beyond" to accept personal responsibility for meeting your needs as a customer. If the service was extraordinarily bad, write a letter to the owner of the business explaining how an employee shirked personal responsibility and created a poor experience for you as a customer.

6. Psychologist Albert Ellis said that irrational beliefs (which he called "stinkin' thinkin'") cause many of our problems. In an essay for your classmates, report on some of your own irrational beliefs that have gotten you off course and lowered your self-esteem. Offer rational beliefs that you could take on to dispute your stinkin' thinkin'.

7. Using the "One Student's Story" essays in *On Course* as a model, write an essay about how you used a strategy from Chapter 2 to overcome a problem in your life—academic, personal, or even at work. First, explain the problem; then discuss the specific strategy you used and how you put it into action; finally, identify what happened. Your instructor may submit your essay for possible publication in the next edition of *On Course*. Additional directions for writing and submitting these essays can be found at http://oncourseworkshop.com/course-textbook/essay-contest/

Discovering Self-Motivation

Concept

Choosing a meaningful purpose gives our lives a direction and creates inner motivation. Many students have not defined a personally meaningful purpose for being in college, let alone for being in a particular course. Unfocused, these students are more likely to drift **from** rather than **to** academic success. By offering them the opportunity to choose personally meaningful outcomes that they would like to achieve in college or in life, we assist students to create internal motivation and thus positively impact their persistence in the face of life's inevitable obstacles.

EMPOWERS STUDENTS TO . . .

1. Design a life plan that replaces external motivation with internal motivation.
2. Create a sense of "self" founded on their unique combination of personal roles, goals, and dreams.
3. Revise or upgrade their personal goals and dreams as a result of being exposed to the variety of aspirations held by other students.
4. Persist when they encounter obstacles that stand between them and their college education (or any other major goal).
5. Develop positive, affirming self-talk and powerful visualizations that will support them in pursuing their goals and dreams in the face of both internal and external obstacles.
6. Make and keep commitments to themselves.

Remember also to use the all-purpose exercises mentioned in the introduction, actively engaging students in the exploration of JOURNAL ENTRIES, CASE STUDIES, ONE STUDENT'S STORY, ON COURSE AT WORK, QUOTATIONS, CARTOONS, FOCUS QUESTIONS, CHAPTER-OPENING CHARTS, and TECH TIPS. Remind students to use letters to label any in-class writing they do in their journals.

Case Study in Critical Thinking: Popson's Dilemma

Purpose

To develop critical thinking skills by exploring a real-life situation concerning self-motivation.

Supplies and Setup

"Popson's Dilemma" in *On Course*

Directions

1. [Have students read "Popson's Dilemma." One way to be sure everyone has read the selection before taking the next step is to have one student read the first paragraph aloud, another student read the second, and so on until the reading is complete. Then have students put in their scores for the eight professors.] [5 minutes]

2. [Find out by a show of hands how many students have picked each professor as number one—the best advice for motivating Professor Popson's students. If two or more characters are chosen as number one, move on to Step 3. In the unlikely event that everyone chooses the same character as number one (or there is otherwise little diversity in opinion), ask how many students have picked each character as number eight—the worst advice for motivating Professor Popson's students. Often there is more diversity of opinion here.] [5 minutes]

3. [Create groups of like-minded students.] *Because you agree in your group about whose advice is best (or worst) for motivating Professor Popson's students, decide how you are going to persuade other groups to agree with you.* [5–10 minutes]

4. [Have a spokesperson from each group present the group's position; then lead a debate on the issue by moving the discussion from group to group, allowing students to explain their positions in more detail and rebut opposing views. Invite students to demonstrate a change in their opinions by getting up and going to the group with which they now agree.] [5–20 minutes]

5. [Quick-Write and/or Class Discussion] *What did you learn from this discussion about self-motivation? What motivates you? If, similar to the student in the case study, you begin to lose your motivation in college, what could you do to get it back? What's the life lesson here for you?* [e.g., "No one else can really motivate us; we're each responsible for creating our own motivation."] [5–10 minutes]

Approximate time: 25–50 minutes

Instructor Notes

1. So as not to stifle discussion, I don't tell students what my scores are.
2. This class discussion is an excellent prewriting activity to be followed by students writing a persuasion essay supporting their opinion in the debate. Because students are now sharply aware of opposing views, they often write much more thorough and persuasive essays than would be the case without the debate.
3. An optional step for this activity is to ask students to do a Quick-Write and then a discussion about the Diving Deeper question: Is there an approach not mentioned by one of the eight professors that would be even more motivating to you?

Journal Entry ⑧ Creating Inner Motivation

EXERCISE 8-1: V × E = M

Purpose

To help students identify courses in which they have low motivation and provide them with an opportunity to find ways to increase their motivation.

Supplies and Setup

A copy of the "V × E = M" handout. Students should have completed Journal Entry 8.

Directions

1. [Have students individually fill out the "V × E = M" handout.] [5 minutes]
2. [Have students get in pairs.] *Partner A, show your handout to Partner B and identify the course in which your motivation score is the lowest and explain why. Partner B, give suggestions to Partner A about how to raise his or her inner motivation. Apply what you know about the motivating power of the value and expectation of success.* [5–10 minutes]
3. *Now reverse roles. Partner B, show your handout to Partner A and identify the course in which your motivation score is the lowest and explain why. Partner A, give suggestions to Partner B about how to raise his or her inner motivation. Apply what you know about the motivating power of the value and expectation of success.* [5–10 minutes]
4. [Quick-Write and/or Class Discussion] *What was your experience of this activity? Who found that they were able to raise their motivation for a course? How? What did you learn or relearn from this discussion about self-motivation?* [e.g., "I can actually increase my motivation by thinking differently about the value I place on passing a course or learning the content of a course."] [5–10 minutes]

Approximate time: 20–30 minutes

Instructor Notes

1. If time allows, have students also discuss the course for which they have their second-lowest score for motivation.
2. List on the board (and perhaps copy and hand out to students) all the ways they found to raise their value and expectancy for success in their courses.

V × E = M

In the "Course" column, list all of the courses you are taking this semester. In the "Value" column, give a score from 0 to 10 (10 high), indicating the value to you of each course (consider the value of both the outcomes and experiences of the course). In the "Expectation" column, give a score from 0 to 10 (10 high), indicating your expectation of being able to achieve your desired outcomes and experiences in each course with a reasonable effort. Multiply the two scores to determine your level of motivation for each course (0–100).

COURSE	VALUE	×	EXPECTATIONS	=	MOTIVATIONS
1.					
2.					
3.					
4.					
5.					
6.					

EXERCISE 8-2: Roles and Dreams

Purpose

To assist students to identify dreams that they have in their various life roles. By showing specifically how college will contribute to these valued outcomes and experiences, we create the conditions for inner motivation to flourish.

Supplies and Setup

A copy of the "Roles and Dreams" handout for each student; students in pairs (Student A and Student B). Post the following three questions on the board or PowerPoint slide: *"What is one of your roles? What outcomes do you want in this role? What experience are you looking for?"*

Directions

1. *We each play many roles in life. A role is any function to which we regularly devote large chunks of time and energy. Write a list of your current roles, beginning with your role as "student." Continue your list with other roles that you play in your life. As you write them down, say them aloud as a reminder to others of their roles.*

2. *Student A, you'll ask student B the following three questions, pausing after each for B to answer: "What is one of your roles? What do you want in this role? What experience are you looking for?" After you have asked the three questions once and they have been answered, ask them again; B can consider the same role or a different one. If B can't think of a desired outcome or experience in a role, ask, "What do you REALLY want in this role? What do you REALLY want to experience in this role?"*

3. *Student B, you'll respond each time to A's question. You can repeat the same role as many times as you want but try to do all of your roles at least once. Any questions? Ready. Begin.* [A demonstration (DEMO) here will help illustrate the process.] [5 minutes]

4. [After both partners have answered the questions aloud.] *Now fill in the boxes on your Roles and Dreams form. Identify your roles and what you really want—your dreams—in each role. What, for example, is your absolute biggest dream as a student? Is it a two-year associate's degree? A four-year bachelor's degree? A master's degree? A doctorate? Don't worry at this time about how you'll do it. What do you really want? Feel free to use words, pictures, symbols whatever. It only has to make sense to you.* [5–10 minutes]

5. *Now we're going to do a milling. "Milling" means to walk around without a particular destination in mind. Take your Roles and Dreams form with you and meet someone. Introduce yourself; then tell one of your roles and a dream.* [DEMO by offering one of your own roles and dreams.] *After each of you has shared a role and dream, move on to another partner and do it again. No one owns a dream, so if you hear one you like, add it to your Roles and Dreams form. Make it your own!* [5–10 minutes, or as long as the energy in the room is high]

6. [Quick-Write and/or Class Discussion] *What's on your mind right now about your dreams? How will college contribute to the achievement of your life dreams? What's the life lesson here for you?* [e.g., "When I realize that college is an important step on the way to my dream, it's easy to stay self-motivated in my classes."] [5–10 minutes]

Approximate time: 20–30 minutes

Instructor Notes

Giving a DEMO of what you want the students to do is essential in this exercise, as it is in many others. If you DEMO the process clearly, the students will move confidently and smoothly through it. Without a good DEMO, the activity often breaks down into confusion and requests for clarification.

Roles and Dreams

Role: _____

My dream:

Role: _____

My dream:

Role: _____

My dream:

Role: _____

My dream:

Role: _____

My dream:

Role: _____

My dream:

EXERCISE 8-3: Guess My Dream

Purpose

To offer students an opportunity to re-evaluate their dreams, make a public statement of their dreams, and hear the dreams of others.

Supplies and Setup

"Guess My Dream" handout; pens; students in groups of four or five

Directions

1. *Finish the 10 sentence stems on the "Guess My Dream" handout.* [5–8 minutes]
2. *Decide who will go first in your group. Read sentences 1 to 9 to the group but don't read sentence 10. After you read sentences 1 to 9, your group will have two minutes to guess your dream. After your group has guessed the dream or time runs out, read sentence 10. I'll let you know when it's time to move on to the next person.* [5 minutes per person]
3. [Quick-Write and/or Class Discussion] *What's on your mind right now about your dreams? What is the value of having dreams? Where do you suppose dreams come from? If you don't have a dream, how could you get one? What's the life lesson here for you?* [e.g., "Some people have a difficult time taking ownership of a big dream."] [5–10 minutes]

Approximate time: 20–40 minutes

Instructor Notes

1. Be sensitive to students who have yet to identify their dreams. Remind them that many successful people took years to find a dream that felt right to them. In the meantime, they set a goal to find a personally meaningful dream.
2. Remind everyone with a dream to stay open to an even more wonderful dream coming along.
3. Remind all students that one of the major values of having a personally meaningful dream is that it motivates us to do the difficult tasks that must be done to achieve success.

Guess My Dream

1. I really love to . . .

2. I'm very good at . . .

3. What I really want to have is . . .

4. What I really want to do is . . .

5. What I really want to be is . . .

6. Something I would do even if I didn't get paid is . . .

7. Someone I really admire for his or her achievements is . . .

8. The best compliment anyone can say to me is . . .

9. After I'm gone, I want to be remembered for . . .

10. One of my biggest dreams is . . .

Journal Entry 9 Designing a Compelling Life Plan

EXERCISE 9-1: Looking Back

Purpose

To offer students an opportunity to consider the quality of their present life plan.

Supplies and Setup

Writing paper and pens; students in pairs (Student A and Student B)

Directions

1. *Partner A, imagine that it is many years from now and you are close to the end of your life. Partner B has come to visit you in the last few days of your life. Partner B will ask, "Have you had a rich and personally fulfilling life?" Partner A, answer "Yes" or "No" and then tell your partner why. Partner B, write your partner's reasons on a sheet of paper. Any questions? If not, begin with Partner B asking, "Have you had a rich and personally fulfilling life?"* [5 minutes]
2. *Now, Partner B will ask the same question. Only this time, Partner A, give the opposite answer. For example, if you said "Yes" before, now say "No, I have not had a rich and personally fulfilling life." Then go on to explain why. Again, Partner B will record your reasons. Any questions? If not, begin. Partner B, ask your friend, "Have you had a rich and personally fulfilling life?"* [5 minutes]
3. [Reverse roles and repeat Steps 1 and 2.] [10 minutes]
4. *Exchange papers and read over the lists that your partner has recorded for you.*
5. [Quick-Write and/or Class Discussion] *What was your experience of doing this activity? What did you learn by doing this exercise? Are there any changes you want to make in your life plan? What's the life lesson here for you?* [e.g., "Many people probably die without having done much more than talk about their dreams. I'm not going to let that happen to me."] [5–15 minutes]

Approximate time: 25–40 minutes

Instructor Notes

1. If possible, it is more effective to have the "dying" partner lying down.
2. If your students are keeping their journals in a journal book, you may want to have their partners record in the journal.

Source: Adapted from Jessica Dibb, Inspiration Seminars

EXERCISE 9-2: Eulogy for Myself

Purpose

To offer students an opportunity to consider the quality of their present life plan.

Supplies and Setup

Paper and pens for each student

Directions

1. *Imagine that you have died. The person who knows you best in life undertakes the task of delivering the eulogy at your funeral. Write the eulogy this person would deliver. Write it neatly enough that someone else can read it. Do not put your name on it.* [10 minutes]
2. [Collect all the eulogies and redistribute them so that no one knows whose eulogy he or she has.]

3. *I'd like a volunteer to come up front and read the eulogy that you have.* [Have as many eulogies read as you have time for: 2–3 minutes each.]
4. [Quick-Write and/or Class Discussion] *How did you feel during this activity? What did you learn from writing and listening to the eulogies? Are there any changes you want to make now in your life plan? What's the life lesson here for you?* [e.g., "I'm not going to live forever, so I better start taking steps to make my life something I'll be proud of."] [5–15 minutes]

Approximate time: 20–45 minutes

Instructor Notes

1. After a eulogy is read, you can have students try to guess whose it is, explaining their choices. Then the true author of the eulogy can identify himself or herself or not.
2. A time-saving alternative is to have students write one sentence they would like carved on their gravestones.
3. Another alternative is to have students imagine that they are at their retirement party and someone is making a speech about them.

EXERCISE 9-3: Practicing the DAPPS Rule

Purpose

To give students an opportunity to practice creating goals that use the DAPPS rule.

Supplies and Setup

Students have read "Designing a Compelling Life Plan," the section of the *On Course* textbook that discusses the DAPPS rule; create DAPPS rule scenarios on index cards, with one scenario per card (see sample scenarios in Step 2 of the directions); students in four groups.

Directions

1. *The DAPPS rule is a tool that can help you create effective goals that often lead to successful completion. Let's review what each of the letters stands for.* [Review DAPPS] [5 minutes]
2. [Give each group a scenario card. Here are some examples:
    a. This job is terrible! I'd quit, but I have bills to pay.
    b. I need to lose weight, but I don't know how to begin!
    c. I'm panicked because I have to give a presentation in two weeks! I can't talk in front of a group!
    d. I'm tired of being single. I can't find a decent person at these clubs!]

    With a fifth scenario, DEMO what you will ask students to do in Step 3. [5 minutes]
3. *Using the DAPPS Rule, please create a goal that would help the person in your scenario solve his or her problem.* [Give students several minutes to create an effective goal for their scenario using the DAPPS rule. Walk around and assist students.] [5–10 minutes]
4. [When finished, invite groups to choose a spokesperson to read the scenario and then the effective goal, written using the DAPPS rule. After the reading of each scenario and goal, have members of other groups offer helpful feedback. For example, did the group cover each of the five elements of the DAPPS rule? Is the group's goal achievable based on the date and actions given for completing the goal? Are there other specific actions that could also be taken to complete the goal?] [Approximately 5 minutes for each group]

Approximate time: 30–35 minutes

Instructor Notes

1. At this point, I have created only four scenarios and at times have had to have more than one group working separately on the same scenario. Feel free to create your own scenarios.
2. By having the debriefing questions printed on a handout or placed on the board, the class response could be done in writing. Groups could even rate each other on this form, which often enhances performance when announced at the beginning of the activity.

Source: Submitted by Debra Ford, Davidson County Community College, NC

Journal Entry 10 Committing to Your Goals and Dreams

EXERCISE 10-1: Draw Your Dreams

Purpose

To assist students to visualize their dreams, thus creating greater commitment to the dreams.

Supplies and Setup

Dozens of felt-tip pens of various colors; journal books (or blank sheets of paper); students in groups of four to six

Directions

1. [Pass around the felt-tip pens and ask students to take some. Later they can exchange with others if they want other colors.]
2. *Turn to the next clean page in your journal (or take out a blank sheet of paper). Using the colored markers, draw a picture or symbol of your greatest dream or dreams in life. You don't have to be a good artist; just use your imagination to create a picture of your dream.* [10 minutes]
3. *Each person in turn, show your drawing to your group and explain what your dream is. Be sure to (1) use present-tense verbs, (2) be specific and concrete in describing your drawing, and (3) present it with the energy and emotion that it deserves. If you finish describing your dream before I indicate it's time to move on, the other members of your group can ask you questions about your dream. Each person will have four minutes.* [15–25 minutes, depending on group size]
4. [Quick-Write and/or Class Discussion] *What was your experience of doing this activity? What's the life lesson here for you?* [e.g., "When people talk about their dreams in the present tense, they often describe them as if they already exist."] [5–10 minutes]

Approximate time: 25–40 minutes

Instructor Notes

1. Some Inner Critics will say, "But I can't draw. I'm no artist." Make it very clear that this is not an art contest. It is simply an opportunity to create a visual image of their dreams, something that they are all perfectly capable of doing.
2. An alternative to drawing is to have students create a collage.
3. Students will enjoy seeing your picture and hearing you explain it as well! Drawing your dream is powerful, and I urge you to get some of the power for yourself. I have pictures of my dreams framed and hanging in my bedroom for inspiration.
4. If you have a student with a particularly powerful dream, consider videotaping him or her explaining it and use the tape to inspire future classes.

EXERCISE 10-2: I Have a Dream

Purpose

To offer students an illustration of the motivating power of commitment to a dream.

Supplies and Setup

Video of Dr. Martin Luther King's "I Have a Dream" speech. Most likely your college library has (or can get) a copy. As of this writing, a number of videos of Dr. King's speech are available on YouTube. The full speech is about 17 minutes long.

Directions

1. *I'd like to introduce you to someone who had one of the most motivating dreams of the 20th century.* [Explain the context for students who are unaware of the racial strife in 1968. Show all or part of "I Have a Dream." The last six or seven minutes are particularly stirring.] [6–15 minutes]
2. [Quick-Write and/or Class Discussion] *What's on your mind or in your heart after hearing Dr. King's dream? How committed do you suppose Dr. King was to his dream? How do you suppose he developed such a commitment to his dream? What did his dream motivate him to do? What difference do you suppose Martin Luther King's dream made in the quality of his life? If you have a dream, how committed are you to its fulfillment? How do you suppose you could strengthen your commitment? What difference would increasing your commitment to your dream make to your life? What's the life lesson here for you?* [e.g., "Dreams give you the courage to make difficult choices."] [10–20 minutes]

Approximate time: 15–30 minutes

Instructor Notes

I have watched this speech numerous times, and it never fails to move me. In addition to the moral imperative of his message, I'm also strongly affected by the reality that Dr. King had such a commitment to his dream that he was motivated to present it to a quarter of a million people at the Lincoln Memorial and to untold millions more on film and video. Dr. King's example causes me to ask myself, "What dream do I have about which I feel that much passion and commitment?"

EXERCISE 10-3: Dream Puzzles

Purpose

To review information about self-motivation and to encourage students to visualize their dreams.

Supplies and Setup

- In the previous class, assign students to read the article "Committing to Your Goals and Dreams" and write Journal Entry 10.
- Prepare questions about the content of the article on "Committing to Your Goals and Dreams."
- Large blank puzzle pieces (can be ordered from http://thecommunitypuzzle.com) one for each student.
- Write a question on the back of half of the puzzle pieces and the answers on the back of the 10 connecting puzzle pieces. For example, if you have 20 students, write 10 questions and 10 corresponding answers.
- Colorful permanent markers

Directions

1. [Place all the pieces on a table. Shuffle. As the students enter the classroom, have them pick up a puzzle piece and read the question or answer on the back. Ask students to find their match, pair up, and sit together.] [5 minutes]
2. [Ask each pair to share their dreams and on the front side of the puzzle piece draw symbols to represent their dreams.] [10 minutes]
3. [Afterward, all students connect their puzzle pieces. Additional pieces may be added to form a border. If desired, the instructor can glue, frame, and hang the dream puzzle in class.] [10 minutes]

4. [Finally, give students time to reflect and do a Quick-Write in their journals focusing on the following questions:]
   - *Did you feel prepared to participate in matching the questions and answers related to your homework assignment? If not, why?*
   - *You drew a symbol to represent your dream on the front side of the puzzle. What steps are you taking now to make sure your dream will become a reality?*
   - *Who will you include in your support system to help you along the journey?* [10 minutes]
5. [DISCUSSION: Ask students to share answers to the three debriefing questions.] [10 minutes]

Approximate time: 45 minutes

Source: Submitted by Essie Childers, Blinn College, TX

Journal Entry 11 Believing in Yourself: Write a Personal Affirmation

EXERCISE 11-1: Revising Toxic Messages

Purpose

To demonstrate how affirmations can dispute the toxic messages of the Inner Critic.

Supplies and Setup

Journals or paper and pen; students in pairs (Student A and Student B)

Directions

1. *Draw a line down the middle of the next clean page in your journal.*
2. *What you are about to write will NOT be shared with anyone unless you choose to. On the left-hand side of the page, write any criticisms you can ever recall hearing from significant adults in your life. Skip a line after each one. For example, maybe your mother once told you, "You're the most selfish child I've ever known." Or your father told you, "You're the laziest child in the world." Or your teacher told you, "Your writing is poor." [Pause as they write.] What criticisms do you recall about your thinking ability? . . . Your emotions? . . . Your body? . . . Your schoolwork? . . . Your physical abilities? . . . The kind of person you are?* [5 minutes]
3. *What you are about to write WILL be shared with others. Now, write in the right-hand column a positive statement that reclaims the quality that you were criticized for. For example, if the criticism is "You're lazy," you'd counter with "I am a hard worker." If the criticism is "You're stupid," you'd counter with "I am intelligent."* [5 minutes]
4. *Partner A, read only your positive statements to Partner B. Partner B, listen carefully, and when your partner is done, tell your partner what you heard: "I heard you say that you are a hard worker and you are intelligent."* [2–4 minutes, based on the energy level of the room]
5. *Now reverse roles. Partner B, you read your positive statements, and, Partner A, you say what you heard.* [2–4 minutes]
6. [Quick-Write and/or Class Discussion] *How did it feel to say those positive statements? What did it feel like to listen to your partner's positive statements? How have the negative voices in your head hindered you in the past? How would your life be different if you heard the positive statements more? What's the life lesson here for you?* [e.g., "If I refuse to allow negative thoughts to occupy my mind, I'll feel a lot better about myself, and I'll probably get a lot more done, too."] [5–15 minutes]

Approximate time: 20–35 minutes

Instructor Notes

This activity makes a great setup for the affirmation writing process in Journal Entry 11.

EXERCISE 11-2: Affirmation Milling

Purpose

To take ownership of one's personal affirmations and hear other people's affirmations. This activity also builds a sense of community in the classroom.

Supplies and Setup

3 × 5 cards, two per student. Students need to have already completed Journal Entry 11, having written their personal affirmations.

Directions

1. *Open your journals to the page where you wrote your affirmations for Journal Entry 11. Make two copies of your affirmation on the 3 × 5 cards.*
2. *Now we're going to get up, walk around the room and greet other people in the room with our names and our affirmations. You can take your cards if you want.*
3. *Here's what it will look like: You'll walk up to someone like this.* [DEMO this by actually going up to a student.] *Then you'll shake hands and say your name and affirmation like this: "Hi, my name is Skip, and I am a bold, happy, loving man." Your partner will respond, "Yes, you are!" And you reply, "I know!"* [Encourage the student you're demonstrating with to say that to you.] *Now your partner will say his or her name and affirmation, and you'll respond, "Yes, you are!" and your partner will reply, "I know!"* [Encourage the student you're demonstrating with to say his or her affirmation, and you respond with a rousing "Yes, you are!" Ham it up and be lighthearted!] [2 minutes]
4. *Okay, let's do it. And have fun! Keep meeting people with your affirmation until I call stop.* [2–4 minutes]
5. [Quick-Write and/or Class Discussion] *What was your experience of doing this activity? How do you feel right now? What's on your mind? Were you aware of any voices in your head while you were doing it? What were they saying? Whose voices were they? When would be great times to say your affirmation to yourself? What's the life lesson here for you?* [e.g., "The more I say positive things about myself, the more I believe them, and when I believe them, I start acting like they are true."]

Approximate time: 10–20 minutes

Instructor Notes

1. The messages students often hear in their heads while doing this activity are "I feel stupid doing this" or "Others will think I'm weird." This is the voice of the Inner Critic. Other messages might include "The teacher is stupid for making us do this" or "This activity is the dumbest thing I've ever experienced." This is the voice of the Inner Defender. Help students acknowledge these voices without judgment so they can begin to hear the more supportive voices of their Inner Guides in their affirmations.
2. Very rarely (in my experience), a student will not want to share his or her affirmation with classmates. (Some cultures, for example, frown on saying such positive things about oneself.) Remind students that they can always pass on doing an exercise.
3. I collect one card with the students' affirmations from each student. I print the affirmations on certificates or paper frames (available from office supply stores) and give them out at the next class. Students love to get this official-looking copy of their affirmations!

Chapter 3: Quiz Questions

(The Answer Key to Chapter 3: Quiz Questions appears at the end of this Facilitator's Manual. Please visit the Instructor Companion Site for *On Course* at login.cengage.com for a digital version of this quiz and its answer key.)

Creating Inner Motivation

1. In two major surveys, college and university educators identified lack of _____ as the number one barrier to student success.

2. According to American College Testing (ACT), in public four-year colleges in the United States, about _____ percent of students fail to return for their second year.

   A. 10

   B. 20

   C. 33

   D. 50

3. According to American College Testing (ACT), in public two-year colleges in the United States, about _____ percent of students fail to return for their second year.

   A. 10

   B. 20

   C. 33

   D. 50

4. In the formula $V \times E =$ Motivation, the letter E stands for _____.

   A. energy

   B. effort

   C. evidence

   D. expectation

5. According to recent U.S. Census Bureau data, how much more do Americans with a four-year college degree earn in a lifetime, on average, than people with a high school degree?

   A. $400,000

   B. $900,000

   C. $1,600,000

   D. $2,100,000

Designing a Compelling Life Plan

1. According to psychologist Brian Tracy, many people resist setting life goals because they don't know how.
   TRUE   FALSE

2. A "life role" is an activity to which we regularly devote large amounts of _____ and energy.

3. The DAPPS rule is an acronym, a memory device to assist us in remembering the five qualities of an effective
   _____.

4. The five letters in DAPPS stand for Dated, Achievable, Personal, Positive, and _____.[Capital-
   ize the word.]

5. Which of the following is the most effective goal, according to the criteria of the DAPPS rule?

   A. Do well academically this semester.

   B. Work hard to get good grades.

   C. Achieve a grade point average of 3.5 or better this semester.

   D. Have more fun.

Committing to Your Goals and Dreams

1. A(n) _____ is an unbending intention, a single-mindedness of purpose that promises to overcome all obstacles regardless of how you may feel at any particular moment.

2. When it comes to accomplishing goals and dreams, commitment creates _____.

3. Because of his commitment to return to Hawaii to visit his new girlfriend, the author earned money for the trip by
   selling magazine subscriptions door to door.   TRUE   FALSE

4. Cathy Turner used visualizations to help her win two Olympic gold medals in speed skating.   TRUE   FALSE

5. Which of the following is NOT a key to effective visualizing?

   A. Relaxing

   B. Using present-tense verbs

   C. Being specific

   D. Feeling your feelings

   E. Listening to your favorite music

On Course at Work: Self-Motivation at Work

1. Designing my career path has nothing to do with writing goals.   TRUE   FALSE

2. A motivating career goal need not have the DAPPS qualities.   TRUE   FALSE

3. To stay self-motivated, you'll want to match your career choice and college major with your parents' recommenda-
   tions and desired income level.   TRUE   FALSE

4. After you have begun your career, you

    A. will continue to find self-motivating strategies helpful.

    B. will no longer need to use your life plan (you've arrived).

    C. will never be asked to set goals or create work plans.

    D. all of the above.

    E. none of the above.

5. Some of the most motivated students we see in college are those who view college as

    A. an easy way to fill the time until they determine what they "really" want to do.

    B. the way to win the heart of someone they love.

    C. the next logical step on the path to their career goals.

    D. a way to win their parents' approval.

Believing in Yourself: Write a Personal Affirmation

1. As adults, we must depend on others to tell us what we should believe about ourselves.   TRUE   FALSE

2. A personal _____ is a statement about ourselves in which we claim our desired qualities as if we already have them in abundance.

3. If your affirmation seems like a lie, remind yourself that when you say your affirmation, you are prematurely telling the _____.

4. If you want to strengthen your affirmation, which of the following would you NOT do?

    A. Realize that you already possess the qualities you desire.

    B. Listen to your Inner Critic.

    C. Repeat your affirmation over and over as a reminder.

    D. Make choices consistent with your affirmation qualities.

5. If you want to further strengthen your affirmation, which of the following would you NOT do?

    A. Criticize other people before they criticize you.

    B. Be careful about the words you use to describe yourself.

    C. Say your affirmation when life tests you and then act consistently with your affirmation qualities.

    D. Record your affirmation and listen to it often.

Chapter 3: Essay Topics

1. Many students are unsuccessful in college because they don't see how college is going to help them create the life they want to live. Write an essay in which you define both what you want to accomplish in your life and how college is going to be an important steppingstone to that success.

2. Some critics suggest that today's college students have no sense of commitment to causes bigger than themselves. If this is an unfair criticism of you as a college student, write a letter to the editor of your local newspaper in which you define exactly what important cause(s) you feel committed to and why.

3. The ability to have a clear picture of the future you want to create is a great help in creating it. Write an essay in which you describe in detail what you would like to have, do, and be 20 years from now.

4. Personal affirmations are helpful for countering the negative self-talk of our Inner Critic. Write an essay in which you explore the messages you consistently get from your Inner Critic, where you think you got them from, and the kind of self-talk that you plan to engage in to minimize the negative effect your self-judgments will have on your success.

5. Some people find it extremely difficult to identify their personal goals and dreams. If this is true for you, write a formal letter to your teacher describing your lack of goals and dreams; speculate on why this is so; explain how you feel about it; and suggest what, if anything, you plan to do about this situation.

6. Using the "One Student's Story" essays in *On Course* as a model, write an essay about how you used a strategy from Chapter 3 to overcome a problem in your life—academic, personal, or even at work. First, explain the problem; then discuss the specific strategy you used and how you put it into action; finally, identify what happened. Your instructor may submit your essay for possible publication in the next edition of *On Course*. Additional directions for writing and submitting these essays can be found at http://oncourseworkshop.com/course-textbook/essay-contest/.

Chapter

4

Mastering Self-Management

Concept

Most major life goals, such as earning a college degree, are achieved by taking purposeful actions consistently over time. Raised in a culture that relishes instant gratification, many students have not learned the rewards of taking persistent, small steps toward a distant personal goal. Without an effective action plan, many students fail to initiate the steps they are perfectly capable of taking to achieve their goals. By regularly offering them an opportunity to identify, record, and take their next-action steps and by acknowledging them for taking these actions (regardless of the outcome), we help students develop effective self-management and reap the benefits of taking persistent, purposeful actions.

EMPOWERS STUDENTS TO . . .

1. Live life actively, rather than passively, understanding that the key to effectiveness is not time management but self-management.
2. Choose, prioritize, and schedule purposeful actions that will move them toward their goals and dreams.
3. Use effective self-management tools (e.g., monthly and weekly planners, next-actions lists, tracking forms, waiting-for lists, 32-day commitments) to get and stay on course.
4. Replace compliance with or defiance against outer rules with cooperation with inner rules that, over time, develop into supportive habits.
5. Develop self-discipline, including the abilities to focus and to persist in the face of obstacles.
6. Raise personal standards about the quality of the work they do.
7. Visualize themselves successfully doing purposeful actions.

Remember also to use the all-purpose exercises mentioned in the introduction, actively engaging students in the exploration of JOURNAL ENTRIES, CASE STUDIES, ONE STUDENT'S STORY, ON COURSE AT WORK, QUOTATIONS, CARTOONS, FOCUS QUESTIONS, CHAPTER-OPENING CHARTS, and TECH TIPS. Remind students to use letters to label any in-class writing they do in their journals.

Case Study in Critical Thinking: The Procrastinators

Purpose

To develop critical thinking skills by exploring a real-life situation concerning self-management.

Supplies and Setup

"The Procrastinators" in *On Course*

Directions

1. [Have students read "The Procrastinators." One way to be sure everyone has read the selection before taking the next step is to have one student read the first paragraph aloud, another student read the second, and so on until the reading is complete.] [5 minutes]
2. [Find out by a show of hands how many students have picked each character as having the more challenging self-management problem. In the unlikely event that everyone chooses the same character, attempt to sway some students by playing devil's advocate. When you have a reasonable diversity of opinion, move on to Step 3.] [5 minutes]
3. [Create two groups of like-minded students.] *Because you agree in your group about which student has the more challenging self-management problem, decide how you are going to persuade members of the other group to agree.* [5–10 minutes]
4. [Have a spokesperson from each group present the group's position; then lead a debate on the issue by moving the discussion back and forth, allowing students to explain their positions in more detail and rebut opposing views. When possible, elicit students' personal experiences with self-management problems. Ask them to explain their self-management system—that is, how they get done what they need to do to achieve their goals and dreams. Invite students to demonstrate a change in their opinion by getting up and going to the other group.] [5–20 minutes]
5. [Create the role-play suggested in the second question of "The Procrastinators." One student role-plays Tracy or Ricardo; another student role-plays a mentor suggesting specific self-management strategies that Tracy or Ricardo could use to get on course in college.] [5–15 minutes]
6. [Quick-Write and/or Class Discussion] *What did you learn from this discussion about self-management? What changes will you make in your self-management system? What's the life lesson here for you?* [e.g., "Feeling overwhelmed can be the result of bad self-management decisions."] [5–10 minutes]

Approximate time: 30–65 minutes

Instructor Notes

1. So as not to stifle discussion, I don't reveal which student I think has the more challenging self-management problem.
2. This class discussion is an excellent prewriting activity to be followed by students writing a persuasion essay that supports their opinion in the debate. Because students are now sharply aware of views opposing their own, they often write much more thorough and persuasive essays than would be the case without the debate.
3. An optional step for this activity is to ask students to do a Quick-Write and then a discussion about the Diving Deeper question: Which person's situation, Ricardo's or Tracy's, is more like yours? Explain the similarity and identify what you do to keep up with all of the things you need to do.

Journal Entry 12 Acting on Purpose

EXERCISE 12-1: Time Wasters

Purpose

To raise students' awareness about how they waste time in Quadrants III and IV and to offer students an opportunity to experience a week in which they consciously avoid one of their most common unpurposeful behaviors.

Supplies and Setup

Students in groups of five. One person in each group needs a pen and paper. Write the following on the whiteboard (or put on a PowerPoint slide): **I waste time by . . .**

Directions

1. *Decide who will be your group's recorder. That person needs a pen and paper. The person to the left of your recorder will go first. That person will complete the following sentence stem: "I waste time by. . . ." Going clockwise, the next person will complete the sentence again. Keep going around and around until I say stop. It's perfectly okay to repeat what someone else has said, but try not to repeat yourself. The recorder will make a list of all the different ways that people in your group waste time.* [5 minutes]

2. *Let's hear from the recorder in each group. What are the top three ways people in your group waste time?* [You may want to record the responses on the whiteboard or easel pad. Continue with all groups.] [5–10 minutes, depending on number of groups]

3. [Quick-Write and/or Class Discussion] *What did you learn from this exchange of ideas? What Quadrant III and IV actions are habits of yours? Which ones would most benefit you to eliminate? What's the life lesson here for you?* [e.g., "When I'm not working on a goal that is important to me, I waste a lot of time."] [5–15 minutes]

4. *I'd like to invite you to try an experiment this week, an experiment that could change the quality of your life. The experiment is to say "No" to one Quadrant III or Quadrant IV action that is a habit of yours. You can use the Embracing Change form in this chapter to track your results. Keeping this commitment will free up time for actions in Quadrants I and II. Remember, this is for just one week. After that you can decide if you want to stop completely. So, who'd be willing to make the commitment to yourself to give up one unpurposeful action for a week?* [You may wish to keep a record of the commitments and follow up on them in a subsequent class.] [5–10 minutes]

Approximate time: 20–35 minutes

Instructor Notes

1. Make sure students are clear about the kinds of behaviors that occur in each of the four quadrants: Quadrant I (Important and Urgent), Quadrant II (Important and Not Urgent), Quadrant III (Unimportant and Urgent), and Quadrant IV (Unimportant and Not Urgent).

2. Additionally, help students understand that what makes an action "Important" is whether or not it moves them toward a desired outcome or experience (not someone else's opinion).

EXERCISE 12-2: Who Wants This Prize?

Purpose

To demonstrate that wanting something is not enough; one also has to take purposeful actions.

Supplies and Setup

A prize of value to your students. (A sure bet is a dollar bill, but you can probably be more creative than that—perhaps a student planner or gift card.)

Directions

1. [Hold up the prize.] *I have a prize here.* [Describe it, making it very desirable.] *Who would like it?* [Keep asking the question until someone comes up and takes it from you or until a few minutes go by.] [3–4 minutes]

2. [Quick-Write and/or Class Discussion] *How many of you wanted the prize? Who got it? What did he or she do that no one else did? What is the life lesson here for you?* [e.g., "It's not enough to just want something; you have to take positive actions or you won't get it."] [5–10 minutes]

3. [In preparation for a later consideration of personal rules for success, valuable groundwork can be laid and an interesting discussion begun with the following questions.] *For all of you who didn't come forward to take the prize, what messages do you have in your heads that stopped you? Where did you get these rules? In what circumstances will these rules help you? Hinder you? What's the life lesson here for you?* [e.g., "Some of the things I believe are the very things that will keep me from taking the actions I need to take to succeed."] [5–10 minutes]

Approximate time: 10–25 minutes

EXERCISE 12-3: Rocks and Sugar

Purpose

To demonstrate the value of doing purposeful actions first.

Supplies and Setup

Two 1-quart glass jars, one empty and the other about three-fourths full of sugar; enough irregularly shaped rocks to nearly fill the empty glass jar

Directions

1. *Imagine that this empty glass jar represents a day in your life. The sugar represents unimportant actions: Quadrant III and IV actions. They are sweet at the moment, but they don't move us toward our goals and dreams. They provide instant gratification with no long-term benefit. What are some examples of these low-priority actions?* [e.g., talking for hours on the phone, watching TV, playing video games, surfing social networking sites, partying every night] *These rocks represent your important actions: Quadrant I and II actions. Important actions move us steadily toward our goals and dreams. Important actions build a strong foundation for success. What are some examples of important actions?* [e.g., studying for a test, going to classes, applying for a job, exercising]

2. *Now I'm going to pour the sugar into this empty jar which—keep in mind—represents a day in your life. So on this day, you're choosing to do unimportant actions first. Now, I'm going to add the rocks, which represent your important actions. What do you notice?* [Very few of the rocks will fit in the jar.]

3. *Now, we'll do it a different way. First, I'll put all the rocks into the empty jar. This represents choosing to do your purposeful actions first. Now, I'm going to pour the sugar into the jar after the rocks. What do you notice this time?* [The sugar fills in between the rocks, and much, perhaps all, of the sugar will go into the jar.] [5 minutes for the whole demonstration]

4. [Quick-Write and/or Class Discussion] *What is the life lesson in the rocks and sugar demonstration for you? What is one way you could apply this lesson?* [e.g., "When you do your important tasks first, you can accomplish more toward your goals and dreams. I will prioritize my next-actions list so that I am doing important tasks first."] [5–10 minutes]

Approximate time: 10–15 minutes

Instructor Notes

1. The key to a successful demonstration is having rocks that are so irregular that they do not sit tight against one another in the jar, thus leaving room for the sugar to settle in between them.

2. Worth stressing: We can't manage time, but we can manage our own actions. The key is making wise choices. Doing important actions first is a wise choice.

3. A video with a similar message is titled "Keep Priorities Straight—A Jar of Life." You can view it (and many others) at http://www.oncourseworkshop.com. Click on the Video Gallery in the "Educator Resources Tab."

Source: Adapted from a demonstration by Stephen Covey.

Journal Entry 13 Creating a Leak-Proof Self-Management System

EXERCISE 13-1: Apps for Self-Management

Purpose

To identify and share applications for phones and computers that provide help with managing tasks.

Supplies and Setup

Computers and/or cell phones [Instructors, please note: Make sure all students in your class use or have access to a computer, tablet, or smartphone before doing this activity.]

Directions

1. *Do you use your computer, cell phone, or other technology to help manage your time more efficiently? Let's look into applications that save us time and share these helpful resources with each other!*
2. *There are hundreds of FREE applications for phones and computers, and many of them involve self-management and productivity. Select a free application and review it. (If you do an Internet search for "free time management applications" or "free productivity applications" you will find thousands of hits.)*

   Review Format:
   1. What is the name of the application, and how can others find it?
   2. Describe what the application does to help a person save time.
   3. Rate this application on a scale of 1 (not helpful) to 10 (extremely helpful). Consider the following in your rating: How easy was this application to install and use? Does it do what it is supposed to do?
   4. Would you recommend this application to others? Why or why not?
3. Have students present their findings in class.

Approximate time: 20 minutes to find and load the application; one week to test the application; 20–30 minutes for students to present their findings

Instructor Notes

This assignment can be used as an online (e.g., Moodle Forum) assignment. Students may post their application reviews and respond to other student posts.

Source: Submitted by Laura Marlow, Sue Heath Olesiuk, Shelly Blackburn, and Barbara Brownsmith Campbell, Asheville-Buncombe Technical Community College, NC

EXERCISE 13-2: Time Savers

Purpose

To discover specific strategies for making the most of every 24 hours.

Supplies and Setup

Groups of four to five students. The group recorder needs a pen and paper.

Directions

1. *Almost everyone has developed strategies for saving time. In your group, have a discussion of your best ideas for saving time and have one person record each suggestion. Here are a few examples:*
   - *I record my favorite television shows on my digital recorder and watch them later at night when I'm too tired to study. Also, I can fast forward through the commercials, allowing me to watch an hour show in about 40 minutes. I figure this saves me at least two hours each week.*
   - *I carry a list of telephone calls that I have to make. Any time I have a few minutes, I pull out my list and make a call. I figure this saves me at least an hour each week.*
   - *On Sundays, I cook large batches of food and freeze them in sizes just right for one meal. During the week, I pull out a frozen meal, heat it, and eat. I figure this saves me about three to four hours per week. This strategy saves me money as well as time because with meals already prepared, I'm much less inclined to go out to eat.*
   So, your job is to come up with a list of great ways to save time. Any questions? Okay, begin. [5–10 minutes]
2. *Now let's have the recorder report each group's best ideas.* [You may want to write them on the board or easel pad.] [5–10 minutes]
3. [Quick-Write and/or Class Discussion] *Which of these time savers will you try this week? What's the life lesson here for you?* [e.g., "I may not be able to add hours to a day, but I can take actions that will make it seem like I have more time."] [5–15 minutes]

Approximate time: 20–30 minutes

Instructor Notes

Worth stressing: We can't manage time, but we can manage our own actions. The key is making wise choices.

Journal Entry **14** Developing Self-Discipline

EXERCISE 14-1: Focused Hands

Purpose

To demonstrate the importance of staying focused on the task at hand.

Supplies and Setup

Pairs of students (Student A and Student B) standing facing one another

Directions

1. *Place your hands in front of you, palms facing and about one inch from your partner's but not touching. Partner A, your job is to move your hands up, down, back, forward, around—any way you want (but you can't move your feet). Partner B, your job is to follow your partner's hands, always keeping your palms about one inch from your partner's palms. Your hands should never touch.* [Demonstrate (DEMO) the process with a student.] *Any questions? Okay, go.* [2 minutes]
2. *What did you notice?* [3 minutes]
3. [Switch roles and repeat Steps 1 and 2.] [5 minutes]
4. [Quick-Write and/or Class Discussion] *What's the life lesson here for you?* [Almost always someone will write or express the idea of "focus." With that comment as a transition, lead the discussion to an in-depth consideration of "focus" with questions like these:] *What happened when you lost focus on your goal? What caused you to lose focus? How did you regain focus? When have you lost focus in your life? What happened? How strong is your focus right now on college? What could you do to strengthen your focus?* [5–15 minutes]

Approximate time: 10–25 minutes

Source: Various presenters. The first time I saw this exercise, it was led by David Ellis.

EXERCISE 14-2: The Graduation Game

Purpose

To demonstrate that graduation—similar to other major successes in life—is usually the result of students taking small, purposeful actions persistently over time. This activity takes a bit more setup than most in this manual, but it's well worth it. Students will be talking about 3-foot tosses the rest of the semester.

Supplies and Setup

Ring toss set (use 1 post and 3–6 rings); tape on the floor marking 30 feet at 3-foot intervals; markers and white board or easel pad on which to keep score. You can purchase a ring toss set at http://www.myndworksedu.com.

Directions

1. *What's a big project you want to complete or goal you want to achieve?* [List some responses on the board.] *The question we're going to address is, "What's the best way for you to successfully complete all of the steps that need to be taken to complete this project or achieve this goal?"*
2. *First, though, we're going to play the Graduation Game. This game teaches an important lesson about HOW to complete a project or achieve an important goal, such as earning a college degree.*

3. *I need three volunteers to play.* [You can play with any number from 2 to 30, but the more players there are, the longer the game takes.]
4. *Every player has the same goal in this game—to graduate as quickly as possible.*
5. *In this game, you graduate when you earn 30 or more credits.*
6. *You earn credits by making a ringer. Each ringer earns credits equal to the distance thrown, and you can throw from any distance you choose. For example, a ringer from 6 feet earns 6 credits; a ringer from 24 feet earns 24 credits, and so on. You can throw from the same distance every time or you can change the distance every time—it's your choice.*
7. *Everyone playing will take turns tossing the rings until someone earns 30 or more credits and graduates. Before you toss each time, I'll write on the board the number representing the distance from which you're choosing to toss. After you toss, I'll circle the number if you get a ringer. The first person to total 30 or more credits graduates!* [When someone gets 30 or more credits and "graduates," allow everyone to complete the same number of tosses, then stop the game.]
8. [Quick-Write and/or Class Discussion] *So, what lesson does the ring-toss game teach us about successfully completing a large project, goal, or dream?* [e.g., "Life is a breeze in persistent 3-foot tosses . . . Life is hard by the yard but a cinch by the inch . . . You can eat a whale if you do it one bite at a time . . . You have to climb a mountain one step at a time."] *What would a 30-foot toss look like in college?* [e.g., "Not studying all semester and then cramming the night before an exam; taking 20 credits in one semester while working full time."] *What would a 3-foot toss look like in college?* [e.g., "Coming to every class; handing in every assignment when due; asking questions when you have them."] [Some students will argue that 3-foot tosses are no challenge and that it's more exciting to take longer tosses. In the likely event that the person who graduated first took many 3-foot tosses, point that out. Remind them that they have every right to choose the excitement of a 30-foot toss, but it might be at the expense of achieving their goals or dreams. It's a strange choice to pick adrenalin over success, but, sadly, many people do it.] *Now let's apply this lesson to the rest of our lives: In life, what distance do you typically toss from? Are you a 30-foot tosser, a 15-foot tosser, a 3-foot tosser? Are you happy with the outcomes and experiences you've been creating this way? Are there any changes you plan to make in the way you pursue your goals and dreams? Let's look at the large projects we listed earlier. What are some 3-foot tosses for each of these projects?*

Approximate time: 30–55 minutes, depending most on the length of discussion

Instructor Notes

1. In my experience, the person with the most 3-foot tosses almost always wins, but even if another person wins, you can make the point that sometimes someone wins the lottery, too. The fact remains that most of the time, 3-foot tosses lead to success, so it still comes down to a choice of which way we will pursue our goals and dreams. Do you want to trust your future success to one lucky 30-foot toss or a series of effective 3-foot tosses?
2. Another point to make is the value of knowing one's skill level. For some people, a 9-foot toss might be as easy as a 3-foot toss for someone else. Also, there is value in stretching a bit beyond our skill level by taking a "reasonable risk" in the service of learning and growth.
3. This game creates a powerful metaphor to which you can return over and over. When someone is pondering an action to take toward his or her goal, you can say, "So what would a 3-foot toss look like in this situation?" or "That sounds like a 30-foot toss to me. Could you break that into smaller, 3-foot tosses?
4. Consider asking players to say their names and affirmations before tossing the ring. In the process, classmates learn one another's names and affirmations.
5. When one student has reached 30 credits, allow all other students one more toss. Some will need to take a desperation toss from 15 to 30 feet. Ask, *"What is the equivalent desperation toss in a class when you have fallen way behind?"* Answers: Staying up all night cramming for a test or even buying a paper from the Internet. Poor self-management can force a student to choose between failing and cheating.
6. Listen for negative self-talk and do some coaching. For example, a student may say, "I can't do this." You might reply, "If you keep saying 'I can't do this,' do you think that helps or hinders you in your efforts to make a ringer? What comment would be more helpful?"

Source: This is a variation on a demonstration I first saw done by Ron and Mary Hulnick at the University of Santa Monica.

Journal Entry 15 Believing in Yourself: Develop Self-Confidence

EXERCISE 15-1: Victory Deck

Purpose

To offer students an opportunity to acknowledge their successes, thus building self-confidence.

Supplies and Setup

Chime, students sitting in pairs (Student A and Student B), a pen and 25 index cards for each student

Directions

1. *Everyone has accomplished goals, and each goal—whether large or small—is a personal victory. Victims focus on what they have not accomplished in life; Creators acknowledge their victories in life. What are some victories you have experienced in the past year?* [Elicit some examples of victories, large and small—for example, graduation from high school, turned in English paper on time.] [1 minute]
2. *Working alone for now, create your own personal victory deck by writing one victory on each card.* [10 minutes]
3. *When I say go, start telling your partners about some of your victories in life. Alternate back and forth, sharing as many victories as you can as fast as you can. If you think of another of your victories, write it quickly on a blank card. After a minute or so, I'll ring the chime and call for either A's or B's to "FLY." All A's or B's will leap up, find an empty seat, sit down with a new partner, and immediately start exchanging victories. Again, go back and forth, telling each other about victories you have created in your life. Then I'll ring the chime and shout for A's or B's to "FLY" again, and one of you will dash off to a new partner to do it all over again.* [DEMO the process, telling your victories quickly to model a sense of urgency.] [3–5 minutes]
4. *So, any questions? Get ready and start telling your victories NOW!* [6–10 minutes, depending on how many partner changes you want]
5. [Quick-Write and/or Class Discussion] *What was your experience? What was it like to hear your partner telling you about victories? What was it like to speak of your own victories? Did your Inner Critic try to block you from telling your victories? How? How do you feel right now? What would it do for your self-confidence if you acknowledged your victories more often? What's the life lesson here for you?* [e.g., "I've got more victories than I thought I did, and saying them out loud makes me feel proud of what I've accomplished."] *What could you do with your "victory deck" beyond this class?* [e.g., "Keep adding victories to it every day. Read the cards every day."] [10–20 minutes]

Approximate time: 30–40 minutes

Instructor Notes

1. Some Inner Critics will accuse the students of "bragging." I acknowledge to students that they might not want to go around telling everyone about their victories, but they surely would get value from acknowledging them to close friends and to themselves.
2. You can use the same process to have students acknowledge their talents, skills, and personal strengths.

EXERCISE 15-2: Visualizing My Success

Purpose

To practice visualizing successfully doing a purposeful action.

Supplies and Setup

Groups of five to six students standing in a circle [Equipment for optional step: video camera and TV and DVD player for playback]

Directions

1. *Think of one of your most challenging goals. Now think of a **purpose**ful action that you need to take to achieve this goal. Even better is to think of a **purpose**ful action that you've been avoiding for some reason.* [After 1–2 minutes, ask.] *Has everyone thought of a **purpose**ful action you could take?* [Give more time or coaching, as needed.]

2. *Each of you will act out your **purpose**ful action, and your group will try to guess what it is that you're doing. Each person will have 2 minutes.* [You might want to DEMO acting out one of your own purposeful actions, such as sitting down to grade a set of exams or painting your living room.] [10 minutes]

3. [Optional: Make a video recording of one or more students from each group acting out their visualizations. You can then show the scenes to the whole class for discussion. With the students' permission, you can also use these recordings as a DEMO for a future class.]

4. [Quick-Write and/or Class Discussion] *What did you learn about visualizing from this exercise? What's the life lesson here for you?* [e.g., "Visualizing myself doing something scary makes it seem less intimidating."] [5–10 minutes]

Approximate time: 15–25 minutes

Instructor Notes

Here's an alternative that requires time outside of class. Put students in pairs. Give each student the assignment to choose and actually carry out a purposeful action that will move him or her toward an important goal, especially one he or she has been postponing. With a video camera or smartphone, partners record each other doing the action (e.g., going to see a teacher for a conference or studying for a math test). With this approach, you can show the recordings in class and then discuss the power of actually seeing the purposeful action being done. You could later post videos on a class website or YouTube channel.

EXERCISE 15-3: Talents

Purpose

To offer students an opportunity to acknowledge their talents and skills.

Supplies and Setup

Entire class standing in a large circle

Directions

1. *Creators raise their self-esteem by acknowledging their talents and skills, at least to themselves. They're good at certain things and, without being conceited, they know it. So be a Creator and think of a talent or a skill that you have. You don't need to be an expert; just think of something that you're fairly good at.* [2 minutes]

2. *When you're ready, you'll walk into the middle of the circle and tell us one thing that you're good at. Anyone else with that same talent will also step into the circle. We'll applaud to acknowledge you all for your talents and skills. Then return to the outside circle, and someone else will step into the circle and tell us one of his or her talents. You can go as many times as you want; just be aware of those who haven't had a chance to go. Notice if your Inner Critic or Inner Defender tries to block you from telling us or acknowledging your talents.* [2 minutes for directions]

3. *So, I'll start. "I'm good at . . ."* [Tell something you're good at; then invite others with the same talent or skill to step into the circle with you and urge those in the outside circle to give resounding applause. Encourage an enthusiastic response to set the pattern for students who follow you. Then take your place in the circle and wait for others to do what you've modeled.] [5–15 minutes, depending on the size of the group and energy generated by the exercise]

4. [Quick-Write and/or Class Discussion] *What was your experience? What was it like to tell about your talents? What was it like to acknowledge that you have talents that someone else named? What was it like to be applauded for your talents? To applaud others? Did your Inner Critic or Inner Defender try to block you from telling or acknowledging your talents? What was the chatter in your head? How did you respond? How do you feel right now? What would it do for your self-confidence if you acknowledged your talents often? What's the life lesson here for you?* [e.g., "It's a lot easier to acknowledge other people for their talents than it is to acknowledge myself for my own talents."]

Approximate time: 20–30 minutes

Instructor Notes

By this time in the semester, most students will be comfortable coming into the circle. If you have a few shy students, you might (near the end of the allotted time) say, "Some of you haven't chosen to go yet, and that's okay. But this is a great opportunity for you to experiment with a bold new behavior. What do you say? We'll give you extra applause. C'mon, you can do it!" The key here is to be encouraging without singling anyone out. Almost always a few shy students will say, "Oh, all right . . .," and you've helped them choose an empowering new behavior.

Chapter 4: Quiz Questions

(The Answer Key to Chapter 4: Quiz Questions appears at the end of this Facilitator's Manual. Please visit the Instructor Companion Site for *On Course* at login.cengage.com for a digital version of this quiz and its answer key.)

Acting on Purpose

For questions 1–4, choose one of the following to fill in the blanks: IMPORTANT, UNIMPORTANT, URGENT, NOT URGENT [Capitalize all answers.]

1. Quadrant I actions are IMPORTANT and _____.

2. Quadrant II actions are IMPORTANT and _____.

3. Quadrant III actions are UNIMPORTANT and _____.

4. Quadrant IV actions are UNIMPORTANT and _____.

5. Creators spend as much time as possible in Quadrant

    A. I.

    B. II.

    C. III.

    D. IV.

Mastering Effective Self-Management

1. It is possible to manage time.   TRUE   FALSE

2. A self-management tool that provides an overview of upcoming commitments, appointments, and assignments by dates is a

    A. next-actions list.

    B. tracking form.

    C. monthly calendar.

3. A self-management tool that records, by life roles, all important tasks to do that day or as soon as possible afterward is a

    A. next-actions list.

    B. tracking form.

    C. weekly calendar.

4. A self-management tool that records and tracks, for two weeks, all of the outer and inner actions that need to be done repeatedly to reach a particular goal is called a

    A. project folder.

    B. tracking form.

    C. calendar.

5. Researchers at the University of Georgia found that students' self-management skills and attitudes are even better predictors of their grades in college than their Scholastic Aptitude Test (SAT) scores.   TRUE   FALSE

Developing Self-Discipline

1. Self-discipline is commitment made visible through purposeful actions.   TRUE   FALSE

2. Self-discipline has three essential ingredients: commitment, focus, and creativity.   TRUE   FALSE.

3. According to *On Course*, for many college and university students, the time to beware of losing focus is at midterm.   TRUE   FALSE

4. A self-management tool for tracking the daily completion of one action long enough to create or eliminate a habit is called a

   A. 32-day commitment.

   B. next-actions list.

   C. tracking form.

   D. weekly calendar.

5. People are either born with self-discipline or they're not.   TRUE   FALSE

On Course at Work: Self-Management at Work

1. The self-management skills you learn in this course will make success in the workplace more likely.   TRUE   FALSE

2. These Quadrant II actions will look great on your resume: volunteer work, internships, and club memberships related to your future career.   TRUE   FALSE

3. Success in the workplace means having the self-discipline to spend the majority of your time in Quadrant III.   TRUE   FALSE

4. When beginning a job search, which of the following self-management tools will serve you well?

   A. Tracking form for directing your outer and inner action steps toward your employment goals

   B. Next-actions list for keeping track of essential one-time actions such as returning calls or sending thank-you notes after an interview

   C. Monthly calendars for avoiding the embarrassment of arriving late or having to cancel an interview because of a scheduling conflict

   D. All of the above

   E. None of the above

5. Imagine that you have a big project at work that is due tomorrow. It's after dinner, and you're about ready to write the final draft of the report when your married friend calls. His wife is out of town, and he asks you to watch their kids (ages three, four, and seven years) while he goes to his high school reunion that night. If you agree to watch his children instead of finishing your project, which Quadrant will you be in?

   A. I

   B. II

   C. III

   D. IV

Believing in Yourself: Develop Self-Confidence

1. Self-esteem is strengthened by increased self-confidence.   TRUE   FALSE

2. Self-confidence is the core belief that I _____. [Capitalize all letters.]

3. By creating one small success after another, eventually you create a success identity, which is one way to build your self-confidence.   TRUE   FALSE

4. Which of the three following groups, studied by psychologist Charles Garfield, improved the most in speechmaking abilities?

    A. **Group 1** read and studied how to give public speeches but delivered no actual speeches.

    B. **Group 2** read about speechmaking and gave two talks each week to small audiences of classmates and friends.

    C. **Group 3** read about effective speaking and gave one talk each week to small groups. This group also watched videotapes of effective speakers and, twice a day, mentally rehearsed giving effective speeches of their own.

5. Genuine self-confidence results from a history of trying to be successful.   TRUE   FALSE

Chapter 4: Essay Topics

1. Students new to college are often overwhelmed by their newfound freedom to make almost unlimited choices. As a result of bad choices, some first-year students do much less well than they are capable of doing. Write an essay in which you warn these students about the bad choices they will probably be tempted to make and recommend the most important actions they should take to resist those temptations and be successful in college.

2. Choosing to do a 32-day commitment offers you an intense learning experience. Write an essay for your classmates in which you discuss your experience with a 32-day commitment, including the life lessons you learned from the experience. Consider, among other things, how your thoughts, feelings, and actions changed over the course of the 32 days. It is not necessary that you had a successful 32-day commitment to write this essay. In fact, there will be much to learn from a 32-day commitment that you had trouble keeping.

3. Many people find that they don't get as much accomplished in their lives as they want. Yet they resist undertaking any sort of self-management system, saying they aren't comfortable using tools such as a monthly calendar, next-action list, 32-day commitment, or tracking form. Write an essay for people who have difficulty using a written self-management plan, suggesting how they might accomplish more in their lives with self-management strategies that are consistent with their personalities. As much as possible, use your own experience to support your opinions.

4. There are numerous electronic and paper self-management tools on the market today. Some are described in the "Tech Tips" section of this chapter. Write a consumer report essay in which you discuss the strengths and weaknesses of one of these tools. You can report on a tool that you own and use, or you can go to a website, app store, or office supply store and familiarize yourself with one of the tools there. Award the product 1 to 5 (high) stars for its value and then explain your reasons for the score.

5. One of the ways that people build confidence is by taking positive risks. Write an essay in which you fully describe the biggest risk(s) you have taken in your life, what you learned from your experience(s), and how your overall confidence has been affected.

6. People's confidence in their ability to succeed at something has a great deal to do with the level of their eventual success. Write an essay for fellow college students in which you explain how confident you feel about succeeding in college. Fully explore what you believe are the causes of your present level of academic confidence and propose what you will do to raise your confidence higher.

7. Using the "One Student's Story" essays in *On Course* as a model, write an essay about how you used a strategy from Chapter 4 to overcome a problem in your life—academic, personal, or even at work. First, explain the problem; then discuss the specific strategy you used and how you put it into action; finally, identify what happened. Your instructor may submit your essay for possible publication in the next edition of *On Course*. Additional directions for writing and submitting these essays can be found at http://oncourseworkshop.com/course-textbook/essay-contest/.

Employing Interdependence

Concept

The world provides valuable resources for those who choose interdependence over independence, dependence, or code-pendence. Many students, however, do not utilize the abundant human resources available to assist them to achieve their goals more easily and enjoyably. Worse, many students are entangled in a web of toxic relationships. Without positive assistance, many students find the achievement of personal, academic, and professional goals to be difficult, even impossible. By offering students the skills to build and nurture mutually supportive relationships, we empower them to benefit from resources that might otherwise go untapped, to experience the uplift of giving and receiving assistance, and to achieve goals that otherwise might be difficult or even impossible. Additionally, in a world that is becoming increasingly diverse, students' academic and life success is affected by their cultural intelligence, which Brooks Peterson, author of *Cultural Intelligence: A Guide to Working with People from Other Cultures*, defines as

> Knowledge about cultures (facts and cultural traits)
>
> + Awareness (of yourself and others)
>
> + Specific skills (behaviors)

EMPOWERS STUDENTS TO . . .

1. Develop interdependence, reinforcing mutual cooperation rather than competition.
2. Identify valuable resources that can assist them in reaching their goals.
3. Request assistance in achieving their goals.
4. Create a network of support for college and beyond.
5. Develop personal bonds of friendship and appreciation that can support them to persist in a course or in college.
6. Communicate more effectively both as speakers and listeners.
7. Develop cultural intelligence and respect for differences.
8. Reduce anxiety and reluctance about trusting others, increasing a sense of safety and willingness to interact positively with the people in their lives.

Remember also to use the all-purpose exercises mentioned in the introduction, actively engaging students in the exploration of JOURNAL ENTRIES, CASE STUDIES, ONE STUDENT'S STORY, ON COURSE AT WORK, QUOTATIONS, CARTOONS, FOCUS QUESTIONS, CHAPTER-OPENING CHARTS, and TECH TIPS. Remind students to use letters to label any in-class writing they do in their journals.

Case Study in Critical Thinking: Professor Rogers's Trial

Purpose

To develop critical thinking skills by exploring a real-life situation concerning interdependence and the ability to work well with others.

Supplies and Setup

"Professor Rogers' Trial" in *On Course*

Directions

1. [Have students read "Professor Rogers's Trial." One way to be sure everyone has read the selection before taking the next step is to have one student read the first paragraph aloud, another student read the second, and so on until the reading is complete. Then have students put in their scores for the four characters.] [5 minutes]
2. [Find out by a show of hands how many students have picked each character as number one—having the greatest responsibility for the team's grade of D. If two or more characters are chosen as number one, move on to Step 3. In the unlikely event that everyone chooses the same character as number one (or there is otherwise little diversity in opinion), ask how many students have picked each character as number four—having the least responsibility for the team's grade of D. Typically, there will be more differences of opinion here.] [5 minutes]
3. [Create groups of like-minded students.] *Choose a spokesperson for your group. Then provide your spokesperson with evidence from the story that will persuade others to agree with your group.* [5–10 minutes]
4. [Have a spokesperson from each group present the group's position; then lead a debate by moving the discussion from group to group, allowing students to explain their positions in more detail and rebut opposing views. Invite students to demonstrate a change in their opinions by getting up and going to the group with which they now agree.] [5–20 minutes]
5. [Quick-Write and/or Class Discussion] *What is the life lesson here about interdependence and working collaboratively? How will you use this insight to improve your next group experience?* [e.g., "Groups sometimes have members who are not contributors. Other group members can use a Creator mindset and still make the most of the group experience."] [5–10 minutes]

Approximate time: 25–50 minutes

Instructor Notes

1. So as not to stifle discussion, I don't tell students what my scores are.
2. This class discussion is an excellent prewriting activity to be followed by students writing a persuasion essay supporting their opinions in the debate. Because students are now sharply aware of views opposed to their own, they often write much more thorough and persuasive essays than would be the case without the debate.
3. An optional step for this activity is to ask students to do a Quick-Write and/or Group Discussion about the Diving Deeper question: *Imagine that you have been assigned to a group project in one of your college courses and that the student whom you scored as most responsible for the group's grade of D (Anthony, Silvia, or Donald) is in your group. What positive actions could you take to help your group be a success despite this person?* One by one, make a list of positive options for dealing with difficult group members like Anthony (a bossy dictator), Silvia (an emotional time bomb), and Donald (a disengaged loafer).
4. One aspect that helps the effectiveness of this activity is the creation of a vocabulary that allows students to address group problems effectively. Students will say to each other, "You're starting to act bossy like Anthony" or "Don't be a Donald—help us out here." This shorthand helps some groups solve problems that might otherwise sabotage their collaborative efforts.

Journal Entry **16** Creating a Support System

EXERCISE 16-1: The Chair Lift

Purpose

To demonstrate that some goals are difficult, or even impossible, to achieve alone, but they are relatively easy to accomplish with help.

Supplies and Setup

Two volunteers (ideally Volunteer A is larger than Volunteer B); one chair. Have Volunteer A (the larger person) sit in the chair and Volunteer B stand behind the chair.

Directions

1. *Everyone in the room will have a goal during this activity.* [To the class] *Your goal is to listen to the goal I give to B and decide how you would attempt to accomplish the goal.* [To A] *You've got the easiest goal of all. Your goal is to stay seated in the chair. You may not stand up. Can you handle that?* [To B] *Your goal is to cause the chair with A sitting in it to be at least two feet in the air as soon as possible. That is, every part of the chair and A, including feet, must be at least 24 inches in the air. Ready? Go.* [It's important that you say "cause the chair," not "lift the chair." Also, it helps to put your hand at about two feet off the floor to indicate the height you are expecting the chair to be raised.] [2 minutes]

2. [Listen for B's self-talk. B's Inner Critic may say things like, "I can't do that" or "I'm not strong enough." B's Inner Defender may say, "That's just ridiculous. No one could do that." Whatever B says, for now simply repeat the directions.] *Remember, your goal is to cause the chair with A sitting in it to be at least two feet in the air as soon as possible. That is, every part of the chair and A, including feet, must be at least 24 inches in the air. Ready? Go.* [3–5 minutes]

3. [Now, encourage B, saying that the goal *can* be accomplished with the right approach. If B doesn't achieve the goal after a couple of minutes, ask B if the class can offer suggestions. Eventually, someone will suggest that B needs help. If B asks, "Can I ask for help?" simply repeat the directions, stressing "**cause** the chair." Notice that you have never told B to lift the chair. Eventually, you will have volunteers come to help B lift the chair with A in it. **IMPORTANT:** Be sure there are at least four strong people lifting and ask each one if his or her back is okay. Tell them to lift with their legs, not their backs. The point here is to guard against injury. I have done this activity many times, and no one has ever gotten hurt—but I am always very careful!] [2–5 minutes]

4. [Quick-Write and/or Class Discussion] [To B] *What beliefs originally kept you from achieving your goal?* [e.g., "I had to lift the chair by myself."] *So, what's the life lesson for you of the chair-lift exercise?* [e.g., "A goal that I couldn't accomplish alone became easy with help."] *Can you identify other goals you have that are difficult because you're trying to accomplish them alone? Whom could you ask for help? Will you? When is it best to be independent, and when is it best to be interdependent?* [These same questions can also be asked of the rest of the students.] [5–10 minutes]

Approximate time: 10–25 minutes

Instructor Notes

If you noticed some self-talk, which is clearly B's Inner Critic or Inner Defender, you might want to spend a few minutes discussing how those voices interfered with his or her success and how to work with that inner voice.

EXERCISE 16-2: The Scavenger Hunt

Purpose

To assist students to learn about your college's resources for student success and to demonstrate that some goals are impossible to achieve alone but are relatively easy to achieve with help.

Supplies and Setup

"The Scavenger Hunt" handout (next page). Give each student a handout as the students arrive.

Directions

[IMPORTANT: Read Steps 1–5 of the directions exactly as given.]

1. *The way **you all** can win the Scavenger Hunt is by accumulating the maximum number of points available.*
2. *The way **you each** accumulate points is to fill in the correct answer in any of the three columns. You earn one point for each box you fill in with the correct information.*
3. *If **you** are a winner, you will win a prize.*
4. *Let's synchronize our watches. It's now ____. You must be back in this room by ____ to be a winner.* [Allow about 20 minutes for the Scavenger Hunt.]
5. *The Scavenger Hunt will not start until everyone is ready. Are you ready?* [This is the time when students could form teams so they could all be winners; chances are, however, they will dash out of the door, operating independently and competitively.] *Remember, you must be back in this room by ____. Ready? Okay, let the Scavenger Hunt begin.* [Steps 1–5: 3–5 minutes]
6. [Upon students' return, go over the resources they have discovered.] [10–15 minutes]
7. *Now let's see who won the Scavenger Hunt. Remember, I said, "The way **you all** can win the Scavenger Hunt is by accumulating the maximum number of points available." What is the maximum number of points available?* [72 points—there are 72 boxes to be filled in on the Scavenger Hunt form.] *Did anyone accumulate the maximum number of points available? What is the only way you could win this game?* [The only way to win the game is by working cooperatively with others. Discuss the students' assumption that they were in competition with one another and that only one person could be a winner when, in fact, the directions allow everyone to be a winner. In what other areas of their lives do they compete, even when cooperation would be more beneficial?] [10 minutes]
8. [Quick-Write and/or Class Discussion] *What is the life lesson for you of the Scavenger Hunt? What will you do as a result of this insight?* [e.g., "For some tasks, many people can accomplish with ease what one person cannot accomplish alone. One of the challenges in life is choosing when it is better to be independent and when it is better to be interdependent. I will be more careful about that choice."] [5–10 minutes]

Approximate time: 30–50 minutes

Instructor Notes

You may want to prepare a Scavenger Hunt handout with all of the correct information filled in. Encourage students to keep the handout for future reference.

Scavenger Hunt

YOUR DESIRE OR PROBLEM	NAME OF COLLEGE OFFICE OR RESOURCE	LOCATION	PERSON TO SEE
1. Need money for tuition and books			
2. Can't decide what major to choose			
3. Want to drop a course			
4. Need help with writing skills			
5. Want to participate in clubs and activities			
6. Need to withdraw from a course			
7. Have a problem with a college bill			
8. Feel physically ill			
9. Need information about transferring to another college			
10. Need to exchange textbooks			
11. Have a personal problem			
12. Need a computer to type an essay			
13. Want career information			
14. Want to write for the school newspaper			
15. Need tutoring in reading			
16. Want services for disabled students			
17. Want to serve in student government			
18. Need books for a research paper			
19. Want to transfer credits to another college			
20. Need a part-time job			
21. Need a parking permit			
22. Want to play intramural sports			
23. Need tutoring in math			
24. Have complaint about a teacher			

EXERCISE 16-3: The Interdependence Game

Purpose

To demonstrate the power of interdependence to solve problems.

Supplies and Setup

One volunteer up front; one recorder with pen and paper. You may wish to post the three sentence stems (Step 1 below) on the board or on a PowerPoint slide.

Directions

1. [To the student volunteer] *We're going to play the Interdependence Game. This is a game in which you can get immediate help on a problem you have. You could leave here today with one of your problems solved. Here's how the game works. All you need to do is complete these three sentence stems:* **My goal is . . . My problem is . . . The help I'd like is . . . .** *What specific help do you need to solve your problem? Do you need information? Advice? Assistance?* [Demonstrate (DEMO) the Interdependence Game process with a problem of your own, or you could tell a story of how the Interdependence Game helped someone in a previous class. For example, Vicki's **goal** was to move to a new apartment at the end of the semester; her **problem** was that she had to paint her old apartment before she could get her deposit back; the **help** she wanted was for classmates to come to a painting party and help her paint the inside of her old apartment. Three people showed up that day and helped her paint her apartment. One of the people helping that day was a man Vicki had never met; he had come along with his friend. Vicki and the man started dating. So Vicki not only got a painted apartment; she got a new relationship as well. The life lesson: You never know what you'll get when you start asking for help.] [5 minutes]
2. [To the class] *After a volunteer explains the situation, if you have information, advice, or assistance to offer, raise your hand and the volunteer will call on you. You have 30 seconds to respond, and our recorder will write down your ideas. If your idea will take longer, give a brief explanation and invite the volunteer to meet you after class for the full version. We'll try to get 10 ideas in 5 minutes.* [Do as many additional volunteers as time allows, about 5–6 minutes each.]
3. [Quick-Write and/or Class Discussion] *What is the life lesson for you of the Interdependence Game? Given that insight, what will you do that you have never done before?* [e.g., "To get the help you need, sometimes all you need to do is ask for it. To solve my problem, I will ask for help from a math tutor."] [5–10 minutes]

Approximate time: About 10–35 minutes

Instructor Notes

A key to the success of the Interdependence Game is to keep it moving. Don't let any suggestion for help last more than 30 seconds before you say, "What a great idea . . . how about meeting after class to finish explaining your idea. Now, quick, let's get another great idea." For the same reason, the person with the problem should not respond to those who are giving suggestions.

EXERCISE 16-4: Study-Team Bingo

Purpose

To help students find possible study-team members.

Supplies and Setup

"Study-Team Bingo" handout (next page)

Directions

1. *In the empty boxes on the top row of your Study-Team Bingo sheet, put the names of the courses you are taking this semester, including this one. If you don't have enough courses to fill in all four columns, put our course at the top of more than one column. If you have more than four courses, write your four most challenging courses.* [2 minutes]
2. *Now we're going to play Study-Team Bingo. Your goal is first to find someone in our class who is taking one of your courses written at the top of any column. Next, go down that column and see if the person has any of the qualities described in the boxes by asking questions such as, "Are you a part-time student? Have you attended another college? Do you exercise regularly?"* [1 minute]
3. *If the person answers "Yes," write the person's full name (first **and** last) in the box. You may use the same person in more than one box in a column if the description applies. Move on to another person and then another. The person who has the most boxes filled in when time is called is the winner.* [10 minutes]
4. [Ring a chime or call "Stop."] *Count the number of boxes you've filled in.* [Optional: Have the winner(s) come up front and read the name and information in each of the filled-in boxes, inviting the named person to stand. This assists everyone to learn who's in the class and what some of their skills and experiences are.]
5. [Quick-Write and/or Class Discussion] *What's the life lesson here for you?* [e.g., "Many people around me have the skills and talents to help me achieve my goals."] *How could you apply this lesson to be more successful in college and in life? Are you willing to do that? How?* [5–15 minutes]
6. *I hope you'll create a study team with the people who are in your classes. Remember, there are four steps to creating a helpful study team: (1) Choose the team yourself. (2) Agree on team goals. (3) Agree on meeting times, dates, and place. (4) Create team rules (e.g., to each meeting bring 10 questions on index cards with answers and sources on back).*

Approximate time: 15–30 minutes

Instructor Notes

The movie *Stand and Deliver*—available from most DVD rental services—dramatizes the value of belonging to a supportive study group and choosing a wise and caring mentor. You might want to show parts of the movie in class to generate additional Quick-Writes and class discussions.

Study-Team Bingo

Course 1	Course 2	Course 3	Course 4
is a part-time student	is a part-time student	is a part-time student	is a part-time student
is a full-time student	is a full-time student	is a full-time student	is a full-time student
loves going to college	loves going to college	loves going to college	loves going to college
types 30 wpm or more	types 30 wpm or more	types 30 wpm or more	types 30 wpm or more
has a child younger than 10 years	has a child younger than 10 years	has a child younger than 10 years	has a child younger than 10 years
has scholarship aid	has scholarship aid	has scholarship aid	has scholarship aid
good with computers	good with computers	good with computers	good with computers
drives to school	drives to school	drives to school	drives to school
will get a 4-year degree	will get a 4-year degree	will get a 4-year degree	will get a 4-year degree
lives in your zip code	lives in your zip code	lives in your zip code	lives in your zip code
works full time	works full time	works full time	works full time
has a work-study job	has a work-study job	has a work-study job	has a work-study job
belongs to a study group	belongs to a study group	belongs to a study group	belongs to a study group
has the same career goal as you	has the same career goal as you	has the same career goal as you	has the same career goal as you
is good at math	is good at math	is good at math	is good at math
out of school 10+ years	out of school 10+ years	out of school 10+ years	out of school 10+ years
exercises regularly	exercises regularly	exercises regularly	exercises regularly
is a grandparent	is a grandparent	is a grandparent	is a grandparent
has 20+ college credits	has 20+ college credits	has 20+ college credits	has 20+ college credits

EXERCISE 16-5: Your Relationship Bank Account

Purpose

To demonstrate how we make deposits and withdrawals from the relationship bank accounts we have with family, friends, and associates in our support network.

Supplies and Setup

Pen and paper

Directions

1. *I want you to think about one of your best friends. Create a picture of this person in your mind. Now, on a sheet of paper, write the number 100. This represents the present balance that your friend has in a relationship bank account with you.*

2. *I'll now ask you to imagine that your friend did the actions that I'm about to read to you. After you hear each one, make an appropriate deposit or withdrawal from your friendship account. For example, if your friend does something that strengthens your relationship, you might add 10 or 20 points to his or her account. If your friend does something that weakens your relationship, you might subtract points from the account. Here's the first situation:*

   A. *You and your friend agree to meet for lunch at noon. Your friend shows up an hour late and offers no explanation.* [After reading each situation, remind students to make a deposit or a withdrawal—that is, add or subtract from the starting balance of 100.]

   B. *You mention to your friend that you're having difficulty understanding one of your college courses. Your friend says, "I passed that course last semester. I'll be glad to give you some help." Your friend comes to your house the next day and tutors you for two hours.*

   C. *Your friend introduces you to a new group of people, telling them that you are the best friend he or she has in the world.*

   D. *On Friday, you and your friend agree to meet at the library at 4:00 on Monday for a study session. On the way to the library on Monday, you see your friend talking and laughing with a group of people. Your friend never shows up at the library as promised. Later your friend apologizes, "I'm really sorry I didn't meet you. I tried to get there, but I was in a conference with my history teacher, and he just kept talking. There was nothing I could do."*

   E. *You're moving to a new place to live, and you've decided to move the furniture yourself. You mention to your friend that you've asked about 10 people to come over on Saturday morning to help you move. Your friend doesn't offer to assist and doesn't show up on Saturday.*

   F. *A person you barely know tells you that some people were criticizing you, and your friend stood up for you.* [5 minutes]

3. [Quick-Write and/or Class Discussion] *After these six interactions with your friend, what is the present balance in your friendship account with this person? What behavior caused you to make the biggest withdrawal from your friend's account? Why? What rule of yours did your friend keep or break? What behavior caused you to make the biggest deposit? Why? What rule of yours did your friend keep or break? If you were a college professor, what behaviors would make a large deposit in your relationship account with a student? What behaviors would make a large withdrawal in your relationship account with a student? What is the life lesson here for you?* [e.g., "Behaviors that greatly bother one person in a relationship may not bother another person much at all." Or "I never realized how my choices might affect how my professors think and feel about me."] [10–25 minutes]

Approximate time: 15–30 minutes

Instructor Notes

Points worth stressing: We deposit points when a friend lives by our rules, and we withdraw points when a friend defies our rules. You can use this exercise to preview the discussion of beliefs and rules in Chapter 6.

EXERCISE 16-6: Tootsie Roll Pops

Purpose

To help students increase respect for differences and gain a deeper understanding of universal similarities.

Supplies and Setup

Tootsie Roll Pops—one per student; two columns on the board, labeled "On the Outside" and "On the Inside"; one Tootsie Roll Pop cracked open (for students who have never seen one)

Directions

1. [Hold up both a Tootsie Roll Pop and a cracked one.] *A Tootsie Roll Pop is a candy-coated sucker on the outside with chewy chocolate on the inside. On a piece of paper, write words or phrases that describe both the outside* [e.g., hard, different-colored wrappers, different flavors, requires 600–800 licks to get to the center] *and on the inside* [e.g., soft, chewy, supported by a lollipop stick]. [3 minutes]
2. *Call out some of the words and phrases written as I record them on the board.*
3. [Quick Write and/or Class Discussion] *How are Tootsie Roll Pops like people—on the outside and on the inside? How can you compare the different flavors of Tootsie Roll Pops with outer differences among people? If you choose Tootsie Roll Pops by the wrapper color, do you also select friends by appearance (clothes, hairstyle)? Why do Tootsie Roll Pops and people have a hard exterior? Just as you look forward to reaching the Tootsie Roll Pop's sweet center, what reward do you get from making the effort to get to know new people? Think about a time you judged someone from the outside and then later found that the person was different on the inside. Just as the Tootsie Roll Pop gets "held up" by the lollipop stick, who are some people in your life you use for support? Do you try different flavors of Tootsie Roll Pops? Do you always choose the same types of friends, or do you sometimes move outside of your comfort zone to get to know new people? What's the life lesson here for you?* [e.g., "I want to find the 'soft centers' of several of my classmates who seem unfriendly." Or "I wish to melt my 'hard shell' so that other students can see I really am sweet on the inside." Or "I usually hang out with people who are similar to me on the outside, and now I want to find people who are like me on the inside."] [10 minutes]
4. *Enjoy eating your Tootsie Roll Pop—a sweet ending for our life lesson!*

Approximate time: 20 minutes

Instructor Notes

1. A summary of the main concepts may include the following. *Everyone has something valuable inside that we may not see at first. The "soft center" of people represents what we all have in common: feelings, hopes, dreams, fears, and insecurities. To feel safe and protected, people often use a hard outside to hide their soft cores. However, a tough outer shell may prevent others from getting to know what is truly special about us. Making the effort to get to know what makes someone special on the inside helps us learn, grow, and practice tolerance.*
2. For students with special dietary needs: Tootsie Roll Pops are a gluten-free, peanut-free, nut-product-free, and Kosher-certified product.

Source: Submitted by Cris Davis and LuAnn Wood, Century College, MN; adapted from Lois Rothberg, retired from Pikesville Middle School, Pikesville, Maryland, *www.tolerance.org*

EXERCISE 16-7: Team Juggling

Purpose

To experience an activity that illustrates the empowerment possible when people in a group work interdependently versus trying to do the activity independently.

Supplies and Setup

Five tennis balls. This is an activity that can be done outside.

RULES: [Post on board or PowerPoint]

1. Always call your partner's name before you toss to him or her.
2. Always have eye contact before you toss.
3. Always toss underhanded.
4. If you drop the ball, don't leave the circle to retrieve it—just keep going.

Directions

1. [Have all students form a circle, standing and facing the center, with their hands raised in the air. Choose a "toss partner" on the other side of the circle and ask the person his or her name and toss him or her a tennis ball (after which the person leaves his or her hands down). Have that person choose a "toss" partner in the same way and continue until the last person names you as his or her "toss partner" and tosses the ball to you. Now everyone has a different "toss partner."

2. **WARM UP:** As a warm-up, begin the game by starting with one ball. Each person catches and tosses the ball to his or her "toss partner," following the rules (call partner's name, eye contact, and toss underhanded), establishing a pattern. One person calls the name of and tosses the ball to his or her "toss to" partner on the other side of the circle. That person then tosses the ball to his or her "toss to" partner and so on until everyone has tossed and caught the ball once. The last catcher tosses the ball back to the facilitator who began the first throw, and the group runs through the sequence again for practice. Now the real juggling can begin.

3. **THE GAME:** With one ball on its way around the circle, the facilitator adds another, so that there are now two balls in the air following the catch-and-toss pattern. The facilitator then adds another ball until all five balls are in play. After the balls are in play for a few minutes, players should be watching carefully for midair collisions, trying to toss the balls so that the intended receivers can catch it. The facilitator may stop the game (by collecting all five balls as they are tossed to him or her) to process what's happening (see processing questions) and remind players that they should keep in mind that this is an interdependent venture. The objective is to keep as many balls in the air as possible. If one ball drops, pick it up quickly if possible or, if not, let it go to keep the pattern going.

Approximate time: 20 minutes

Instructor Notes

1. After processing of the following questions has been completed, the facilitator again tosses the ball to his or her partner and begins the patterns until all five balls are again in play. The facilitator stops the action to process every so often. It's fun to ask the group a few questions as you "pause" the game, such as:
   A. What's working?
   B. What's not working?
   C. Is there anything you'd like to change to make it work better?
   D. Is there anything you'd like to say to your partner that would help you to be a better team player?
   E. If something isn't working, what can you do to fix it? (e.g., Slow down or speed up your throw to make the multitasking more manageable.)
   F. Does the group want more of a challenge? (e.g., Add more balls, speed up the process, eliminate calling of names to see if the group members can keep the focus and pattern going.)
   G. What are some results we notice when as a team, we creatively change the rules?

Additional Process Questions

   H. What was that like for you? What are your reactions to this game?
   I. What are some "team" aspects of this game?

   [e.g., "If everyone doesn't do their part, the objective isn't achieved."]

   [e.g., "If everyone does their small part well—paying attention and following the rules—we work together to create something amazing that we couldn't create alone."]

   J. What worked? Give examples.
   K. What didn't work? Give examples and share—how did you problem solve this?
   L. Was it challenging to enlist the support of teammates to make the process work more smoothly? Why or why not?
   M. How does this game relate to our lives and working dependently, independently, or interdependently?

   N. What have you learned about your role as a team player?

   O. What could we learn from this game to apply to our own experiences (at home, at work with coworkers, at work with customers, with fellow students and instructors)?

   P. What have you learned about interdependence?

   Q. What's the life lesson?

2. Later, for more of a challenge, break the whole group into smaller groups. The smaller the group, the greater the challenge.

Source: Submitted by Sherry Lichte-Baird, Rio Salado College, AZ

Journal Entry 17 Strengthening Relationships with Active Listening

EXERCISE 17-1: Circle of Reflection

Purposes

To practice listening actively; to explore thoughts and feelings about asking for assistance.

Supplies and Setup

Students sitting in trios (Students A, B, and C)

Directions

1. *We're going to practice listening actively. Here's how it works: Person A speaks a thought to B about the topic of asking for help. This "thought" can be an experience, opinion, or anything having to do with asking for help. B reflects A's thoughts and feelings. A confirms or corrects. (If A corrects, B now reflects the correction.) When B has accurately reflected A's thought, B speaks a thought to C about asking for help. C reflects B's thoughts and feelings. B confirms or corrects. When C has accurately reflected B's thought, C speaks a thought to A about asking for help. And the process of reflecting keeps going around the circle.* [You may want to provide these directions on a handout or post them on a PowerPoint slide. A sample DEMO follows. Emphasize not changing speakers until the speaker confirms that the listener has gotten the thought and feeling—the complete message—correct.]

2. *Whoever isn't the speaker or the listener is the observer. The observer's job is to identify any talking that doesn't follow the reflecting format. Keep going around your circle until I call stop.* [8–10 minutes]

3. [Quick-Write and/or Class Discussion] *What was your experience when you were the active listener? What was your experience when you were being actively listened to? What did you notice when you were the observer? What did you learn about active listening? What did you learn about asking for help? What is the life lesson here for you? How will this insight influence your behavior in a conversation?* [e.g., "Some people listen without really hearing. I'll use more reflecting when I'm talking with someone."] [10–20 minutes]

Approximate time: 20–30 minutes

Instructor Notes

1. Here's a sample DEMO as a model for the interactions in this activity:

   A to B: I really don't like asking for help. [States thought]

   B to A: What I heard is that you don't like to ask for help. [Reflection]

   A to B: That's right. [Confirms accuracy of B's reflection]

   B to C: Well, I don't mind asking for help. In fact, my brother would probably tell you that I ask for help all the time. Maybe I ask for too much help. [States thought]

   C to B: What I heard is that you don't mind asking for help. [Reflection]

   B to C: Right, but also, sometimes I think I ask for too much help. [Corrects C's reflection]

C to B: Okay, now I've got it. You don't mind asking for help, but you're wondering if you ask for too much help. [Reflection]

B to C: That's it. [Confirms C's reflection]

C to A: Actually, I've never thought much about asking for help.

[The process returns to A for a reflection, and it keeps going around the circle until time is called.]

2. If you want to illustrate how poorly people listen to one another, show a recording of a few minutes from one of the conflict-oriented TV talk shows, such as the *Jerry Springer Show.*

EXERCISE 17-2: The Sounds of Silence

Purpose

To demonstrate the value of silence and careful observation while actively listening.

Supplies and Setup

Chime; students sitting in pairs facing one another, each with journal and a pen

Directions

1. *The first part of this activity is to be done without talking. Please don't say a word until I tell you it's okay to talk again. Sit with your partner in total silence and observe each other. Don't say a word until I ring the chime* [or call "Stop"]. [2 minutes]

2. [Quick-Write] *In your journal, write an answer to this question: What did you observe about your partner during the silence? Be complete. Later, you'll be sharing with your partner what you wrote.* [Many people will report not observing much, feeling rather uncomfortable, and wondering how much longer the silence would last. In other words, they were more aware of themselves than their partners.] [4 minutes]

3. *Now sit with your partner again, and this time, see what you can learn about him or her just by observing him or her in silence. Use your powers of observation and intuition. Don't say a word until I ring the chime* [or call "Stop"]. [2 minutes]

4. [Quick Write] *In your journal, write an answer to this question: What did you observe about your partner this time? Be complete.* [Many people will report more meaningful observations about their partners this time.] [3 minutes]

5. *Alternate reading your first entry to one another. Then read your second entry to one another. Then take a few minutes to have a conversation about what you observed and learned about each other.* [7 minutes]

6. [Quick-Write and/or Class Discussion] *What was the experience like for you? How might silence contribute to a more complete communication? What can you look for in another person that tells you something about that person or what he or she is experiencing at the moment? What is the life lesson here for you? How will this insight affect how you interact with other?* [e.g., "You can look at a person without really seeing him or her. I will pay much more attention to the person I'm talking with."] [5–15 minutes]

Approximate time: 25–40 minutes

Journal Entry 18 Respecting Cultural Differences

EXERCISE 18-1: What's in a Name?

Purpose

To enable students to get to know their classmates—including their cultures—and begin to create a comfortable learning community where students feel safe to risk new behaviors and adopt new beliefs and attitudes.

Supplies and Setup

Pens and paper (journals, if available)

Directions

1. *Write your full name on the top of a blank page in your journal. Now, write the story of your name. Where did it come from? How do you feel about it? How do you think your name has influenced who you are? Does your name reflect the culture with which you most identify; if so, how? Add anything else that comes to mind about your name as you write.* [Teacher DEMOs by telling the story of his or her name.] [5–8 minutes]
2. [Move students into groups of four.] *The person in your group who will have the next birthday goes first. That person reads the story of his or her name to the group. Then go clockwise around your group until each person has read. When everyone has finished reading, have a discussion about any patterns that you notice about the names in your group. For example, perhaps you'll find that many of you in your group were named for a relative or that most of you prefer a different name. Later, one of you will report on what your group discovered about your names, so be sure to take notes about your group members' names. You have 10 minutes. What questions do you have?* [Respond to questions, if any.] *Please begin.* [10 minutes]
3. *Let's hear from someone in each group. What did you learn about the names of the people in your group? Any patterns? Any discoveries about the cultures of your group members? Any surprises? Any unusual stories?* [5–15 minutes]

Approximate time: 20–30 minutes

Instructor Notes

This activity is also a great first-day ice breaker, generating lively discussions. Most people enjoy talking about their names. Some people discover thoughts and feelings about their names that they didn't realize they had.

Source: This activity is a variation of an exercise I learned from Barbara Jaffe of El Camino College, CA

EXERCISE 18-2: Examining Stereotypes

Purpose

To help students become aware of the hurtful nature of stereotypes as well as ways to combat stereotypes.

Supplies and Setup

Index cards (five for each student)

Directions

1. *Each of us has an identity that is composed of the many aspects that make us who we are. It is the unique combination of these aspects that makes us similar to some people as well as different from every other person. On each of the five index cards, write an important part of your identity. No one else will know which cards are yours. Here are some examples of aspects of identity. If you hear one that is important to your identity, write it on a card: woman, college student, Democrat, middle class, Asian, man, Republican, middle-aged, learning disabled, athlete, immigrant, black, southerner, Muslim, tall, white, Jewish, large, Native American, teenager, gay, Latino/a, surfer, jazz musician, Goth, "A" student, elderly, working class. What are some other aspects of identity?* [Ask students to brainstorm aloud.] [5–7 minutes]
2. *According to the* On Course *text, "A stereotype is a generalization about a group of people based on limited or even faulty evidence. Once we accept a generalization as true, we have a tendency to apply it to all individuals we encounter from that group. . . . Stereotypes about any group disrespect individuals from that group, denying them their uniqueness." On the back of each of your five index cards, write a stereotype you have heard about people who have the aspect as part of their identity. These stereotypes could be seemingly negative, such as "Women are weak." Or these stereotypes could be seemingly positive, such as "Asians are good at math." If you honestly can't think of a stereotype for an aspect of your identity, leave the back of the card blank. Remember, don't put your name on any of the cards."* [5–8 minutes]
3. [Collect only the cards that have both an aspect of identity on one side and a stereotype on the other. Shuffle the cards and pass them all out to students. Each student will likely have two or three cards.] [2 minutes]
4. [To a volunteer:] *Please read the identity on one of your cards.* [To the class:] *See if you can predict what stereotype is written on the back of the card.* [Ask the volunteer to read the stereotype.] *How do you suppose a person would feel to*

be stereotyped in that manner? [Repeat as often as time allows, providing about three minutes for each card.] [3–30 minutes]

5. [Optional if time allows] [Collect the cards that have an aspect of identity on one side but no stereotype written on the other. Shuffle the cards and pass them all out to students. Ask volunteers to read an aspect from a card and ask the class to offer stereotypes they have heard about people with this aspect.] *How do you suppose a person would feel to be stereotyped in that manner?* [Repeat as often as time allows, providing about three minutes for each card.] [3–15 minutes]

6. *What ideas do you have for eliminating stereotypes in your own thinking?* [Example: "Don't assume someone either fits a stereotype or can speak for a whole culture."] [5–10 minutes]

Approximate time: 25–70 minutes

Source: Adapted from an activity posted on the Teaching Tolerance website, www.tolerance.org

EXERCISE 18-3: The Ladder of Prejudice

Purpose

To help students learn the range of harmful behaviors caused by prejudice and how to combat them.

Supplies and Setup

Post-it Notes (all the same color, five for each student). Post the following Ladder of Prejudice on the board or an easel pad (make the ladder large so that a number of Post-it Notes can be placed on the ladder during the activity).

The Ladder of Prejudice

> The Fifth Rung: Extermination
>
> The Fourth Rung: Physical Attack
>
> The Third Rung: Discrimination
>
> The Second Rung: Avoidance
>
> The First Rung: Spoken Abuse

The ladder should be positioned so that students can place Post-it Notes on it unseen (like the privacy of a voting booth). For example, if the Ladder of Prejudice is on an easel pad, turn the pad to face away from the class. If the Ladder of Prejudice is on the board, move a screen in front of the board (or lower a screen from a ceiling mount if available). In either case, have students come up one at a time and place their Post-its without anyone seeing where they place them.

Directions

1. *What is your understanding of the meaning of "prejudice"? Write a definition of "prejudice."* [3 minutes]
2. *Here's one definition: "Prejudice is prejudgment, that is, a judgment or opinion (usually negative) that is formed without the benefit of knowledge or an examination of the facts." In other words, even though we don't have good reasons for it, we believe something is true, so we make choices as if it is true.* [2 minutes]
3. *Psychologist Gordon Allport, in his book* The Nature of Prejudice, *describes the hurtful choices that are the result of prejudice. He called this the "Ladder of Prejudice."* [Show the "Ladder of Prejudice."] *Let's start with the first rung: "Spoken Abuse." What's an example of a behavior on this rung?* [e.g., calling people insulting names] *The second rung is "Avoidance." What's an example of this rung?* [e.g., not going to places where people are different from you] *The third rung is "Discrimination." What's an example?* [e.g., not hiring someone for a job because of her age, race, or sexual orientation.] *The fourth rung is "Physical Attack." What's an example?* [e.g., pushing and shoving someone because he or she is different.] *And the fifth rung of Allport's Ladder of Prejudice is "Extermination." What's an example?* [e.g., U.S. government/Native Americans; Nazis/Jews] [5 minutes]

4. *Working by yourself, write on a Post-it Note something that happened here at school, in your community, or in the world that could be posted somewhere on the ladder. Don't put your name on the notes; they will remain anonymous. When you have completed a Post-it Note, please come up one at a time and stick it on the appropriate rung of the Ladder of Prejudice. Only one person may come up at a time so that everyone has complete privacy. You are welcome to add more than one Post-it if you wish.* [10 minutes]

5. [Reveal the Ladder of Prejudice with the Post-it Notes attached. Have a volunteer read Post-its on each rung, starting with Rung 1. Pause after each to ask, *What did you hear that you expected? What did you hear that you didn't expect? What can we do to make sure these things don't happen in our class? On our campus?* [Consider sharing this quotation from anthropologist Margaret Mead: "Never doubt that a small group of thoughtful, committed citizens can change the world; indeed, it is the only thing that ever has."] [20–30 minutes]

Approximate time: 40–50 minutes

Instructor Notes

Stress that prejudice is a judgment made by the Inner Defender.

Source: This is a variation of an activity by Stefanie Fox of Kingsway Middle School posted at www.tolerance.org/activity/ladder-prejudice.

EXERCISE 18-4: Microaggressions

Purpose

To identify microaggressions and understand what messages they send to members of minority groups.

Supplies and Setup

"Microaggressions" handout (following this exercise) and whiteboard with markers. Place students in groups of four to six. (This is a great activity for success teams if you use them.)

Directions

1. *One of the ways we can work toward better intercultural communication is to be aware of when we use commonplace (intentional or unintentional) microaggressions in our interactions with others. Microaggressions are brief slights and insults that send demeaning messages to members of minority groups. This activity will help us identify these messages and understand what they subtly say to others, especially to groups that are racially, ethnically, or otherwise different from the majority culture. Taking personal responsibility for using correct terminology and avoiding microaggressions is an important step in building trust and respect between and among various cultures.* [If possible, show the brief video mentioned in the Instructor Notes section. It provides a good explanation and examples of microaggressions.] [5 minutes]

2. [Give out the Microaggressions handout.] *In your group, read through the rows together. In each row there is a blank cell. Discuss and fill in what you think the missing theme, action, or message is. When you are done filling out the sheet, write your responses on the board or poster paper that corresponds to the blank space in each row of your handout.* [15 minutes]

3. [Large-Group Discussion: First, talk through the examples the students offered, as well as adding any statements from the possible answers provided below the handout. Then discuss the following questions:] *Why are microaggressions hurtful? Are there any other examples of microaggressions you would be willing to share from your own personal and cultural background? What should someone do if he or she experiences a microaggression? What will you do with this information?* [15 minutes]

Approximate time: 35 minutes (40 minutes if adding the video mentioned in the Instructor Notes)

Instructor Notes

1. Depending on the reading level of your students, you may need to explicitly explain some of the vocabulary used. As with any discussion on race and any "ism," it is important to have built a classroom of trust and respect. Reviewing your classroom civility rules prior to this activity helps set a Creator tone for this activity. We stress "listen deeply, avoid assumptions, and turn to wonder" to set the stage for this activity.

2. You may wish to introduce microaggressions by showing a four-minute video on YouTube by Derald Wing Sue, professor of psychology and education at Teacher's College, Columbia University. Sue explains what a microaggression is (with examples), how it manifests itself, how it impacts people, and what can be done to address it. You can access it at http://www.OnCourseWorkshop.com → Educator Resources → Video Gallery → Interdependence.

3. Possible answers for blanks in each row:
   1. You are not American. You are a foreigner.
   2. You are a credit to your race. You are so articulate. Asking an Asian person for help with a math or science problem.
   3. Statements that indicate that a white person does not want to acknowledge race.
   4. I am immune to racism because I have friends of color. Your racial oppression is not different than my gender oppression. I can't be a racist. I'm like you.
   5. Assimilate to the dominate culture. Leave your cultural baggage outside.
   6. People of color are given extra unfair benefits because of their race. People of color are lazy and/or incompetent and need to work harder.

Source: Submitted by LuAnn Wood and Cris Davis, Century College, MN, based on and adapted from work by Tracey Wyman, Century College, MN

Microaggressions

Microaggressions are commonplace verbal or behavioral indignities, whether intentional or unintentional, that communicate hostile, derogatory, or negative slights and insults to people because of their membership in a cultural subgroup.

THEME	MICROAGGRESSION	MESSAGE
1. Alien in Own Land When Asian Americans and Latino Americans are assumed to be foreign born	"Where are you from?" "Where were you born?" "You speak good English." A person asking an Asian American to teach him or her words in his or her native language.	
2. Ascription of Intelligence Assigning intelligence to a person of color on the basis of his or her race		People of color are generally not as intelligent as whites. It is unusual for someone of your race to be intelligent. All Asians are intelligent and good in math and science.
3. Color Blindness	"When I look at you, I don't see color." "America is a melting pot." "There is only one race, the human race."	Denying a person of color's racial/ethnic experiences Assimilate/acculturate to the dominant culture. Denying the individual as a racial/cultural being
4. Denial of Individual Racism A statement made when whites deny their racial biases	"I'm not a racist. I have several black friends." "As a woman, I know what you go through as a racial minority."	
5. Pathologizing Cultural Values/ Communication Styles The notion that the values and communication styles of the dominant/ white culture are ideal	Asking a black person, "Why do you have to be so loud or animated? Just calm down." To an Asian or Latino person: "Why are you so quiet? We want to know what you think. Be more verbal. Speak up more." Dismissing an individual who brings up race or culture in a work or school setting.	
6. Myth of Meritocracy Statements asserting that race does not play a role in life successes	"I believe the most qualified person should get the job." "Everyone can succeed in this society if they work hard enough."	

Note: We are all going to make mistakes. Be genuine, be honest, apologize, and learn from the mistake. Recognize and accept that your worldview is only one of many ways to understand and experience the world.

Journal Entry 19 Believing in Yourself: Be Assertive

EXERCISE 19-1: The Party

Purpose

To better understand placating, blaming, and leveling as communication styles.

Supplies and Setup

Chime (or another way to get the students' attention). Students should have read/written Journal Entry 19.

Directions

1. *According to family therapist Virginia Satir, the two most common patterns of ineffective communication are **placating** and **blaming**. Both perpetuate low self-esteem. In a few moments, we're going to have a party of placaters, blamers, and levelers. Let's examine how placaters, blamers, and levelers typically communicate.* [DEMO each of these three communication styles: **Placate:** "Even though I'm extremely busy, I'll be glad to drop everything I need to do in order to do what you want me to do." **Blame:** "You never make time for me; you are a terrible friend." **Level:** "I miss the times we used to spend together. Would you be willing to meet for coffee on Thursday or Friday?" Explain that these are the voices of the Inner Critic (placating), Inner Defender (blaming), and Inner Guide (leveling).]

2. *During our party, everyone born in January, February, March, or April will communicate as a placater. Those born in May, June, July, or August, your style of communication will be blaming. If you were born in September, October, November, or December, your style of communication will be leveling. When you talk to people at this party, communicate in your assigned style.* [5–8 minutes]

3. *You can talk about anything you want to: sports, college, what you did this weekend, whatever you might talk about at a party. Okay, let the party begin!* [3–5 minutes]

4. [Ring the chime or call "Stop!"] *Stop where you are; close your eyes; and become aware of your breathing, thoughts, feelings, and body sensations.* [Pause] *How do you feel about yourself?* [Pause] *How do you feel about the people you have been talking to?* [Pause] *Now we're going to start the party again. But you're going to change communication styles. If you were placating, now use blaming. If you were blaming, now use leveling. If you were leveling, now use placating. Okay, let the party resume!* [5 minutes]

5. [Ring the chime or call "Stop!"] *Stop where you are; close your eyes; and again become aware of your breathing, thoughts, feelings, and body sensations.* [Pause] *How do you feel about yourself now?* [Pause] *How do you feel about the people you have been talking to?* [Pause] *In a moment, we're going to start the party again. But you're going to change communication styles one last time. If you were placating, now use blaming. If you were blaming, now use leveling. If you were leveling, now use placating. Okay, let the party resume!* [5 minutes]

6. [Ring the chime or call "Stop!"] *Stop where you are; close your eyes; and one more time become aware of your breathing, thoughts, feelings, and body sensations.* [Pause] *How do you feel about yourself now?* [Pause] *How do you feel about the people you have been talking to?* [Pause] *Okay, return to your seats.* [5 minutes]

7. [Quick-Write and/or Class Discussion] *What was your experience at this party? How did you feel about yourself as you spoke as a placater? As a blamer? As a leveler? How did you feel about other people as they used these three styles to communicate with you? Did you have a sense that any of these communication styles is the one you use most often? What is the life lesson here for you?* [e.g., "Speaking as a placater and blamer is exhausting."] [10–20 minutes]

Approximate time: 30–50 minutes

EXERCISE 19-2: Make a Request—Now!

Purpose

To assist students to be more assertive about making requests, especially at college.

Supplies and Setup

Pen and paper

Directions

1. *Write down a problem that you are having here at college. For example, perhaps you're having a problem with a particular course, with a particular assignment, or with finding a book you need. Okay, let's hear some of the problems you have.* [Having some students share their problems will assist others to think of one of their own. Make sure everyone has thought of a problem before moving on to Step 2.] [5 minutes]

2. *Now make a list of requests you could make to assist you to solve this problem. For example, if your problem is that you're confused in your math course, you could request an appointment with your math teacher or a tutor to get help.* [5 minutes]

3. *Okay, let's hear your problem and the requests for help that you could make.* [As students read their lists of possible requests, listen for one in each list that the student could do immediately. Without telling them why, instruct each to put a star next to one request—the one you picked because the request could be made immediately.] [10 minutes]

4. [Each student should now have a request starred that he or she could make immediately.] *Get together with a partner. You have five minutes to practice your request related to the problem you starred.* [5 minutes]

5. *Okay, now I want you to leave the class and go and make the request that has a star next to it. Return in 15 minutes to report on your experience, no matter what it is.* [15 minutes]

6. [Quick-Write and/or Class Discussion] *What was your experience? Were you aware of your Inner Critic or Inner Defender talking to you as you went to make your request? How did you feel as you went to make the request? How did you feel after making the request (if you were able to)? What is the life lesson here for you?* [e.g., "Making a request that is important to me is a great way to take care of myself."] [15 minutes]

Approximate time: 50 minutes

Instructor Notes

Some students may not have been able (either because of inner or outer barriers) to make their requests. Be sure to remind them that they don't have to judge themselves for not succeeding this time. You may even want to suggest that they create a plan to try it again and report their results in the next class period. This activity is another of life's learning opportunities, not a reason to beat themselves up.

Chapter 5: Quiz Questions

(The Answer Key to Chapter 5: Quiz Questions appears at the end of this Facilitator's Manual. Please visit the Instructor Companion Site for *On Course* at login.cengage.com for a digital version of this quiz and its answer key.)

Creating a Support System

1. Individualistic cultures, such as mainstream North American culture, have an "I/me" orientation, and independence is highly regarded.   TRUE   FALSE

2. Collectivistic cultures, such as Latino, Asian, and Native American cultures, have a "we/us" orientation, and independence is highly regarded.   TRUE   FALSE

3. Most college and university instructors hold office hours when students can visit them to ask questions about the course.   TRUE   FALSE

4. Certain steps must be taken to create an effective study group. Which of the following suggestions is NOT suggested in *On Course*?

   A. Choose only Creators.

   B. Choose group goals.

   C. Choose a group name.

   D. Choose group rules.

5. If you were having academic problems in a math class, which college resource would likely offer the most effective help?

   A. Student Activities Office

   B. Career Center

   C. Tutoring Lab or Learning Center

   D. Financial Aid Office

Strengthening Relationships with Active Listening

1. Good listeners clear their minds and listen for the entire message, including words, tone of voice, gestures, and facial expressions.   TRUE   FALSE

2. Suppose that you are listening to someone and you ask, "Could you say more about that?" You are using an active listening strategy called "reflection."   TRUE   FALSE

3. You are actively listening when you're actively waiting for the first opportunity to offer your own opinion on what the other person is saying.   TRUE   FALSE

4. Active listening is a way to demonstrate the high esteem with which you value the other person.   TRUE   FALSE

5. Listening effectively means that you accept 50 percent of the responsibility for receiving the same message that the speaker is sending, uncontaminated by your own thoughts or feelings.   TRUE   FALSE

Respecting Cultural Differences

1. According to the Pew Research Center, whites will make up less than half of the population of the United States by 2050.   TRUE   FALSE

2. Although there are many different verbal languages on Earth, nonverbal languages (e.g., the meaning of gestures) are pretty much the same for all people.   TRUE   FALSE

3. Ethnocentrism is the belief that

    A. all people are created equal.

    B. the way we do things is superior to the way they do things.

    C. prejudice is inherited, just like skin color.

    D. other people are usually right.

4. Jean Moule, an African American professor at Oregon State University, described the following experiences: "A man saw my face as I walked into the store and subconsciously checked his wallet." This experience is an example of a _____.

5. If you witness or are the target of discrimination, bigotry, or hate crimes, which of the following is NOT a recommended choice in *On Course*?

    A. Ignore the incident.

    B. Report the offense to campus officials.

    C. Follow up to see that something is done.

    D. Request help from a group that has experience dealing with such injustices.

On Course at Work: Interdependence at Work

1. One advantage of choosing good attendance and completed assignments is that instructors will be more willing to help with job references or letters of recommendation.   TRUE   FALSE

2. A good choice for collaboration during your job search is to get to know individuals who are already working in your field of interest.   TRUE   FALSE

3. A mentor is someone further along in his or her career development who is willing to assist newer employees.   TRUE   FALSE

4. In what ways will mutually supportive relationships assist you during a job search?

    A. They may be a source for good letters of recommendation or references.

    B. They may be a source of job openings that are unpublished or "invisible."

    C. They may assist you in staying on course when the job search is frustrating.

    D. All of the above

    E. None of the above

5. Once you are on the job (and let's imagine that it's your dream job), you can be sure that

    A. your work with collaboration has ended.

    B. your bosses will value those workers who "fly solo" and work independently.

    C. your ability to develop strong support networks at work may make you a "star."

    D. your coworkers will not be interested in your active listening skills or interdependent values.

Believing in Yourself: Be Assertive

1. Victims who _____ are placing themselves below others. They protect themselves from the sting of criticism and rejection by saying whatever they think will gain approval.

    A. blame

    B. level

    C. placate

2. Victims who _____ are placing themselves above others. They protect themselves from wounds of disappointment and failure by making others responsible for their problems.

    A. blame

    B. level

    C. placate

3. Creators who _____ (a term used by family therapist Virginia Satir) are telling the truth as they see it.

    A. blame

    B. level

    C. placate

4. Which of the following problems could you probably get help with at your college if you made a request to the proper person?

    A. Academic problems

    B. Money problems

    C. Health problems

    D. Problems deciding on a career

    E. All of the above

5. The DAPPS rule, which we use to remember the qualities of an effective goal, can also be used to remember the qualities of an effective request. The letters in DAPPS stand for Dated, Achievable, Personal, Positive, and _____.

Chapter 5: Essay Topics

1. Many college students are very proud of being INDEPENDENT. Write an essay in which you persuade them that they would actually be better off if they were INTERDEPENDENT.

2. Whereas the deep culture of some students promotes independence (individualism), the deep culture of other students promotes interdependence (collectivism). Write an opinion piece for your college newspaper in which you explore the advantages and disadvantages of each belief. Conclude by explaining when it would be beneficial for college students to choose to be independent and when it would be beneficial to choose to be interdependent.

3. Successful students often create study groups. Write a formal letter to three to five fellow students in one of your present classes persuading them to join you in forming a study group. Be sure to explain what a study group is, why one is important, and how you see the group working for mutual success.

4. Very few people are truly active listeners. Do a personal research project to answer the question: What behaviors typically interfere with listening well? You should be able to gather a great deal of information simply by observing people while they are engaged in a conversation. Feel free to gather information in any way that seems appropriate to answer your question. Write an essay revealing your discoveries.

5. Describe a time when you experienced a culture different from your own. Explain the differences in surface and/or deep cultures. Relate any challenges you had while interacting with others in this culture, how you dealt with the challenges, and what you learned.

6. There are times in most people's lives when they said "Yes" because they were not assertive enough to say "No." Write an essay about a time when you said "Yes" when "No" would have been a wiser choice. Explain the situation, including your thoughts that led to saying "Yes." Describe the consequences of your "Yes" in terms of the price you later paid. End your essay by explaining what you have learned about the power of saying "No" and how you expect this discovery to affect your life in the future.

7. Using the "One Student's Story" essays in *On Course* as a model, write an essay about how you used a strategy from Chapter 5 to overcome a problem in your life—academic, personal, or even at work. First, explain the problem; then, discuss the specific strategy you used and how you put it into action; finally, identify what happened. Your instructor may submit your essay for possible publication in the next edition of *On Course*. Additional directions for writing and submitting these essays can be found at http://oncourseworkshop.com/course-textbook/essay-contest/.

Gaining Self-Awareness

Concept

When discussing self-awareness, the thought that usually pops most quickly to mind is awareness of one's strengths and weaknesses, inclinations and disinclinations. However, there is another realm of self-awareness that may play an even bigger role than these characteristics in determining one's outcomes and experiences. Many people, despite their conscious intentions, make choices that sabotage their success. As a result of their self-defeating habit patterns (including behaviors, thoughts, emotions) and unconscious limiting beliefs, students with great potential can thwart the achievement of their most cherished goals and dreams. As a result, these students are their own greatest obstacle. By assisting students to become aware of their unconscious self-defeating habit patterns and limiting beliefs, we empower them to rewrite outdated life scripts and change their lives for the better.

EMPOWERS STUDENTS TO . . .

1. Recognize when they are off course from their goals and dreams.
2. Identify their self-defeating habit patterns of thought, behavior, and emotion.
3. Identify their unconscious limiting beliefs about themselves, other people, and the world.
4. Revise their outdated scripts, thereby becoming the authors of their futures.
5. Consciously take charge of the outcomes and experiences of their lives.

Remember also to use the all-purpose exercises mentioned in the introduction, actively engaging students in the exploration of JOURNAL ENTRIES, CASE STUDIES, ONE STUDENT'S STORY, ON COURSE AT WORK, QUOTATIONS, CARTOONS, FOCUS QUESTIONS, CHAPTER-OPENING CHARTS, and TECH TIPS. Remind students to use letters to label any in-class writing they do in their journals.

Case Study in Critical Thinking: Strange Choices

Purpose

To develop critical thinking skills by exploring a real-life situation concerning self-awareness and the power of scripts to affect our choices.

Supplies and Setup

"Strange Choices" in *On Course*

Directions

1. [Have students read "Strange Choices." One way to be sure everyone has read the selection before taking the next step is to have one student read the first paragraph aloud, another student read the second, and so on until the reading is complete. Then have students put in their scores for the six professors' students.] [5 minutes]

2. [Find out by a show of hands how many students have picked each professor's student as number 1—demonstrating the strangest choices (or, as we will see later, the most self-sabotaging script). If two or more characters are chosen as number 1, move on to step 3. In the unlikely event that everyone chooses the same character as number 1 (or there is otherwise little diversity in opinion), ask how many students have picked each character as number 6—demonstrating the least self-sabotaging script. Sometimes there is more diversity of opinion here.] [5 minutes]

3. [Create groups of like-minded students.] *Because you agree in your group about which student demonstrated the strangest choice, decide how you are going to persuade other groups to agree with you.* [5–10 minutes]

4. [Have a spokesperson from each group present the group's position; then lead a debate on the issue by moving the discussion from group to group, allowing students to explain their positions in more detail and rebut opposing views. Invite students to demonstrate a change in their opinions by getting up and going to the group with which they now agree. If spokespersons don't offer reasons for the student's "strange choice," encourage them to speculate on the causes. See if you can guide them to discover that unconscious beliefs are sometimes the cause of strange choices and that, as long as people are unaware of these beliefs, they will make "strange" and perhaps self-sabotaging choices.] [5–20 minutes]

5. [Quick-Write and/or Class Discussion] *What did you learn from this discussion about strange choices? What's the life lesson here for you?* [e.g., "People sometimes make choices that seem strange to others because the choices sabotage the very goals the people say they want, such as getting a college degree" Or "Sometimes we make bad choices, and we don't even know why."] [5–10 minutes]

Approximate time: 25–50 minutes

Instructor Notes

1. So as not to stifle discussion, I don't tell students what my scores are.
2. This class discussion is an excellent prewriting activity to be followed by students writing a persuasion essay supporting their opinions in the debate. Because students are now sharply aware of opposing views to their own, they often write much more thorough and persuasive essays than would be the case without the debate.
3. An optional step for this activity is to ask students to do a Quick-Write and then a discussion about the Diving Deeper question: Recall a course you once took in which you made a choice that your instructor might describe as "strange." Explain why you made that choice. Dive deep, exploring what *really* caused your choice.

Journal Entry 20 Recognizing When You Are Off Course

EXERCISE 20-1: On Course—Off Course

Purpose

To become conscious of whether one is on course or off course in the pursuit of one's goals and dreams.

Supplies and Setup

Students in pairs (Student A and Student B). Display on a PowerPoint slide or write on the board the following four listening skills that students learned in the article in Chapter 5, "Strengthening Relationships with Active Listening" (Journal 17):

- *Listen to understand.*
- *Clear your mind and remain silent.*
- *Ask the person to expand or clarify.*
- *Reflect the other person's thoughts and feelings.*

Directions

1. *Make a list of all of your life roles. Refer to Journal Entry 9 to remind yourself of the life roles you've chosen.* [3 minutes]
2. *On a scale of 0–10, rate how on course you are toward your goals and dreams in each of your life roles. A score of 0 means that you are totally off course in this role. A score of 10 means that you are totally on course in this role. Scores in between indicate various degrees of being on course or off course. Listen to the information available to you from your Inner Guide and score yourself now.* [3 minutes]
3. *Partner A, tell Partner B your life roles and the scores you have given each one. Explain each score. You have five minutes.* [Display and review the four listening skills.] *B, use your best active listening skills.* [10 minutes]
4. *Now switch roles. Partner B, you explain your scores to Partner A, who will use his or her best listening skills. You have five minutes.* [10 minutes]
5. [Quick-Write and/or Class Discussion] *What did you discover? In what roles are you on course? In what roles are you off course? What self-sabotaging habits may have gotten you off course? What could you do about these habits? What is the life lesson here for you?* [e.g., "If I don't pay close attention, I can get far off course, and my Inner Defender won't even let me admit it."] [5–15 minutes]

Approximate time: 30–40 minutes

EXERCISE 20-2: The Air Traffic Controller

Purpose

To demonstrate the value of responding as a Creator when receiving feedback about being off course.

Supplies and Setup

Have a volunteer stand on the opposite side of the room from you.

Directions

1. [To the volunteer] *Let's imagine for this demonstration that I'm an airplane pilot, and I am trying to fly to your airport in a terrible storm. You're the air traffic controller, and it's your job to guide me safely to your airport. If I'm headed toward you, say, "On course, on course, on course . . ." If I'm not headed toward you, say, "Off course, off course, off course . . ." Now I'm going to close my eyes because there's a storm in my life, and I can't see very well.* [Head toward the volunteer and make sure he continually says, "On course, on course . . ." Now head away from the volunteer and make sure he

says, "Off course, off course . . ." After you have him or her trained as an air traffic controller, you can go into your DEMO of what people often do when they receive feedback that they're off course.]

2. *Notice that I'm now getting feedback saying I'm off course. How do people often act when they're told they're off course?* [Elicit and dramatize various responses: anger, blame, tears, complaints, self-criticism, excuses, or just sitting down and giving up.] *Are any of these responses helping me get back on course?* [Naturally, the answer is NO.]

3. *Life constantly gives us feedback when we are off course. What kind of feedback might we get that we're off course in college?* [An F on a test.] *On a job?* [Demoted or fired.] *Concerning our health?* [We get sick or have a heart attack.] *In a relationship?* [Someone we love decides to leave us.] *Many people, when they get feedback that they're off course, resist the feedback. Does it help us get back on course to get angry, cry, blame, complain, make excuses, or quit? Whose voices are these, anyway?* [It's the Victim reacting from his or her Inner Defender and Inner Critic.]

4. *What would be a more effective way to respond to feedback that tells us we're off course?* [As a Creator listening to his or her Inner Guide.] *Would someone like to demonstrate how a Creator, listening to his her Inner Guide, would respond to the feedback from the air traffic controller?* [Have someone take your place. Have the person close his or her eyes and role-play the pilot of a plane moving on course and off course as it makes its way toward its destination. Ideally, the student will simply take the off-course feedback and use it to change direction to get back on course.]

5. [Quick-Write and/or Class Discussion] *What's the life lesson here for you?* [e.g., "Even feedback that is uncomfortable to hear can be helpful in getting me back on course."] *How do you most often respond to feedback that you're off course? Are there any changes you wish to make? Have you received any off course feedback from an instructor? How did you respond?* [5–10 minutes]

Approximate time: 10–20 minutes

EXERCISE 20-3: Can We Be Trained to Lose and Then Learn to Win?

Purpose

To help students learn that failures teach us about ourselves and prepare us for our successes in life.

Supplies and Setup

Pens and journals or paper; computer, projector, or Internet access; prepare to show "Seabiscuit (1/10) Movie CLIP— The History of Seabiscuit (2003) HD" available on YouTube (less than 3 minutes); prepare reflective questions to be displayed on the white board, handout or PowerPoint slide.

Directions

1. [Introduce the activity to the students.] *We have all failed at something. Some people say that failures teach us more than successes do. Failures can actually prepare us for our successes. In this activity, you will view a clip from the movie* Seabiscuit *and reflect on times in your life when you felt like a failure and/or victim. You will then explore the positives that actually came from the experience and what you learned.*

2. Show the video. Then post the questions below and lead a discussion.
   A. In the clip, the narrator explains that when Seabiscuit would not perform like the horses labeled as champions, he was instead trained to lose. When he began racing again, Seabiscuit did what he had been trained to do. He lost. Write about a time when you experienced failure at something because you were "trained to lose."
   B. As we now know, Seabiscuit went on to become a champion. Were you able to get back on track after failing? How? If not, why do you think that is? What would you do differently now?

Approximate time: 25–55 minutes (depending on the length of discussion)

Instructor Notes

1. This discussion can tie into self-awareness, self-esteem, choices students make, and so forth. It also opens up a good discussion about Victims and Creators. Students can continue to blame someone else who may very well have trained them to lose, but they will be the ones to suffer. There are many different directions you can go with this discussion.

Source: Submitted by Katy Goforth, from Tri-County Technical College, SC

EXERCISE 20-4: What Color Are Your "Lenses"?

Purpose

To help students understand that the way we "view" the world has a huge impact on the choices we make at forks in the road.

Supplies and Setup

Several pairs of "fashion" glasses painted with differently colored lenses. Pebeo's Vitrea 160 transparent paints are available at Michael's and Hobby Lobby.

Directions

1. Bring to class several pairs of "fashion" glasses, their lenses painted with different transparent colors.
2. Ask for several student volunteers to participate in the activity. Each student is given a different pair of glasses to wear.
3. When the students are wearing the glasses, show them different items, starting with a plain white sheet of paper and ask them to describe the color. The color they describe SHOULD correspond to the color of the lenses in their glasses.
4. After all of the students have given their responses, discuss how our beliefs are similar to the "lenses" through which we see the world and how these "lenses" can color everything we see. If we see the world through the colored lens of an Inner Victim or Inner Defender, things will look much different than if we view them through the clear lens of the Inner Guide, thereby coloring the choices we make.

Approximate time: 50 minutes. This activity can easily be completed during a regular 50-minute class period, although the discussion can be extended for as long as necessary.

Instructor Notes

1. I find that students understand the concepts of mindsets better when we have done this literal, physical exercise of seeing the world through different colors.
2. I sometimes give the students a journal assignment to write about the different "lenses" through which they see the world.

Source: Submitted by Lory Conrad, University of Arkansas—Fort Smith, AR

Journal Entry **21** Identifying Your Scripts

EXERCISE 21-1: What's Your Pattern?

Purpose

To dramatize and raise students' awareness about self-defeating patterns.

Supplies and Setup

Students in groups of three; "Situation Cards" handout (following this exercise) cut into eight slips of paper, each with one situation on it. You may want to create your own Situation Cards based on a topical issue at your campus or in your class.

Directions

1. [Have someone from each group pick a Situation Card containing the cast and situation for the skit.] *Each group has five minutes to assign each person in the group to one of the roles in the skit. Your skit will be ____ minutes long.*

[See Instructor Note 1 about length of skits.] *The character listed first on the Situation Card will always say the first line of the skit, and the other two characters will simply play off that character's lead.*

2. *Whatever your role is, your character is to demonstrate a self-defeating pattern. You can choose one from the list of Self-Defeating Habit Patterns in the text immediately before Journal Entry 21, or you can simply role-play a self-defeating pattern you're familiar with. Before each skit, character 1 will read the Situation Card to the audience so we know what role each person is playing. After each skit, we'll try to guess what each character's self-defeating pattern is.* [During the preparation time check with each group to confirm that they are, indeed, choosing self-defeating patterns to dramatize.] [5–8 minutes]

3. [Get the actors in each skit to the front of the room and turn them loose to role-play. Remind them to read their Situation Cards aloud to the audience. Time the skits and stop them if they exceed your allotted time. After each skit, have the audience guess what self-defeating patterns each person was dramatizing.]

4. [Quick-Write and/or Class Discussion] *What did you learn about self-defeating habit patterns? Did you recognize yourself in any of the skits? Did you discover any habit patterns of thought, behavior, or emotions that you want to change? What's the life lesson here for you?* [e.g., "It's easier to see someone else's self-defeating habit patterns than it is to see my own."] [10–25 minutes]

Approximate time: 10–60 minutes, depending on how many groups and the length of each skit

Instructor Notes

1. Determine the length of each skit by the amount of time you have available for the presentation and discussion of all skits. If you have 30 minutes available for all skits and six groups, then allot five minutes per group. That would allow about three minutes for acting out the skit and two minutes for guessing the self-defeating pattern. With any luck, the point about the self-defeating patterns will be made before you need to stop the skit.

2. To create Situation Cards for class, simply duplicate the next page and cut it into eighths. If you need more than 8 Situation Cards, make two copies of the page and create 16 cards. It is interesting to have two groups do the same skit to see the differences.

3. You could give out Situation Cards in one class period and do the skits in class at the next meeting. You could also carry some skits over to another day if your students get really involved.

4. When students are familiar with this activity, you could have each team create its own Situation Cards.

Situation Cards

1. **STUDENT A:** Has just gotten word that he or she has been turned down for a scholarship.

2. **DIRECTOR OF FINANCIAL AID:** This is the person who turned down Student A's application for a scholarship.

3. **STUDENT B:** The boyfriend or girlfriend of Student A. Just got a huge scholarship from the same director of financial aid.

---

1. **FRIEND 1:** Promised two other friends to buy them lottery tickets for Christmas. Asked them to each pick a number, bought the tickets, and held on to them. The ticket bought for Friend 2 wins $1,000,000. Friend 1's spouse threatens a divorce if Friend 1 gives the winning ticket to Friend 2.

2. **FRIEND 2**

3. **FRIEND 3**

---

1. **THE BOSS:** Owns a huge business, is looking for a vice president, and has narrowed the field to Applicants A and B. The boss has invited both applicants in at the same time for a final interview.

2. **APPLICANT A**

3. **APPLICANT B**

---

1. **STUDENT 1:** Organized these three students into a study group for a very difficult course. Always comes to the group prepared.

2. **STUDENT 2:** Sometimes comes to the group prepared.

3. **STUDENT 3:** Never comes to the group prepared and often misses the meetings.

---

1. **MOTHER:** Has discovered that her teenager has not been attending high school for the past three weeks. She has no idea where her teenager has been going every day.

2. **FATHER:** Dropped out of high school when he was a teenager.

3. **TEENAGER**

---

1. **SPOUSE 1:** Wants to return to college. Has been out of school for 10 years. Presently earns more money than Spouse 2 but dislikes the job.

2. **SPOUSE 2:** Worried about their family having enough money if Spouse 1 goes to college.

3. **PARENT OF SPOUSE 2:** Visiting from another state.

---

1. **DRIVER 1:** Was backing out of a parking space in a mall parking lot and was struck in the rear door by Driver 2, who was also backing out of a parking space. Driver 1's car has a huge dent. Driver 2's car is unhurt.

2. **DRIVER 2:** Thinks that Driver 1 is at fault for backing out so fast.

3. **POLICE OFFICER**

---

1. **STUDENT:** Has failed the professor's class; believes that the professor graded unfairly after the student disagreed with the professor in front of the class; has appealed the grade to the department chairperson.

2. **PROFESSOR**

3. **DEPARTMENT CHAIRPERSON**

EXERCISE 21-2: The Puzzle

Purpose

To discover self-defeating patterns and their underlying limiting beliefs.

Supplies and Setup

Have one jigsaw puzzle of about 35 pieces for each 10 to 12 students. Thus, for a group of 35 students, have three puzzles available.

Directions

1. [Have students count off so that you form groups of 10–12 students. Thus, if you have 35 students, have them count off by three's. Place the puzzles, one for each group, where they can be picked up by students—perhaps on the front desk. Do not hand them to any particular student.] *Your goal is to assemble these puzzles. Please begin.* [If anyone asks a question, simply repeat the directions. Record what students are doing and saying as they work on the puzzles. Also note if there are any emotions that surface during the puzzle assembly (e.g., one student getting upset with another). Start recording from the time you put out the puzzles until you stop the puzzle assembly.] [5–10 minutes]

2. [When all puzzles are assembled, introduce the next part as follows.] *What's the value of heightened awareness?* [e.g., "Awareness allows us to see when we are off course and what options we have for getting back on course. Without awareness we will just keep heading off course without even realizing it. Awareness allows us to change so that we can achieve our goals and dreams."] *So our goal here is to see if we can each become aware of one or more patterns in our lives, especially habits that may keep us from achieving the outcomes and experiences we desire. If we can become more aware of what we are doing that isn't working, then we have the option of making different choices that get us more of the outcomes and experiences we want.* [5 minutes]

3. *Some psychologists believe that the microcosm of our lives (the little things) sometimes reveal the macrocosm of our lives (the big things). For example, the way you go through the grocery store may reveal how you live your life. Do you go up and down every aisle or go right to what you need? Do you buy whatever brand you want or only the ones on sale? Do you chat in the check-out line or are you all business about finishing your shopping? For today, you're going to see what you can learn about how you live your life by examining how you did the puzzle. It's important to realize that none of this exploration is about "right" and "wrong." It's merely about becoming aware of how we live our lives. No one did the puzzle right, and no one did the puzzle wrong. You just did the puzzle, and we're going to examine what that looks like for each of us.* [Without naming names, give examples of what you saw, heard, and recorded as the puzzles were being assembled.] [5 minutes]

4. [Solo Quick-Write] *Now we're going to begin a little experiment in self-awareness. Title a page in your journal: "How I did the puzzle is how I do my life." Then write as much as you can to prove that this statement is true. Don't worry about whether it really IS true; for now, just pretend it is and make your case by giving examples wherever possible. Consider questions such as "What were you thinking, feeling, and doing while your group was working on the puzzle? Where else in your life do you think, feel, or do that?" You'll have about eight minutes to write; then you'll share what you wrote with someone else. By the way, everybody "did the puzzle." Whatever you did from the time I put the puzzles out until the puzzles were put together (even if you were out of the room) is "how you did the puzzle." And, again, please understand that this is not about whether you did this activity "right" or "wrong." This is only about seeing how aware you are about what you were thinking, saying, doing, and feeling during the puzzle . . . and then seeing if you can find examples of how you have done the same thing at other times in your life. So go ahead and make a case for the idea, "How I did the puzzle is how I do my life."* [10 minutes]

5. [Pair] *Now meet with a partner and read and discuss what you wrote. See if either of you found any truth to the idea that "How I did the puzzle is how I do my life."* [10 minutes]

6. [Class Discussion] *So, did anyone find truth in the statement that "How I did the puzzle is how I do my life"? Do these habit patterns support or limit you in achieving your desired outcomes and experiences? Are there any changes you'd like to make in your beliefs, behaviors, thoughts, or feelings? What is the life lesson here for you?* [e.g., "Self-aware people make choices with minimal contamination from their past experiences."] [10–20 minutes]

Approximate time: 45–65 minutes

Instructor Notes

1. This puzzle exercise is a very powerful means of generating discussion and insight about habit patterns and their underlying beliefs. Given time, many people will make extraordinary discoveries about their scripts.
2. Keep the puzzle groups large enough—10 to 12 people—so that it is difficult for everyone to work on the puzzle at the same time. This arrangement creates some stress and tends to cause habitual scripts to emerge. Among other discoveries, participants may notice their patterns of participating or withdrawing and of competing or cooperating.

EXERCISE 21-3: What's in Your Backpack?

Purpose

Students bring a great deal of attitudinal baggage with them when they arrive at college, yet many are unaware of how these past attitudes will affect their present behavior and beliefs. Some are weighed down with past failures and negative academic experiences, making it challenging for them to stay motivated when encountering life's inevitable obstacles. This strategy helps students:

1. identify some of the internal baggage that weighs them down, gaining greater self-awareness about the attitudes and choices that take them off course.
2. become aware of ways to 'fill their backpacks' with the confidence and grit that will help them achieve their goals.

Supplies and Setup

For each student, have one brown paper bag (lunch bag size) and in each one put a . . .

- rock
- button
- sheet of paper with the outline of a hand on it
- plastic fork
- small energy bar

These are just samples; have fun coming up with your own metaphors!

Directions

1. [Create groups of three or four students.]
2. *Students arrive at college with backpacks filled with objects such as pencils, laptops, and notebooks. In a different kind of backpack, students also arrive with ideas, beliefs, and attitudes about their education. Those ideas, beliefs, and attitudes will have a powerful impact on success at college, so today we're going to examine: "What's in your backpack?"* [2 minutes]
3. [Hand out a brown bag "backpack" to each student.] *Let's look at this backpack and how it represents some of your beliefs, attitudes, and expectations of success for college. Please take out the rock that is in your backpack. This rock represents some of the negative attitudes that can "weigh" you down. For example, when I went to college, my "rock" was* [provide your own example such as: "I didn't think I was college material, or "I thought I could never pass the math requirements"]. [5 minutes]
4. *Share with your group one negative attitude that might be in your backpack and how that negative attitude might weigh you down in the weeks, months, and years ahead. When you encounter that attitude, remind yourself, "I don't need that attitude weighing me down; I can take that rock out of my backpack!"* [6–8 minutes]
5. *Now please take the button out of the bag. We all have a full range of emotions—happy, sad, upset, feeling overwhelmed. To be successful at college, we need to know what kinds of things "press our buttons" in such a way that we allow our emotions to take us off course. For example . . .* [again provide your own personal example such as: "If I'm feeling overwhelmed by all of my homework, it's easy for me to procrastinate by playing video games instead of attending to what needs to be done."] *Share with your group what one of your buttons is and how you can deal with that emotion more effectively in the future if your button get pressed.* [6–8 minutes]

6. *Our belief about asking for help when we need it will greatly affect our likelihood of success. Students who are willing to ask for help are more likely to be successful. Please take out the sheet of paper with the helping hand outlined on it. Your task is to come up with five people that you can "reach out to" for help this semester. You can include staff, family, friends, instructors . . . and put their names on the hand.* [Note: Students who can't think of five people may be at risk if they encounter problems in the semester ahead. Work with these students individually to help them identify college resources they can add to their helping hands!] [6–8 minutes]

7. *Now take the fork out of the bag. This fork stands for the wise choices you have made in your life. Let it remind you that you have the ability to make wise choices at every fork in the road. Share with your group one of the wisest choices you've made in your life.* [6–8 minutes]

8. *The last thing in your bag is an energy bar. The road ahead is long, and there may be times when you feel tired and think of giving up. What helps you get re-energized? For example, when I'm feeling low energy, I [provide your own example]. Share with your group some of the ways you get re-energized and recommitted to your goals.* [6–8 minutes]

9. Discuss as a group what they experienced, discovered, and learned from this experience. Remind them of the challenges they've faced in the past and how these challenges have helped them develop inner resources to meet challenges ahead. Invite students to write in their journals about the experience and any Aha! moments they had in the process. [6–8 minutes]

Approximate time: This strategy can be completed in a 50-minute class. With students who are able to dive deeper, I've used two class periods to complete the strategy along with more group discussion along the way.

Instructor Notes

This activity is easily adaptable to the needs of your class, so consider: How can I use or adapt this? What other objects could I use?

Source: Submitted by Robin Middleton, Jamestown Community College, NY

Journal Entry 22 Rewriting Your Outdated Scripts

EXERCISE 22-1: What I Did Instead

Purpose

To raise students' awareness about limiting core beliefs that may cause them to make unwise choices and help students see how they can revise these beliefs.

Supplies and Setup

Each student needs a pen and a piece of paper.

Directions

1. *Think of a time when you missed or were late to a class for a poor reason. On a piece of paper, write what you did instead of attending or getting to class on time. Don't put your name on the paper. For example, you might write, "Instead of going to math class, I stayed home to watch television." Or, "Instead of arriving on time to my English class, I stopped in the cafeteria, got into a conversation with a friend, and talked too long."* [3 minutes]

2. [Collect the papers and redistribute them so no one knows whose paper he or she has.] [2 minutes]

3. *Look at what the person chose to do instead of attending class or being on time. Write a list of possible **limiting core beliefs** that may have led to this choice. In other words, why do you think the student REALLY was late or absent? For example, if the paper says, "Instead of going to English class on time, I continued talking with a friend in the cafeteria," you might suggest the following possible core beliefs:*

"I'm not smart enough to pass this class."

"Going to college is a waste of time."

"Teachers don't care whether I do well in college."

"When I'm tired, I'm not motivated to go to class."

"It doesn't matter if I'm late."

"I can't be rude and just walk away from a conversation." [5 minutes]

4. *Now get a partner. Partner A, read the core beliefs on your list to your partner. After reading each belief, Partner A tell Partner B whether this core belief is actually one of your own. Partner B, ask questions to help A explore each core belief and take ownership if appropriate. Discuss what would be a more empowering core belief to adopt. When I ring the chime, reverse roles.* [10–15 minutes]

5. [Quick-Write and/or Class Discussion] *What did you learn about your limiting core beliefs from this activity? Did you discover a limiting core belief that you will actively seek to rewrite? What's the life lesson here for you?* [e.g., "Core beliefs that I'm not even aware of can cause me to make unwise choices. I need to become more aware of my core beliefs."] [5–15 minutes]

Approximate time: 30–40 minutes

Instructor Notes

When students are speculating in Step 3 about the other person's limiting core beliefs, they may be projecting their own scripts onto another. So it is likely that at least some, if not all, of the core beliefs on their lists are actually their own.

EXERCISE 22-2: Author, Author

Purpose

To practice changing a limiting script into an empowering script.

Supplies and Setup

Ten index cards for each student

Directions

1. *By now you're probably aware of some of your limiting beliefs. As you know, if you revise your limiting beliefs, you'll change your patterns of thought, behavior, and emotion.*

2. *Write five of your limiting beliefs, one each on five index cards. No one will ever see these cards, so be honest with yourself. Write limiting beliefs you have about life, about people, and especially about yourself. For example, one of the students mentioned in* On Course *believed, "I am the half-brain in the family, so I'll never be able to go to college." If you can't think of five limiting beliefs, then make some up so that you have five cards, each with a limiting belief. Please note, however, that you'll get much more value from this activity if you use your own limiting beliefs.* [5–8 minutes]

3. *Next, translate each of your limiting beliefs into empowering beliefs. Write each empowering belief on a separate index card. For example, the student in* On Course *might have revised her limiting belief to read, "I am smart and doing great in college."* [5–10 minutes]

4. *Now, rip up and throw your limiting beliefs into the trash can. Who would like to read one [or more] of their empowering beliefs to the class?* [5 minutes]

5. [Quick-Write and/or Class Discussion] *When are times that it might be particularly important to remind yourself of these empowering beliefs? How can you remember to think these beliefs even at the most difficult times? So, what's the life lesson here for you?* [e.g., "It isn't easy, but I can change my core beliefs."] [10–20 minutes]

Approximate time: 20–40 minutes

Instructor Notes

Suggest that students carry their empowering belief cards with them or post them at home where they will see them often.

EXERCISE 22-3: Making Academic Course Corrections

Purpose

To help students become aware of and revise self-defeating behaviors, beliefs, and attitudes that get them off course in challenging college courses.

Supplies and Setup

"Making Academic Course Corrections" handout (next page); students in pairs [Student A and Student B]

Directions

1. *Decide which of your present college courses is the most challenging for you. Then complete each of the 13 sentences on the handout as it relates to this challenging course. For example, if your most challenging course this semester is Math 110, you'd write "So far in Math 110 . . . (1) I've been absent four times." You will be sharing your answers with a partner. Obviously, to get value from this exercise, you must be honest.* [10 minutes]

2. *Partner A, read your completed sentences to Partner B. Afterward, Partner B, tell your partner any behaviors, beliefs, or attitudes you heard that might sabotage his or her success. When possible, suggest more empowering behaviors, beliefs, or attitudes that your partner could choose.* [10 minutes]

3. *Switch roles and repeat the same process.* [10 minutes]

4. [Quick-Write and/or Class Discussion] *Are there any changes you intend to make in your behaviors, beliefs, or attitudes? Why? What is the life lesson here for you?* [e.g., "If I don't notice when I am off course and make a course correction, then I become my own worst enemy."] [5–10 minutes]

Approximate time: 25–30 minutes

Making Academic Course Corrections

Complete the sentence below:

The most challenging course I am taking is _____ [course name]

Now complete the following sentences about your efforts in that challenging course; let your Inner Guide tell the truth.

1. I've been absent _____ times.

2. I've been late _____ times.

3. I've studied for this course an average of _____ hours per week.

4. I've completed _____ percent of the assignments.

5. I've done my work at _____ percent of my best effort.

6. I've participated actively in _____ percent of the classes I've attended.

7. I've attended _____ study group meetings.

8. I've attended _____ conferences with my instructor.

9. I've gotten tutoring for this subject _____ times this semester.

10. If I keep doing what I've been doing, the grade I'll probably get in this course is _____.

11. The advantages of my doing well in this course are . . .

12. The disadvantages of my doing poorly in this course are . . .

13. Changes I will make to improve my results in this course are . . .

EXERCISE 22-4: The Party Game

Purpose

To get students interacting with one another; to orient students to the importance of preferred people-environments in thinking about future careers; and to help students find potential study buddies and/or study groups.

Supplies and Setup

Create six pieces of paper with one of the following letters on each: R I A S E C; post these papers in six different spaces in the room; handout of "The Party Game" (next page)

Directions

1. [Announce to the class that they are all going to go to a "party." This should elicit cheers. Distribute "The Party Game" handouts. Ask the students to read the six descriptors, and then go to the "lettered" area of the room where they would most like to "party" with people who share the same interests.] [5 minutes]
2. [After they are at a letter, ask the students to introduce themselves to their fellow partygoers. Ask them to discuss why they chose that party. If there are any students standing alone by a letter, go over and have the same conversation with them. When it appears that a good chat has occurred, give the next set of directions.] [5 minutes]
3. *Now imagine that everyone at your party leaves for another party across town, except you. Find another party here to join. Again discuss why you chose that party.* [5 minutes]
4. [When it appears that this has occurred, repeat the instructions one last time.] [5 minutes]
5. [After the third round, ask students to return to their seats and write down all three letters of the "corners" in the order that they visited. Guide the conversation about what they observed—did they encounter the same student(s) in all three groups? Could one of them be a potential study buddy or study team member?] [5 minutes]
6. *The three letters you just chose, in the three steps, are called your "Holland Code."* [Then, if you wish, you can take this conversation further and talk about possible careers or majors, calling on a variety of websites that discuss Holland codes.] [10 minutes]

Approximate time: 30–35 minutes

Instructor Notes

1. I really play this up in the introduction of the activity as a fun party. I also suggest to students that they really do know the type of environment with which they are comfortable and to trust their instincts.
2. Dick Bolles, author of *What Color Is Your Parachute?*, has written about the importance of environmental factors as a part of career planning. Learning about the environment in which we would most like to work, including the kind of people we are surrounded by, is a fun activity for the next class meeting after the activity.
3. The late Dr. John L. Holland believed that there are six primary people/environments. They are referenced in your *On Course* textbook in the "Self-Awareness at Work" section. Dr. Holland also created the *Self-Directed Search* assessment, also referenced in the text.

Source: Submitted by Lea Beth Lewis, California State Fullerton, CA. Adapted from *What Color Is Your Parachute?* by Richard Nelson Bolles.

The Party Game

Realistic:
People who have athletic or mechanical ability, prefer to work with objects, machines, tools, or animals, or prefer to be outdoors.

Investigative:
People who like to observe, learn, investigate, analyze, evaluate, or solve problems.

Conventional:
People who like to work with data, have clerical or numerical ability, and who carry things out in detail or follow through on others' instructions.

Artistic:
People who have artistic, innovating, or intuitive abilities, and like to work in unstructured situations, using their imagination or creativity.

Enterprising:
People who like to work with people—influencing, persuading or performing, or leading or managing for organizational goals or for economic gain.

Social:
People who like to work with people—to inform, enlighten, help, train, develop, or cure them, or who are skilled with words.

Journal Entry 23 Believing in Yourself: Write Your Own Rules

EXERCISE 23-1: Changing Habits

Purpose

To see that rules followed over time become habits; to identify and modify self-defeating habits and rules.

Supplies and Setup

Students sitting in pairs (Student A and Student B). Write the following three sentence stems on the board or display on a PowerPoint slide):
1. One habit I have that supports my success is . . .
2. One habit I have that hinders my success is . . .
3. One habit I would benefit from having is . . .

Directions

1. *Partner A will read and complete the three sentences until I call "Stop." For example, you might say . . .*
   A. *One habit I have that supports my success is . . . I always get places on time.*
   B. *One habit I have that hinders my success is . . . smoking cigarettes.*
   C. *One habit I would benefit from having is . . . exercising more.*

   Remember that habits include behaviors, thoughts, feelings, and beliefs. Keep going until I call stop.
2. *Partner B, tell Partner A what you heard him or her say. For example, "I heard you say that your smoking is a habit that hinders your success. And I heard you say that you always get places on time." [3–5 minutes]*
3. *[Reverse roles and repeat steps 1 and 2.] [3–5 minutes]*
4. *[Quick-Write and/or Class Discussion] What are some of the habits you mentioned that support your success? That hinder your success? Are there any habits that you would like to get rid of? Are there any new habits that you would like to adopt? How could you do that? [e.g., doing a 32-day commitment] How are habits like rules? What is the life lesson here for you? [e.g., "I need to make a habit of not letting negative habits run my life."] [10–15 minutes]*

Approximate time: 15–30 minutes

Instructor Notes

An important point to bring out in the discussion is that the rules we adopt—whether consciously or unconsciously—eventually turn into habits. It isn't easy to adopt a new habit or eliminate an old habit, but with the exercise of intention and self-discipline, we can choose to do that. You may wish to conclude this activity by inviting students to make a 32-day commitment (Journal Entry 14) to create a new empowering habit or extinguish an old self-sabotaging one.

EXERCISE 23-2: Role Model Rules

Purpose

To identify a role model who demonstrates excellence in the way he or she lives and to determine the habits or rules this person uses to create success.

Supplies and Setup

Students in groups of three with pens and journals or paper

Directions

1. *Write the name of a person who, in your opinion, has created success. This role model can be anyone, whether you know the person or not.* [1–2 minutes]

2. *Under your role model's name, list all of the reasons why you chose this person. In other words, what has this person accomplished, and what does this person do consistently that impresses you?* [5 minutes]

3. *Given what your role model has accomplished and what this person does consistently, what are most likely his or her habits or rules for life? Make a list. For example, your role model's rules might include: "Do all tasks with excellence. Perform good deeds for others. Be cheerful."*

4. *Now, each person in your group reads aloud what you wrote, both why you chose your role model and what his or her rules may be. Choose one person to start and go clockwise until everyone has had a chance to read.* [10 minutes]

5. [Quick-Write and/or Class Discussion] *What did you learn about creating greater success in your life? Is there a rule you identified or heard that you would* not *want to adopt? Why? Is there one new success rule you would benefit from adopting today? Why? What's the life lesson here for you?* [e.g., "People don't get to be successful by accident; instead, they operate by personal rules that act as an inner compass, and this compass keeps them on course."] [5–15 minutes]

Approximate time: 25–40 minutes

Chapter 6: Quiz Questions

(The Answer Key to Chapter 6: Quiz Questions appears at the end of this Facilitator's Manual. Please visit the Instructor Companion Site for *On Course* at login.cengage.com for a digital version of this quiz and its answer key.)

Recognizing When You Are Off Course

1. Leverrier predicted that an invisible planet was pulling the planet Uranus off its predicted course around the sun. Likewise, human beings are pulled off course by the invisible forces of their

   A. conscious minds.

   B. unconscious minds.

   C. Inner Guides.

2. Some people sabotage their goals and dreams by unconsciously choosing actions, thoughts, and/or emotions that get them off course from their goals and dreams.   TRUE   FALSE

3. When Creators are off course, they tend to deny it, make excuses, blame others, or give up.   TRUE   FALSE

4. One characteristic of Creators is that they are able to recognize and acknowledge when they are off course. TRUE   FALSE

5. The story of Jerome, the accounting student, illustrates that when a person has a clear goal, he or she will not get off course.   TRUE   FALSE

Identifying Your Scripts

1. Eric Berne, the creator of a mode of counseling called Transactional Analysis, referred to our invisible inner forces as

   A. defense mechanisms.

   B. patterns.

   C. habits.

   D. scripts.

2. As part of our individual script, each of us has developed three kinds of habit patterns: behaviors, thoughts, and emotions.   TRUE   FALSE

3. Our habit patterns are motivated by our unconscious core _____.

4. We seem to create our scripts as a result of

   A. how others responded to us.

   B. what significant adults said to us.

   C. observing the behavior of significant adults in our lives.

   D. all of the above.

5. The purpose of our scripts is to maximize our pain and minimize our pleasure.   TRUE   FALSE

Rewriting Your Outdated Scripts

1. Diana, the student in the author's writing course, had a script from her childhood that said her brain didn't work well.   TRUE   FALSE

2. When our core beliefs about ourselves, about other people, or about the world are inaccurate, they can sabotage our success.   TRUE   FALSE

3. Diana's core beliefs about her inability to think caused her to hear what she expected to hear rather than what her teacher actually said.   TRUE   FALSE

4. Although it is not easy, human beings can revise their limiting beliefs and change their self-defeating habit patterns.   TRUE   FALSE

5. The parts of our scripts that are available to our conscious minds are our patterns of self-defeating actions, thoughts, and emotions. By revising these three patterns, we can help revise our limiting core _____.

On Course at Work: Self-Awareness at Work

1. "Hard skills" are the special-knowledge skills that you've learned to do throughout your life—for example, swimming, writing, solving math problems, building a house, creating a budget, backpacking, playing chess, and reading.   TRUE   FALSE

2. "Soft skills" are the ones you have developed to cope with all areas of life—for example, making choices as a Creator, motivating yourself, being persistent, developing mutually supportive relationships, and believing in yourself.   TRUE   FALSE

3. The Holland Code is an inventory of personal preferences that can assist you in understanding your outdated scripts.   TRUE   FALSE

4. If you have not yet declared a major, where can you go on campus to take one of the inventories recommended in *On Course*?

   A. Your advisor's office

   B. The Registrar's office

   C. The Student Union

   D. The Career Center

5. Becoming aware of the match between _____ improves your chances of finding a satisfying career match.

   A. your desired income level and your preferred location

   B. your interests and your personality

   C. your family's plans and your need to work near them

   D. your personality and your desired income level

Believing in Yourself: Write Your Own Rules

1. According to psychologist Virginia Satir, we are all living by rules, although we may not be aware of them. TRUE   FALSE

2. All of the unconscious rules that we live by need to be revised.   TRUE   FALSE

3. The author of *On Course* has polled thousands of college instructors who identify three behaviors that their most successful students do consistently. Which of the following is NOT one of these top three behaviors of successful students (although it may be a good rule nonetheless)?

    A. Attend every class from beginning to end.

    B. Seek help from tutors.

    C. Do their best work on all assignments.

    D. Participate actively in class.

4. At Baltimore City Community College, a study found that, on average, the more classes that students *missed*, the higher their grades were, especially in introductory courses.   TRUE   FALSE

5. A personal rule is your conscious intention. You may need to break one of your rules if something of a higher _____ conflicts with it.

Chapter 6: Essay Topics

1. One of the most valuable skills of successful people is their ability to identify the life roles in which they are off course and design a plan to get back on course. Write an essay in which you identify the life role in which you are the most off course. Discuss what you believe is the underlying cause (self-defeating patterns and limiting core beliefs) of your being off course in this role and present a detailed plan of action for getting back on course. Let your plan contain both outer steps (changes in behaviors) and inner steps (changes in beliefs and attitudes).

2. We human beings are creatures of habit. Whereas some of our habits (or patterns) support our success, others get us off course from our goals and dreams. Write an essay in which you thoroughly explore one of your limiting patterns of behaviors, thoughts, or feelings. Then discuss how you may have come to adopt this pattern and explain how this pattern hinders you in the pursuit of a rich, personally fulfilling life. Finally, discuss a plan for changing this pattern so that you can stay on course to your goals and dreams.

3. We adopted many of our present beliefs during our childhoods. We learned these beliefs from our parents and other significant adults. These beliefs—some empowering, some disempowering—often remain unconscious, and they control what we do, think, and feel. Identify one or more of your limiting beliefs, discuss how you may have come to believe it, and explain how it has limited you in the past. Finally, explain what you plan to do to revise this belief so that you can change the outcome of your future.

4. Too many people set goals for themselves that are below what they are capable of achieving. Examine your present goals and consider if you have undershot your true potential. If you now believe that you have chosen goals that are too modest, write an essay in which you explore your belief system to uncover the limiting core beliefs that are holding you back. Explore where these beliefs may have come from and suggest what you plan to do to raise your goals in line with your true abilities.

5. Olympic gold medalist Jesse Owens said, "The battles that count aren't the ones for gold medals. The struggles within yourself—the invisible, inevitable battles inside all of us—that's where it's at." In an essay to be read by your classmates in this course, explore your own inner struggles. What inner forces have you done battle with, what has the battle been about, which side is presently winning, and what do you plan to do to triumph?

6. Children learn many of their inner rules from parents, other significant adults, and from others in their culture. Identify a child who is important to you (perhaps even one not yet born) and write a formal essay that you will present on his or her 21st birthday. In this essay, inform him or her about the most important rules you have chosen to create a rich, personally fulfilling life.

7. We learn our scripts not only from individuals but also from our cultures. In this essay, inform your classmates about a script of yours that you realize is a result of your culture. Explain whether you believe this script does or does not support you to create the outcomes and experiences that you want in life and why. If you conclude that the script does not support you, what do you plan to do about it?

8. Using the "One Student's Story" essays in *On Course* as a model, write an essay about how you used a strategy from Chapter 6 to overcome a problem in your life—academic, personal, or even at work. First, explain the problem; then, discuss the specific strategy you used and how you put it into action; finally, identify what happened. Your instructor may submit your essay for possible publication in the next edition of *On Course*. Additional directions for writing and submitting these essays can be found at http://oncourseworkshop.com/course-textbook/essay-contest/.

Adopting Lifelong Learning

Concept

Many students have lost the insatiable curiosity and effective learning strategies that served them so well as young children. For them, exciting forays into the mysteries of the unknown have been replaced by boredom, anxiety, and/or self-doubt. By (re)familiarizing struggling students with the skills of effective learners, we offer them the opportunity to replace their ineffective choices with more effective choices that can enable them to reach their potential. Additionally, by helping struggling students replace a fixed mindset (in which they believe there's little they can do to improve their academic success) with a growth mindset (in which they believe that hard work and persistence will improve their academic success), we empower them to make choices that improve their learning and academic success. In other words, in addition to teaching academic content, we need to help struggling students regain a learner's mindset and master the study skills they need to be a success in college . . . and a lifelong learner in the years beyond graduation.

EMPOWERS STUDENTS TO . . .

1. Adopt a learning orientation to life, willingly changing approaches that get them off course and actively learning new approaches that keep them on course.
2. Exchange a fixed mindset for a growth mindset.
3. Discover their preferred way of learning.
4. Become critical thinkers.
5. Learn what they need to know to accomplish their greatest goals and dreams.

Remember also to use the all-purpose exercises mentioned in the introduction, actively engaging students in the exploration of JOURNAL ENTRIES, CASE STUDIES, ONE STUDENT'S STORY, ON COURSE AT WORK, QUOTATIONS, CARTOONS, FOCUS QUESTIONS, CHAPTER-OPENING CHARTS, and TECH TIPS. Remind students to use letters to label any in-class writing they do in their journals.

Case Study in Critical Thinking: A Fish Story

Purpose

To use critical thinking skills and a growth mindset to practice extracting valuable lessons from every experience, thus developing into effective lifelong learners.

Supplies and Setup

"A Fish Story" in *On Course;* journals or writing paper; chime

Directions

1. [Have students read "A Fish Story." One way to be sure everyone has read the selection before taking the next step is to have one student read the first paragraph aloud, another student read the second, and so on until the reading is complete.] [5 minutes]
2. *Write an answer to the question at the bottom of the story: "If you had been in this biology lab class, what lessons about college and life would you have learned from the experience?"* [5 minutes]
3. [Put *students* in pairs.] *Partner A, read to your partner the lessons you learned about college and life. Partner B, respond with your best active listening skills, reflecting what you heard and asking for clarification or expansion. When I ring the chime, change roles: B reads, and A is the active listener.* [5 minutes]
4. [*Have A's switch partners, creating new pairs, and repeat step 3 with their new partners. Switch and repeat step 3 as often as time allows.*] [5–25 minutes]
5. *Look at what you wrote originally and take a few minutes to see if you can now dive deeper. Write new insights you think you could have learned from the experience with the fish.* [5 minutes]
6. [Quick-Write and/or Class Discussion] *What is the most important lesson that you drew from the experience in the biology lab? What lessons did others draw from the experience that you didn't think of? What did you learn from this discussion about how people create meaning from experience? What is the life lesson for you?* [e.g., "The deeper I dive, the richer are the learning rewards."] [5–10 minutes]

Approximate time: 30–55 minutes

Instructor Notes

1. Point worth making: Human beings are "meaning makers." When we have an experience, we invent what it means to us. We see a present experience through the lens of our past experiences, and that shapes the meaning we make. Many "meanings" are embedded in any one experience, and Creators seek the meaning that best supports their success. This will occasionally require them to revise their answers or beliefs about themselves, other people, or the world.
2. A variation is to have students write new insights and discoveries (step 5) after each pair discussion.
3. See Exercise 2-3 for another use of "A Fish Story."

Journal Entry **24** Developing a Learning Orientation to Life

EXERCISE 24-1: The Choice Evaluation Process

Purpose

To gain important life lessons from a past mistake or a broken commitment.

Supplies and Setup

Handouts listing the six steps of the Choice Evaluation Process (in the Instructor Notes section), one for each student; students sitting in pairs (Partner A and Partner B); journals or writing paper

Directions

1. *What is a mistake?* [Guide the discussion to the idea that a mistake is a choice that gets us off course.] *Everyone makes mistakes. Victims rarely learn anything from their mistakes, so they keep making them over and over. Creators, on the other hand, learn from their mistakes, so they seldom repeat the same mistake. Their course corrections typically get Creators quickly back on course and teach them important life lessons.* [To illustrate this perspective on mistakes, consider sharing a mistake that you have made in your life, especially as an undergraduate, to get students thinking about the mistakes they have made. An alternative is to remind students about the mistakes that the authors of the One Student's Story essays report making.] [5 minutes]

2. *Now I'd like you to describe briefly in writing a mistake that you have made in your life. If possible, choose a mistake you made this semester in college. You will be sharing your mistake with one other person.* [5 minutes]

3. *In a moment you and your partner will use the Choice Evaluation Process to explore a mistake that one of you made. If you are the person asking the questions of the Choice Evaluation Process, use your active listening skills to help your partner dive deep into exploring the mistake. Here's what this might look like.* [Do a DEMO of the Choice Evaluation Process, perhaps using one of your own mistakes.] *You'll have 20 minutes with your partner, which may be only enough time to explore one person's mistake. However, if you get through quickly, feel free to switch roles and examine the other person's mistake. Any questions? Ready, begin.* [20 minutes]

4. [Quick-Write and/or Class Discussion] *What was your experience of doing the Choice Evaluation Process? What lesson did you learn from your mistake?* [e.g., "Sometimes I make choices based on what is convenient at the time rather than on what is best for accomplishing my goals."] [10–20 minutes]

Approximate time: 40–50 minutes

Instructor Notes

1. Here are the six steps of the Choice Evaluation Process:
   1. What mistake did you make?
   2. What other choices could you have made?
   3. What's the likely outcome of each other choice?
   4. What choice(s) will you make if you face a similar situation in the future?
   5. Have you ever made a similar choice in the past? In other words, is this choice part of a pattern in your life?
   6. What's the life lesson for you?

2. You'll notice that the Choice Evaluation Process is similar to the Wise Choice Process from Chapter 2. Whereas the Wise Choice Process helps students make a wise choice in the *future*, the Choice Evaluation Process helps them examine a *past* choice and (A) discover more positive options and (B) learn an important life lesson (so they don't repeat a self-sabotaging choice in the future). If students have difficulty coming up with an answer for step 1 (a mistake they made), they may be able to find one by revisiting their answers to "Making Academic Course Corrections" in Exercise 22-3. Or you might suggest a questionable choice that you have seen the student make: "I notice you've been absent five times already this semester. Could that be a mistake?"

3. A variation of the Choice Evaluation Process creates valuable lessons from a broken commitment. This is particularly appropriate if you had your students create course commitments earlier in the semester. The only change is in step 1.
   1. What commitment did you break?
   2. (Continue with steps 2–6 above.)

4. Another variation of the Choice Evaluation Process can be used to debrief the One Student's Story essays. Thanks to June Poman of Union County College (NJ) for this suggestion:
   1. What mistake did the student in the essay make?
   2. What other choices could he or she have made?
   3. What would be the likely outcome of each of these other choices?
   4. Have you ever made a choice like the one the student in the essay made? Is this choice part of a pattern in your life?
   5. What choice would you make if you face a similar situation in your life?
   6. What's the life lesson for you?

EXERCISE 24-2: The Failure Toss

Purpose

To gain valuable insights from a failure.

Supplies and Setup

Pen and paper for each student; trash can; students in groups of five

Directions

1. *Everyone has failed at something. Victims rarely learn anything from their failures; worse, they may develop a fixed mindset—a belief that their learning ability is fixed and cannot grow. Creators, on the other hand, learn from their failures and develop a growth mindset—a belief that hard work and perseverance will help them learn nearly anything they need to know.* [1 minute]

2. *Before we do this activity, let's define a "failure." What do you think a failure is?* [A definition I like is "A failure is what your Inner Critic calls those times when you didn't create a goal or dream exactly on schedule." This definition keeps the Inner Critic at bay. After discussing the definition of a failure, consider sharing a failure of your own and what you learned from it. This will DEMO for students what they are about to do.] [5 minutes]

3. *Please fold your sheet of paper in half vertically, creating two columns. At the top of the left-hand column, write the word FAILURES. Below that, write a list of your failures in school and in life. No one else is going to see your failures, so you can be totally honest with yourself. Number each failure.* [5 minutes]

4. *At the top of the right-hand column, write the word LIFE LESSONS. In that column, write the valuable life lesson you learned from each of your failures. For example, maybe failure 1 was "My first marriage ended after only eight months." Next to that you might write that life lesson 1 was "I learned that I can never depend on someone else to create my sense of security." Maybe failure 2 was "I flunked out of college the first time I enrolled five years ago." Next to that you might write that life lesson 2 was "I need to choose friends who have the same goals that I do." Add as many life lessons as you learned from each failure.* [5–10 minutes]

5. *Choose someone in your group to read one life lesson . . . but not the failure. Then keep going around your group clockwise, with each person reading one life lesson. Remember, don't mention how you learned the life lesson; just state it. Keep going around your group until all in your group have presented all of their life lessons or until I call time.* [5 minutes]

6. *Now tear your paper in half along the fold. This leaves you with your FAILURES in one hand and your LIFE LESSONS in the other. Now make a choice. You can:*
   1. *Keep both your FAILURES and your LIFE LESSONS.*
   2. *Throw away your FAILURES and keep your LIFE LESSONS.*
   3. *Keep your FAILURES and throw away your LIFE LESSONS.*
   4. *Throw away both your FAILURES and your LIFE LESSONS.*

   Make that choice and do it now. If you choose to throw anything away, toss it into the trash can. [3 minutes]

7. [Quick-Write and/or Class Discussion] *What choice did you make? Why? What is the life lesson here for you?* [e.g., "Every failure can be a powerful teacher, and I want to hang on to my hard-earned life lessons."] [10–20 minutes]

Approximate time: 25–35 minutes

Instructor Notes

As a variation, you can have students title the left-hand column with any or all of these: Failures, Mistakes, Challenges, Obstacles, Adversities.

EXERCISE 24-3: Lessons from Your Obstacle

Purpose

To gain wisdom from an obstacle.

Supplies and Setup

Journals or writing paper; chime. You may wish to play relaxing instrumental music during this activity.

Directions

1. *First, we're going to do a relaxation exercise. Then I am going to take you on a journey in your minds. So get comfortable in your chairs, close your eyes, and prepare to relax.* [Do a progressive relaxation technique. One of my favorites is to ask students to breathe deeply and rhythmically while you invite them to tighten muscle groups one by one from the tips of their toes to the tops of their heads.] [5 minutes]

2. [After the relaxation, begin reading the following guided visualization, waiting about 10 seconds for any ellipses . . . and waiting about 20–30 seconds at a PAUSE.] *Now, in your mind, imagine that you are walking along a path at the foot of a majestic mountain . . . notice all the natural beauty that is around you . . . See the tall, green trees . . . Hear the birds singing . . . Smell the wonderful piney odor . . . Feel the soft grass beneath your feet . . . Now look up at the top of the mountain. There in the distance at the top of the mountain you see one of your most important goals. Get a clear picture of your goal waiting for you at the top of this beautiful mountain. Picture it clearly and exactly as it will look when you have achieved it.* [PAUSE] *Now notice that there is a path that leads from where you are now, a path that goes all the way up the mountain to your goal . . . As your eyes follow the path up, notice any challenging obstacle on your path to your goal: perhaps the obstacle is a person in your way . . . perhaps it is a health problem . . . or not enough time . . . or lack of money . . . Perhaps your obstacle is a self-defeating behavior pattern such as procrastination, or substance abuse, or watching too much television . . . Perhaps it is a self-defeating thought pattern such as negative self-talk, self-judgments, or self-criticism . . . Perhaps it is a self-defeating emotional pattern such as constant anger or sadness or depression . . . Or perhaps it is a limiting belief about yourself, about other people, or about the world . . . What is the biggest, most challenging obstacle standing in the way of reaching your goal? What does it look like? Picture it clearly now.* [PAUSE] *What if your obstacle were actually a great teacher that has come to teach you an important lesson? What would this teacher say to you? Take time right now to really listen to your obstacle . . . Listen for one sentence of advice from your obstacle . . . What lesson does your obstacle have to teach you? Listen now.* [PAUSE] *When you are ready, bring your awareness back to this room and open your eyes. Write any advice that your obstacle gave you.* [10 minutes]

3. [Have half of the students stand and move their chairs or desks to the edges of the room. This will leave half of the students sitting down with enough space between their chairs for the others to walk.]

4. *In a moment, those of you who are standing are going to whisper the wise advice your obstacle gave you to the people sitting. As soon as you have whispered your obstacle's advice to one person, move on to another person and whisper it again and then move to another and another.* [DEMO so students can see exactly what this will look like] *For example, suppose your obstacle told you, "You would be happier and more successful if you stayed away from people who constantly criticize you."* [Whisper this advice into one student's ear, and then, modeling what the students will do, move on and repeat the same advice to another student, and another.] *Try to get to everyone, and if you do, then keep going, whispering to people a second time. Many people find that is helps to close their eyes while listening to the whispered advice.* [5 minutes]

5. *When you hear the chime, reverse places. Those of you sitting will stand and move behind the chair you were sitting in, and those of you standing will sit in the first empty chair you see. The people now standing will immediately begin whispering their obstacle's wise advice to the people sitting. Keep whispering the same advice to different people until you hear the chime a second time. Then find a seat and take a few moments to think about the wisdom you've just heard from your obstacle and the obstacles of others. Feel free to write any of this wisdom. Are there any questions?* [The success of this activity requires that everyone understands the directions before beginning, so be extra sure everyone is ready.] *Ready, begin.* [3 minutes]

6. [Let the first round of whispering go for about three or four minutes. Ring the chime to signal reversing roles and allow another three or four minutes for the second round. Then ring the chime a last time and give students a few minutes to relax and reflect on the wisdom they have heard.] [8 minutes]

7. [Quick-Write and/or Class Discussion] *What was that experience like for you? What wisdom did you hear from your obstacle? From other people's obstacles? What is the life lesson here for you?* [e.g., "I have a powerful Inner Guide, but I need to take the time to listen to its wisdom."] [10–20 minutes]

Approximate time: 45–50 minutes

Instructor Notes

This activity sets up the "Affirmation Whisper" activity later in the course. The Affirmation Whisper—one of my students' favorites—will be even more powerful with this preparation.

Journal Entry 25 Discovering Your Preferred Ways of Learning

EXERCISE 25-1: My Favorite Teacher

Purpose

To discover ways of learning effectively when an instructor does not teach to the student's preferred way(s) of learning.

Supplies and Setup

Students take the *On Course* Learning Preference Self-Assessment in Chapter 7. This self-assessment is also available online in the MindTap College Success for *On Course*; optional: show scene from *Ferris Bueller's Day Off*. As of this writing, the scene "Boring Economics Teacher" (1:13 minutes) is available on YouTube.

Directions

1. *Think of your favorite teacher of all time and make a list of what you specifically liked about his or her teaching method. For example, maybe you liked that this teacher had you do group projects or maybe you liked that the teacher would eat lunch with students in the cafeteria and showed a personal interest in you.* [5 minutes]
2. *Now think of your least favorite teacher of all time and make a list of what you specifically disliked about his or her teaching method. For example, maybe you disliked that this teacher lectured for the entire class period in a boring monotone voice or you disliked that this teacher made the class do too much group work.* [Optional: Here you might show the very brief and funny scene from *Ferris Bueller's Day Off* in which a teacher, played by Ben Stein, is lecturing badly on voodoo economics.] [5 minutes]
3. [Place students in four groups according to their preferred way of learning, as determined by their scores on the self-assessment.] *As a group, combine your lists of what you liked about your favorite teachers and create one list. Then combine your lists of what you disliked about your least favorite teachers and create a second list.* [10 minutes]
4. *Now, imagine that you are taking a class with an instructor who exhibits some or all of the characteristics of your least favorite teachers. Being Creators and using what you know about preferred ways of learning, come up with a list of what* **you** *could do in this class to learn the subject well and get a good grade in the course despite how the instructor teaches.* [10 minutes]
5. [Group reports: Have volunteers from each group present a summary of their preferred way of learning and one strategy for learning when an instructor isn't teaching to that preferred way of learning. If there is time, have each group present a second strategy for how to learn when an instructor isn't teaching to their preferred way of learning.] [10–20 minutes]
6. [Quick-Write and/or Class Discussion] *Which of these ideas will you try? Why?* [5–15 minutes]

Approximate time: 45–65 minutes

Instructor Notes

In step 5, you may wish to point out those instances when one group says it doesn't like a teaching approach but another group says that it does.

EXERCISE 25-2: Fine-Tuning Study Methods

Purpose

To discover new and appealing study strategies for maximizing learning in college.

Supplies and Setup

Students in groups of four to five, each with pen and paper; whiteboard or easel pad and marker

Directions

1. *Most students have developed at least some strategies to help them study effectively. In your group, discuss your favorite study strategies. Later, one person will share some of your group's best ideas with the whole class. You won't know who the group reporter is until I call on you, so everyone needs to record all suggestions. This is a good time to practice your best note-taking techniques.* [10–15 minutes]
2. *Now let's have a spokesperson report each group's best ideas.* [Choose a spokesperson from each group to report. As you record the ideas on the whiteboard or on an easel pad, you may want to have a student recorder make a copy that could later be copied and distributed. Consider grouping strategies into categories of *before*, *while*, and *after* studying.] [10–15 minutes]
3. [Quick-Write and/or Class Discussion] *Which of these study strategies will you try? What appeals to you about this strategy? How well does this study strategy complement your preferred ways of learning?* [10–15 minutes]

Approximate time: 30–45 minutes

Journal Entry 26 Employing Critical Thinking

EXERCISE 26-1: The Logic of Advertising

Purpose

To practice analyzing a persuasive argument.

Supplies and Setup

A handout for each student with a copy of a magazine or newspaper advertisement duplicated on the upper half of the page. On the bottom half of the page, create three stacked rectangles (like a triple-layer cake) labeled REASONS (top rectangle), EVIDENCE (middle rectangle), and CONCLUSION (bottom rectangle). Place students in groups of three or four. Before this activity, students should have completed reading and writing Journal Entry 26.

Directions

1. [Distribute the handout.] *You'll recall from your reading in* On Course *that an argument is made up of Reasons, Evidence, and Conclusions. To what conclusion does this advertisement want you to come?* [Buy the particular product or service in the advertisement.] *Go ahead and write that in the box labeled "Conclusion." Now we're going to see how well the logic of this advertisement stands up to critical thinking.* [5 minutes]
2. *In your groups, fill in the boxes for Reasons and Evidence. In other words, in the advertisement, what reasons are given for buying this product or service? And what evidence is offered that the product or service will address those reasons? After you have filled in the Reasons and Evidence boxes, see if the conclusion is logical.* [A DEMO here is very helpful. For example, you could offer another advertisement—perhaps projected on a PowerPoint slide—and explain the reasons, evidence, and conclusions presented or not presented in it. Point out that sometimes reasons or evidence are only implied, not stated.] [15 minutes]

3. [Lead a discussion regarding the logic of the advertisement. Keep emphasizing the importance of finding the unstated reasons, of identifying and assessing the evidence offered, and of evaluating the logic of the argument. Be sure that students consider both the verbal (text) and nonverbal (visual) elements of the advertisement. Help students see how the advertisement may appeal more to emotion than to logic. (e.g., If you buy this car, you'll be more popular.)] [10–20 minutes]

4. [Quick-Write and/or Class Discussion] *What is the life lesson here for you?* [e.g., "Much advertising is not logical at all. Instead it seeks to create a positive experience and have consumers associate that positive experience with the product."] [5–15 minutes]

Approximate time: 35–55 minutes

Instructor Notes

1. After having students analyze the logic of print ads, you can have them do the same thing with television commercials. You can either play a recorded commercial or show one found on YouTube. You may need to play the advertisement a couple of times to help students see the subtle and quick-moving persuasive strategies used in commercials. One commercial available on YouTube that I like for this purpose is titled "Six Flags 'It's Playtime' commercial" (1:28 minutes).

2. Another option is to show a scene from a television show or Hollywood movie in which an argument is presented. For example, YouTube has a number of scenes from the classic film *Twelve Angry Men,* in which jurors present one argument after another to persuade others of the guilt or innocence of a boy accused of killing his father. It makes a fascinating case study for critical thinking.

EXERCISE 26-2: RateMyProfessors.com

Purpose

To practice asking probing questions.

Supplies and Setup

"RateMyProfessors.com" handout (following this exercise). Before this activity, students should have completed Journal Entry 26.

Directions

1. *How many of you are familiar with the website RateMyProfessors.com? Who'll tell us about this site?* [Have a volunteer explain that this website offers students the opportunity to rate professors on a scale of 1 (low) to 5 (high) for the following criteria: Easiness, Helpfulness, Clarity, and Overall Quality. Students can then add any comments they wish in order to explain their ratings.] [5 minutes]

2. [Place students in pairs and provide the handout.] *By way of example, here are ratings and comments posted on Rate-MyProfessors.com for two professors. Professor 1 received an average rating of 5 for Overall Quality, the highest score possible. Professor 2 received an average rating of 1 for Overall Quality, the lowest score possible. Let's take a look at the comments that students said about these professors.* [Have volunteers read the six comments aloud.] *It might appear easy to decide to take a course with Professor 1 and to avoid a course taught by Professor 2. However, a critical thinker would want additional information and would use probing questions to gather that information.* [5 minutes]

3. *You'll recall from your reading assignment that arguments are made up of reasons, evidence, and conclusions.* [Write these three terms on the board for reference.] *With your partner, brainstorm a list of probing questions that you might ask the students who wrote these comments. The goal of your questions is to uncover any information that would provide a reason to reject the conclusions of the raters. In other words, you are seeking to uncover a hidden truth.* [10 minutes]

4. *Now let's make a list on the board of your probing questions.* [As students offer questions, ask them to explain what they are after—are they questioning the reasons, evidence, and/or conclusions? What do they hope to discover that might contradict the high or low scores? For example, a question might be "What grade did you get in the course?"

This question is designed to determine if the student is praising the teacher because of a high grade or criticizing the teacher because of a low grade. In other words, the reason for the student's comment is the grade, not the professor's ability to teach.] [10–20 minutes]

5. [Quick-Write and/or Class Discussion] *What is the life lesson here for you?* [e.g., "Probing questions can poke holes in what appears to be the truth."] [5–15 minutes]

Approximate time: 35–55 minutes

Instructor Notes

If you have Internet access in your classroom, you may want to take (or send) students to the **www.RateMyProfessors .com** website and have them look for and question reasons that students give for their ratings. Also, at the time of this writing, there is a link to "Professors Strike Back" in the blog section. Here you'll find videos of professors responding to their students' comments. Some of the professors offer interesting "rebuttals" to students' criticisms, rebuttals that, too, can be scrutinized for their logic.

RateMyProfessors.com

With your partner, brainstorm a list of probing questions that you might ask the students who wrote the comments below. The goal of your questions is to uncover any information that would provide a reason to reject the conclusions of the raters. In other words, you are seeking to uncover a hidden truth.

Professor 1. This professor's average rating for Overall Quality (13 votes) is 5.0, the *highest* score possible. Here are comments from three of the raters (all grammar and spelling mistakes are in the original):

1. Very fun class. She is very clear about her expectations and expects you to do your best. Assignments were fun. Tests are multiple choice with no surprises. Final was not cumulative. I would definitely recommend her!

2. [She] is an awesome teacher. She kept the class interesting for us. She grades *fairly* and doesn't ask too much of her students. The class was very fun. She is good at what she does and is very helpful and knowledgeable in her chosen field. I would take her class over and over again.

3. Take her class she is a hottie. I probably wouldn't have stayed awake if it weren't for that.

Professor 2. This professor's average rating for Overall Quality (3 votes) is 1.0, the *lowest* score possible. Here are comments from the three raters (all grammar and spelling mistakes are in the original):

1. HORRIBLE—possibly the worst professor I have EVER had! Presents—doesn't teach. He skips around and doesn't really make clear what you really need to know. Assumes that students should be able to understand right away as he doesn't dwell long on any one topic. Save yourself the headache and DON'T take this class!

2. Barely got a c last sem. he sucke

3. accuses the class of not studying. assumes that we don't because the class is failing. out of about 25, only a handful are passing. he's not helpful and grades too hard.

Diving Deeper: Would it make any difference to you if you knew what subjects each of these instructors teach? Why or why not?

Source: Comments are from www.RateMyProfessors.com.

EXERCISE 26-3: Timeless Wisdom Quotes

Purpose

Encourage students to think critically and make connections to specific course concepts and their lives through the use of Timeless Wisdom quotations.

Supplies and Setup

A list of quotations on one topic—for an example, see "Timeless Wisdom—Diversity" quotes handout (next page); electronic discussion board, blog, or wiki

Directions

1. *There are two parts to this online assignment. Part 1 is the electronic discussion board, and Part 2 is a personal reflection paper. You will have seven days to complete this assignment, five days to post your chosen quote and analysis, and then two additional days to reply to three of your classmates' postings. You are required to read 10 of your classmates' postings. You will have three days after the discussion board closes to Dropbox (or turn in) your personal reflection paper.*

2. ONLINE ACTIVITY:
   - *Read the Timeless Wisdom quotations. Choose the quote that most resonates with you. In other words, which quote did you most agree with or make a connection to? If you did not find a quote that made you say, "Wow!" you can find your own quote about the topic. If you chose your own quote, you will need to check with your instructor first before posting.*
   - *Open the discussion board entitled Timeless Wisdom.*
   - *Type your chosen quote, including the author's name. Then state why you chose the quote—what personal connections did you make to the quote, what does the quote remind you of, and/or why do you think this quote is significant? Submit your posting.*
   - *Read at least 10 of your classmates' postings. Then reply to three of your classmates' postings. Indicate whether you agree, disagree, or made a similar connection to each student's posting. All replies must be respectful and well thought out.*

3. PERSONAL REFLECTION PAPER: *How did this online assignment make you think about the topic of the quotations? What insights did you learn from the online discussion with your classmates? What connections did you make between this topic and the* On Course *principles we have been exploring in class?*

Approximate time: 50–60 minutes for online discussion board

Source: Cris Davis and LuAnn Wood, Century College, MN

Instructor Notes

Any of the Timeless Wisdom quotes from the *On Course* I Workshop or from the margins of the *On Course* text can be used for this activity. This activity could easily be altered to use as an in-class exercise.

Timeless Wisdom—Diversity

1. "We may have different religions, different languages, different colored skin, but we all belong to one human race."—Kofi Annan

2. "What we have to do . . . is to find a way to celebrate our diversity and debate our differences without fracturing our communities."—Hillary Clinton

3. "It is time for parents to teach young people early on that in diversity there is beauty and strength."—Maya Angelou

4. "Diversity may be the hardest thing for a society to live with, and perhaps the most dangerous thing for a society to be without."—William Sloane Coffin, Jr.

5. "Toward no crimes have men shown themselves so cold-bloodedly cruel as in punishing differences of belief."—James Russell Lowell

6. "Human diversity makes tolerance more than a virtue; it makes it a requirement for survival."—Rene Dubos

7. "We have become not a melting pot but a beautiful mosaic. Different people, different beliefs, different yearnings, different hopes, different dreams."—Jimmy Carter

8. "Differences challenge assumptions."—Anne Wilson Schaef

9. "Since when do you have to agree with people to defend them from injustice?"—Lillian Hellman

10. "Tolerance is the positive and cordial effort to understand another's beliefs, practices, and habits without necessarily sharing or accepting them."—Joshua Liebman

11. "Every human being, of whatever origin, of whatever station, deserves respect. We must each respect others even as we respect ourselves."—U. Thant

12. "Don't ever let them pull you down so low as to hate them."—Booker T. Washington

13. "I swore never to be silent whenever human beings endure suffering and humiliation. We must always take sides. Neutrality helps the oppressor, never the victim. Silence encourages the tormentor, never the tormented."—Elie Weisel

14. "Let all bear in mind that a society is judged not so much by the standards attained by its more affluent and privileged members as by the quality of life which it is able to assure for its weakest members."—H. E. Javier Perez de Cuellar

15. "No single tradition monopolizes the truth. We must glean the best values of all traditions and work together to remove the tensions between traditions in order to give peace a chance."—Thich Nhat Hanh

Journal Entry 27 Believing in Yourself: Develop Self-Respect

EXERCISE 27-1: Claiming Respect

Purpose

To identify qualities that students respect in someone else and to own these projections.

Supplies and Setup

Journals or writing paper; students sitting in pairs (Partner A and Partner B). Write the following sentence stem on the board or project it on a PowerPoint slide: **I respect ____ because . . .**

Directions

1. *Think of a person for whom you have great respect. This person can be a family member, a coworker, a friend, someone on our campus, someone famous you haven't ever met . . . absolutely anyone you respect.* [2 minutes]

2. *Copy the sentence stem from the board, inserting the name of the person you respect:* **I respect (person's name) because . . .** *Then complete the sentence five or more times, giving a different reason each time for why you respect that person. Focus on HOW the person lives his or her life rather than his or her accomplishments. For example, I might write, "I respect my sister Holly because she has experienced a great deal of physical and emotional pain in her life, yet she remains one of the most positive, loving, and caring people I know."* [5–8 minutes]

3. *Partner A, read your sentences to Partner B. But when you read the sentence, you're going to substitute* **yourself** *for the person about whom you originally wrote. So, I would say,* **"I respect myself because I** *have experienced a great deal of physical and emotional pain in* **my** *life, yet* **I** *remain one of the most positive, loving, and caring people I know." Partner B, when your partner has read all the sentences, reflect what you heard him or her say. Partner A, be aware of any thoughts or feelings you have as you read or listen to feedback from your partner.* [8–10 minutes]

4. *Switch roles. Partner B, you read now, and remember to substitute "myself" for the person about whom you originally wrote. Afterward, Partner A, reflect what you heard your partner say. And Partner B, remember to be aware of any thoughts or feelings you have as you read or listen to feedback from your partner.* [8–10 minutes]

5. [*Quick-Write and/or Class Discussion*] *Did you find that what you respect in the other person is a quality you have as well? What was it like to claim the quality for yourself that you respect in the other person? Did your Inner Critic have anything to say? How about your Inner Guide? How do you feel right now? What would it do for your self-confidence if you acknowledged respect for* **how** *you live your life? What is the life lesson here for you?* [e.g., "My level of self-respect is determined not only by the goals I achieve but also by how I achieve them."] [10–20 minutes]

Approximate time: 40–50 minutes

Instructor Notes

You may wish to point out that we often project our own thoughts onto others. So respecting someone for a particular quality may suggest that we either have or want to have that same quality. Emphasize that self-respect is about having admiration for HOW we live life.

EXERCISE 27-2: Symbol of Self-Respect

Purpose

To acknowledge and express self-respect.

Supplies and Setup

Set up this activity in a previous class by requesting that students bring in an item of which they're proud. This item might be a sports trophy, a grade report, a scholarship letter, a wedding ring, a picture they painted, and so on. If they can't bring in the item, they can bring a photo or a sketch of it, or they can describe it to the class. Whatever it is, it should be a tangible object. Write two sentence stems on a whiteboard or project them on a PowerPoint slide: **I am proud of this item because . . . What this item reveals about how I live my life is . . .** Have students form groups of three.

Directions

1. *The people who go first in each group will show the item they brought and (if necessary) explain what it is. Next, speaking to your group, complete the two sentence stems on the chalkboard. After the first person has gone, move clockwise around your group until everyone has finished.* [5–10 minutes]

2. *Now we are going to do the same exercise again. This time, go to your very deepest level of honesty. Let your Inner Guide suggest the deepest truth about why you are proud of this item and what it reveals about you. If you are proud of this item, it suggests a very deep self-respect. Honor yourself by expressing that deep self-respect. Don't worry about bragging. Bragging is encouraged, even required, in this activity.* [5–10 minutes]

3. [Quick-Write and/or Class Discussion] *What was it like to tell about what you deeply respect about yourself? What thoughts or feelings did you have as you explained yourself each time? Did your Inner Critic try to interfere? How do you feel right now? What would it do for your self-esteem if you fully acknowledge what you respect about yourself? What is the life lesson here for you?* [e.g., "All of my accomplishments are a window into my soul, revealing not only what is important to me but also how I live my life."] [10–20 minutes]

Approximate time: 20–40 minutes

Instructor Notes

Emphasize that self-respect is about having admiration and pride for HOW we live our lives.

Chapter 7: Quiz Questions

(The Answer Key to Chapter 7: Quiz Questions appears at the end of this Facilitator's Manual. Please visit the Instructor Companion Site for *On Course* at login.cengage.com for a digital version of this quiz and its answer key.)

Developing a Learning Orientation to Life

1. Learners with a _____ **mindset** believe people are either born intelligent or they are not. They avoid a challenge because they fear their intelligence may not be up to the task.

2. Learners with a _____ **mindset** believe that intelligence is like a muscle—it gets stronger the more it's used. They accept challenges, work hard, learn from mistakes, change course if needed, and keep going despite setbacks and failures.

3. According to psychologist Carol Dweck, which of the following statements would be more likely to help someone develop a growth mindset?

    A. *You did so well in math. You're obviously very smart!*

    B. *You did so well in math. You're obviously a hard worker!*

    C. *You did so well in math. I'm so proud of you!*

    D. *You did so well in math. You obviously cheated!*

4. A *learning* goal would be to earn an A in a writing course. A *performance* goal would be to learn three ways to write an effective introductory paragraph.   TRUE   FALSE

5. Which of the following would NOT help you develop a growth mindset?

    A. Think of your brain as a muscle.

    B. Set performance goals (rather than learning goals).

    C. Seek feedback.

    D. Change course when needed.

Discovering Your Preferred Ways of Learning

1. Our preferred ways of learning are the only ways we can learn new information or skills.   TRUE   FALSE

2. Traditional college teaching—characterized by lectures and textbook assignments—MOST favors the learning preference of

    A. Thinkers.

    B. Doers.

    C. Feelers.

    D. Innovators.

3. Traditional college teaching—characterized by lectures and textbook assignments—LEAST favors the learning preference of

    A. Thinkers and Doers.

    B. Doers and Feelers.

    C. Feelers and Innovators.

    D. Innovators and Thinkers.

4. If an instructor does not teach to our preferred ways of learning, we cannot expect to learn the subject.   TRUE   FALSE

5. Knowing our preferred ways of learning suggests the kind of deep-processing strategies that might be best for us in creating strong neural networks in our brains and therefore, more deep and lasting learning.   TRUE   FALSE

Employing Critical Thinking

1. Critical thinking helps with making wise choices as well as constructing and analyzing persuasive arguments.   TRUE   FALSE

2. Which of the following is NOT one of the components of a logical argument?

   A. Reasons

   B. Evidence

   C. Probing Questions

   D. Conclusions

3. Probing questions can be helpful for challenging a conclusion.   TRUE   FALSE

4. If someone tells you that a movie is great and you ask why, you are asking the person to provide you with a logical conclusion.   TRUE   FALSE

5. A characteristic of evidence is that, if true, its accuracy can be verified.   TRUE   FALSE

On Course at Work: Lifelong Learning at Work

1. After graduation, when you have secured a job, you will finally be able to stop studying and learning.   TRUE   FALSE

2. Soft skills, such as those you are learning in *On Course*, are in such high demand in the workplace that some training consultants charge many thousands of dollars *per day* to teach these skills to employees of American businesses.   TRUE   FALSE

3. Studies suggest that company executives who failed and did not learn from their mistakes and shortcomings rebounded and resumed successful careers.   TRUE   FALSE

4. Your college provides many resources for learning about careers. One such source on your campus is _____ .

5. Ned Herrmann, creator of the Brain Dominance Inventory, suggests that alignment of what two things is predictive of success and satisfaction in a job?

   A. Your learning preferences and compatible careers

   B. Desired careers and income levels

   C. Enjoyable hobbies and time off from work

   D. Your learning preferences and level of self-esteem

Believing in Yourself: Develop Self-Respect

1. If self-confidence is the result of *what* I do, then self-respect is the result of _____ I do it.

2. When we have a foundation of personal values, we create integrity by choosing words and actions consistent with those values.   TRUE   FALSE

3. Each time you make a choice that goes against your own values, you make a deposit in your self-respect account.
   TRUE   FALSE

4. When you break a promise (especially to yourself), you make a withdrawal from your self-respect account.
   TRUE   FALSE

5. Which of the following does NOT help you to keep commitments?

   A. Make your agreements unconsciously.

   B. Make your agreements important—write them down.

   C. Create a plan; then do everything in your power to carry it out!

   D. If a problem arises or you change your mind, renegotiate.

Chapter 7: Essay Topics

1. Psychologist Carol Dweck and her colleagues have studied the causes and effects of two mindsets: growth and fixed. In an essay for college students, compare and contrast these two mindsets. Then explain which mindset you think you have and how you came to have it. Finally, explain any actions you plan to take to develop or strengthen a growth mindset.

2. Recall your favorite teacher or subject. With what you now know about preferred ways of learning, write an essay in which you explain why you liked this teacher or subject so much.

3. Students new to college are often stuck in old habit patterns that sabotage their academic success. In an essay for first-year college students, offer your suggestions for the most important behaviors, beliefs, and attitudes necessary for academic success. Suggest ways your readers could make a course correction if they need to. Use your own experience wherever possible.

4. In a letter to the board of education members where you went to high school, persuade them to make one signifi cant change to help future students. Use your critical thinking skills to make a logical case for the change you suggest. Consider using your understanding of how the human brain learns best and your knowledge of individual learning preferences to develop your argument.

5. Educational philosopher John Dewey wrote, "The most important attitude that can be formed is that of the desire to go on learning." In an essay for new parents, discuss what they can do to preserve and nurture their children's love of learning. Use your understanding of how the human brain learns best and your knowledge of personal learning preferences.

6. Taking a personal inventory is often the first step toward improving an area of one's life. Write an essay in which you explore your strengths and weaknesses as a learner (both in school and out of school). End your essay by proposing changes that you could make to become a more effective learner.

7. Psychologist Mihaly Csikszentmihalyi wrote, "The ability to persevere despite obstacles and setbacks is the quality people most admire in others. . . ." Your perseverance through difficulties not only causes others to respect you; it also raises your own self-respect. In an essay for a general audience, describe a time in your life when you persevered against inner and/or outer obstacles to reach a goal or dream of great importance to you. Conclude by telling what you learned from your experience and how it affected your sense of self-respect.

8. Using the student essays in *On Course* as a model, write an essay about how you used a strategy from Chapter 7 to overcome a problem in your life—academic, personal, or even at work. First explain the problem; then discuss the strategy you used and how; finally, identify what happened. Your instructor may submit your essay for possible publication in the next edition of *On Course*. Additional directions for writing and submitting these essays can be found at http://oncourseworkshop.com.

Chapter 8

Developing Emotional Intelligence

Concept

People in the grip of overwhelming emotions are seldom effective. Consequently, one of the most essential components of success—by some accounts more important than academic intelligence—is emotional intelligence. Emotional intelligence is the ability to manage emotions—our own and those of others—and stay on course even when navigating life's most challenging storms. Just as we are responsible for the quality of our outer lives, we are responsible for the quality of our inner lives as well. In fact, cognitive psychologists suggest that we can only perceive what is going on outside of us through the lens of what is going on inside of us. Belief systems and inner conversations create our interpretation of the events going on around us, and in this way, our thoughts actually create our "reality." People who are emotionally intelligent are skilled at controlling the content of their consciousness. This skill allows them to make wise choices in the throes of emotional storms while others struggle merely to survive. When we assist students to gain greater emotional intelligence, we empower them not only to be more effective in the pursuit of their dreams but also to experience happiness, joy, and peace of mind on their journey.

EMPOWERS STUDENTS TO . . .

1. Take responsibility for the quality of their inner experience of life.
2. Honor their emotions, seeing both pleasant and unpleasant emotions as important feedback for keeping them on course.
3. More consciously choose the content of their consciousness, thinking and speaking more positively about themselves, others, and their world, thus creating an experience of greater optimism, joy, and happiness.
4. Avoid emotional hijackings, thus persisting in the face of challenges and setbacks.
5. Manage and reduce stress.
6. Learn how to create more happiness in their lives.
7. Improve relationships through empathy for and an understanding of the emotions of others.
8. Postpone instant gratification for future rewards.

Remember also to use the all-purpose exercises mentioned in the introduction, actively engaging students in the exploration of JOURNAL ENTRIES, CASE STUDIES, ONE STUDENT'S STORY, ON COURSE AT WORK, QUOTATIONS, CARTOONS, FOCUS QUESTIONS, CHAPTER-OPENING CHARTS, and TECH TIPS. Remind students to use letters to label any in-class writing they do in their journals.

Case Study in Critical Thinking: After Math

Purpose

To develop critical thinking skills by exploring a real-life situation concerning emotional intelligence.

Supplies and Setup

"After Math" in *On Course*

Directions

1. [Have students read "After Math." One way to be sure everyone has read the selection before taking the next step is to have one student read the first paragraph aloud, another student read the second, and so on until the reading is complete. Alternately, have six volunteers play the roles of the five characters and a narrator; then present the case study as a play.] [5–10 minutes]

2. [Before students score the characters, have them turn to the next section after the case study titled "Understanding Emotional Intelligence" and read about the four components of emotional intelligence. Again, you may want to have volunteers read the four components aloud. This information enables your students to make more informed choices.] [5 minutes]

3. [Here is an alternative to having students rank all of the characters from 1–5 on their emotional intelligence as the directions in the case study suggest. Divide your students into five groups and assign one character to each group.] *Your task is to rate your character's emotional intelligence on a score from 1 (low) to 10 (high emotional intelligence). When your spokesperson reports on the number you have chosen for your character, I'll ask him or her to provide specific evidence from the story that justifies your group's score.* [10–15 minutes]

4. [Have each group's spokesperson give the group's emotional intelligence score for its character while you write the five characters' names and scores on the board or easel pad. Now return to each group one by one and ask the spokesperson to offer specific evidence from the case study that led to each character's score. The key is to elicit specific behaviors that explain scores based on the four components of emotional intelligence. Thus, the explanations are far more important than the scores. For example, Professor Bishop may get a low score because he demonstrated poor relationship management when he announced Scott's low test score in front of the entire class.] [15 minutes]

5. [Quick-Write and/or Class Discussion] *What did you learn from this discussion about emotional intelligence and its importance for achieving your goals and dreams? What is the life lesson here for you?* [e.g., "If I manage my emotions, I will have a far better life than if I let my emotions manage me."] [5–10 minutes]

Approximate time: 35–55 minutes

Instructor Notes

1. So as not to stifle discussion, I don't tell students what my scores are.

2. This class discussion is an excellent prewriting activity to be followed by students writing a persuasion essay supporting their opinions in the debate. Because students are now sharply aware of views opposed to their own, they often write much more thorough and persuasive essays than would be the case without the debate.

3. You might ask students to relate an experience they have witnessed in which someone (perhaps themselves) became hijacked by emotions and tell what happened as a result. Afterward, ask, "What could this person have done that would have been more emotionally intelligent?"

4. An optional step for this activity is to ask students to do a quick-write about and then participate a discussion of the Diving Deeper question: "Imagine that you have been asked to mentor the person whom you ranked number 5 (least emotionally intelligent). Other than recommending a counselor, how would you suggest that this person handle his or her upset in a more emotionally intelligent manner?"

5. An optional follow-up is to ask students to rewrite the case study; in their rewrite, they are to have all of the characters make emotionally wise choices.

Journal Entry 28 Understanding Emotional Intelligence

EXERCISE 28-1: I'm Willing to Feel . . .

Purpose
To help students become more conscious of the emotions they accept and those they reject.

Supplies and Setup
Students in pairs (Student A and Student B). Post the list of "I'm willing . . ." statements on a PowerPoint slide, whiteboard, or easel pad. (See Instructor Notes for list.)

Directions
1. *Healthy emotions tell us when we're on course or off course. Most people were raised to be comfortable with some emotions but uncomfortable with others. This exercise is designed to help you become more conscious of how comfortable you are with various emotions.* [2 minutes]
2. *Partner A will read one of the "I'm willing . . ." statements. Use your best acting skills to display the emotion you are mentioning. Partner B will respond, "I can accept you when you are feeling ___."* [Fill in the emotion that Partner A has just mentioned.] *Be conscious of how you feel as you say your part.* [DEMO the process, demonstrating the appropriate emotion.] *You may find that you feel comfortable when you express anger but uncomfortable when your partner expresses anger. There is no "right" or "wrong" way to feel. Just be sensitive to how you feel as you say or hear each of these statements about feeling your emotions. Watch for any feedback from your body, such as a flutter in your stomach. If you finish before I call time, go back to the top of the list and repeat the list. Any questions? Okay, Partner A, begin.* [5 minutes]
3. *Now switch roles. Partner B, you read the statement, and Partner A responds, "I can accept you when you are feeling ___." Again, the key here is to be aware of how you feel as you express these ideas.* [5 minutes]
4. [Quick-Write and/or Class Discussion] *Did you notice emotions that you are more comfortable with feeling? Less comfortable with feeling? What emotions are you comfortable with others expressing? Uncomfortable with others expressing? What do you suppose is the value for you of this awareness? What is the life lesson here for you?* [e.g., "My emotions show up in my body long before they show up in my mind."] [5–20 minutes]

Approximate time: 15–35 minutes

Instructor Notes
Here are the statements to put on the whiteboard or PowerPoint slide:

I'm willing to feel all of my anger.

I'm willing to feel all of my anxiety.

I'm willing to feel all of my fear.

I'm willing to feel all of my sadness.

I'm willing to feel all of my guilt.

I'm willing to feel all of my resentment.

I'm willing to feel all of my depression.

I'm willing to feel all of my love.

I'm willing to feel all of my joy.

Source: This is a variation of an exercise by Gay and Kathlyn Hendricks.

EXERCISE 28-2: Right Now I Feel . . .

Purpose

To improve students' ability to be aware of their emotions and to dramatize how the words that we think affect how we feel.

Supplies and Setup

Students in groups of three. Write the list of sentence stems on the board or project with a PowerPoint slide. (See Instructor Notes for the sentence stems.)

Directions

1. *For many people, staying in touch with their feelings is a great challenge. This exercise is designed to assist us to become more aware of our feelings.*

2. *Before we start, let's list as many feelings as we can think of. Call them out.* [Record the list of emotions on the chalkboard, further exploring suggestions that are not really feelings, such as "stupid." "Stupid" is not a feeling, but you may feel "embarrassed" when you think that you did something stupid.] *What's the difference between fear and anxiety? Between sadness and depression? Between anger and fury?* [10 minutes]

3. *The person in your group who has the next birthday goes first. That person will read and complete the first sentence stem. Moving clockwise, the other two people also read and complete the first sentence stem. Then the first person will read and complete the second sentence stem and so on until all the sentences have been read and completed by each person. Be very conscious of how you feel as you say how you feel.* [DEMO the process.] *Any questions? Okay, decide who will go first, and begin.* [5–10 minutes]

4. [Quick-Write and/or Class Discussion] *What did you learn about your relationship to the various emotions you discussed? Did you notice your emotions changing as you said you feel a particular emotion? What does this suggest about how we can manage our emotions? What is the life lesson here for you?* [e.g., "The thoughts that I allow to linger in my mind create emotions that show up in my heart."] [10–20 minutes]

Approximate time: 25–40 minutes

Instructor Notes

1. Here are the statements to put on the board or PowerPoint slide:

   Right now I feel . . .

   I feel angry when . . .

   I feel afraid when . . .

   I feel sad when . . .

   Right now I feel . . .

   I feel calm when . . .

   I feel peaceful when . . .

   I feel contented when . . .

   Right now I feel . . .

   I feel happy when . . .

   I feel joyful when . . .

   I feel loved when . . .

   Right now I feel . . .

2. An important point to bring out in the discussion is that the thoughts we allow in our consciousness greatly influence how we feel. Typically, recalling a past event that generated an emotion causes the emotion in the present. (This is a method many actors use to generate emotions for a part they are playing.) The stems in this activity are set up to move students from negative emotions to tranquil emotions to positive emotions.

3. A variation is to have students complete the sentence stems in writing (instead of speaking them). In this way, they will create a kind of poem about their emotions. If you have them both speak and write these sentences, you can explore whether they experienced a difference emotionally in the two mediums.

Journal Entry **29** Reducing Stress

EXERCISE 29-1: Up on the Roof

Purpose

To experience how changing the content of one's consciousness changes the quality of one's experience.

Directions

1. *I'd like you to stand up and position yourself so you can spread out your arms without touching anyone else. In a moment, I'm going to invite you to close your eyes, and I'm going to guide you through a mental experience with words. If you involve yourself totally in the experience, you may discover a powerful way to reduce stress in your life. When you're ready, close your eyes, take a deep breath, and here we go.* [1 minute]

2. *Picture yourself walking along a sidewalk in a large city. Above you, tall buildings tower as you weave your way through the crowd on the sidewalk. Now see yourself walking up to a huge building with a revolving door. As you push on the glass door, it glides open, and you find yourself entering an expansive lobby. Walk across the smooth marble floor to the elevator and push the UP button. The doors open, and when you are inside the empty elevator, you push the top button marked "ROOF." Hear the elevator music and then feel the light sensation in your stomach as the elevator begins rushing you upward. After a long ride, the elevator doors open, and you step out into a deserted hallway. Look down at the end of the hall . . . notice a door down there. Walk down the hall to the door, turn the handle, and push the door open. Now step into the dimly lit stairway. Take the stairs up until you come to another door. Push on the horizontal bar and feel the latch opening and the door swinging open. The brightness of the sun causes you to squint your eyes, and the breeze blows across your face as you step out onto the crunchy gravel of the roof. Birds are flying overhead, and the sky is dotted with a few white clouds. Notice that the edge of the building has a little parapet, a one-foot-high cement wall that runs around the entire edge of the roof. Walk over to the parapet, again feeling the strong breeze nudging you forward. As you reach the parapet, step up on it. That's right—lift your foot and step right up on that little wall that runs around the very edge of the roof. Look over into the canyon between the buildings . . . notice the tiny people way down below . . . listen to the far-off sounds of automobile horns honking in the city . . . . Now, see how far out over the edge you can lean, and be aware of how you are feeling as you lean out over that open space below you. . . . Be careful! That wind is blowing harder now. Feel it pushing on your back. Don't let it blow you over the edge. . . . Okay, now step back down to the roof, feeling the gravel crunch beneath your shoes again.* [5 minutes]

3. *Now as you stand on the roof, an amazing thing begins to happen. You feel a tingle on your back. Something is growing out of each of your shoulder blades. In a moment, you realize that wings are coming right through your clothing, and they keep growing until they are large and strong. Strangely, these wings feel very familiar to you, as if you have had them all of your life. Flap your wings a few times. Notice that you have full control of them. Feel yourself confidently lift off of the roof a few feet and then settle back down. Now that you have your wings and you feel confident in their use, step back up on the little parapet, the cement wall running around the edge of the roof. Again, feel the wind blowing at your back, see the birds flying overhead, and look down at the tiny people and cars far below. Try leaning out again, and this time, if you want, let yourself soar off of the roof and fly around with the birds high into the white clouds. Soar around as high as you wish to go; then, after an exhilarating flight, come back and land again on the parapet. Step off the parapet and feel the gravel again beneath your shoes. In a moment, I'll be inviting you to open your eyes and return to this room, but before you do, you have something to decide. You need to decide if you will bring your wings back here with you or leave them behind. So, when you have decided whether or not to keep your wings, take a deep breath, let your eyes come open, and have a seat.* [5 minutes]

4. [Quick-Write and/or Class Discussion] *What did you experience when you stepped up on the parapet for the first time?* [Some people report fear or concern about being on the roof.] *Was your experience different when you got your wings?* [Many people report a more positive experience when they got their wings.] *How many of you had a more positive experience on the roof after you got your wings? Where did your wings come from?* [They created them with their thoughts.] *What is the life lesson about how to create a more positive experience of life?* [By consciously choosing to occupy the content of our consciousness with positive thoughts, we change our experience of life for the better. We can reduce stress by changing our thoughts.] *What is an area of your life where you could apply this wisdom?* [10–20 minutes]

Approximate time: 20–30 minutes

Instructor Notes

This visualization can lead to some great discoveries. After this visualization, one participant said, "Thanks for reminding me that I have wings and that I can fly." You could follow the activity by playing the song "I Believe I Can Fly" by R. Kelly.

EXERCISE 29-2: Resolving Incompletions

Purpose

To give participants the stress-reducing experience of an outer world completion.

Supplies and Setup

Journal or writing paper; Step 1 is done in one class period; step 2 is done in the following class period

Directions

1. *Open your journal to a blank page. Make a list of incompletions that exist in your outer world—things you have been meaning to do but keep putting off. For example, you might include incompletions such as (1) make a dentist appointment, (2) get my car tuned up, (3) tell my boyfriend that I am upset with him, (4) complete term paper for history, or (5) complete my taxes. Circle one of these incompletions that you are willing to complete before our next class meeting. Now I'd like each person to announce what he or she is going to complete. You'll get to report your results in our next class.* [Allow students to "pass" and not announce what they plan to complete.] [10 minutes]
2. [Next class period] [Quick-Write and/or Class Discussion] *What did you promise yourself to complete? How successful were you? How do you feel right now about completing or not completing it? If you did complete it, does your Inner Guide have anything to say about your success? If you didn't complete the action, what did you make more important than doing it? Does your Inner Critic or Inner Defender have anything to say about your failure to complete it? What does your Inner Guide have to say? Are you willing to recommit to doing it? What is the life lesson here for you?* [e.g., "Resolving incompletions is a great way to reduce stress that is caused by feeling overwhelmed by my to-do list."] [10–30 minutes]

Approximate time: 20–40 minutes [spread over two classes]

EXERCISE 29-3: Happy Music

Purpose

To demonstrate that what we choose as the content of our consciousness influences the quality of our experience.

Supplies and Setup

Compact disc player. In the previous class, ask students to bring a song on a CD that lifts their spirits or otherwise makes them feel happy, or the instructor can bring a variety of songs. If a number of students keep their music on a smartphone, provide speakers.

Directions

1. [Invite volunteers to play their songs.] [3–5 minutes for each song]
2. [Quick-Write and/or Class Discussion] *How do you feel right now? Do you feel better or worse than before you heard the music? What is it about the music that created this feeling? How can you apply this idea in other ways besides music? What is the life lesson about changing your emotional state?* [e.g., "I can manage my emotions by making wise choices about the music I listen to . . . and the books I read . . . and the friends I have . . . and by all that I allow into my mind."] [5–10 minutes]

Approximate time: 5–45 minutes [depending on how many songs you play]

Instructor Notes

1. This is a good exercise to carry over to other class periods. You can begin and/or end a class with one or two uplifting songs.
2. This exercise can also be a good diversity exercise. Invite students to bring in music that represents the very best of their culture, music that inspires them or generates positive feelings.
3. After playing a number of songs (either in one class or over a number of classes), have students nominate and then vote on a "class song," one that inspires them to do their very best in the quest for their academic goals.

Journal Entry 30 Increasing Happiness

EXERCISE 30-1: Acts of Kindness

Purpose

To introduce students to another scientifically studied strategy for increasing happiness.

Supplies and Setup

Students should have completed reading and writing Journal Entry 30, "Increasing Happiness." Whiteboard and markers. Journals or writing paper. This activity is conducted in parts in two different class sessions. In class one, be prepared to show a video on the Internet titled *The Science of Happiness–Operation Kindness* (8:15). Find this video at OnCourse-Workshop.com → Educator Resources → Video Gallery → "The Science of Happiness–Operation Kindness." An alternative is to assign viewing the video as homework.

Directions

Day 1

1. *In* On Course, *you read about a number of strategies for increasing happiness that positive psychologists have studied. We are going to experiment with another. We are going to test the hypothesis that "Performing acts of kindness increases happiness." First, we are going to brainstorm a list of Acts of Kindness we could do between now and our next class. They can be small acts such as giving someone a compliment. Or they could be large acts such as giving a $100 bill to a homeless person. Remember, we're just brainstorming acts of kindness. You are not committing to doing anything on this list. Okay, let's begin. Please make a list of your own as I record them on the board.* [Record the list of suggestions on the board, making sure that students are creating their own list.] [10 minutes]
2. *Now let's watch a short video (8:15) about doing kind things for others and the impact it has on people's happiness.* [Show the video "The Science of Happiness–Operation Kindness."] [10 minutes]
3. *Did watching the video suggest any other acts of kindness we could add to our list?* [Add suggestions to the list.] [5 minutes]

4. *Your homework is to do 3 acts of kindness as close together in time as possible. Afterward write answers to the following questions:*
   A. *Before performing your acts of kindness, where would you score yourself on a Happiness scale from 1–10, with 10 being the highest?*
   B. *What three acts of kindness did you perform?*
   C. *Which, if any, of the acts of kindness lifted your mood and made you feel happier?*
   D. *After performing your acts of kindness, where would you score yourself on a Happiness scale from 1–10, with 10 being the highest?*

[It would be wise to write the questions on the board.] *What questions do you have about this assignment? Your written answers to these questions will be your ticket to enter the next class. No ticket . . . no admittance.* [5 minutes]

Day 2

1. [Place students in pairs.] *Please read your answers to each other regarding your experiment with kindness. Remember, the hypothesis we are testing is, "Performing acts of kindness increases happiness." Discuss whether your experience suggests that the hypothesis is true or false. Please be honest because it is now believed by positive psychologists that no one happiness activity works to increase happiness for everyone.* [10–15 minutes]
2. [Large-Group Discussion] *Now let's hear what you experienced. Please share your answers to the four questions and then tell us whether or not the hypothesis was true for you.* [You may want to ask students to nominate their partners to share.] [10–15 minutes]
3. [Consider recording all pre- and post-experiment scores and determining the results for the entire class.]
4. *What is the life lesson from this experiment? What new things, if any, will you do to increase your happiness?* [5–10 minutes]

Approximate time: Day 1: 30 minutes; Day 2: 25–40 minutes

Instructor Notes

Emphasize that individual "happiness" activities typically do not work for everyone; thus, each of us must find what works for us as individuals. If it's not doing acts of kindness (as experimented with here), perhaps a student's happiness will be increased by savoring pleasures or expressing gratitude or exercising or any number of other possibilities.

EXERCISE 30-2: Creating Flow

Purpose

To help students become aware of how they have created "flow" states in the past so they can create them in the future, especially in higher education.

Supplies and Setup

Students in pairs; journals or writing paper; students have read "Increasing Happiness" in *On Course*; chime or other way to signal transitions. Put the following characteristics of a flow state on the board, handout, or PowerPoint slide:
A) total absorption in the effort to achieve a challenging goal
B) a sense that one's skill level is equal to or only slightly below the challenge level
C) immediate feedback on effectiveness
D) loss of thoughts or concern about oneself
E) a distorted sense of time

Directions

1. *Much research has been done on "flow" experiences, in which time seems to stop and the participant is totally and positively absorbed in the pursuit of a challenging goal.* [Explain the five characteristics of a flow state. See Instructor's Notes for a video you could use to supplement your explanation.] *Think of a time when you experienced flow yourself and jot down what you were doing and what the experience was like for you.* [5–8 minutes]

2. *In your pair, each person should take four minutes to describe to your partners the flow experience you recall. Describe in detail what you were doing and what the experience was like for you.* [Ring chime to signal switching roles 4 minutes] [10 minutes]

3. *If your partner convinced you that he or she truly experienced a "flow" state, nominate him or her to share it with all of us.* [During presentations, point out the characteristics of a flow state.] [5–20 minutes, depending on how many students you want to present their flow experience.]

4. *Psychologist Daniel Goleman wrote, "Being able to enter flow is emotional intelligence at its best; flow represents perhaps the ultimate in harnessing the emotions in the service of performance and learning." How could you create more flow experiences here in college? First discuss the question with your partner and then we'll explore it as a group."* [5–8 minutes]

5. [Group Discussion] [Draw out possible ways that students could create flow experiences in college. As a possible DEMO, give an example of a flow experience from your own undergraduate experience.] [5–15 minutes]

Approximate time: 30–60 minutes

Instructor Notes

Optional: In your introduction, show a video (3:47) titled "Flow" found at OnCourseWorkshop.com → Educator Resources → Video Gallery → Emotional Intelligence.

EXERCISE 30-3: Clump

Purpose

To offer participants an opportunity to explore their relationship with play. (Note: This is a great energizer and mood lightener, too.)

Supplies and Setup

Chairs pushed to the sides of the room; students standing in the middle of the room

Directions

1. *We're going to play a very silly child's game called Clump. Be aware of what you tell yourself and how you feel both as I describe the game and as you play it. Here's the way to play Clump. First, everyone walks randomly around the room. As you walk, I'll call out "Clump" plus a number, such as "Clump 4." As soon as you hear "Clump 4," your goal is to grab hold of three others to form a clump of four people, no more, no less. Any questions? Okay, let the Clumping begin.* [Vary the Clump number each time: Clump 2, Clump 6, Clump 3, and so on.] [5–10 minutes, depending on size of the group]

2. [Quick-Write and/or Class Discussion] *What did you tell yourself when you heard how to play Clump? What did you tell yourself while you were playing? How did you feel while playing? How do you feel right now? Do you like to play? What kind of play do you like? Why do you suppose some people lose the urge to play as they grow older? What gets in their way? What might their Inner Critics or Inner Defenders have to say? Is there any change you'd like to make in your life regarding play? What is the life lesson here for you?* [e.g., "Playing keeps me young at heart."] [5–10 minutes]

Approximate time: 10–20 minutes

Instructor Notes

1. *Optional:* Video record a group of children playing Clump. Show the video and talk about the difference between the way the children and the adults played. Explore: Why the difference?

2. Be particularly sensitive to the people who don't want to participate in this playful activity. Without judgment, ask them to become aware of what their Inner Critic or Inner Defender is telling them. Note also that some people confuse play with competition: If there's no competition, there's no play. Help them tease these two concepts apart. Also, you may need to adapt the game to the physical limitations of some of your students.

3. To *add* a level of challenge, you can change the directions so that you offer only a hint about how many people should clump. For example, "Clump the number of blind mice" (3) or "Clump the number of basketball players from one team who play at one time" (5). You can invite students to offer their own "Clump" directions.

4. Be sensitive to students with a physical challenge that may make this activity difficult for them.

EXERCISE 30-4: Work Becomes Play

Purpose

To explore how we can bring more of the advantages of play into our work.

Supplies and Setup

Whiteboard or easel pad; students in groups of four to five

Directions

1. *What are the positive characteristics of play? What makes play fun and enjoyable?* [Make a list of answers on a whiteboard or easel pad. For example, ideas might include "Games allow you to start over often," "You get to choose your teammates," "You decide when to play," "There are immediate rewards for your skills," "Rules keep the players honest," "It's exciting to compete," "Winning is fun," or "Each time you play, you improve your skills."] [5–10 minutes]

2. [Assign each group a small number of the listed items to discuss.] *Your goal is to figure out how to have your present or future work take on the characteristics of play that are on your list. For example, if play offers immediate rewards for your skills, think of how you could experience that same characteristic in your work.* [10–15 minutes]

3. *Let's have a report from each group on some of your best ideas.* [10–15 minutes]

4. [Quick-Write and/or Class Discussion] *What did you learn about enjoying work? Why do you suppose some people hate the work they do? How do you feel about the work you do now or plan to do in the future? Is there any change you'd like to make in your life regarding work? What is the life lesson here for you?* [e.g., "I can make choices that make my work more like play."] [10–20 minutes]

Approximate time: 25–35 minutes

EXERCISE 30-5: Instructors Who Create Flow

Purpose

To have students develop a list of instructors who create "flow," so that they can make wiser choices when registering for future semesters. Students should have completed Journal Entry 30 so they can understand the concept of "flow."

Supplies and Setup

"Instructors Who Create Flow" handout (following this exercise); students sitting in pairs; chime (or other way to signal a change of partners)

Directions

1. *Many students sign up for classes based only on college requirements and times that courses are offered. Often a more important factor is who is teaching the course. We're going to do an activity that will enable you to learn about some of the outstanding instructors at our college. The next time you register, you will have more information with which to make wiser choices about your course selection. From the handout, I'd like five different volunteers to each read aloud one of the qualities of "Instructors Who Create Flow." As you hear these qualities, think of the instructors you have had here at this college who rate high in these qualities.* [5 minutes]

2. *Fill in Line 1 with your nomination of one instructor who creates flow for you. Next you will be sharing your nomination with other students. If by any chance you can't think of an instructor who creates flow, then leave the line blank.* [5 minutes]

3. [Put students in pairs.] *You will now have a few minutes to exchange nominations with your partner. On your own form, write down your partner's nomination, both the instructor's name and courses taught. If you have time, go on to share more about how these instructors create flow for you. After a couple of minutes, I'll ring a chime and you will find a new partner and exchange instructors again. You'll get to meet with a number of partners so you'll learn about a number of instructors.* [10–25 minutes, depending on how many partner exchanges you create]

4. [Quick-Write and/or Class Discussion] *Were there any instructors whose names you encountered a number of times? What is it about them that your classmates appreciated? What is the life lesson here for you?* [e.g., "I can create a more positive experience in college by making wise choices about my instructors."] [5–10 minutes]

Approximate time: 25–45 minutes

Instructor Notes

Some students may want to talk about their "lousy" instructors. I highly recommend that you keep them focused on the best instructors, the ones who create flow for their students.

Instructors Who Create Flow . . .

1. Demonstrate a deep knowledge of their subject.
2. Show great enthusiasm for the value of their subject.
3. Set challenging but reasonable learning goals for their students.
4. Offer learning experiences that appeal to a variety of learning preferences.
5. Provide a combination of academic and emotional support that gives their students high expectations of success.

Instructor's Name	Courses This Instructor Teaches
1.	
2.	
3.	
4.	
5.	
6.	
7.	
8.	
9.	
10.	
11.	
12.	

EXERCISE 30-6: Random Acts of Kindness

Purpose

To understand the power of random acts of kindness and their consequences for oneself and others.

Supplies and Setup

A piece of paper and a writing utensil for each participant

Directions

1. [Select a person who will be located nearby during your class session, perhaps a college employee with an office near your classroom (e.g., a counselor, custodian, dean, faculty member). Tell your students about that person and why you think he or she is worthy of positive attention. For instance . . .] *I would like to introduce you to the division administrative assistant, Ruth. She is always so helpful with students and exudes a positive attitude no matter what else is going on.* [Continue describing what this person does and her admirable positive attributes. It is important to alleviate any trepidation students may have about writing a "thank you" note to someone they don't even know. Remind students that it is the intention of the action that really matters and that if we were the recipients of a random act of kindness we wouldn't mind whether the act was done as an assignment or whether it was done "freely." What matters are the action itself and the nature of the experience. At the very least, you can tell students why you believe this person is worthy of recognition and that you need their help in accomplishing this goal.] [5–10 minutes]

2. [Have students take out pen and paper.] *You will be writing a brief but positive note of praise to _____ (recipient's name). The intent of this letter is to make him or her feel good and have a positive experience. You will be personally delivering this note to _____ (the recipient).* [During this time (while students are writing), you may want to check to see if the person is available and ready to receive your students. Of course, this exercise is best done as a surprise, hence the reason you should select someone likely to be in a specific place at a specific time.] [5 minutes]

3. *Okay, now that we are all finished, we will be walking over to the office, and you will deliver your note with a smile and a "thank you." Remember to be aware of two things during this experiment: First, what is the reaction of the person receiving the letter? Second, what are your own internal feelings while you are doing this exercise?* [2 minutes]

4. [Lead the students to wherever this person is located. After you have confirmed that the person is ready, have the students approach the person in a single file and deliver their notes, keeping in mind the reaction of the person and an awareness of one's own feelings.] [5–10 minutes]

5. [Return to the classroom and debrief.] *How did the person receiving the notes react? How do you feel about giving the note to the person?* [In my experience, students are willing and eager to share their experiences. The intention of the act causes the recipient to experience a powerful emotion (effect), and the giver (cause) also experiences something positive. I often go off on a hypothetical tangent in which I bring their actions back to them (similar to throwing sand up in the air, it will eventually fall back on your head).] *Ruth will be so happy that she will go home and tell her husband. He will be so happy that he'll take her out to celebrate. They will patronize the restaurant where you work. She will recognize you and leave you a generous tip. Misery begets misery, and happiness begets happiness. When we realize that our emotions, experiences, and lives are interconnected, we will become more aware of the power of causality, especially the impact it has on our relationships with other people."* [Keep the focus of the topic on how our actions influence both others and ourselves.] [15 minutes]

Approximate time: about 30–40 minutes

Source: Submitted by Christian Bauer, Folsom Lake College, CA

Journal Entry 31 Believing in Yourself: Develop Self-Acceptance

EXERCISE 31-1: What I Appreciate About Myself

Purpose

To acknowledge and appreciate one's positive characteristics.

Supplies and Setup

Students sitting in pairs (Student A and Student B)

Directions

1. *For the next little while, you're going to have an exchange with your partner about your good qualities. Whoever starts will say, "What I appreciate about myself is . . ." and finish the sentence. Then the other person will say, "What I appreciate about myself is . . ." and finish the sentence. Go back and forth. Take your time. Think deeply and feel deeply. Trust your Inner Guide and don't hold back.* [You might want to do a DEMO by sharing some of the things you appreciate about yourself. If you sense that some students are uncomfortable, encourage them by saying that "truthful bragging" is definitely encouraged in this activity.] [5 minutes]

2. [Quick-Write and/or Class Discussion] *What was that experience like for you? What was it like to hear your partner expressing appreciation for him- or herself? What was it like to say what you appreciate about yourself? What thoughts or feelings did you have as you expressed yourself each time? Did your Inner Critic try to interfere? How do you feel right now? What would it do for your self-esteem if you fully acknowledged all your positive traits? What is the life lesson here for you?* [e.g., "Loving and appreciating myself are the secret ingredients of my success."] [10–20 minutes]

Approximate time: 15–25 minutes

Instructor Notes

1. In pairing students for this activity, you might want to suggest that students choose a partner with whom they have felt a close connection during the semester. This closeness can free people to be more expressive of their appreciation for themselves.

2. An alternative structure for this activity begins with students standing in a circle. Invite any student to step into the middle of the circle and say, "What I appreciate about myself is . . ." and finish the sentence. Do a DEMO to show what this will look like. Any students who also appreciate that same thing about themselves also move into the middle of the circle. Then reform the circle and repeat.

EXERCISE 31-2: What is Self-Esteem?

Purpose

To understand the important contribution of self-esteem to success as well as identify choices for increasing self-esteem.

Supplies and Setup

Journals; students in groups of three. Optional: Show a scene from *Dead Poets Society* (available on YouTube by searching for "My favorite scene from Dead Poets Society.")

Directions

1. [Step 1 is optional but recommended: Show the scene from *Dead Poets Society* in which the teacher (played by Robin Williams) has asked his students to read the poems they wrote for homework. He asks Todd to read his poem, and Todd says he didn't write one, although earlier in the film he is shown trying to write the poem and

throwing away every draft. After showing the scene . . .] *On a scale of 1–10 (with 10 being the highest), how strong do you think Todd's self-esteem is? How can you tell? How successful do you think Todd will be in life if he doesn't increase his self-esteem? Why is strong self-esteem important to success?* [10 minutes]

2. *In your journal, write your personal definition of* self-esteem. *You'll have an opportunity to revise your definition later if you wish.* [5 minutes]

3. *Read your definition of* self-esteem *to your group. Also, see if you can identify someone you know who has high self-esteem according to your definition.* [4–6 minutes]

4. *In your group, decide on three things a person can do to raise his or her self-esteem. Pick a group reporter to share your ideas with the class.* [5–10 minutes]

5. [Invite group reporters to tell each group's suggestions for raising self-esteem. Record suggestions on the whiteboard or on an overhead transparency.] [5–10 minutes]

6. [Quick-Write and/or Class Discussion] *What is your definition of* self-esteem? *What do you think are good ways for a person to raise his or her self-esteem? What part does self-acceptance play in self-esteem? What's the life lesson here for you?* [e.g., "I always thought that I was stuck with my self-esteem; now I feel hopeful that I can learn how to make it stronger."] [5–10 minutes]

Approximate time: 35–45 minutes

Instructor Notes

Here are five definitions of self-esteem that you could share with students to promote conversation:

- "Self-esteem is the ability to value one's self and to treat oneself with dignity, love, and reality."—Virginia Satir
- "Self-esteem is the experience of being capable of managing life's challenges and being worthy of happiness."—National Council for Self-Esteem
- "Self-esteem is the capacity to experience maximal self-love and joy whether or not you are successful at any point in your life."—David Burns
- "Self-esteem is the feeling that we are worthwhile in our personal, social, and work lives. It comes from feeling loved and respected as a child in our family, by friends, and at school."—Jeffrey E. Young and Janet S. Klosko
- "Self-esteem is the reputation we have with ourselves."—Nathaniel Brandon

EXERCISE 31-3: Overheard Praise

Purpose

To expose students to the positive perceptions others have of them and to encourage them to begin accepting these positive qualities.

Supplies and Setup

Journals or writing paper; chime; students sitting in groups of five to six in a circle, facing toward the center of the circle. In each group, one student turns his or her chair around so it is facing away from the center of the circle. All students have their journals or writing paper on their laps, ready to write.

Directions

1. *Title a page "Overheard Praise." Keep your writing paper and pen with you throughout this exercise.* [1 minute]

2. *Notice that one person has his or her back to your group. Imagine that this person isn't here today. In his or her absence, your group is going to talk about all the things you like and admire about that person. Whenever possible, recall specific events to explain what you're saying about the person. For example, I might say, "I admire Joe because he always comes to class prepared. He has turned in every assignment on time." Or, "I appreciate Joanne because she has the ability to see the best in everyone. Last week I heard her telling Robert what a good writer he is." While this conversation is going on, the person who is "absent" writes everything the other people say about him or her. Don't choose; record everything. Each time I ring the chime, everyone moves one chair to the right. Then the group will begin talking about the new person whose back is to the group. Any questions? Okay, begin.* [4 minutes for directions; 2–3 minutes for the group to discuss each person] [15–20 minutes]

3. *Take a moment now to reread the overheard praise that you recorded. Let it sink in.* [2 minutes]
4. [Quick-Write and/or Class Discussion] *What was that experience like for you? What was it like to give praise and appreciation? Was it difficult or easy to decide what to say? What was it like to hear praise and appreciation of yourself? Is it difficult or easy for you to accept the praise? How do you feel right now? What can you do to feel like this more often? What's the life lesson here for you?* [e.g., "I'm going to be sure to give more praise to the people I love."] [10–20 minutes]

Approximate time: 25–40 minutes

Instructor Notes

If you create success teams in your class, this is a good activity to do in those groups.

EXERCISE 31-4: Ways to Love and Accept Myself

Purpose

To create dozens of options for treating oneself with love.

Supplies and Setup

Journals or writing paper; "32-Day Commitment" handout (next page). Four easel pad markers and four easel pad pages, each titled with one of the following words: PHYSICAL, MENTAL, EMOTIONAL, SPIRITUAL. Post these pages in various places in the room.

Directions

1. *Some of us are better at loving and accepting other people than we are at loving and accepting ourselves. Sometimes that's because we're just not sure how to love ourselves; nobody ever taught us. So, today we're going to create a list of ways we can be loving to ourselves. Notice the four topics posted around the room: Physical, Mental, Emotional, and Spiritual. Go to whichever one you choose.* [Give each group one of the markers.] [3 minutes]
2. *Your group's goal is to come up with a list of as many ways as possible to be loving to yourself in the realm you've chosen. For example, what ways can you be loving to yourself physically?* [Elicit examples, such as get a massage, eat a healthy meal.] *What ways can you be loving to yourself mentally?* [e.g., listen to my Inner Guide and not my Inner Critic, read a good book] *What ways can you be loving to yourself emotionally?* [e.g., spend time with people I love, express anger in a healthy way] *What ways can you be loving to yourself spiritually?* [e.g., say a prayer, spend time in nature] *Write your ideas on the easel pad page. Remember, the goal here is quantity. As many as possible—ready, go!* [During the activity, you may want to assist a group that gets stuck.] [10 minutes]
3. *Now we're going to hear some of your ideas for showing love to ourselves. In your journal or on a sheet of paper, title a page WAYS TO LOVE MYSELF. I suggest that you make a list of all the suggestions, even the ones you don't think you'll ever do. Maybe you'll read this list five years from now and find a suggestion that will be just perfect for you then. Now, let's have a reporter present each group's suggestions.* [20 minutes]
4. [Quick-Write and/or Class Discussion] *What would your life be like if you treated yourself with these loving actions when you are going through a challenge or a crisis in your life? What would it do for your self-esteem if you treated yourself better every day? What is the life lesson here for you?* [e.g., "If I consistently treat myself with love and acceptance, I'll have plenty of overflow for the important people in my life."] [10–20 minutes]
5. *Here's a 32-Day Commitment Form. Consider making a commitment to do one of these loving things for yourself every day for 32 days.* [Pause for students to write a commitment.] *Is there anyone who would like to publicly announce a 32-day commitment?* [5 minutes]

Approximate time: 45–55 minutes

Instructor Notes

Students may disagree about where to place some ideas for loving oneself (e.g., does "Meditate" belong under Mental or Spiritual?). I allow all suggestions to stay wherever they are placed; if an item comes up in two or more realms, that's fine, too. (Thus, "Meditate" might be in the list for Mental *and* Spiritual.) The point is that students leave class with a menu of options for self-care.

32-Day Commitment

Because I know that this commitment will keep me on course to my goals, I promise myself that every day for the next 32 days, I will take the following action: _____

Day 1	Day 17
Day 2	Day 18
Day 3	Day 19
Day 4	Day 20
Day 5	Day 21
Day 6	Day 22
Day 7	Day 23
Day 8	Day 24
Day 9	Day 25
Day 10	Day 26
Day 11	Day 27
Day 12	Day 28
Day 13	Day 29
Day 14	Day 30
Day 15	Day 31
Day 16	Day 32

"By making and keeping promises to ourselves and others, little by little, our honor becomes greater than our moods."—Stephen Covey

"Success is . . . the long-term consequence of making and keeping promises—promises to others . . . and promises to yourself . . . the more you exercise your self-discipline, the stronger it gets."—Harvey Cook

EXERCISE 31-5: Affirmation Whisper

Purpose

To demonstrate the power of self-affirming statements and give students' self-worth a boost.

Supplies and Setup

Chime. Students need to know their personal affirmation (Journal Entry 11) by heart or have it written on an index card. Arrange the room so that half of the students are sitting in chairs (randomly placed about the room) and half of the students are standing behind the chairs in which students are sitting. Be sure there is enough space between the chairs so that the standing students can walk about without bumping into anyone. I recommend soothing instrumental music as background; "Angelic Music" by Iasos is my choice.

Directions

1. [Give all directions—steps 1 to 3—before starting the activity. You may want to project abbreviated directions on a PowerPoint slide for students to reference throughout the activity.] *In a moment, those of you who are standing are going to whisper your affirmation to the people sitting down. But instead of saying, "I am a bold, generous, joyful man," you will say "**You** are a bold, generous, joyful . . . **man or woman**," whichever gender is appropriate. It helps also to say the person's name first.* [DEMO by whispering your affirmation into one student's ear and then moving on and repeating it.] *As soon as you have whispered your affirmation to one person, move on to another person and whisper your affirmation again. Keep whispering until you hear the chime ring, even if that means you repeat your affirmation for some people. And here's a last thought for those of you sitting down—it seems to enrich the experience if you close your eyes.* [Make sure that everyone knows how to pronounce everyone's name correctly. You may also wish to determine if there is a student with a hearing challenge who would prefer to have the affirmations spoken in a particular ear.]

2. *When you hear the chime, reverse roles. Those of you sitting will stand and walk behind your chair, and those of you standing will sit in the first empty chair you see. As before, the standing people will immediately begin whispering their affirmations to the sitting people. Start whispering as soon as someone sits in the chair in front of you and keep moving around the room whispering to other people until you hear the chime ring, even if that means you repeat your affirmation for some people.*

3. *When the chime rings a second time, simply relax. Find a comfortable position anywhere in the room, sitting or lying down, and take a few minutes to think about what that experience was like for you. What questions do you have?* [The success of this activity requires that everyone understands the directions before beginning, so be extra sure everyone is clear.] *Ready, begin.* [Steps 1–3 will take about 10 minutes.]

4. [Let the first round of whispered affirmations go for about three to four minutes. Ring the chime to signal reversing roles and allow about three to four more minutes for the second round (allow a little extra time for the second group to switch roles). Then ring the chime a last time and give students about two or three minutes in silence to relax and take in and think about the affirmations they have just heard.] [10 minutes]

5. [Quick-Write and/or Class Discussion] *What was that experience like for you? How do you feel right now? What can you do to feel like this more often? What did you hear? What is the life lesson here for you?* [e.g., I'll never forget one of my students saying, "How different, warmer, sweeter this life might have been, if only once each day I might have heard these loving words so gently spoken."] [10–20 minutes]

Approximate time: 30–40 minutes

Instructor Notes

This powerful activity is one of my students' all-time favorites. It often creates an experience for some students that is nothing short of sacred. I take great precautions that no one ruins that experience for the class. Occasionally, there is someone who gets uncomfortable and wants to make a joke of the activity. If you sense there is someone in your class who might do this, give everyone the opportunity to opt out.

Chapter 8: Quiz Questions

(The Answer Key to Chapter 8: Quiz Questions appears at the end of this Facilitator's Manual. Please visit the Instructor Companion Site for *On Course* at login.cengage.com for a digital version of this quiz and its answer key.)

Understanding Emotional Intelligence

1. Having mental intelligence (a high IQ) is all one needs to create great success in college and in life.   TRUE   FALSE

2. In an experiment during the 1960s, young children were divided into two groups on their ability (or lack of ability) to postpone the immediate gratification of eating one marshmallow in order to get two marshmallows later. Years later the group that was able to postpone gratification scored, on average, 210 points higher on the SAT (Scholastic Aptitude Test) than did the group that chose immediate gratification.   TRUE   FALSE

3. Writing a term paper instead of attending a party that you'd love to go to is an example of

    A. emotional self-awareness (knowing your feelings in the moment).

    B. emotional self-management (managing strong feelings).

    C. social awareness (empathizing accurately with other people's emotions).

    D. relationship management (handling emotions in relationship with skill and harmony).

4. Noticing when someone else is experiencing sadness or anxiety is an example of

    A. emotional self-awareness (knowing your feelings in the moment).

    B. emotional self-management (managing strong feelings).

    C. social awareness (empathizing accurately with other people's emotions).

    D. relationship management (handling emotions in relationship with skill and harmony).

5. Making an effort to help someone feel comfortable in a situation that is new to him or her is an example of

    A. emotional self-awareness (knowing your feelings in the moment).

    B. emotional self-management (managing strong feelings).

    C. social awareness (empathizing accurately with other people's emotions).

    D. relationship management (handling emotions in relationship with skill and harmony).

Reducing Stress

1. Creators accept responsibility not only for the results they create in their outer world but also for the emotions they experience in their inner world.   TRUE   FALSE

2. When stress persists, stress hormones (cortisol and epinephrine) remain active in the body's systems, damaging almost every part of the body.   TRUE   FALSE

3. To reduce stress of many kinds, you can choose new behaviors and/or new thoughts.   TRUE   FALSE

4. Feeling overwhelmed is probably the most common stressor for college students. To begin reducing this feeling, you can use the following self-management tool to list and prioritize everything you need to do in each of your life roles (then you can begin doing the high-priority tasks one by one).

   A. Next actions list

   B. Tracking form

   C. 32-day commitment

   D. Calendar

5. High stress has a positive impact on memory and other mental skills such as creativity, concentration, and attention to details.   TRUE   FALSE

Increasing Happiness

1. About 50 percent of our happiness is determined by a genetically fixed set point.   TRUE   FALSE

2. We can influence about 50 percent of our happiness by the quality of the choices we make.   TRUE   FALSE

3. Pleasures created by such experiences as eating a fine meal, receiving a massage, or viewing a beautiful sunset soon fade because of . . .

   A. flow states.

   B. the hormone dopamine.

   C. hedonic adaptation.

   D. gratitude.

4. Which of the following would not describe an instructor who is likely to help you experience "flow" as a student

   A. demonstrates a deep knowledge of their subject.

   B. shows great enthusiasm for the value of their subject.

   C. sets challenging but reasonable learning objectives for their students.

   D. is an easy grader.

   E. offers engaging learning experiences that appeal to diverse learning preferences.

   F. provides a combination of academic and emotional support that gives their students high expectations of success.

5. According to the author of *On Course*, experiencing any of the following might be called a _____ moment:
   1. creating and savoring a momentary pleasure
   2. feeling gratitude for what we have rather than distress for what we don't
   3. engaging in flow
   4. showing kindness to someone who is facing one problem after another

On Course at Work: Emotional Intelligence at Work

1. Responding impulsively to the actions of bosses or coworkers shows a lack of the emotional intelligence component called emotional self-management.   TRUE   FALSE

2. Embarrassing a coworker by pointing out his or her poor performance in a meeting with coworkers shows a lack of the emotional intelligence component called emotional self-awareness.   TRUE   FALSE

3. In fields such as engineering, medicine, computer science, and the law, emotional intelligence has little importance in getting and keeping the job.   TRUE   FALSE

4. To be an outstanding leader, one must be able to resolve conflicts that happen in the workplace. In emotional intelligence terms, this skill is called

    A. emotional self-awareness.

    B. emotional self-management.

    C. social awareness.

    D. relationship management.

5. Imagine that you are the leader of a team at work. One member of the team is always late, never meets deadlines, and angers her teammates. You feel your temper rising every time you think about this person's poor work habits. Which of the following choices demonstrates the most professional behavior?

    A. In the next team meeting, confront the offending team member with the evidence of her poor teamwork.

    B. While you are still motivated by your anger, send an email about this coworker's lack of motivation to your boss.

    C. When calm, meet with the offending team member alone, share your feelings about her behaviors, and make a request for a change in behavior that will help the team function more effectively.

    D. Stop sending her notices of when and where your team is meeting.

Believing in Yourself: Develop Self-Acceptance

1. Self-esteem is the reputation we have with others.   TRUE   FALSE

2. Self-esteem is strengthened by increased self-acceptance.   TRUE   FALSE

3. Accepting our weaknesses means

    A. we are content to stay as we are.

    B. we can now begin to strengthen the things about ourselves that can be changed.

    C. we are weak.

4. Successful people are usually willing to

    A. admit their personal weaknesses.

    B. set a goal to change.

    C. manage their actions to bring about change.

    D. look at feedback about their efforts to change.

    E. have the courage to change.

    F. do all of the above.

5. We are born with a certain level of self-esteem, and it remains that way throughout our lives.   TRUE   FALSE

Chapter 8: Essay Topics

1. Misfortune happens to every human being. Whereas Victims often get overwhelmed by their distressing emotions, Creators move on to more positive futures. Using your knowledge of emotional intelligence and strategies for reducing stress, write an essay comparing how you dealt with a misfortune in your past with how you might deal with that same misfortune today.

2. Few people are fully conscious of the chatter of their inner aspects such as their Inner Defender, Inner Critic, and Inner Guide. In an essay for college students, explain how these inner aspects impact the quality of their inner experience. Present your readers with methods for dealing positively with their inner voices.

3. Author William Saroyan advised, "Try as much as possible to be wholly alive. . . . You will be dead soon enough." In an essay for a general audience, explain what specific steps one can take to create the experience of feeling "wholly alive."

4. Many people focus on what is wrong in their lives, but others radiate a positive outlook on life. In an essay for a mass-circulation magazine (e.g., *Reader's Digest*), tell about the most positive person you have ever known.

5. Self-esteem is an important concept but one that is difficult to define. In an essay for a national magazine read by college students, write about a person you know who demonstrates high self-esteem. In this way, offer your readers your best definition of high self-esteem and how to achieve it.

6. Using the "One Student's Story" essays in *On Course* as a model, write an essay about how you used a strategy from Chapter 8 to overcome a problem in your life—academic, personal, or even at work. First, explain the problem; then, discuss the specific strategy you used and how you put it into action; finally, identify what happened. Your instructor may submit your essay for possible publication in the next edition of *On Course*. Additional directions for writing and submitting these essays can be found at http://oncourseworkshop.com/course-textbook/essay-contest/.

Staying On Course to Your Success

Chapter
9

Concept

Staying on course to a rich, personally fulfilling life is one of a human being's greatest challenges. Forces both outside of us and inside of us seemingly conspire to divert us from this achievement. By assisting students to plan and take their next steps, we not only remind them of the changes they have made to empower themselves and better their lives, but we also help them keep their sights on both a positive future and the wise choices that will guide them there. As we bid our students farewell for now, we give them the momentum to head off into great lives of their own creation.

EMPOWERS STUDENTS TO . . .

1. Review what they have learned about themselves in this course.
2. Assess the changes they have made to improve the outcomes of their lives.
3. Identify additional changes they wish to make in the near and distant future.
4. Plan their next steps toward creating a rich, personally fulfilling life.

Journal Entry 32 Planning Your Next Steps

EXERCISE 32-1: Self-Assessment Revisited

Purpose

To have students acknowledge the changes they have created in their lives during this course and to decide what additional changes they want to make.

Supplies and Setup

Journal Entry 32 completed; students sitting in pairs (Student A and Student B)

Directions

1. *Partner A, read to your partner what you wrote for Step 2 of Journal Entry 32. When Partner A is finished, Partner B will respond, "What I heard you say in your journal entry is . . . ." Partner B can then add any other comments or observations that come to mind.* [5 minutes]
2. *Now, Partner B, you read Step 2 of your Journal Entry 32. Afterward, Partner A will respond, "What I heard you say in your journal entry is . . ." and then add any other comments or observations that seem appropriate.* [5 minutes]

3. [Repeat steps 1 and 2 above for Step 3 of Journal Entry 32.] [10 minutes for both partners to read and respond]
4. [Repeat steps 1 and 2 above for Step 4 of Journal Entry 32.] [10 minutes for both partners to read and respond]
5. [Repeat steps 1 and 2 for Step 5 of Journal Entry 32.] [10 minutes for both partners to read and respond.]
6. [Quick-Write and/or Class Discussion] *What important discoveries have you made in this course? What changes have you made in your life? What additional changes do you plan to make in the future? What life lessons do you want to remember from this course?* [e.g., I will remember to pause before important choices I make and ask, "Which choice will help me create my goals and dreams?"] [10–20 minutes]

Approximate time: 50–60 minutes

EXERCISE 32-2: Commencement

Purpose

To offer an opportunity for students to review and reflect on what they have learned in this course.

Supplies and Setup

A beach ball (or other large, light ball) with key terms written on it with a permanent marker: SELF-RESPONSIBILITY, SELF-MOTIVATION, SELF-MANAGEMENT, INTERDEPENDENCE, SELF-AWARENESS, LIFELONG LEARNING, EMOTIONAL INTELLIGENCE, BELIEVE IN YOURSELF, WISE CHOICES, CRITICAL THINKING, CORE, and any other concepts you want to review. Write four sentence stems on the board or project them on a PowerPoint slide. (See Instructor Notes for the sentence stems.) Paper and pens. Optional: video recorder.

Directions

1. [You may wish to have students standing in a circle for this step.] *Let's take a few minutes to review where we've been this semester. I'm going to toss this ball to someone. When you catch it, read the first word or words that you see and tell us the most important thing you have learned or relearned about that topic. You can tell us what the concept means to you, about a strategy you learned or an experience you had that illustrates this concept, or whatever feels appropriate to you. There is no right or wrong answer. When you're done, toss the ball to another person, and that person will do the same thing. It's fine if you talk about the same topic that someone else discussed. Each topic will probably be discussed a number of times in different ways.* [10–15 minutes or until you sense that the key points of the course have been adequately reviewed]
2. *On a sheet of paper, complete the four sentence stems you see written on the whiteboard. I will be collecting this as feedback to me about your experience in the course. Be as complete as possible.* [Collect what the students have written. Collecting these forms prevents students from merely reading from them in the next part.] [10–15 minutes]
3. *Now we're going to have a commencement exercise for our class. To commence means to "begin." So this exercise is the beginning of the rest of your lives. I invite you to come to the front of the room and talk to us from your heart for a couple of minutes. Tell us the most important things you've learned in this course; tell us what you want in your life; tell us what you know are the keys to your success; tell us anything else that you want us to know. When one person finishes, the next person can come right up. I'm just going to sit here and listen. Who would like to be first?* [There may be a couple of long periods when no one comes to the front to speak. If you are patient with the silence, most times someone will come forward.] [10–25 minutes]

Approximate time: 30–55 minutes

Instructor Notes

1. Post the following four sentence stems:
   1. Important goals and dreams in my life include . . .
   2. The success strategies I will use to achieve them include . . .
   3. Changes I would make in this course include . . .
   4. Most of all from this course I want to remember . . .

2. I recommend video recording the commencement presentations. Students in your class will enjoy watching themselves later, and the video is great to show at the beginning of future classes to show new students the amazing journey they are about to undertake. You can also use the video for recruiting new students to take your course and for demonstrating to colleagues and administrators the value students are getting from the course.

3. You might want to mention that some students' Inner Critics or Inner Defenders will give them all sorts of reasons why they should not go to the front of the room and speak. That's why doing so is such a great boost to their self-esteem: They get to show their Inner Critics and Inner Defenders who is making the choices that matter.

EXERCISE 32-3: Appreciations

Purpose

To experience an avalanche of affirming thoughts that can boost the students' sense of self-worth.

Supplies and Setup

Journals; chime; students sitting in circles of 8–10. Write the words APPRECIATE, ADMIRE, RESPECT on the board or project them on a PowerPoint slide.

Directions

1. *Open your journal to a clean page and write your name at the top of the page. Now pass your journal to the person on your right.* [1 minute] [For students who don't have their journal, a piece of paper will do.]

2. *When you get your neighbor's journal, write a short note telling what you **appreciate, admire,** and **respect** about him or her. You'll have only one minute, so get right to the heart of what you wish to say. When I ring the chime, sign your name and pass the journal to your right. Keep writing and passing until your journal comes back to you. Then read what people wrote to you.* [20–30 minutes]

3. [Quick-Write and/or Class Discussion] *What was it like to write appreciations to others? What was it like to read the appreciations written to you? How do you feel right now? What would it do for your success if you fully acknowledged all the aspects of yourself that others appreciate, admire, and respect? What is the life lesson here for you?* [e.g., "I am having more of an impact on other people's lives than my Inner Critic ever let me realize."] [10–20 minutes]

Approximate time: 30–50 minutes

EXERCISE 32-4: *On Course* in the Movies

Purpose

For students to reflect on *On Course* concepts and see how they are applied in Hollywood films.

Supplies and Setup

"*On Course* in the Movies" handout that lists films (next page)

Directions

1. *For this assignment, you will watch a movie and analyze how it illustrates concepts we have covered in our course this semester.*

2. *Don't simply give a plot summary of the movie; instead choose certain scenes and/or key themes that relate to any of the Eight Choices of Successful Students (found on the inside front cover of your* On Course *textbook) and/or related ideas presented in the book. Rather than try to tie in all eight choices, you might focus on two or three areas that you think stand out the most in the movie. You may choose to analyze one character in particular, or you may give examples of things that many characters in the movie did that demonstrated (or did not demonstrate) patterns of thought, emotion, and behavior consistent with a particular* On Course *principle.*

Source: Submitted by Lisa Marks, Ozarks Technical Community College, MO

On Course in the Movies

Choose from the following films:

The Blind Side	*Rain Man*	*Gifted Hands*
Any *Star Wars* movie	*Lean on Me*	*To Sir with Love*
For the Love of the Game	*Tuesdays with Morrie*	*Paper Chase*
Rocky IV	*12 Angry Men*	*Precious*
Hoosiers	*Yes Man*	*Music of the Heart*
The Karate Kid	*Forrest Gump*	*Freedom Writers*
Dead Poet's Society	*Homeless to Harvard*	*Educating Rita*
Mr. Holland's Opus	*The Bucket List*	*Me Again*
Good Will Hunting	*Stand and Deliver*	*Peaceful Warrior*
Finding Forrester	*Pay It Forward*	*Rise of the Guardians*
Breakfast Club	*Slumdog Millionaire*	*The Ultimate Gift*
Dangerous Minds	*Patch Adams*	*Fireproof*
Antwone Fisher	Any *Harry Potter* movie	*Groundhog Day*
Akeelah and the Bee	*The King's Speech*	*The Pursuit of Happyness*
Tangled	*Coach Carter*	*Chariots of Fire*

EXERCISE 32-5: Letter to the Next Class

Purpose

To offer students an opportunity to evaluate and identify the changes they have experienced as a result of the course and to impart to future students a description of the course and advice from a student's perspective.

Supplies and Setup

Students can either use pen and paper or submit letters in an electronic format. Provide on a handout the four questions that students will answer in their essay (included in Direction #1 below).

Directions

1. [At the end of the course, have students write letters to future students by answering each of the following questions in the form of a paragraph:
   A. Evaluate the choices you made before this course. What were some of the consequences of those choices?
   B. What have you learned from the course about yourself that will change the choices you will make in the future?
   C. How would you describe this course to someone else?
   D. What advice would you give to future students about what students can expect to learn in the course? In what ways can the course help them obtain the strategies necessary to be successful not only in college but also in life?]
2. [Have students present their completed letters to their classmates. Additionally, retain copies of the letters so they may be read by future students in the first week of the course.]

Approximate time: Time may vary depending on whether students complete their letters outside of class or within the classroom. The critical thinking is much deeper when students are given the opportunity to complete the assignment outside the classroom.

Instructor Notes

Instructors may want to ask students to type the letters and submit in electronic format to ensure the readability and accessibility of each letter. In addition, the student's last name is removed from the letter when it is shared with future classes. Finally, at our institution because the course is mandatory, reading letters from past students seems to help them keep more of an open mind about the course. Example letters begin on the next page. [Author's note: A similar positive impact can be obtained by showing videos of students reading their "One Student's Story" essays, found at http://OnCourseWorkshop.com → Educator Resources → Video Gallery.]

Source: Submitted by Dana J. Kermanian, Grayson College, TX

Example Letters to the Next Class

Dear Future Students,

Before taking this course, I made some poor decisions that honestly hurt my future and personal character. I constantly made excuses and blamed others for my failures, especially in school. If I did poorly on a test, I also said, "That test was too hard; there is no way I could have done better," or "The teacher did not teach anything that was on the test. What is the point of going to class? I am going to do bad anyways." These choices led to me give up on that class and on myself. I felt like it was not my fault; I was blind. I did not realize that by doing this I was only hurting myself.

Something I learned from this course about myself that will change the choices I will make in the future is I learned that it is okay to make mistakes as long as I take it as an opportunity to make improvements in my life. I used to make mistakes, then try to avoid them; now, I make a mistake and learn how to improve that area and not repeat the same thing over. I learned to grow as a person. I learned to be more open to change and acknowledgement of my own problems and successes.

I would describe this class as a guide for college learning and self-awareness. This course gets you closer to yourself and more aware of how to be successful in college. This course is great for helping that transition from high school to a higher education. The course teaches you how to be more aware of your choices and the effects they have on not only yourself but others.

The advice I would give to future students about what they should learn in this class is themselves. You will learn more about yourself, your strengths and weaknesses. This course will also teach you how to improve those areas. This class will bring you closer to your true self than you knew was possible. The advice I would give about how you can be successful not only in college but in life is to keep learning. Never stop learning, and learn at a deep meaningful level. Learn in way that you will always remember. Connect new learning with old memories. As long as you are learning, you are growing as a person, improving.

Sincerely,
Keri

To the next class,

Before beginning this class, Learning Frameworks, you would have found me struggling with my classes. I would have been pulling my hair out, stressed from procrastinating assignments and projects, listening to the voice inside of me, that you will learn is your inner critic, telling me I'm not good enough, and choosing activities I find fun over what I really should be doing . . . my homework. Before this class I was extremely disorganized and chose to do the easy things on my to-do list over something bigger and more important.

This course has helped turn that all around. You can expect to learn your personal learning preference or preferences, how to plan out important tasks that lead you down a path to success, find out what your habits and beliefs are that get in your way of true success, and a multitude of other things. This class does require you to pull memories and emotions that you may normally want to hide and not think of, but I advise you not to hold back. Coming into this class I thought, this is just a class I'm required to take and an easy A. This class is easy in that there isn't as much work as maybe some of your other classes, but it's hard because you are asked to open up and dive deep.

If you DO NOT hold anything back, you will be surprised to discover some of the things that trigger your inner critic or beliefs that could hinder your success. So as I said don't hold back. Be open to the learning and lessons of this class; you will not regret it! The things you learn in this class can be used not only in school but also in your career, relationships, etc. for the rest of your life.

Because of this course I am much more confident that I will reach my goals in life and be successful. I still have a long ways to go and more things to learn about myself but I am not where I used to be. I now know some of the beliefs and habits that stand in my path to success. I know how I learn at my best and how to learn at my best even if my teacher or boss isn't teaching me the way I prefer. I know what triggers my inner critic to open its judgmental mouth and how I can turn that off. I have learned a multitude of things and am surely not done learning either. I personally will take the lessons I have learned in this class outside of my school life, to be as successful as I can be.

Onward!
Tayler

Dear Future Students,

Before I decided to go back to college after being out for 7 years, I was a horrible student. In fact, I now realize that I was just a horrible person in general. I lacked serious motivation and life skills. It's not fun when you realize that you have been leading an unsuccessful life and have to reevaluate your entire way of thinking. Before this class my study habits were terrible, my test taking lacked serious effort, and my college career was an all-around failure.

I had gone to college the first four years after high school and dropped several classes and ended up with a very low grade point average. In fact it was less than 2.0. This is the main reason I quit attending. I thought I was just not college material. When I decided this year to go back to college and I found out I had to take this course, honestly I was a little disappointed. I thought "I'm 31 years old; I know how to be a student!!" But now I realize that I may have known how to be a student, just not a successful one.

This class has taught me more than I ever imagined. The main thing it taught me was how to change my way of thinking. I now understand the concept of "digging deep" into my brain and evaluating my thought processing. Not only can this help in college but in my job and personal life as well. I used to overlook things and I also had a tendency to ignore things. I now feel confident in my college career. I feel like I know how to prepare for exams, write better papers, and study effectively. I have also learned not to blame others for my own mistakes. It wasn't the professor's fault I failed algebra the first time I took it. It was my fault. I didn't study the correct way and didn't put forth an effort to try and understand the subject.

The most important thing I can pass on to future students is to have an open mind when you take this class. Don't think this class is useless and a waste of time, like I did. I ended up learning far more than I ever expected. Thanks to this class I am currently passing college algebra, the class I failed out of twice before. I now have a better understanding of college skills and I am looking forward to using these skills in the future, not only in college but in my overall life.

Sincerely,
Andrea

Chapter 9: Essay Topics

1. Almost everyone would agree that they want to live a rich, personally fulfilling life—yet few people know what they mean by the idea, let alone how to create such a life. In an essay for *Success Magazine,* define what you consider to be a rich, personally fulfilling life and explain how you plan to create such a life.

2. In an essay to be given to your children (or grandchildren) on their 21st birthdays, present your philosophy of living a successful life. Be specific about what defines a successful life for you and how you plan to create it.

3. In an essay for the author of our textbook, *On Course,* explain what parts of the book you found most valuable and any that you found less valuable, along with your reasons. Please send a copy of your essay to Skip Downing, c/o Product Assistant, Developmental Studies/College Success, Cengage Learning, 500 Terry A. Francois Blvd., Second Floor, San Francisco, CA 94158.

4. Using the "One Student's Story" essays in *On Course* as a model, write an essay about how you used a strategy from anywhere in the book to overcome a problem in your life—academic, personal, or even at work. First, explain the problem; then discuss the specific strategy you used and how you put it into action; finally, identify what happened. Your instructor may submit your essay for possible publication in the next edition of *On Course.* Additional directions for writing and submitting these essays can be found at http://oncourseworkshop.com/course-textbook/essay-contest/.

Study Skills: A Toolbox for Active Learners

A. Becoming an Active Learner

EXERCISE A-1: The Learning Game

Purpose

To identify the value of being an active learner and paying close attention to feedback.

Supplies and Setup

A dollar bill folded into a very small square; one volunteer (A)

Directions

1. *Do you remember how you loved to learn as a child and how good you were at it? Many adults have lost both this love of learning and the effective way they went about learning when they were children. Today we're going to play a game to see if we can rediscover some of that lost love and the natural learning process we can use even today to maximize our learning.* [To Volunteer A:] *I'm going to ask you to go out of the room for a few minutes while we set up a learning game for you to play.*

2. [To the class after A has left the room:] *I'd like someone to hide this folded dollar bill somewhere in the room. It's important that everyone knows where the dollar is, so watch carefully where it's being hidden. When A returns, I'll tell her that her goal is to learn where the dollar is hidden. Notice how this situation is similar to coming into a new course. Whether the course is history, English, math, or another subject, your job as a student is to figure out where the valuable information is hidden. In this activity, your job is to be scientists and figure out some choices that enhance learning and those that diminish learning. To do that, watch and listen for everything that A does or says. See what she does that works to learn where the dollar is and what she does that doesn't work.*

   There are two parts to this activity. First, we'll just let A look for the dollar without any help. If she asks you a question, don't answer in any way. Second, after a couple of minutes, I'll fold my arms across my chest like this. That will be your signal to start giving A some feedback. Do you remember the kids' game called "Hot and Cold"? Well, as A gets closer to the dollar bill, we'll all start to hum like this: "Hmmm . . . ." If she gets closer to the dollar, we'll hum louder. If A stops or turns away from the dollar, we'll immediately stop humming. Watch very carefully what A does both before and after we give her feedback by humming. Write down everything she says or does. Remember, you're trying to figure out what behaviors help people learn something. [5 minutes]

3. [To A after returning to the room:] *We've hidden a dollar bill somewhere in this room. Your goal is to learn where it is as fast as possible. Please verbalize what you are thinking so we can understand how you learn where the dollar is. When you find the dollar, it's yours to keep. Any questions?* [No matter what the volunteer says, merely repeat these same directions. After a while, the volunteer will get the point and probably start looking.] [2 minutes]

4. [As the volunteer is looking for the dollar, you want to do two things: (1) Ask the volunteer to think out loud—explain what she is doing to learn where the dollar is. (2) Keep comparing what the volunteer is doing to what happens to many students in college. For example, if the volunteer gets frustrated because she is getting no answers

to her questions, ask, "Have you ever had a teacher who didn't seem to give you helpful feedback? What did you do?" If the volunteer just stands and does nothing, ask, "Have you ever gotten stuck in a course and found it hard to do anything? Did doing *nothing* ever help you learn? What did it help you learn?" If the volunteer says, "I quit. I just can't find it," ask, "Have you ever felt like quitting a difficult course?" The possibilities of the volunteer's actions and comments are many, so to facilitate this activity well, you need to stay alert.] [3–8 minutes] [Cut the activity shorter if the volunteer is getting too frustrated. Most volunteers will go as long as you wish, so you can gauge the duration on how long you think the class is getting value from observing the activity.]

5. [After a couple of minutes of A's searching, fold your arms to let the class members know it's time for them to give feedback to the volunteer by humming. Keep asking the volunteer to think out loud: "How are you now going about trying to learn where the dollar is?" Also keep relating the present events to the students' experiences in college: "Is it possible that you had a teacher who was giving you great information and feedback about how to learn a subject, but you just didn't realize what he was doing?"] [3–8 minutes, again gauging the timing on the value present]

6. [After the volunteer has found the dollar and the class has given a huge round of applause—which is usually spontaneous in this activity—then comes a Quick-Write and/or Class Discussion. Lead students to identify one or more of the components of the CORE Learning System.] *What did you learn about learning? What actions help people learn?* [There are many "right" answers here, but a few you may want to highlight are (1) ask Creator questions, (2) collect relevant information, (3) organize information into empowering answers, (4) evaluate your present answers, (5) heed feedback, and (6) revise your answers when incorrect.] *What actions hinder learning? What thoughts help people learn? What thoughts hinder learning? What emotions help people learn? What emotions hinder learning? What beliefs help people learn? What beliefs hinder learning? Are there any changes you could make to become a better learner? What is the life lesson here for you?* [e.g., "Learning is a skill that requires my active engagement, and I can learn to learn better than I do now."] [10–25 minutes]

Approximate time: 25–60 minutes

Instructor Notes

1. Don't let the lengthy directions scare you. This is one of my favorite classroom activities. Students love it, and it never fails to generate fascinating discoveries about learning and about life. The Learning Game has turned out somewhat differently every time I've done it. I find this unpredictability to be part of the magic of this activity. You just need to keep your goal (discovering how people learn) in mind and go with the flow. Let the learning be yours, too.

2. The directions here are very important. It is essential that the class members understand that they are to hum as the volunteer moves *toward* the dollar and to stay quiet when the volunteer *stops* or *moves away* from the dollar. If, during the game, it becomes apparent that the class is sending confusing feedback to the volunteer, ask the volunteer to leave the room again and clarify the directions for the class.

3. The volunteer will likely get frustrated after a few minutes. That's usually OK, but be sensitive not to let the frustration go on too long. Keep giving the volunteer praise and support. Don't let the volunteer stop without the experience of success in finding the dollar bill—even if you have to virtually lead him or her to it (which isn't likely).

4. One of the most fascinating experiences I have had with this game occurred when the class was sitting in a circle and the dollar bill was hidden outside the circle. The volunteer came into the circle and, ignoring all feedback from the group, would not venture outside of the circle of chairs to look for the dollar. Afterward, students engaged in an insightful discussion about how we limit our learning because of mistaken beliefs that we hold—in this case that the dollar had to be hidden within the circle. Ultimately, the discussion led to a listing of limiting beliefs that students may hold: *I can't do math; I can't bother an instructor outside of class; I'm born with a certain writing ability, and there's nothing I can do to improve it;* and so on. Identifying these beliefs laid a helpful foundation for a later discussion of beliefs and scripts in Chapter 6.

EXERCISE A-2: Beautiful Questions

Purpose

(1) To offer practice in actively asking beautiful Creator questions, rekindling curiosity and wonderment and (2) to have students identify the important questions for each academic course they are taking.

Supplies and Setup

Journals; five 3 × 5 index cards for each student; students in groups of four

Directions

1. *The poet e.e. cummings wrote, "Always the beautiful answer / Who asks a more beautiful question." Open your journal to a clean page and title the page "BEAUTIFUL QUESTIONS." Now make a list of some of the beautiful questions that you'd like to find answers to during your life. You have five minutes to make your list of questions. To help yourself invent questions, think of your life roles. What do you want to know about being a student, a parent, a spouse, an employee, an athlete? Think of questions you'll need to answer in order to reach your goals and dreams.* [5 minutes]

2. [Have volunteers share some of their questions with the class. Invite students to add to their lists when they hear questions they also want answered during their lives. When appropriate, ask . . .] *Can you think of a college class in which you might learn the answer to that question?* [10 minutes]

3. *Perhaps you never realized that what makes one college course different from another is its intention to answer different questions. A psychology course, for example, answers different questions from those a history course does. Turn to the next clean page in your journal and title it "BEAUTIFUL ACADEMIC QUESTIONS." On that page, list the courses you're taking this semester, starting with this course. Leave five blank lines under each course. Beneath each course, write what you think are the three most important questions the course is designed to answer.* [10 minutes]

4. [Lead a discussion in which students share the questions they think various courses are designed to answer. Ask for students who are taking the same courses to compare their questions. Consider recording the questions by course on the whiteboard.] [15 minutes]

5. [Quick-Write and/or Class Discussion] *What advantage is it for you to know what the key questions are for all your courses? How would you go about determining what questions a teacher might ask on a test? What do you think makes one question more beautiful than another? What is the life lesson here for you?* [e.g., "If I ask the wrong question, I might get the 'right' answer, but it won't be much help to me."] [10 20 minutes]

Approximate time: 50–60 minutes

Instructor Notes

I like to point out that the root word of *question* is "quest," and a quest requires action. Additionally, the quality of any quest is determined by the quality of the question that starts it.

Active Learning: Quiz Questions

(The Answer Key to Active Learning: Quiz Questions appears at the end of this Facilitator's Manual. Please visit the Instructor Companion Site for *On Course* at login.cengage.com for a digital version of this quiz and its answer key.)

1. To excel as a learner, you need to create as many strong neural networks (connections) in your brain as possible.   TRUE   FALSE

2. To create strong neural networks (connections) in your brain, you've got to _____ the learning process.

   A. participate actively in

   B. read about

   C. remember

   D. listen to a lecture about

3. Brain research reveals that when you connect what you are learning now to previously stored information (e.g., already formed neural networks), you learn the information or skill more slowly and less deeply.   TRUE   FALSE

4. The human brain learns best when learning efforts are done in

   A. one long marathon session using one method of deep processing.

   B. frequent sessions distributed over time using one method of deep processing.

   C. one long marathon session using a variety of deep-processing strategies.

   D. frequent sessions distributed over time using a variety of deep-processing strategies.

5. The four components of the CORE Learning System are <u>C</u>ollect, <u>O</u>rganize, <u>R</u>ehearse, and _____.

Active Learning: Essay Topic

Using the "One Student's Story" essays in *On Course* as models, write an essay about how you used active learning strategies (especially the C.O.R.E. Learning System) to overcome an academic challenge in college. First explain the academic challenge; then discuss the specific active learning strategy or strategies you used; finally, identify the outcome of your efforts. Your instructor may submit your essay for possible publication in the next edition of *On Course*, where it could inspire tens of thousands of your fellow students. Additional directions for writing and submitting your essay may be found at http://oncourseworkshop.com/course-textbook/essay-contest/.

B. Reading

EXERCISE B-1: Academic Coaches (Option 1)

Purpose

To help students identify reading challenges in college and possible solutions to those problems.

Supplies and Setup

4 × 6 index cards (one for each student); students have previously read the "Reading" section in Study Skills: A Toolbox for Active Learners.

Directions

Note—this activity can be repeated with each study skill.

1. [Students in pairs] *The purpose of most reading assignments in a college class is to inform you about three things: (A) a key concept, (B) main ideas about that concept, and (C) supporting details about the main ideas. Brainstorm with your partner and list possible challenges that could keep you from fully understanding a reading assignment. For example, one problem might be that your mind keeps wandering when you read. After you together come up with five reading challenges, each of you choose one of the problems (not the same one) and write it on a 4 × 6 card. You'll get the most value from this activity if you choose a reading problem that has been a challenge for you.* [10 minutes]

2. *Decide which of you will be a "coach" and which will be a "client."* [Make sure that every pair of students has one coach and one client and encourage them to recall which they are.] *In a few moments, I'm going to say, "Clients, get a coach," and everyone who has chosen to be a client, stand up and move to a new partner. Coaches, you stay seated and wave your hand in the air to let clients know that you need a partner. When a new partner joins you, put down your hand. You'll be with each partner for a five-minute conversation, and then I'll say, "Clients, get a new coach." Clients will move to a new partner, and coaches will stay seated, waving their hands to let clients know they need a new partner.* [It helps to demonstrate exactly what this way of changing partners will look like.] *So, what will you talk about with your partners? When clients get to their coach, share the reading challenge on your card. Your partner will then coach you on how you might overcome this problem. Coaches, you may refer to the reading strategies in* On Course *if you wish. Clients, take notes on the suggestions.* [It helps to demonstrate exactly what the conversation might sound like, with the client stating the reading problem and the coach offering a suggested solution from the text or personal experience.] *What questions do you have? Ready . . . Clients get a coach!* [10–25 minutes, depending on how many times you have students move to a new partner.]

3. [Have students reverse roles: Coaches become clients, and clients become coaches. Continue the process of changing partners as in Step 2.] [10–25 minutes]

4. [Discussion] *What's a reading challenge that you or one of your partners identified? What is one way to overcome this challenge? Can anyone think of another way to overcome this challenge?* [10–20 minutes]

Approximate time: 40–80 minutes

Instructor Notes

1. If you have participated in an On Course Workshop, you will recognize that this activity is an adaptation of a structure called "Eagles and Hawks."
2. Give directions carefully (including a physical demonstration of how students change partners).
3. If you have an uneven number of students, you can designate one student as an "observer." This student joins any pair that he or she chooses.
4. This activity could be spread over two class periods by dropping Step 3 on day 1. On day 2, start with Step 3 and finish, as previously, with Step 4.

EXERCISE B-2: Marking and Annotating

Purpose

To provide students with an opportunity to practice marking and annotating a reading assignment.

Supplies and Setup

Whiteboard; handout: Copy a page from *On Course* (or another text) that students have not yet read. Make three copies for every two students. In a previous class, assign students to bring with them the note-taking tools that they use when they read class assignments (e.g., pencils, pens, highlighters). Students have previously read the "Reading" section in Study Skills: A Toolbox for Active Learners.

Directions

1. [Discussion] *When you read an assignment for one of your classes, what is your purpose?* [To accurately and completely identify the key concepts, main ideas, secondary ideas, major supporting details, and minor supporting details.] *The question is, how do you remember what's important so you don't have to read all of your assignments again before a test?* [Marking and annotating what you read.] *Marking and annotating allows you to return later and* C*ollect the key concepts, important ideas, and supporting details without rereading the whole assignment.* [5 minutes]
2. *Let's brainstorm a list of helpful ways to mark or annotate your reading assignments.* [Record a list on the whiteboard: for instance, circle key concepts, underline or highlight main ideas, write comments in the margin, write questions in the margin alongside their answers in the text, use different-color highlighters for ideas of different levels of importance, write questions in the margin that you will ask in class, underline or highlight examples, put stars next to very important ideas.] [5 minutes]
3. [Distribute the handout, one to each student; hold the additional handouts for later.] *Read this text and do the best job you know how to mark and annotate it so that the key concepts, important ideas, and supporting ideas are easily seen.* [10 minutes]
4. *Now pair up with a partner.* [If there is an extra student, create one trio. Give each pair or trio a third unmarked copy of the handout.] *With your partner(s), mark and annotate this new handout by combining the best from what each of you did earlier. Remember, your goal is to mark and annotate it so that the key concepts, important ideas, and supporting ideas are easily seen.* [10 minutes]
5. *Now, each pair, join another pair.* [If there is an extra pair, create one sextet.] [Collect the just-completed handouts from each group. Mix up the handouts and redistribute two handouts to each group, making sure that no group gets a handout created by any of its members.] *Choose a group spokesperson. The spokesperson's job will be to tell us which handout you think has the better marking and annotating . . . and why. That means you'll be explaining specific examples of effective marking and annotating. And, if there's something that you think would improve the marking and annotating, tell us that as well.* [10 minutes]
6. [Call on team spokespersons to present the positive marking and annotating features their groups found in their chosen handout. Urge each presenter to be specific about what positive techniques were used and what concepts, ideas, or details were highlighted. Ask the presenter if there is anything the group thought would improve the marking and highlighting.] [10–20 minutes]

Approximate time: 50–60 minutes

Instructor Notes

1. In my experience, some students are initially reluctant to write in their college books. Sometimes this is a carryover from high school where they were forbidden to write in their school-owned books. Sometimes it is because students plan to sell their books after the course and don't want to lower their value by writing in them. If you face such reluctance, consider reminding students that now they (not the school) own their books and should use them for maximum learning and high grades. Additionally, they will receive only a small fraction of their purchase price back, and it would be a false economy to trade deep and lasting learning for a few extra dollars in used book sales, especially when the cost of books is such a small percentage of their investment of money and time to earn their education.
2. If you mix up the handouts well in Step 5, no student or group will know who created the handouts not chosen. Thus, no student should experience being the "loser" of a competition.

EXERCISE B-3: My Academic Skills Plan for Reading

Purpose

Using the Wise Choice Process (from *On Course*, Chapter 2), each student designs a Personal Academic Skills plan to overcome a specific challenge he or she has with reading. The goal of this Academic Skills Plan is for each student to identify one or more specific strategies that he or she will experiment with to improve reading skills. By using this powerful decision-making model, students not only solve a problem with reading; they also strengthen critical and creative thinking skills that will empower them to solve many other problems in their lives.

Supplies and Setup

Students have completed reading the section in Study Skills: A Toolbox for Active Learners titled "Reading." Handouts: 1) "Sample Academic Skills Plan for Reading" and 2) "My Academic Skills Plan for Reading" [blank] following this exercise, one of each for all students. You may want to have extra blank forms on hand in case students need a clean form.

Directions

1. *In this activity, you'll use the six steps of the Wise Choice Process to design a personal academic skills plan for improving your reading. In your plan, you'll identify a specific strategy you will experiment with to improve this important study skill. For an example of how to complete each of the six steps, refer to the handout titled "Sample Academic Skills Plan for Reading."* [5 minutes]

2. *On your blank "My Academic Skills Plan for Reading," complete Step 1:* **What is your present situation?** *In the box, write the biggest challenge you have with reading. For suggestions, refer to the list of "Challenges with Reading" in* On Course. *Remember, for an example of how to complete all of the six steps, refer to the "Sample Academic Skills Plan for Reading."* [5 minutes]

3. *Complete Step 2:* **How would you like your situation to be?** *In Step 1, you identified the biggest challenge you are having with reading. Now shift your attention from the challenge to how you would like your situation to be regarding this study skill. In the second row on your Academic Skills Plan, write one or more goals for reading. State a goal in the present tense as if it already exists (e.g., I understand . . . rather than I will understand . . . or . . . I enjoy . . . rather than I will enjoy . . .).* [5 minutes]

4. *Complete Step 3:* **What are my possible choices?** *Revisit the list of strategies for reading in* On Course. *Choose three strategies you think would help you overcome the challenge that you identified in Step 1 and help you achieve the desired situation (goals) you identified in Step 2. Write one strategy in Box 1, another strategy in Box 2, and a third strategy in Box 3.* [10 minutes]

5. *Complete Step 4:* **What's the likely outcome of each possible choice?** *Imagine yourself actually doing each of the three strategies you chose in Step 3. Write on your Academic Skills Plan what you think would be the likely outcome of doing each strategy.* [5 minutes]

6. *Complete Step 5:* **Which choice(s) will I commit to doing?** *It's now time to decide which one of the three strategies you think will best improve your learning and grades. Write the strategy on Step 5 of "My Academic Skills Plan for Reading."* [5 minutes]

7. *Complete Step 6:* **When and how will I evaluate my Academic Skills Plan for Reading?** *An effective way to evaluate any plan is to choose a future date and, at that time, compare your situation then with how you would like it to be. If at that future time you have achieved your goal(s) as described in Step 2, consider your plan a success. If your results in the future fall short of your goal(s), then the plan isn't working and needs revision. To evaluate accurately, it is helpful to make your goals as specific as possible. Because some goals are inherently general and difficult to measure (e.g., I enjoy taking notes), it helps if you create a scale (e.g., 1–10) on which to assess these general goals. Write your criteria for deciding whether or not your Academic Skills Plan for Reading is a success.* [5 minutes]

8. DISCUSSION: Invite students to share their Academic Skills Plans. If time allows, start with a Pair-Share and then move to a Whole-Group Discussion; if short of time, start with a Whole-Group Discussion. [10–20 minutes]

Approximate time: 50–60 minutes

Instructor Notes

Consider having students turn in a written assessment of their experiment with new study skills.

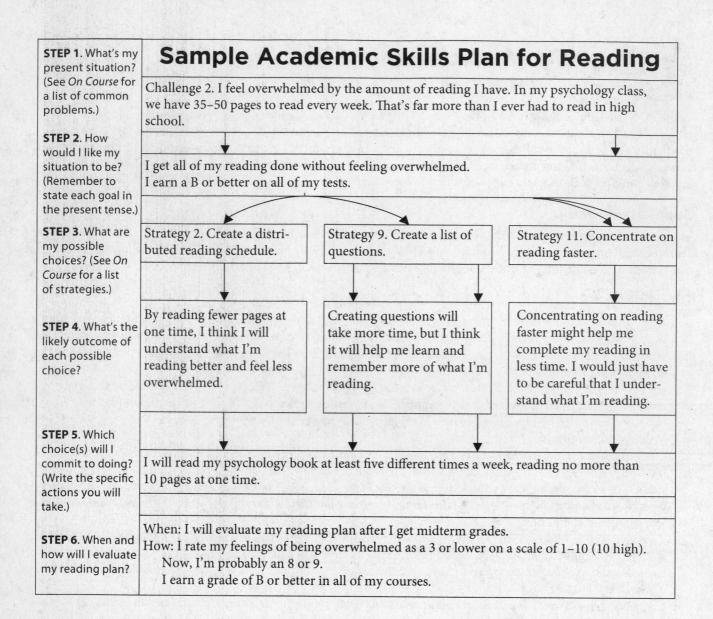

STEP 1. What's my present situation? (See *On Course* for a list of common problems.)

STEP 2. How would I like my situation to be? (Remember to state each goal in the present tense.)

STEP 3. What are my possible choices? (See *On Course* for a list of strategies.)

STEP 4. What's the likely outcome of each possible choice?

STEP 5. Which choice(s) will I commit to doing? (Write the specific actions you will take.)

STEP 6. When and how will I evaluate my reading plan?

Sample Academic Skills Plan for Reading

Challenge 2. I feel overwhelmed by the amount of reading I have. In my psychology class, we have 35–50 pages to read every week. That's far more than I ever had to read in high school.

I get all of my reading done without feeling overwhelmed.
I earn a B or better on all of my tests.

Strategy 2. Create a distributed reading schedule.

Strategy 9. Create a list of questions.

Strategy 11. Concentrate on reading faster.

By reading fewer pages at one time, I think I will understand what I'm reading better and feel less overwhelmed.

Creating questions will take more time, but I think it will help me learn and remember more of what I'm reading.

Concentrating on reading faster might help me complete my reading in less time. I would just have to be careful that I understand what I'm reading.

I will read my psychology book at least five different times a week, reading no more than 10 pages at one time.

When: I will evaluate my reading plan after I get midterm grades.
How: I rate my feelings of being overwhelmed as a 3 or lower on a scale of 1–10 (10 high).
　　 Now, I'm probably an 8 or 9.
　　 I earn a grade of B or better in all of my courses.

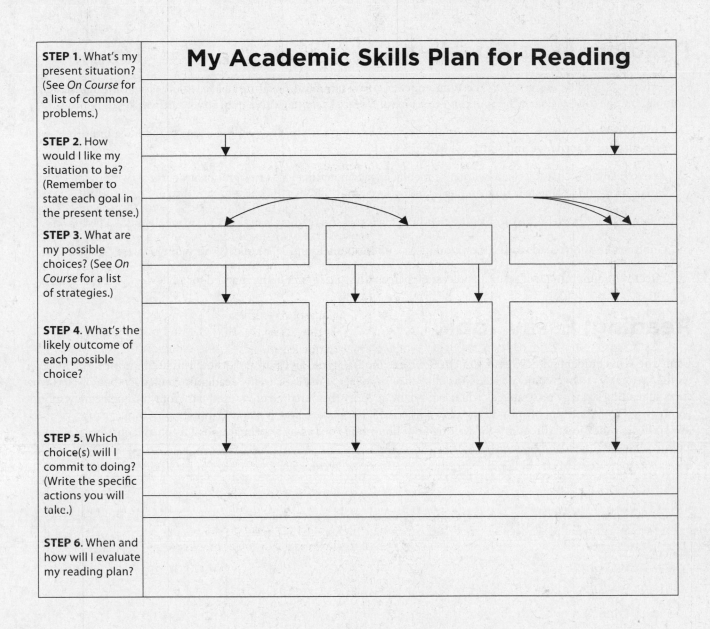

My Academic Skills Plan for Reading

STEP 1. What's my present situation? (See *On Course* for a list of common problems.)

STEP 2. How would I like my situation to be? (Remember to state each goal in the present tense.)

STEP 3. What are my possible choices? (See *On Course* for a list of strategies.)

STEP 4. What's the likely outcome of each possible choice?

STEP 5. Which choice(s) will I commit to doing? (Write the specific actions you will take.)

STEP 6. When and how will I evaluate my reading plan?

Reading: Quiz Questions

(The Answer Key to Reading: Quiz Questions appears at the end of this Facilitator's Manual. Please visit the Instructor Companion Site for *On Course* at login.cengage.com for a digital version of this quiz and its answer key.)

1. **C**ollecting knowledge is the first step in the CORE Learning System, and reading is one of the most important ways of **C**ollecting knowledge and skills.   TRUE   FALSE

2. Active reading is characterized by intense mental engagement that leads to significant neural activity in the brain, assists deep and lasting learning, and leads to high grades.   TRUE   FALSE

3. When reading actively, the most significant information in the reading is in the supporting details.   TRUE   FALSE

4. Good readers don't read words; they read ideas, and ideas are found in chunks (groups of words).   TRUE   FALSE

5. Effective highlighting will result in at least 60 percent of a paragraph being marked for review.   TRUE   FALSE

Reading: Essay Topic

Using the "One Student's Story" essays in *On Course* as models, write an essay about how you used one or more new reading strategies to overcome an academic challenge in college. First explain the academic challenge; then discuss what specific reading strategy or strategies you used; finally, identify the outcome of your efforts. Your instructor may submit your essay for possible publication in the next edition of *On Course*, where it could inspire tens of thousands of your fellow students. Additional directions for writing and submitting your essay may be found at http://oncourseworkshop .com/course-textbook/essay-contest/.

C. Taking Notes

EXERCISE C-1: Academic Coaches (Option 2)

Purpose

To help students identify note-taking challenges in college classes and possible solutions to those problems.

Supplies and Setup

Whiteboard or easel pad for recording ideas from brainstorm. This activity is done over two class periods.

Directions

Note: Tis activity can be repeated with each study skill. It uses a learning structure called the "Jigsaw." Numerous websites discuss other ways to use this multipurpose structure.

Day 1:

1. [Students in pairs] *With your partner, make a list of the challenges a student might face when trying to take complete and accurate notes during a college class. For example, one challenge is misunderstanding what the main idea of the class session is. Another challenge occurs when the professor talks very fast. List as many note-taking challenges as you can in five minutes. Begin!* [5 minutes]

2. [Conduct a class brainstorm of the challenges of taking complete and accurate notes during a college class. Encourage students to identify challenges that might occur during lectures, class discussions, class activities, and labs. Record the items on a whiteboard or easel pad.] [10 minutes]

3. *In a moment, I'm going to ask you each to vote for the four challenges that are most like your own. So look over the list and decide which four you will vote for.* [Pause while students decide. Then ask them to vote for four and tally the votes for each challenge. Identify the four challenges that received the most votes.] [5–10 minutes]

4. [Have each pair join another pair, creating groups of four students. Extra students make a group of five.] *You are now in your "home group." Decide who will become your home group's Academic Coach for each of the four note-taking challenges. This person will learn strategies for overcoming the challenge and coach the rest of you at our next class. Because teaching something is a great way to learn it, you might want to choose the note-taking challenge that gives you the most difficulty. If you have five in your group, two people double up on one of the challenges.* [5 minutes]

5. [Assign homework to read "Wise Choices in College: Taking Notes."] As you read, look for the best strategies for overcoming the note-taking challenge so you can coach your home team on them in our next class. Obviously if you're absent or unprepared, your group is going to suffer. What questions do you have? [5 minutes]

Day 2:

6. [Have students re-form their home groups so they will know where to go in Step 7.] *Before you do any coaching, you're going to leave your home group and meet with other coaches who chose the same note-taking challenge that you did. You'll have 15 minutes in your expert coaches' group to exchange ideas and come up with the very best strategies. Then you'll return to your home group to coach others in the strategies that you have learned.* [Indicate corners of the room where each group of expert coaches is to work and have students move to their group.] [20 minutes]

7. *Return to your home group. Go around the group, with each coach teaching just one strategy to the group. If there's time, keep going around the group, sharing only one strategy at a time.* [20 minutes]

8. [Class Discussion] *What were the best solutions you learned for our first note-taking challenge? The second note-taking challenge? The third? The fourth? How did it affect your learning to know that you were going to be coaching your group?* [10–20 minutes]

Approximate time: Class 1: 20–35 minutes; **Class 2**: 50–60 minutes

EXERCISE C-2: The Lecture

Purpose

To offer students an opportunity to assess their note-taking skills.

Supplies and Setup

You will need the ability to show a lecture, using either a DVD or the Internet. The advantage of using a pre-recorded lecture (as opposed to presenting one live) is that students can go back later and see where they missed key concepts, main ideas, and supporting details. Here are some of the many lectures that can be viewed on the Internet:

- www.YouTube.com: Search for **Psych 1—General Psychology—Lecture 2** (approximately 40 minutes). This is one of a series of lectures from University of California–Berkeley and is the most academic of the lectures listed here.
- www.YouTube.com: Search for **Randy Pausch Last Lecture**. This is the most inspirational of the lectures listed here. It does a great job of reinforcing many of the concepts presented in *On Course*. The full version runs well over an hour. One edited version of 44 minutes will fit into a class period.
- www.Ted.com: Search for **Ken Robinson says schools kill creativity** (approximately 20 minutes).
- www.Ted.com: Search for **Robert Wright: How cooperation (eventually) trumps conflict** (approximately 20 minutes). This lecture is also a good one to show in Chapter 5: Interdependence.

Note: The directions assume that you will show the lecture during class. As an alternative, you can assign Step 1 for homework, which will save class time for having students assess and discuss their notes. Of course, to save time, you could also choose to show only part of the lecture.

Directions

1. *I am going to show a video of a lecture. As you listen, please take the very best notes you know how. Make every effort to record completely and accurately the key concepts, main ideas, and supporting details.* [If some students don't have note-taking materials, you may want to discuss the importance of bringing such materials to every class.] [Show the video.] [10–60 minutes, depending on the length of the lecture and how much you choose to show]
2. [Place students in pairs. I recommend putting the following directions on the board, a handout, or a PowerPoint slide, rather than giving them orally.] *Compare notes with your partner and . . .*
   A. *Identify at least two similarities.*
   B. *Identify at least two differences.*
   C. *Identify at least two strengths for each person's notes.*
   D. *Identify at least two areas for improvement for each person's notes.*
   E. *Identify your greatest challenges in taking good notes on this lecture.*
   F. *On a scale of 0–10 (with 10 high), rate the completeness and accuracy of your own notes.* [10–15 minutes]
3. [Journal Writing and/or Class Discussion] *What happened while you were taking notes? What difficulties did you encounter? If you were to sum up the speaker's lecture in one sentence, what would you say? What similarities did you notice between your notes and your partner's notes? What differences? What strengths did you find in your notes? What score did you give your own notes and why? What areas for improvement did you find in your own notes? Regarding note-taking, what will you do differently?* [10–25 minutes]

Approximate time: 30–105 minutes (depending on whether you show the lecture video in class)

Instructor Notes

You can have students do this activity before and/or after they read about note-taking in the text. If the activity is done both before and after students read about note taking, they can assess changes (and hopefully improvements) in their note-taking skills.

EXERCISE C-3: A Picture is Worth a Thousand Words

Purpose

Students typically struggle with taking notes from a graph, chart, or map. When an entire slide in a presentation consists of a graph, chart, or map, the students look at it in class and listen to the professor speak, but they either don't know what to write or don't write anything in their notebooks. This exercise will help students understand not only the importance of writing something but also knowing what to write.

Supplies and Setup

A premade PowerPoint presentation consisting of three or four slides. Use at least one graph, one map, and one chart (some suggestions follow). Before class, the instructor should study each one so that he or she can speak for a minute or two on each slide, essentially replicating a lecture.

Directions

1. Tell the students you will be discussing three or four slides in class that are important and then proceed through the slides and your one- to two-minute lecture on each.
2. When finished, have students pair up and compare notes: What is the same? What is different?
3. Get back together in one group and discuss what types of multiple-choice questions could be asked on an exam where the answer would come from these slides.

Approximate time: 25–45 minutes (depending on the length of discussion time)

Instructor Notes

It's important for students to understand the meaning of *purpose*. What is the professor's purpose in showing a graph, chart, or map as opposed to a slide with words? Next, students need to understand the parts of each. For example, does the graph, chart, or map have a title? Are there words on it? A legend? And, finally, what are the areas that the professor is focusing on during the discussion? Search the Internet to find representative images. Here are some examples:

- A map from Arbor Day detailing changes in hardiness zones (search at www.arborday.org)
- A chart from an Excel spreadsheet tutorial
- A graph from the Business Insider (search at www.businessinsider.com)

Source: Submitted by Melanie Marine, University of Wisconsin–Oshkosh, WI

EXERCISE C-4: Studying is a Process

Purpose

This activity will help students understand that studying in college is a multiple-step process that takes place over time. Over the course of five classes, this activity will give students a practical experience with the C.O.R.E. Learning System.

Supplies and Setup

None

Directions

1. After discussing the note-taking section in class, assign students to submit one full class period's lecture notes to you. (Depending on how often you meet, a general-type class that has an exam in two to three weeks would be best.) Read over these notes and write feedback on them; then give them back to the students in the next class period.

2. In the next class period, discuss the text section in *On Course* on organizing study materials. Then, as an assignment for the next class period, have the students create study materials using strategies from the section on Organizing Study Materials.

3. In the third class period, have the students show their study materials to their classmates and explain two things: why did they choose that particular way to organize and how creating the study materials helped them retain information about that lecture. Then assign students to create three or four test questions that could possibly come from that lecture and have this due for the next class period (just the questions).

4. In the fourth class period, discuss the section on taking tests. During class, have students take the test questions they developed in Step 3 and write each of them as a complete multiple-choice question, like their professor would have on the exam. At the end of class, make sure they turn in these questions.

5. At the beginning of the fifth class period, hand back the quizzes they developed in Step 4 and give them five minutes to take this "pop quiz." After the five minutes, allow them to grade their "quizzes." Then conduct a class discussion on this process. How did they do on the quiz? Why do they feel they got the score they did? What did they like? Not like? Did they discover anything about themselves? About studying?

Approximate time: Portions of five class meeting (depending on the length of your course, as well as how long each class period is)

Instructor Notes

1. If you have access to your students' schedules, you may find that a number of them have courses in common. You can divide them into groups based on courses they have in common and do this assignment but add a "group study" component between weeks 2 and 3 and then again between weeks 3 and 4.

2. The most important part of this long assignment is the discussion at the end. Many of my students constantly say, "I don't have any homework to do." They are still thinking in "high school mode," where class was held every day, they had worksheets to complete on a regular basis, and the teacher told them every single day what needed to be done. Especially if your campus has a high number of first-generation college students, "how to study" can become a serious problem. By taking one lecture step by step through the entire C.O.R.E. Learning System, you are essentially making the students study. Letting them know that this is the process for every lecture in every class will show them what they need to accomplish to be successful students!

Source: Submitted by Melanie Marine, University of Wisconsin–Oshkosh, WI

EXERCISE C-5: My Academic Skills Plan for Taking Notes

Purpose

Using the Wise Choice Process (from *On Course*, Chapter 2), each student designs a Personal Academic Skills plan to overcome a specific challenge he or she has with taking notes. The goal of this Academic Skills Plan is for each student to identify one or more specific strategies that he or she will experiment with to improve note-taking skills. By using this powerful decision-making model, students not only solve a problem with taking notes; they also strengthen critical and creative thinking skills that will empower them to solve many other problems in their lives.

Supplies and Setup

Students have completed reading the section in Study Skills: A Toolbox for Active Learners titled "Taking Notes." Handouts: 1) "Sample Academic Skills Plan for Taking Notes" and 2) "My Academic Skills Plan for Taking Notes" [blank] following this exercise, one of each for all students. You may want to have extra blank forms on hand in case students need a clean form.

Directions

1. *In this activity, you'll use the six steps of the Wise Choice Process to design a personal academic skills plan for improving your ability to take complete and accurate notes. In your plan, you'll identify a specific strategy you will experiment with to improve this important study skill. For an example of how to complete each of the six steps, refer to the handout titled "Sample Academic Skills Plan for Taking Notes."* [5 minutes]

2. *On your blank "My Academic Skills Plan for Taking Notes," complete Step 1:* **What is your present situation?** *In the box, write the biggest challenge you have with taking notes. For suggestions, refer to the list of "Challenges with Taking Notes" in* On Course. *Remember, for an example of how to complete all of the six steps, refer to the "Sample Academic Skills Plan for Taking Notes."* [5 minutes]

3. *Complete Step 2:* **How would you like your situation to be?** *In Step 1, you identified the biggest challenge you are having with taking notes. Now shift your attention from the challenge to how you would like your situation to be regarding this study skill. In the second row on your Academic Skills Plan, write one or more goals for taking notes. State a goal in the present tense as if it already exists (e.g., I understand . . . rather than I will understand . . . or . . . I enjoy . . . rather than I will enjoy . . .).* [5 minutes]

4. *Complete Step 3:* **What are my possible choices?** *Revisit the list of strategies for taking notes in* On Course. *Choose three strategies you think would help you overcome the challenge that you identified in Step 1 and help you achieve the desired situation (goals) you identified in Step 2. Write one strategy in Box 1, another strategy in Box 2, and a third strategy in Box 3.* [10 minutes]

5. *Complete Step 4:* **What's the likely outcome of each possible choice?** *Imagine yourself actually doing each of the three strategies you chose in Step 3. Write on your Academic Skills Plan what you think would be the likely outcome of doing each strategy.* [5 minutes]

6. *Complete Step 5:* **Which choice(s) will I commit to doing?** *It's now time to decide which one of the three strategies you think will best improve your learning and grades. Write the strategy on Step 5 of "My Academic Skills Plan for Taking Notes."* [5 minutes]

7. *Complete Step 6:* **When and how will I evaluate my Academic Skills Plan for Reading?** *An effective way to evaluate any plan is to choose a future date and, at that time, compare your situation then with how you would like it to be. If at that future time you have achieved your goal(s) as described in Step 2, consider your plan a success. If your results in the future fall short of your goal(s), then the plan isn't working and needs revision. To evaluate accurately, it is helpful to make your goals as specific as possible. Because some goals are inherently general and difficult to measure (e.g., I enjoy taking notes), it helps if you create a scale (e.g., 1–10) on which to assess these general goals. Write your criteria for deciding whether or not your Academic Skills Plan for Reading is a success.* [5 minutes]

8. DISCUSSION: Invite students to share their Academic Skills Plans. If time allows, start with a Pair-Share and then move to a Whole-Group Discussion; if short of time, start with a Whole-Group Discussion. [10–20 minutes]

Approximate time: 50–60 minutes

Instructor Notes

Consider having students turn in a written assessment of their experiment with new study skills.

Sample Academic Skills Plan for Taking Notes

STEP 1. What's my present situation? (See *On Course* for a list of common problems.)	Challenge 22. I like math, but my class notes are worthless when it comes time to study for a test.
STEP 2. How would I like my situation to be? (Remember to state each goal in the present tense.)	I take notes in my math class that are a great help in studying for tests. When I show my notes to my study group, everyone tells me how helpful they are.
STEP 3. What are my possible choices? (See *On Course* for a list of strategies.)	Strategy 3. Complete all reading assignments and homework problems before attending class. / Strategy 18. Use three-column notes for math. / Strategy 22. Compare notes with my study group.
STEP 4. What's the likely outcome of each possible choice?	Coming to class prepared should help me better understand what the instructor is doing when he's solving problems on the board. That should help me take better notes. / Taking three-column notes will help me remember how the instructor solved each step of the problem. It's going to be a little hard at first because I've never done this before. / Comparing notes will show me how my classmates are taking notes. This may give me some other ideas about how to improve my class notes.
STEP 5. Which choice(s) will I' commit to doing? (Write the specific actions you will take.)	Practice three-column notes with my homework. Then use three-column notes for all problems the instructor solves in class. I'll suggest to my study group that we all take three-column notes so we can compare and improve.
STEP 6. When and how will I evaluate my reading plan?	When: I'll evaluate my note-taking plan at each study group meeting and when I study for the next test. How: I will ask my study group to rate the helpfulness of my three-column notes. When I study for each test, I rate my own notes at least an 8 (with 10 high).

STEP 1. What's my present situation? (See *On Course* for a list of common problems.)

STEP 2. How would I like my situation to be? (Remember to state each goal in the present tense.)

STEP 3. What are my possible choices? (See *On Course* for a list of strategies.)

STEP 4. What's the likely outcome of each possible choice?

STEP 5. Which choice(s) will I commit to doing? (Write the specific actions you will take.)

STEP 6. When and how will I evaluate my reading plan?

My Academic Skills Plan for Taking Notes

Taking Notes: Quiz Questions

(The Answer Key to Taking Notes: Quiz Questions appears at the end of this Facilitator's Manual. Please visit the Instructor Companion Site for *On Course* at login.cengage.com for a digital version of this quiz and its answer key.)

1. In the pursuit of a four-year degree, students spend nearly 400 hours in a formal classroom.   TRUE   FALSE

2. The goal of taking notes is to get down "everything that the instructor says."   TRUE   FALSE

3. Victims allow wandering thoughts to sabotage their learning.   TRUE   FALSE

4. In a study by Kenneth Kiewra, it was found that lecture notes taken by first-year students contain, on average, only _____ of the critical ideas presented during a class.

    A. 5 percent

    B. 11 percent

    C. 75 percent

    D. half

    E. the first and last

5. When taking notes in the class of a speed talker, what can you do to be a speed note taker?

    A. Condense: listen for a minute, note the key concept or main idea, and then paraphrase in your own words.

    B. Leave blank spaces for missed material—you can talk with a classmate after class to fill in the blanks.

    C. Create your own personal shorthand—use a system of abbreviations.

    D. All of the above

    E. None of the above

Taking Notes: Essay Topic

Using the "One Student's Story" essays in *On Course* as models, write an essay about how you used one or more new note-taking strategies to overcome an academic challenge in college. First explain the academic challenge; then discuss what specific note-taking strategy or strategies you used; finally, identify the outcome of your efforts. Your instructor may submit your essay for possible publication in the next edition of *On Course*, where it could inspire tens of thousands of your fellow students. Additional directions for writing and submitting these essays may be found at http://oncourseworkshop.com/course-textbook/essay-contest/.

D. Organizing Study Materials

EXERCISE D-1: Concept Maps

Purpose

To provide students with practice in organizing key concepts, main and secondary ideas, and major and minor supporting details with the use of a concept map.

Supplies and Setup

Sticky notes in five colors (about 25 of each color for each group of three or four students); two easel pad pages and markers for each group of students; tape to hang easel pad pages on the wall. Assign students to read Creating a Self-Management System and "Organizing Study Materials" before coming to class. Encourage them to mark and annotate the reading assignment as they learned to do in the "Reading" section in Study Skills: A Toolbox for Active Learners.

Directions

1. [Review with students the idea of levels of significance of information: key concepts, main and secondary ideas, and major and minor supporting details. These ideas were first introduced in the "Reading" section in the Study Skills: A Toolbox for Active Learners.] [5 minutes]
2. [With students in groups, provide each group with sticky notes in five colors (about 25 of each color). Designate a color for each of the five levels of significance. For example:

   Green = Key concept

   Yellow = Main idea

   Blue = Secondary idea

   Orange = Major supporting detail

   Pink = Minor supporting detail] [5 minutes]
3. *Read through Creating a Self-Management System and create a sticky note for each key concept, main idea, secondary idea, major supporting detail, and minor supporting detail. Write the information on the appropriate-color sticky note and post it on one easel pad page.* **During this part of the activity, no one may talk.** [10 minutes]
4. [Review how to create a concept map.] [5 minutes]
5. *Move sticky notes around on your easel pad page until they form a helpful concept map. Then use your markers to draw the concept map on your other easel pad page.* **You may talk during this part of the activity.** *When you are finished, tape your group's concept map on the wall.* [10 minutes]
6. [Gallery Walk: Invite students to walk around, viewing the concept maps of other groups. Ask students to draw a star with a colored marker on the best concept map created by a group other than their own.] [5 minutes]
7. [Class Discussion] [Identify the concept map that has the most stars.] *What do you like about this concept map? What would you add or change to improve it? What did you learn or relearn? How will you use concept maps to organize study materials? Are there courses for which concept maps might be ideal? Less than ideal?* [Time permitting, you could repeat the discussion about the concept map that has the second most stars.] [10–20 minutes]

Approximate time: 50–60 minutes

EXERCISE D-2: Cornell Study Sheets

Purpose

To provide students with practice in creating effective Cornell study sheets.

Supplies and Setup

Students in groups of four (if you have extra students, create one to three groups of five); one 9 × 12 envelope for each group; three blue index cards for each student; three green index cards for each student; two white index cards for each student; one "Cornell Study Sheet" handout (following this exercise) for each student. In a previous class, assign students to read "Believing in Yourself: Develop Self-Confidence" and write Journal Entry 15.

Directions

1. [Give each group one large envelope. Distribute to each student three blue index cards, three green index cards, two white index cards, and one Cornell Study Sheet handout.] [5 minutes]
2. *The first step of creating a Cornell study sheet is to copy your polished notes into Section A. Usually, these notes will be either an outline or a concept map. You can see that Section A of your Cornell Study Sheet handout has already been completed with an informal outline. The second step of creating a Cornell study sheet is writing questions in Section B about the information found in Section A. Take your three blue index cards and write one question on each about the information found in Section A; then place the cards in your group's envelope. This is an individual activity, so there should be no talking at this time.* [5 minutes]
3. *The third step of creating a Cornell study sheet is writing key concepts, terms, or names in Section B alongside their definitions or explanations in Section A. Take your three green index cards and write one key concept, term, or name from Section A on each card; then place the cards in your group's envelope.* [5 minutes]
4. *The fourth step of creating a Cornell study sheet is writing in Section C a summary of the information in Section A. Take one white index card and write a summary of the information in Section A. The second white card is available in case you want to copy over what you wrote on your first card. When you have completed writing your summary, place the white index card in your group's envelope.* [5–10 minutes]
5. *Exchange envelopes with another team. Then exchange again with another team. Empty the contents of the envelope and group the cards by color. Starting with the blue cards, read and discuss each question with your group members. Then each person, individually, choose the questions you think would be most helpful to study this material and write them in Section B on your Cornell Study Sheet handout.* [5–10 minutes]
6. *Now go through the green cards with your group. Again, read and discuss each key term with your group members. Then each person, individually, choose the key terms you think would be most helpful to study this material and write them in Section B on your Cornell Study Sheet handout.* [5 minutes]
7. *Now go through the white cards. Read and discuss each summary. Then each person, individually, choose the summary you think would be most helpful to study this material and write it in Section C on your Cornell Study Sheet handout. Feel free to revise the summary if you think you can improve upon it.* [10 minutes]
8. [Journal Writing and/or Class Discussion] *What did you learn or relearn about using Cornell study sheets to organize your study materials? What is a plus (positive) about Cornell study sheets? What is a minus (negative) about Cornell study sheets? What do you find most interesting about Cornell study sheets?* [10 minutes]

Approximate time: 50–60 minutes

Instructor Notes

1. Obviously, any color index cards will work fine as long as you have three different colors.
2. The purpose of exchanging envelopes twice in Step 5 is to make it highly unlikely that students know whose cards they are working with.
3. You can reduce the time of this activity by reducing the number of students in each group.

Cornell Study Sheet

Section A "Develop Self-Confidence"

Importance of self-confidence: We are unlikely to accomplish more than we believe we can.
  • Example: Student wasn't sure she was "cut out for college."

Three ways to develop greater self-confidence

1. Create a success identity.

  How: Stack one small victory on another.
      • Example: Nathan McCall—After spending time in prison, he built self-confidence by graduating from college, getting a job with newspaper, becoming bureau chief, and publishing best seller. Each victory raised his self-confidence.

2. Celebrate your successes and talents.

  How: Acknowledge small and large victories.
    —Victory cards: Write at least one success per day on an index card and read through the deck every day.
    —Celebrate and reward yourself for successes, even small ones, with dinner out, seeing a movie, and so on.
      • Example: An 8-year-old girl writes praise on her school work.

3. Visualize purposeful actions done well.

  How: Create mental picture using all five senses.
    —Experiment by psychologist Charles Garfield: Visualizing helped a group of nervous speakers improve more than two other groups that didn't visualize.

Result: These actions increase self-confidence and lead to a core belief that says, "I CAN."

EXERCISE D-3: Compare and Contrast Charts

Purpose

Students typically struggle with test questions that use phrases similar to "all of the following are true EXCEPT" and "which of the follow is NOT true." Using a compare and contrast chart to help differentiate between similar information can help students see what they might be tested on.

Supplies and Setup

Copies of the "Compare and Contrast Chart Notes" and the "Compare and Contrast Chart" (following this exercise); enough small wipe boards to give one to each group of two to three students (or students can write the charts on the board in the classroom, or they can write on pieces of paper and use a doc cam to show the other students)

Directions

1. Before class, assign for homework "Organizing Study Materials" in Study Skills: A Toolbox for Active Learners.
2. Place students into pairs or trios. Give each group the sheet with the notes on it. Have the students fill out the blank Compare and Contrast Chart using the notes on the handout.
3. When all students are finished, have one student from each group show the rest of the class the Compare and Contrast Chart that his or her group created. The student must explain to the class HOW each row is either similar or different.

Approximate time: 25–45 minutes (depending on the length of discussion time)

Instructor Notes

1. It's important to point out that empty boxes are okay; that is something that would be remembered on a test (e.g., "Which of the following Indigenous groups did NOT have a writing system?").
2. Additionally, upon completion of the Compare and Contrast Chart, either the instructor or students could give examples of possible test questions—for example, "All of the following are true about the Mayans EXCEPT. . . ."
3. Ideally, if all your students are enrolled in a paired class, asking the instructor of that class to give you notes to go through and then choosing different sections of similar material would be most meaningful. Additionally, you could divide students into groups based on courses they are enrolled in together, have them bring their notebooks from that class, and then have them create the Compare and Contrast Chart for a future exam.

Source: Submitted by Melanie Marine, University of Wisconsin–Oshkosh, WI

Compare and Contrast Chart Notes

	Use the following notes to develop your chart:
The Maya	Developed in Guatemalan highlands
	Spread to Honduras, Belize, and Yucatan
	Architecture: pyramids—Chichen Itza
	Advanced in math, astronomy, calendar
	Writing system (glyphs)
	Collapse: 1. military conflict (most probable), 2. natural disaster, 3. soil exhaustion, 4. epidemic disease
The Aztec	1325 AD establishment of Tenochtitlan on an island in Lake Texcoco
	Adopted Toltec culture
	Subjects had to pay tribute to rulers
	Very militaristic; importance of human sacrifices
	Conquered in 1519 by Cortes: superior weapons, alliances with subjugated tribes, legend predicted return of fair-skinned god assisted by a native woman
The Inca	Large empire stretching from Ecuador to Chile
	Focused on the city of Cuzco
	Taxes were paid through labor (mita)
	Extensive road network with bridges
	Imperial relay runners (Chasqui)
	Sophisticated architecture: mortarless masonry
	Advance agriculture: terracing
	No writing or calendar
	Kept records with strings and knots = Quipus
	Conquered in 1532

Compare and Contrast Chart

Category	Maya	Aztec	Inca
Where developed?			
Agriculture?			
Architecture?			
Tribute/taxes?			
Advanced in/distinguishing characteristic?			
Writing system?			
Focused on what city?			
Collapsed/Conquered?			
Toltecs?			

Example: Completed Compare and Contrast Chart

Category	Mayas	Aztecs	Incas
Where developed?	Developed in Guatemalan highlands in 3000 BC; spread to Honduras, Yucatan Tol Peninsula	Tenochtitlan developed on an island in Lake Texcoco in 1325 AD	Large empire stretching from Ecuador to Chile
Agriculture?	Based on subsistence agriculture		Advanced agriculture = terracing
Architecture?	Architecture = pyramids		Architecture = mortarless masonry
Tribute/taxes?		Subjects had to pay tribute to rulers = taxes	Taxes were paid through labor (mita)
Advanced in/distinguishing characteristic?	Advanced in math, astronomy, and calendars		No calendar
Writing system?	Writing was called glyphs		No writing; kept records with Quipus using imperial relay runners (Chasqui)
Focused on what city?	Focused on city of Chichen Itza in the Yucatan		Focused on city of Cuzco
Collapsed/conquered?	Collapsed because: Military conflict Natural disaster Soil exhaustion Epidemic diseases	Conquest of the Aztec Empire: 1519: Cortes Alliances with subjugated tribes Legend predicted return of a fair-skinned god assisted by a native woman	Conquered in 1532
Toltecs	Much of Mayan area conquered by Toltecs	Aztecs adopted the Toltec culture	

EXERCISE D-4: My Academic Skills Plan for Organizing Study Materials

Purpose

Using the Wise Choice Process (from *On Course*, Chapter 2), each student designs a Personal Academic Skills plan to overcome a specific challenge he or she has with **organizing study materials**. The goal of this Academic Skills Plan is for each student to identify one or more specific strategies that he or she will experiment with to improve **organizing study materials**. By using this powerful decision-making model, students not only solve a problem with **organizing study materials**; they also strengthen critical and creative thinking skills that will empower them to solve many other problems in their lives.

Supplies and Setup

Students have completed reading the section in Study Skills: A Toolbox for Active Learners titled "Organizing Study Materials." Handouts: 1) "Sample Academic Skills Plan for Organizing Study Materials" and 2) "My Academic Skills Plan for Organizing Study Materials" [blank] following this exercise, one of each for all students. You may want to have extra blank forms on hand in case students need a clean form.

Directions

1. *In this activity, you'll use the six steps of the Wise Choice Process to design a personal academic skills plan for improving your ability to organize your study materials. In your plan, you'll identify a specific strategy you will experiment with to improve this important study skill. For an example of how to complete each of the six steps, refer to the handout titled "Sample Academic Skills Plan for Organizing Study Materials." [5 minutes]*

2. *On your blank "My Academic Skills Plan for Organizing Study Materials," complete Step 1: **What is your present situation?** In the box, write the biggest challenge you have with organizing study materials. For suggestions, refer to the list of "Challenges with Organizing Study Materials" in On Course. Remember, for an example of how to complete all of the six steps, refer to the "Sample Academic Skills Plan for Organizing Study Materials." [5 minutes]*

3. *Complete Step 2: **How would you like your situation to be?** In Step 1, you identified the biggest challenge you are having with organizing study materials. Now shift your attention from the challenge to how you would like your situation to be regarding this study skill. In the second row on your Academic Skills Plan, write one or more goals for organizing study materials. State a goal in the present tense as if it already exists (e.g., I understand . . . rather than I will understand . . . or . . . I enjoy . . . rather than I will enjoy . . .). [5 minutes]*

4. *Complete Step 3: **What are my possible choices?** Revisit the list of strategies for organizing study materials in On Course. Choose three strategies you think would help you overcome the challenge that you identified in Step 1 and help you achieve the desired situation (goals) you identified in Step 2. Write one strategy in Box 1, another strategy in Box 2, and a third strategy in Box 3. [10 minutes]*

5. *Complete Step 4: **What's the likely outcome of each possible choice?** Imagine yourself actually doing each of the three strategies you chose in Step 3. Write on your Academic Skills Plan what you think would be the likely outcome of doing each strategy. [5 minutes]*

6. *Complete Step 5: **Which choice(s) will I commit to doing?** It's now time to decide which one of the three strategies you think will best improve your learning and grades. Write the strategy on Step 5 of "My Academic Skills Plan for Organizing Study Materials." [5 minutes]*

7. *Complete Step 6: **When and how will I evaluate my Academic Skills Plan for Organizing Study Materials?** An effective way to evaluate any plan is to choose a future date and, at that time, compare your situation then with how you would like it to be. If at that future time you have achieved your goal(s) as described in Step 2, consider your plan a success. If your results in the future fall short of your goal(s), then the plan isn't working and needs revision. To evaluate accurately, it is helpful to make your goals as specific as possible. Because some goals are inherently general and difficult to measure (e.g., I enjoy taking notes), it helps if you create a scale (e.g., 1–10) on which to assess these general goals. Write your criteria for deciding whether or not your Academic Skills Plan for Reading is a success. [5 minutes]*

8. DISCUSSION: Invite students to share their Academic Skills Plans. If time allows, start with a Pair-Share and then move to a Whole-Group Discussion; if short of time, start with a Whole-Group Discussion. [10–20 minutes]

Approximate time: 50–60 minutes

Instructor Notes

Consider having students turn in a written assessment of their experiment with new study skills.

Sample Academic Skills Plan for Organizing Study Materials

STEP 1. What's my present situation? (See *On Course* for a list of common problems.)

Challenge 19. I study for tests by going over my homework and rereading my class notes. My grades aren't nearly as good as they were in high school, so this approach isn't working.

STEP 2. How would I like my situation to be? (Remember to state each goal in the present tense.)

I have predicted and studied for all of the questions/problems that show up on my tests. My GPA is at least a 3.0.

STEP 3. What are my possible choices? (See *On Course* for a list of strategies.)

Strategy 10. Condense course materials.

Strategy 13. Create test questions.

Strategy 20. Create Cornell study sheets.

STEP 4. What's the likely outcome of each possible choice?

Condensing course materials will help me make sure I am studying all of the important information in the course.

If I get good at creating test questions, I will feel more confident that I am really well prepared for every test.

Filling out a Cornell study sheet will help me figure out what kinds of questions are likely to be on the test.

STEP 5. Which choice(s) will I commit to doing? (Write the specific actions you will take.)

I will to create at least 20 possible questions for each test, answer each one, and check my answers with a tutor in the Learning Center. Before I create the questions, I'll probably condense my course materials and make a Cornell study sheet.

STEP 6. When and how will I evaluate my reading plan?

When: After I get back each test, I will evaluate how well my academic skills plan worked.
How: My confidence going into each test is least an 8 out of 10. Presently, I'm at about a 4.
   I get at least a B on every test.

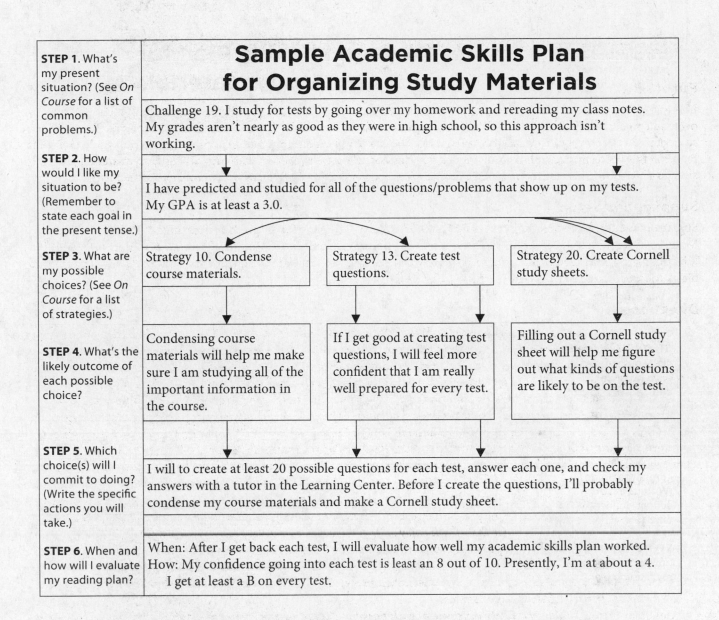

My Academic Skills Plan for Organizing Study Materials

STEP 1. What's my present situation? (See *On Course* for a list of common problems.)

STEP 2. How would I like my situation to be? (Remember to state each goal in the present tense.)

STEP 3. What are my possible choices? (See *On Course* for a list of strategies.)

STEP 4. What's the likely outcome of each possible choice?

STEP 5. Which choice(s) will I commit to doing? (Write the specific actions you will take.)

STEP 6. When and how will I evaluate my reading plan?

Organizing Study Materials: Quiz Questions

(The Answer Key to Organizing Study Materials: Quiz Questions appears at the end of this Facilitator's Manual. Please visit the Instructor Companion Site for *On Course* at login.cengage.com for a digital version of this quiz and its answer key.)

1. Quality processing of information leads to a deep understanding of what we are learning.   TRUE   FALSE

2. After **C**ollecting information (e.g., through reading and taking notes) from course materials, we begin to develop a deep understanding of what we are learning by immediately **R**ehearsing the knowledge we have **C**ollected.   TRUE   FALSE

3. The goal of **O**rganizing our **C**ollected information is the creation of many different kinds of effective study materials.   TRUE   FALSE

4. Creators hold the core belief that their ability to learn can be improved.   TRUE   FALSE

5. Good learners condense the information they have **C**ollected (from reading assignments and taking notes) into the key concepts, main ideas, and supporting details of the course.   TRUE   FALSE

Organizing Study Materials: Essay Topic

Using the "One Student's Story" essays in *On Course* as models, write an essay about how you used one or more new strategies for organizing study materials to overcome an academic challenge in college. First explain the academic challenge; then discuss what specific organizing strategy or strategies you used; finally, identify the outcome of your efforts. Your instructor may submit your essay for possible publication in the next edition of *On Course*, where it could inspire tens of thousands of your fellow students. Additional directions for writing and submitting these essays may be found at http://oncourseworkshop.com/course-textbook/essay-contest/.

E. Rehearsing and Memorizing Study Materials

EXERCISE E-1: Quiz Me

Purpose

To offer students the experience of creating flashcards and rehearsing the answers to possible test questions.

Supplies and Setup

In a previous class, assign students to read Chapter 5 in *On Course* (or whatever part of the text you want to cover at this time). Index cards, eight for each student; "Directions for Playing 'Quiz Me'" handout (following this exercise), one for each student. This activity is distributed over three class periods. Optional: Prizes for the winners.

Directions

Class 1:

1. [Discussion] *We're now going to look at a study strategy that will help you create deep and lasting learning . . . and help you earn better test scores. First, what kinds of questions can an instructor ask you on a test?* [List answers on the board: true/false, multiple choice, matching, fill in the blank (completion), short answer (paragraph), essay, problems, and so on. Ask for a definition and example of each kind of question, perhaps putting examples on the board.] [5–10 minutes]

2. [Give out eight index cards to each student and the "Directions for Playing Quiz Me" handout. Have volunteers read aloud the Day 1 part of the directions. Review the directions and make sure that everyone understands.] *Your ticket to play the game in our next class is two identical sets of four flashcards. No cards, no play! If you know of anyone who's not here, tell them what they need to do before our next class. See you then!* [If you plan to give a prize, you could announce what the prize is as an extrinsic motivator for students to come prepared with their flashcards. Remind them again:] *No cards, no play. No play, no prize!* [5 minutes]

Class 2:

3. [As students arrive, collect one set of four cards from each student. Make sure that all cards have a question on one side and—on the other side—an answer, the page number where the answer is found in *On Course*, and the student's name. Now conduct the Quiz Me Game. Have volunteers read aloud the Day 2 part of the Quiz Me directions.] *What questions do you have?* [Respond as appropriate.] *Ready, begin.* [25 minutes]

4. [Determine who has the most cards and award a prize, if you wish. If there is a tie, you can either provide all winners with a prize or have a quiz-off, where each gets to ask the other player(s) to "Quiz me" until there is a winner.] [5 minutes]

5. [Journal Writing and/or Class Discussion] *What happened during the game? For what kind of courses would flashcards be a good way to rehearse information? What did you learn or relearn during the game? How will you use what you learned?* [5–10 minutes]

Class 3:

6. [After Class 2, go through the flashcards you collected, choose the best question from each student, and create a quiz using these questions.]

7. [At the start of Class 3, administer the unannounced quiz. You may want to put a short time limit, such as 30 seconds for each question. Thus, a 20-question quiz would have a 10-minute time limit. After the test, have students exchange and grade quizzes as you elicit a correct answer for each question. Have students receive their quizzes back.] [15–20 minutes]

8. [Journal Writing and/or Class Discussion] *What did you say to yourself during the quiz? How did you feel during the quiz? What was your experience when you saw your own question on the quiz? What would it be like if you could predict all of the questions that an instructor asked on a test?* [If there are students who didn't participate in the previous days' activities—either because of absence or because of not having flashcards—ask them how they did on the quiz. Ask them if they think they would have done better if they had created flashcards and participated in the Quiz Me game.] *How will this affect how you prepare for your next test?* [10–20 minutes]

Approximate time: **Class 1:** 10–15 minutes; **Class 2:** 35–40 minutes; **Class 3:** 25–40 minutes

Instructor Notes

1. Optional: Instead of resolving "fouls" during the game, collect the offending cards and, after the game, have a class discussion about them. The issues will be (1) What is the correct answer? and/or (2) Is this a question that a fair instructor would ask?

2. If you encounter a lot of "fouls" being called, you may want to institute the "frivolous foul" rule. If you judge a foul claim to be frivolous, that player's opponent may take two cards from the player who called the frivolous foul.

Directions for Playing "Quiz Me"

Day 1: Preparation: In our next class, we are going to play a learning game called "Quiz Me." Your homework is to create two identical sets of four flashcards using information in Chapter 5 of *On Course*. Each set of four flashcards must contain one each of the following questions:

- true/false
- multiple choice
- matching
- fill in the blank (completion)

The four questions should be questions that you believe an instructor might actually ask on a test that is **challenging but fair**. In other words, they should be questions about key concepts, main or secondary ideas, or major or minor supporting details. No ridiculous questions that a fair instructor would never ask are allowed, such as "What is the third word on page 143?"

Unfair questions will be penalized. Here's how to create your flashcards. On one side of an index card, write a question. On the other side, write (1) the answer, (2) the page number where the information is found in the book, and (3) your name.

Be sure you create two identical sets of these four cards. To play, you must bring all eight cards to our next class.

Day 2: How to play Quiz Me: Everyone starts with four flashcards. The winner of "Quiz Me" is the person who has the most flashcards at the end of the game. Here's how you collect additional flashcards:

1. During the game, everyone will be walking around. You'll walk up to someone and say, "Quiz me." Your partner shows you the question on a flashcard, and you answer the question. If you answer correctly, you get the card. If you answer the question incorrectly, you do not get the card.
2. Your partner then says either, "Quiz me" or "Quiz me not." If your partner says "Quiz me," you show a question card, and your partner gives an answer. If the answer is correct, you lose your card. If the answer is incorrect, you keep your card. If your partner says, "Quiz me not," you each find another partner.
3. If you run out of cards, sit down.
4. As long as you still have flashcards, keep playing Quiz Me until the time is up.

The game will last a maximum of 20 minutes, and the person with the most flashcards at the end is the winner. Of course, if one person gets all of the cards before 20 minutes is up, that person is the winner.

FOULS: There are three conditions under which you may call a **foul** and ask for a ruling by the referee (the instructor). You can call a foul if you think . . .

(1) the answer on the flashcard is wrong and your answer is correct.
(2) your answer is an acceptable variation of the answer on the flashcard.
(3) the question is ridiculous, one that a fair instructor would never ask.

To call a foul: Raise your hand, and the referee will come and arbitrate the dispute.

Result: If you call a foul and the ruling is in your favor, you get the flashcard. If you call a foul and the ruling goes against you, you must give two flashcards to your partner. (If you have only one or two card left, hand your card(s) over to your partner and exit the game.)

EXERCISE E-2: The Memory Box

Purpose

To have students learn and apply effective rehearsing and memorizing strategies.

Supplies and Setup

One box with 50 different small objects, some common and some not so common (e.g., paperclip, piece of paper, book, comb, plastic bottle, birthday card, packet of sugar, pen, scissors, pencil sharpener, cell phone, index card, calendar page, flower, can of hair spray); have an additional 25 items available as well; table at front of room; students with paper and pens. Optional: prizes for members of the winning team. This activity is done over two class periods.

Directions

Day 1:

1. [Students in teams of five or six.] *We're going to play a game called the Memory Box. I'm going to take 50 objects from this box one at a time and place them on the table. Then I am quickly going to put the items back in the box. Afterward, I will ask you each to make a list of as many of the 50 objects as you can remember.* [If someone asks if they can take notes, the answer is no.] [Remove an item from the box, display it for about five seconds, and then place it on the table where students can still see it. When 50 items are on the table, sweep them quickly back into the box, where students can no longer see them.] [10 minutes]

2. *Now that the objects are back in a box, please make a list of as many of them as you can remember. You have five min-utes, and you must work alone.* [5 minutes]

3. [Help students assess how many items they got right. Take the items out one at a time and have students check those they listed correctly. Each student then adds up the number he or she recalled correctly. Obviously, a perfect score would be 50.] [10 minutes]

4. [Have students create groups of four to six students. It is helpful, but not essential, for the groups to be the same size.] *On a sheet of paper, make a list of each person on your team and the number of items each person remembered correctly.* [To help students assess their lists accurately, take the items out one at a time as students check them off on their lists. Collect the team lists, showing the number of items that each person remembered. Bring these lists back to the next class.] [10 minutes]

5. *In our next class, we are going to play the Memory Box game again with a few variations. I will again take 50 objects out of the box one at a time and place them on a table for viewing. They may be the same objects as last time, or they may be new objects. Next time, however,* **you will each be allowed to take notes as I remove the items from the box.** *After all items are back in the box, you will have 10 minutes working alone to organize, rehearse, and memorize your notes. After 10 minutes, I'll collect your notes, and you'll make a list of as many items as you can remember. Afterward, we'll see which team improved the most.* [Optional: *You now have the rest of the class period to make a plan for how you play next time.*] *You will find many helpful strategies in the "Rehearsing and Memorizing Study Materials" section in* On Course. *Of course your team is welcome to get together outside of class to continue mastering these skills, if you wish.* [5–15 minutes]

Day 2:

6. [Replace 25 of the items in the box with new items. Students should not be sitting with their teams.] *As in our last class, I'm going to take 50 objects from this box one at a time and place them on the table. Then I am going to put them all back in the box. This time you may take notes as I display the items.* [Remember that 25 of these items should be ones that the students have not seen previously. Remove an item from the box, display it for about five seconds, and then place it on the table where students can still see it. When 50 items are on the table, sweep them quickly back into the box, where students can no longer see them.] [10 minutes]

7. *You now have 10 minutes to study your notes before the test. You must work alone.* [Afterward, collect all notes.] [10 minutes]

8. *Now, please make a list of as many objects as you can remember. You have five minutes and you must work alone.* [5 minutes]

9. [Help students assess how many items they got right. Take the items out one at a time and have students check those they listed correctly. Each student then adds up the number he or she recalled correctly. Again, a perfect score would be 50.] [10 minutes]

10. [Have students reconvene their teams. Return to each team the score sheets you collected in the previous class.] *Now figure out how many more items your team remembered today than last time. To get the average improvement of each team member, divide your total improvement by the number of people on your team.* [On the board, record the results—average improvement—of each team.] [5 minutes]

11. [Discussion. Congratulate the team that improved the most. Ask the winning team (and later all teams) to discuss the following questions:] *What did you do differently the second time? How much did it help to take notes this time? Did you do anything to organize the notes you took? What strategies did you use to remember the items in your notes? Did you find it easier to remember items that you saw in both rounds of the game? Why or why not? What does this tell you about memory? What changes will you make in the way you study for tests?* [10–20 minutes]

Approximate time: Class 1: 35–50 minutes; **Class 2:** 40–60 minutes

EXERCISE E-3: My Academic Skills Plan for Rehearsing and Memorizing Study Materials

Purpose

Using the Wise Choice Process (from *On Course*, Chapter 2), each student designs a Personal Academic Skills plan to overcome a specific challenge he or she has with rehearsing and memorizing study materials. The goal of this Academic Skills Plan is for each student to identify one or more specific strategies that he or she will experiment with to improve rehearsing and memorizing skills. By using this powerful decision-making model, students not only solve a problem with rehearsing and memorizing study materials; they also strengthen critical and creative thinking skills that will empower them to solve many other problems in their lives.

Supplies and Setup

Students have completed reading the section in Study Skills: A Toolbox for Active Learners titled "Rehearsing and Memorizing Study Materials." Handouts: 1) "Sample Academic Skills Plan for Rehearsing and Memorizing Study Materials" and 2) "My Academic Skills Plan for Rehearsing and Memorizing Study Materials" [blank] following this exercise, one of each for all students. You may want to have extra blank forms on hand in case students need a clean form.

Directions

1. *In this activity, you'll use the six steps of the Wise Choice Process to design a personal academic skills plan for improving your ability to rehearse and memorize your study materials. In your plan, you'll identify a specific strategy you will experiment with to improve this important study skill. For an example of how to complete each of the six steps, refer to the handout titled "Sample Academic Skills Plan for Rehearsing and Memorizing Study Materials."* [5 minutes]

2. *On your blank "My Academic Skills Plan for Rehearsing and Memorizing Study Materials," complete Step 1:* **What is your present situation?** *In the box, write the biggest challenge you have with rehearsing and memorizing study materials. For suggestions, refer to the list of "Challenges with Rehearsing and Memorizing Study Materials" in On Course. Remember, for an example of how to complete all of the six steps, refer to the "Sample Academic Skills Plan for Rehearsing and Memorizing Study Materials."* [5 minutes]

3. *Complete Step 2:* **How would you like your situation to be?** *In Step 1, you identified the biggest challenge you are having with rehearsing and memorizing study materials. Now shift your attention from the challenge to how you would like your situation to be regarding this study skill. In the second row on your Academic Skills Plan, write one or more goals for rehearsing and memorizing study materials. State a goal in the present tense as if it already exists (e.g., I understand . . . rather than I will understand . . . or . . . I enjoy . . . rather than I will enjoy . . .).* [5 minutes]

4. *Complete Step 3:* **What are my possible choices?** *Revisit the list of strategies for rehearsing and memorizing study materials in On Course. Choose three strategies you think would help you overcome the challenge that you identified in Step 1 and help you achieve the desired situation (goals) you identified in Step 2. Write one strategy in Box 1, another strategy in Box 2, and a third strategy in Box 3.* [10 minutes]

5. Complete Step 4: **What's the likely outcome of each possible choice?** *Imagine yourself actually doing each of the three strategies you chose in Step 3. Write on your Academic Skills Plan what you think would be the likely outcome of doing each strategy.* [5 minutes]

6. Complete Step 5: **Which choice(s) will I commit to doing?** *It's now time to decide which one of the three strategies you think will best improve your learning and grades. Write the strategy on Step 5 of "My Academic Skills Plan for Rehearsing and Memorizing Study Materials."* [5 minutes]

7. Complete Step 6: **When and how will I evaluate my Academic Skills Plan for Rehearsing and Memorizing Study Materials?** *An effective way to evaluate any plan is to choose a future date and, at that time, compare your situation then with how you would like it to be. If at that future time you have achieved your goal(s) as described in Step 2, consider your plan a success. If your results in the future fall short of your goal(s), then the plan isn't working and needs revision. To evaluate accurately, it is helpful to make your goals as specific as possible. Because some goals are inherently general and difficult to measure (e.g., I enjoy studying), it helps if you create a scale (e.g., 1–10) on which to assess these general goals. Write your criteria for deciding whether or not your Academic Skills Plan for Rehearsing and Memorizing Study Materials is a success.* [5 minutes]

8. DISCUSSION: Invite students to share their Academic Skills Plans. If time allows, start with a Pair-Share and then move to a Whole-Group Discussion; if short of time, start with a Whole-Group Discussion. [10–20 minutes]

Approximate time: 50–60 minutes

Instructor Notes

Consider having students turn in a written assessment of their experiment with new study skills.

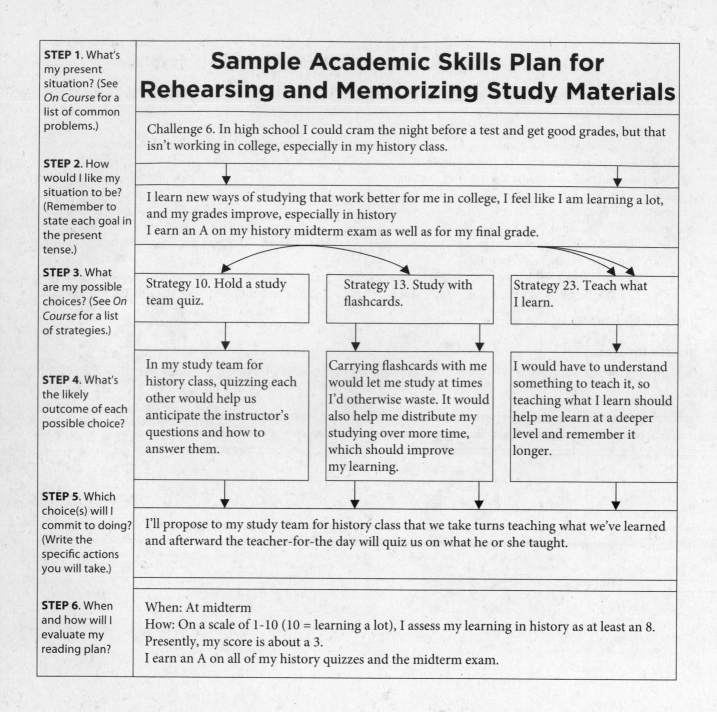

STEP 1. What's my present situation? (See *On Course* for a list of common problems.)

STEP 2. How would I like my situation to be? (Remember to state each goal in the present tense.)

STEP 3. What are my possible choices? (See *On Course* for a list of strategies.)

STEP 4. What's the likely outcome of each possible choice?

STEP 5. Which choice(s) will I commit to doing? (Write the specific actions you will take.)

STEP 6. When and how will I evaluate my reading plan?

Sample Academic Skills Plan for Rehearsing and Memorizing Study Materials

Challenge 6. In high school I could cram the night before a test and get good grades, but that isn't working in college, especially in my history class.

I learn new ways of studying that work better for me in college, I feel like I am learning a lot, and my grades improve, especially in history
I earn an A on my history midterm exam as well as for my final grade.

Strategy 10. Hold a study team quiz.

Strategy 13. Study with flashcards.

Strategy 23. Teach what I learn.

In my study team for history class, quizzing each other would help us anticipate the instructor's questions and how to answer them.

Carrying flashcards with me would let me study at times I'd otherwise waste. It would also help me distribute my studying over more time, which should improve my learning.

I would have to understand something to teach it, so teaching what I learn should help me learn at a deeper level and remember it longer.

I'll propose to my study team for history class that we take turns teaching what we've learned and afterward the teacher-for-the day will quiz us on what he or she taught.

When: At midterm
How: On a scale of 1-10 (10 = learning a lot), I assess my learning in history as at least an 8. Presently, my score is about a 3.
I earn an A on all of my history quizzes and the midterm exam.

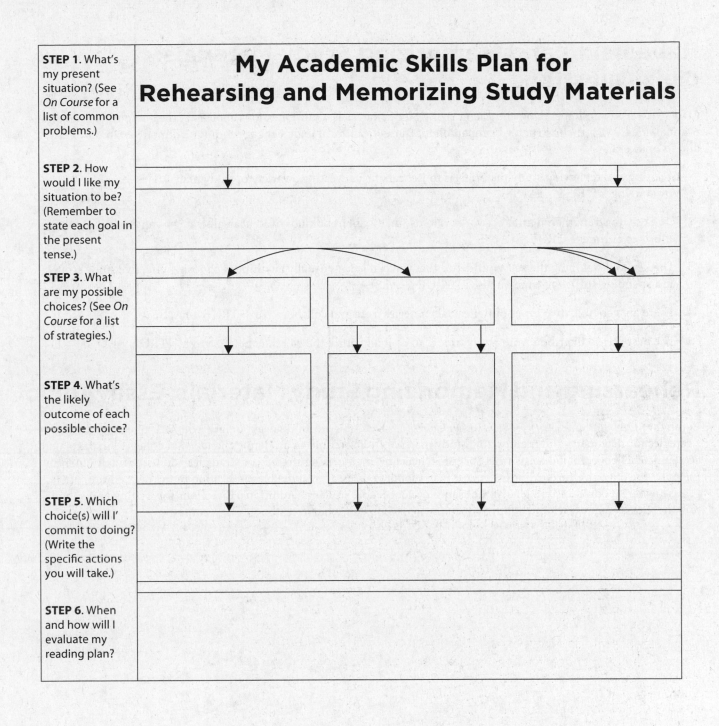

STEP 1. What's my present situation? (See *On Course* for a list of common problems.)

STEP 2. How would I like my situation to be? (Remember to state each goal in the present tense.)

STEP 3. What are my possible choices? (See *On Course* for a list of strategies.)

STEP 4. What's the likely outcome of each possible choice?

STEP 5. Which choice(s) will I' commit to doing? (Write the specific actions you will take.)

STEP 6. When and how will I evaluate my reading plan?

My Academic Skills Plan for Rehearsing and Memorizing Study Materials

Rehearsing and Memorizing Study Materials: Quiz Questions

(The Answer Key to Rehearsing and Memorizing Study Materials: Quiz Questions appears at the end of this Facilitator's Manual. Please visit the Instructor Companion Site for *On Course* at login.cengage.com for a digital version of this quiz and its answer key.)

1. Reciting and reviewing study materials is to **R**ehearsing as creating a variety of study materials is to **O**rganizing.   TRUE   FALSE

2. One way to strengthen neural networks is to use many different kinds of **R**ehearsal strategies and distribute these efforts over time.   TRUE   FALSE

3. The key to developing the self-confidence that you can learn virtually anything is choosing effective study strategies and spending sufficient time on task.   TRUE   FALSE

4. There are generally two types of **R**ehearsal strategies: rote and collaborative.   TRUE   FALSE

5. The best way to distribute your study time is to do it all within the 24 hours before a test.   TRUE   FALSE

Rehearsing and Memorizing Study Materials: Essay Topic

Using the "One Student's Story" essays in *On Course* as models, write an essay about how you used one or more new strategies for rehearsing and memorizing study materials to overcome an academic challenge in college. First explain the academic challenge; then discuss what specific rehearsing/memorizing strategy or strategies you used; finally, identify the outcome of your efforts. Your instructor may submit your essay for possible publication in the next edition of *On Course*, where it could inspire tens of thousands of your fellow students. Additional directions for writing and submitting these essays may be found at http://oncourseworkshop.com/course-textbook/essay-contest/.

F. Taking Tests

EXERCISE F-1: The Test-Smart Game

Purpose

To have students practice creating a test-smart plan.

Supplies and Setup

"Creating a Test-Smart Plan" handout (following this exercise), one copy for each student. You may prefer to project each question (table) one at a time on a PowerPoint slide so students can't work ahead. Optional: prizes for members of the winning team.

Directions

1. [Organize students into six groups. You may want to ask students to name their team. Otherwise give each team a number and place the team name/number on the whiteboard.] [5 minutes]
2. [Discussion] *What does it mean to be "test-smart"?* [Lead discussion to the concept that being test-smart means knowing how to earn the maximum number of points possible on any test. As such, one of the most important elements of creating a test-smart plan is strategically allocating the available time to earn the most points possible. The best approach is to spend more time on high-point and easy questions and less time on low-point and difficult questions.] [5 minutes]
3. [Distribute the handout.] *On your handout, look at the example history test.* [Explain how the numbers in *each* column were derived. Confirm that students understand how to determine the following:

   A. Points available for each section of the test
   B. Percent of total possible points for each section of the test
   C. The number of minutes that should then be allocated for each section of the test] [5 minutes]
4. *We're now going to play the Test-Smart Game. Starting with Test 1: Mathematics, fill in the test-smart answers as a team. When you think you have all the answers correct for Test 1, place your paper face down and stand up. The round will be over when all teams have placed their answer sheets face down and are standing up. I'll keep track of the order of finishers. Starting with the first team done, we'll check the answers. If all of the answers for the test are correct, the first team done will earn points. If any answer is incorrect, we'll move on to the answers of the second team to stand up. We'll keep going until we get to a team with all correct answers or until all teams are eliminated. If a team gets all correct answers, points will be awarded as follows:*

   First team to finish: 10 points

   Second team to finish: 8 points

   Third team to finish: 6 points

   Fourth team to finish: 4 points

   Fifth team to finish: 2 points

   Sixth team (and beyond) to finish: 1 point

   Questions? Start with Test 1: Mathematics Test. Begin! [15 minutes for first round]
5. [Keep track of the order in which teams turn over their answer sheets and stand up. When all teams have stood up, check and discuss answers starting with the first team to stand up. Discuss why answers are correct or incorrect. Track points earned for each team and offer kudos—or prizes—to the winning team.]
6. [Repeat steps 4 and 5 for Tests 2–4. If you wish, give a prize for the winning team.] [10–30 minutes, depending on number of additional rounds]
7. [Discussion] *What's the lesson here for being test-smart?* [The way you take a test can affect your grade a lot.] [5 minutes]

Approximate time: 45–65 minutes

Instructor Notes

You may want to post the scoring chart (found in Step 4) on the board or a PowerPoint slide.

Creating a Test-Smart Plan

Test: History (example) Total Time: 60 minutes; possible points: 100	Points available for this section	Percent of total possible points	Minutes for this section
Part 1: 25 true/false questions (1 point each)	25	25%	15
Part 2: 5 short-answer questions (5 points each)	25	25%	15
Part 3: 2 essay questions (25 points each)	50	50%	30
Total	100	100%	60

Test 1: Mathematics Total Time: 60 minutes; possible points: 100	Points available for this section	Percent of total possible points	Minutes for this section
Part 1: 25 true/false questions (1 point each)			
Part 2: 5 word problems (15 points each)			
Total			

Test 2: Literature Total Time: 60 minutes; possible points: 100	Points available for this section	Percent of total possible points	Minutes for this section
Part 1: 30 matching questions (1 point each)			
Part 2: 5 short-answer questions (10 points each)			
Part 3: 2 essay questions (10 points each)			
Total			

Test 3: Biology Total Time: 80 minutes; possible points: 100	Points available for this section	Percent of total possible points	Minutes for this section
Part 1: 10 fill-in-the-blank questions (5 points each)			
Part 2: 10 short-answer questions (4 points each)			
Part 3: 1 essay question (10 points)			
Total			

Test 4: Sociology Total Time: 100 minutes; possible points: 250	Points available for this section	Percent of total possible points	Minutes for this section
Part 1: 1 essay questions (85 points)			
Part 2: 15 matching questions (3 points each)			
Part 3: 5 short-answer questions (5 points each)			
Part 4: 20 multiple-choice questions (4 points each)			
Part 5: 15 true/false questions (1 point each)			
Total			

Creating a Test-Smart Plan (Answers)

Test: History (example) Total Time: 60 minutes; possible points: 100	Points available for this section	Percent of total possible points	Minutes for this section
Part 1: 25 true/false questions (1 point each)	25	25%	15
Part 2: 5 short-answer questions (5 points each)	25	25%	15
Part 3: 2 essay questions (25 points each)	50	50%	30
Total	100	100%	60

Test 1: Mathematics Total Time: 60 minutes; possible points: 100	Points available for this section	Percent of total possible points	Minutes for this section
Part 1: 25 true/false questions (1 point each)	25	25%	15
Part 2: 5 word problems (15 points each)	75	75%	45
Total	100	100%	60

Test 2: Literature Total Time: 60 minutes; possible points: 100	Points available for this section	Percent of total possible points	Minutes for this section
Part 1: 30 matching questions (1 point each)	30	30%	18
Part 2: 5 short-answer questions (10 points each)	50	50%	30
Part 3: 2 essay questions (10 points each)	20	20%	12
Total	100	100%	60

Test 3: Biology Test Total Time: 80 minutes; possible points: 100	Points available for this section	Percent of total possible points	Minutes for this section
Part 1: 10 fill-in-the-blank questions (5 points each)	50	50%	40
Part 2: 10 short-answer questions (4 points each)	40	40%	32
Part 3: 1 essay questions (10 points)	10	10%	8
Total	100	100%	80

Test 4: Sociology Total Time: 100 minutes; possible points: 250	Points available for this section	Percent of total possible points	Minutes for this section
Part 1: 1 essay questions (85 points)	85	34%	34
Part 2: 15 matching questions (3 points each)	45	18%	18
Part 3: 5 short-answer questions (5 points each)	25	10%	10
Part 4: 20 multiple-choice questions (4 points each)	80	32%	32
Part 5: 15 true/false questions (1 point each)	15	6%	6
Total	250	100%	100

EXERCISE F-2: Test Debrief

Purpose

To have students practice analyzing a past test to determine where points were lost and to make a test-smart plan for improving their score on future tests.

Supplies and Setup

Assign students to bring a copy of a graded test they have taken during the semester. If they have more than one to choose from, they should choose the one on which they got the lowest score. Have students open to the Test Debrief in *On Course* (in Study Skills: A Toolbox for Active Learners, "Taking Tests"). Students sitting in pairs.

Directions

1. *Decide who will be Partner A and who will be Partner B. Partner A will be the interviewer in the first round. Partner A, your role as the interviewer is to use your very best questioning and listening skills to help Partner B honestly and accurately fill in the Points Lost on the Test Debrief sheet. Be sure all points lost total the number of points lost on the actual test. You'll have five minutes.* [5 minutes]
2. *Switch roles. Partner B, interview Partner A and help him or her honestly and accurately fill in the Points Lost on the Test Debrief. Again, be sure all points lost total the same number of points lost on the actual test. You'll have five minutes.* [5 minutes]
3. *Partner A, now help Partner B identify the test-taking problems that cost him or her the most points and make a list of three things to do differently to improve the score on the next test. You'll have 10 minutes.* [10 minutes]
4. *Switch roles. Partner B, now help Partner A identify the test-taking problems that cost him or her the most points and make a list of three things to do differently to improve the score on the next test. You'll have 10 minutes.* [10 minutes]
5. [Discussion] *What were the problems that cost you the most points on the test? Did you uncover any problems that cost you points on the test but are not one of the seven listed on the Test Debrief? What will you do differently to improve your score on the next test?* [10–20 minutes]

Approximate time: 40–50 minutes

Instructor Notes

1. Consider listing on the board the test-taking problems and solutions the students identify during the discussion.
2. Consider asking students to report on the results they create on their next tests, discussing what they did differently and how well their new skills worked to improve their test scores.

EXERCISE F-3: Marking Up Exams

Purpose

Students learn that paying close attention to key words within test questions can help them feel confident in the answers they choose.

Supplies and Setup

Handout "Sample Multiple-Choice Questions" (following this exercise), one for each student

Directions

1. Before class, assign students to read the "Taking Tests" section in Study Skills: A Toolbox for Active Learners.
2. Organize students into five groups. Assign each group a test question from the list of questions. Ask the groups to read "Answer Multiple Choice Questions*"; then decide which strategy/strategies would apply to the test question they were given. Then they discuss how they would mark up this test question to help them reach the answer. [*This strategy is #7 in the regular edition and #10 in the Study Skills Plus edition.]
3. When all students have an answer, one student from each group comes forward with the group's question and explains to the class how and why they are marking up the test question.

Approximate time: 25–45 minutes (depending on the length of discussion time)

Instructor Notes

1. The questions included are the ones I use because they show very common examples of "types" of questions (question 1 has absolute words in three of the responses, all incorrect; question 2, uses the word *conclusively*, which students forget is an absolute word; question 3 is a good example of "choose the *best* answer" as well as "treat the question as a short answer and see if an option matches"; question 4 shows that you only need to prove two things are correct in an "all of the above" question [and that "none of the above" is typically a distracter]; and question 5 is perfect for using the "true/false" technique).
2. Ideally, if all of your students are enrolled in a different class together (e.g., a learning community), asking the other instructor to give you an old exam and choose examples from that exam would be most meaningful. The key is to ask the students to explain *why* a particular option is incorrect.

Source: Submitted by Melanie Marine, University of Wisconsin–Oshkosh, WI

Sample Multiple-Choice Questions

1. Most psychologists agree that

   A. children who grow up in institutions have no chance of succeeding in life.

   B. domestic violence is a behavior that is always found in boys from fatherless homes.

   C. those who receive little love and caring during infancy usually have personality difficulties.

   D. those who were not abused as children never abuse their children.

2. At the present time, there are relatively few women in positions of corporate management. One reason for this is

   A. until five years ago, no women had completed an MBA program.

   B. research has proven conclusively that women do not possess the skills required for corporate leadership.

   C. women have no interest in pursuing careers in management.

   D. there has been a general lack of formal and informal corporate programs for development of women as managers.

3. Milk is considered an excellent food because it

   A. tastes very good to many people.

   B. is relatively cheap considering that it is a superior food product.

   C. contains many vitamins and minerals.

   D. is used in the preparation of a variety of food products.

4. Which of the following cities is (are) in the state of New York?

   A. Syracuse

   B. Rome

   C. Albany

   D. All of the above

   E. None of the above

5. Among the causes of slow reading are

   A. lack of comprehension.

   B. reading word by word rather than in phrases.

   C. poorly developed vocabulary.

   D. too few fixations per line.

   E. A and B.

   F. A, B, and C.

   G. all of the above.

EXERCISE F-4: My Academic Skills Plan for Taking Tests

Purpose

Using the Wise Choice Process (from *On Course*, Chapter 2), each student designs a Personal Academic Skills plan to overcome a specific challenge he or she has with taking tests. The goal of this Academic Skills Plan is for each student to identify one or more specific strategies that he or she will experiment with to improve test scores. By using this powerful decision-making model, students not only solve a problem with taking tests; they also strengthen critical and creative thinking skills that will empower them to solve many other problems in their lives.

Supplies and Setup

Students have completed reading the section in Study Skills: A Toolbox for Active Learners titled "Taking Tests." Handouts: 1) "Sample Academic Skills Plan for Taking Tests" and 2) "My Academic Skills Plan for Taking Tests" [blank] following this exercise, one of each for all students. You may want to have extra blank forms on hand in case students need a clean form.

Directions

1. *In this activity, you'll use the six steps of the Wise Choice Process to design a personal academic skills plan for improving your ability to take tests. In your plan, you'll identify a specific strategy you will experiment with to improve this important skill. For an example of how to complete each of the six steps, refer to the handout titled "Sample Academic Skills Plan for Taking Tests."* [5 minutes]

2. *On your blank "My Academic Skills Plan for Taking Tests," complete Step 1:* **What is your present situation?** *In the box, write the biggest challenge you have with taking tests. For suggestions, refer to the list of "Challenges with Taking Tests" in* On Course. *Remember, for an example of how to complete all of the six steps, refer to the "Sample Academic Skills Plan for Taking Tests."* [5 minutes]

3. *Complete Step 2:* **How would you like your situation to be?** *In Step 1, you identified the biggest challenge you are having with taking tests. Now shift your attention from the challenge to how you would like your situation to be regarding this skill. In the second row on your Academic Skills Plan, write one or more goals for taking tests. State a goal in the present tense as if it already exists (e.g., I understand . . . rather than I will understand . . . or . . . I enjoy . . . rather than I will enjoy. . .).* [5 minutes]

4. *Complete Step 3:* **What are my possible choices?** *Revisit the list of strategies for taking tests in* On Course. *Choose three strategies you think would help you overcome the challenge that you identified in Step 1 and help you achieve the desired situation (goals) you identified in Step 2. Write one strategy in Box 1, another strategy in Box 2, and a third strategy in Box 3.* [10 minutes]

5. *Complete Step 4:* **What's the likely outcome of each possible choice?** *Imagine yourself actually doing each of the three strategies you chose in Step 3. Write on your Academic Skills Plan what you think would be the likely outcome of doing each strategy.* [5 minutes]

6. *Complete Step 5:* **Which choice(s) will I commit to doing?** *It's now time to decide which one of the three strategies you think will best improve your grades on tests. Write the strategy on Step 5 of "My Academic Skills Plan for Taking Tests."* [5 minutes]

7. *Complete Step 6:* **When and how will I evaluate my Academic Skills Plan for Taking Tests?** *An effective way to evaluate any plan is to choose a future date and, at that time, compare your situation then with how you would like it to be. If at that future time you have achieved your goal(s) as described in Step 2, consider your plan a success. If your results in the future fall short of your goal(s), then the plan isn't working and needs revision. To evaluate accurately, it is helpful to make your goals as specific as possible. Because some goals are inherently general and difficult to measure (e.g., I enjoy studying), it helps if you create a scale (e.g., 1–10) on which to assess these general goals. Write your criteria for deciding whether or not your Academic Skills Plan for Taking Tests is a success.* [5 minutes]

8. DISCUSSION: Invite students to share their Academic Skills Plans. If time allows, start with a Pair-Share and then move to a Whole-Group Discussion; if short of time, start with a Whole-Group Discussion. [10–20 minutes]

Approximate time: 50–60 minutes

Instructor Notes

Consider having students turn in a written assessment of their experiment with new test-taking skills.

STEP 1. What's my present situation? (See *On Course* for a list of common problems.)

STEP 2. How would I like my situation to be? (Remember to state each goal in the present tense.)

STEP 3. What are my possible choices? (See *On Course* for a list of strategies.)

STEP 4. What's the likely outcome of each possible choice?

STEP 5. Which choice(s) will I commit to doing? (Write the specific actions you will take.)

STEP 6. When and how will I evaluate my reading plan?

Sample Academic Skills Plan for Taking Tests

Challenge 9. When I study, I feel like I know the material, but I just don't test well. That gets very discouraging and ruins my academic confidence.

My test scores reflect how hard I studied and how much I have learned. I feel very confident in my test-taking abilities.

Strategy 8. Make a test-smart plan.	Strategy 13. Review my answers.	Strategy 23. Analyze my errors.
If I use my time during a test so I can get the most points, my test scores should go up.	Reviewing my answers before turning in a test should help me eliminate careless errors and improve my final test score.	I think doing a Test Debrief would show me how to eliminate errors and do better on future test.

I will practice creating a test-smart plan for every test I have already taken this semester. I'll complete a Test Debrief for every test I have taken this semester and make a list of solutions to the test-taking problems that caused me to lose points.

When: After every test
How: My score on every test is higher than my score on the previous test in that subject. On a scale of 1–10 (10 = very confident), I assess my confidence in test-taking as a 9 or 10. My present confidence is about a 3.

STEP 1. What's my present situation? (See *On Course* for a list of common problems.)

STEP 2. How would I like my situation to be? (Remember to state each goal in the present tense.)

STEP 3. What are my possible choices? (See *On Course* for a list of strategies.)

STEP 4. What's the likely outcome of each possible choice?

STEP 5. Which choice(s) will I commit to doing? (Write the specific actions you will take.)

STEP 6. When and how will I evaluate my reading plan?

My Academic Skills Plan for Taking Tests

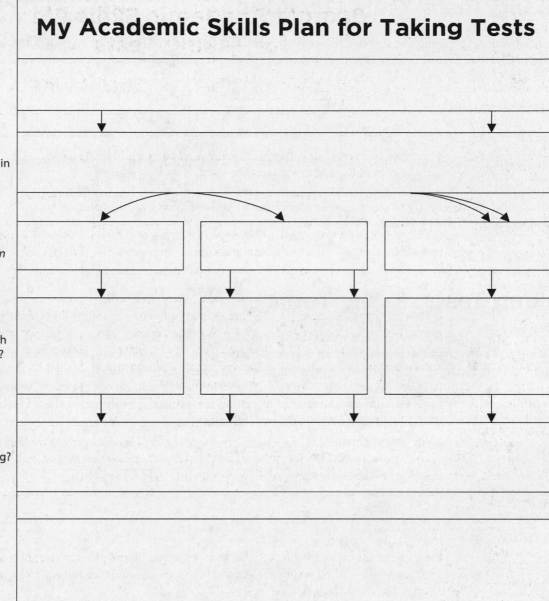

Taking Tests: Quiz Questions

(The Answer Key to Taking Tests: Quiz Questions appears at the end of this Facilitator's Manual. Please visit the Instructor Companion Site for *On Course* at login.cengage.com for a digital version of this quiz and its answer key.)

1. Factors that determine how well you score on tests include preparation for the test, test-taking skills, and use of feedback on prior tests.   TRUE   FALSE

2. Test scores are not a good way of determining if you are off course in college.   TRUE   FALSE

3. Visualizing yourself successfully taking a test prepares you to think, feel, and act positively during that test.   TRUE   FALSE

4. It's a good idea to stay up all night studying before a test and use every available minute for preparation.   TRUE   FALSE

5. Before you begin answering questions on a test, take a few minutes to preview it.   TRUE   FALSE

Taking Tests: Essay Topic

Using the "One Student's Story" essays in *On Course* as models, write an essay about how you used one or more new strategies for taking tests to overcome an academic challenge in college. First explain the academic challenge; then discuss what specific test-taking strategy or strategies you used; finally, identify the outcome of your efforts. Your instructor may submit your essay for possible publication in the next edition of *On Course*, where it could inspire tens of thousands of your fellow students. Additional directions for writing and submitting these essays may be found at http://oncourseworkshop.com/course-textbook/essay-contest/.

G. Writing

EXERCISE G-1: Beautiful Questions

Purpose

To have students experience the value of using their readers' likely questions to organize writing.

Supplies and Setup

Envelopes, one for each student; index cards, 25 for each student; whiteboard and markers. In a previous class, assign students to bring with them a one-sentence thesis statement for an upcoming essay. It is wise to illustrate how a thesis is composed of topic and a claim. For more on this skill, see "Define Your Thesis" in the "Before Writing" section in *Study Skills: A Toolbox for Active Learners*.

Directions

1. [Put students in groups of six or seven, sitting in a circle. Give each student an envelope and 25 index cards. Going around the room, have each student say his or her thesis statement aloud. If needed, help students revise their thesis statements so that they contain a topic and a claim. After all students have a workable thesis statement, ask them to write theirs on the outside of their envelopes.] [5–10 minutes]

2. *Pass your envelope to the person on your left. When you receive an envelope, read the thesis statement written on it. Then pause and think about beautiful questions that you might ask about that statement. The term "beautiful questions" comes from a line in a poem by e.e. cummings, who wrote: "Always the beautiful answer who asks a more beautiful question." What do you think he means by a "beautiful question?"* [Elicit some answers, such as "A beautiful question is one that causes someone to see something in an entirely new way." or "A beautiful question is one that causes someone to dig much deeper into a complex topic."] [5 minutes]

3. *Okay, let's practice asking beautiful questions. Suppose the thesis statement on the envelope reads, "A college degree is essential for success in the 21st century." The topic is "a college degree," and the claim is that "a college degree is essential for success in the 21st century." What beautiful questions would you want to ask the author about this claim?* [Elicit a large number of questions and record them on the whiteboard.] [5 minutes]

4. *Now turn to the thesis statement written on the envelope you're holding. What "beautiful question" comes to your mind about it? Write it on an index card and put it in the envelope. Now think of another beautiful question, write it on a card, and put it in the envelope. And finally, add a third card with a beautiful question. When you've added three questions, pass the envelope to the person on your left. Keep going around your small group until you get your envelope back.* [Completed envelopes should have 18 to 21 cards in them.] [10–15 minutes]

5. *Now that you have your envelope back, take out the cards and organize them in related piles. Perhaps two questions are almost the same, so you put them in the same pile.* [5 minutes]

6. *Now look over your questions and pick your three or four favorites. These are the three or four questions that you think are the most important to answer in your essay. Place them in the order you think they should be answered.* [5 minutes]

7. *Now, on a blank sheet of paper, write your thesis statement, and under it, on separate lines, write the three or four questions in the order you think they should be answered. Below the last question, write, "Conclusion."* [5 minutes]

8. [Journal Writing and/or Class Discussion] *What you have created is a question outline. How have you organized your writing assignments in the past? How helpful do you think this question outline would be in organizing your ideas for an essay? How could you generate a list of questions on your own? What is the advantage of getting questions directly from your potential readers? If you didn't know the answer to a question, where could you find it? What did you learn or relearn about organizing an essay? Could you use a question outline on an essay test? How will you use/or adapt this approach in your other classes?* [10–20 minutes]

Approximate time: 40–65 minutes

Instructor Notes

You might ask each student to nominate the "most beautiful question" he or she received. Then ask the student to explain why the question is the most beautiful. What criteria did he or she use to award that distinction?

EXERCISE G-2: Playing with Style

Purpose

To provide students with an experience of revising the style of their writing. This activity will also help students become more proficient at writing on a computer.

Supplies and Setup

"Playing with Style" handout (following this exercise). Homework is assigned in class 1. Discussion is held in class 2. Students need access to a computer and the *On Course* text.

Directions

1. [Class 1: Distribute and review the handout. Answer questions and assign the activity for homework. Be sure students understand what is meant by "reading level" and how they can use a word-processing program to determine the reading level of prose writing.] [10 minutes]

2. [Class 2:] *What is the reading level of the original essay?* [The original essay has a Flesch-Kincaid reading grade level of 9.4, according to Word.] *So the reading level is about the middle of the first year in high school. Does the reading level of the essay surprise you? Did you think it would be higher or lower than grade 9.4? What do you think is the average reading level of most U.S. newspapers?* [Answer: "about eighth grade," according to Philip Meyer in his book *The Vanishing Newspaper* (2009).] *Does that surprise you? Why do you suppose the reading level of most newspapers is so low?* [5 minutes]

3. [Place students in pairs.] *Read to each other the essay you revised to have a reading level two grades* below *that of the original essay. If you were successful, the reading level of your revision is grade 7.4 or below. Discuss the changes you made to lower the reading level.* [10 minutes]

4. *Now, read to each other the essay you revised to have a reading level two grades* above *the original essay. If you were successful, the reading level is grade 11.4 or above. Discuss the changes you made to raise the reading level.* [10 minutes]

5. [Class Discussion:] *What did you discover about how to lower or raise the reading level of your writing?* [e.g., change the number of sentences or paragraphs, the number of words or sentences, the number of characters or words, the number of passive sentences] *Who would like to nominate their partner to read an essay that has a reading level below grade 7.4?* [Discuss the style of the essay.] *Who would like to nominate their partner to read an essay that has a reading level above grade 11.4?* [Discuss the style of the essay.] *What did you learn or relearn? How will you use this knowledge when you write?* [20–30 minutes, depending on how many essays you discuss.]

Approximate time: **Class 1:** 10 minutes; **Class 2:** 45–55 minutes

Instructor Notes

1. To save students the need of typing the Lindsey Beck essay that they will be modifying, you could send it to them via email or post it on a course management system. You can view a video of Lindsey Beck reading her essay at http://OnCourseWorkshop.com → Educator Resources → Video Gallery → Emotional Intelligence.

2. When assigning the homework, consider pairing students who are computer savvy with students who are not. The computer-savvy students can help their partners with technical problems.

3. When pairing students in the second class, confirm that each has completed the homework. For students without completed homework, consider asking them to leave the room, do the work, and bring it to you by the end of the day. When students learn that your homework assignments have a "no escape" policy, they are more likely to complete them on time.

4. If your course meets in a smart classroom or you have access to a computer lab, it is possible to do the writing part of this activity during class time. However, this approach is less desirable because students finish the initial writing at very different times. If doing the writing part of the activity in class, circulate and help students who are having challenges with either the technology or the writing.

Playing with Style

1. Use the index in the back of *On Course* to find the One Student's Story essay by student Lindsey Beck. Type her essay into a word-processing program on a computer. Then determine the reading level of Lindsey's essay and write that number at the end of the essay.

   To determine the reading level of a piece of writing using Word 2013:
   Click the **File** tab → **Options** → **Proofing**
   Under **When correcting spelling and grammar in Word**, make sure all five boxes are checked.
   Open the file you want to check and click **File** → **Review** → **Spelling and Grammar**. When done with the spell/grammar check, Word will provide the document's Flesch-Kincaid reading level (last number in the results).

2. Make two more copies of Lindsey's essay.

   To make copies using Word 2013:
   Place the cursor at the beginning of the essay.
   Left click the mouse, drag the cursor to the bottom of the essay, and release the left click. (The entire essay will now be highlighted.)
   Left click the "copy" icon on the home tab. (You have now created a copy of the essay in the computer's memory.)
   Now place the cursor where you want to insert a copy of the essay.
   Left click the "paste" icon on the home tab. (A copy of the essay will appear.)
   Repeat this process to create a total of three copies of the essay.

3. Without changing the meaning of Lindsey's essay, revise the first copy until the reading level is at least two whole grades *lower* than the original. For example, if the original essay has a reading level of 8.4, your revision should have a reading level of 6.4 or lower. At the end of the essay, type the reading level of your revised copy.

4. Without changing the meaning of Lindsey's essay, revise the second copy until the reading level is at least two whole grades *higher* than the original. For example, if the original essay has a reading level of 8.4, your revision should have a reading level of 10.4 or higher. At the end of the essay, type the reading level of your revised copy. Then print each essay on a separate piece of paper.

5. Bring completed copies of the three essays to our next class. They are your tickets to *enter*, and you must have all three tickets to attend.

EXERCISE G-3: My Academic Skills Plan for Writing

Purpose

Using the Wise Choice Process (from *On Course*, Chapter 2), each student designs a Personal Academic Skills plan to overcome a specific challenge he or she has with writing. The goal of this Academic Skills Plan is for each student to identify one or more specific strategies that he or she will experiment with to improve writing skills. By employing this powerful decision-making model, students not only solve a problem with writing; they also strengthen critical and creative thinking skills that will empower them to solve many other problems in their lives.

Supplies and Setup

Students have completed reading the section in Study Skills: A Toolbox for Active Learners titled "Writing." Handouts: 1) "Sample Academic Skills Plan for Writing" and 2) "My Academic Skills Plan for Writing" [blank] following this exercise, one of each for all students. You may want to have extra blank forms on hand in case students need a clean form.

Directions

9. *In this activity, you'll use the six steps of the Wise Choice Process to design a personal academic skills plan for improving your writing. In your plan, you'll identify a specific strategy you will experiment with to improve this important study skill. For an example of how to complete each of the six steps, refer to the handout titled "Sample Academic Skills Plan for Writing."* [5 minutes]

10. *On your blank "My Academic Skills Plan for Writing," complete Step 1:* **What is your present situation?** *In the box, write the biggest challenge you have with writing. For suggestions, refer to the list of "Challenges with Writing" in On Course. Remember, for an example of how to complete all of the six steps, refer to the "Sample Academic Skills Plan for Writing."* [5 minutes]

11. *Complete Step 2:* **How would you like your situation to be?** *In Step 1, you identified the biggest challenge you are having with writing. Now shift your attention from the challenge to how you would like your situation to be regarding this study skill. In the second row on your Academic Skills Plan, write one or more goals for writing. State a goal in the present tense as if it already exists (e.g., I understand . . . rather than I will understand . . . or . . . I enjoy . . . rather than I will enjoy . . .).* [5 minutes]

12. *Complete Step 3:* **What are my possible choices?** *Revisit the list of strategies for writing in On Course. Choose three strategies you think would help you overcome the challenge that you identified in Step 1 and help you achieve the desired situation (goals) you identified in Step 2. Write one strategy in Box 1, another strategy in Box 2, and a third strategy in Box 3.* [10 minutes]

13. *Complete Step 4:* **What's the likely outcome of each possible choice?** *Imagine yourself actually doing each of the three strategies you chose in Step 3. Write on your Academic Skills Plan what you think would be the likely outcome of doing each strategy.* [5 minutes]

14. *Complete Step 5:* **Which choice(s) will I commit to doing?** *It's now time to decide which one of the three strategies you think will best improve your learning and grades. Write the strategy on Step 5 of "My Academic Skills Plan for Writing."* [5 minutes]

15. *Complete Step 6:* **When and how will I evaluate my Academic Skills Plan for Writing?** *An effective way to evaluate any plan is to choose a future date and, at that time, compare your situation then with how you would like it to be. If at that future time you have achieved your goal(s) as described in Step 2, consider your plan a success. If your results in the future fall short of your goal(s), then the plan isn't working and needs revision. To evaluate accurately, it is helpful to make your goals as specific as possible. Because some goals are inherently general and difficult to measure (e.g., I enjoy writing), it helps if you create a scale (e.g., 1–10) on which to assess these general goals. Write your criteria for deciding whether or not your Academic Skills Plan for Writing is a success.* [5 minutes]

16. DISCUSSION: Invite students to share their Academic Skills Plans. If time allows, start with a Pair-Share and then move to a Whole-Group Discussion; if short of time, start with a Whole-Group Discussion. [10–20 minutes]

Approximate time: 50–60 minutes

Instructor Notes

Consider having students turn in a written assessment of their experiment with new study skills.

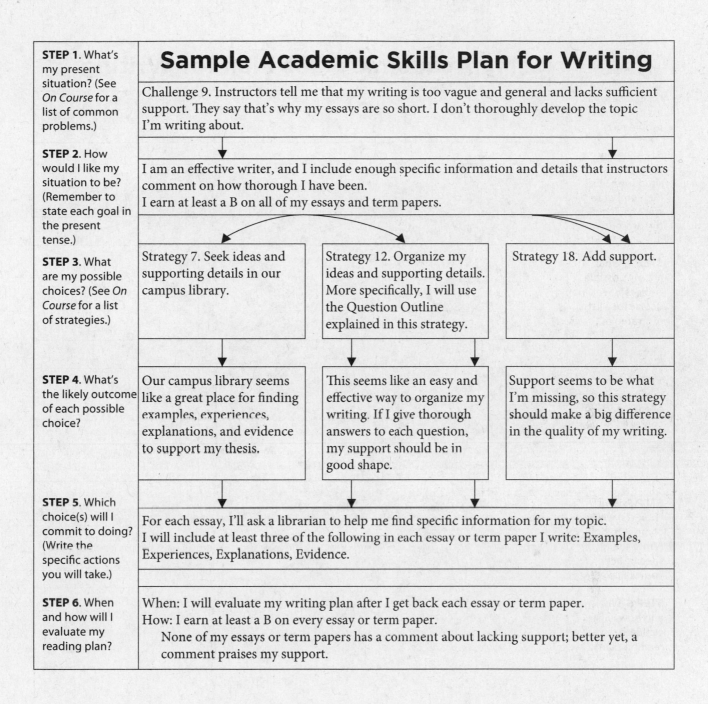

Sample Academic Skills Plan for Writing

STEP 1. What's my present situation? (See *On Course* for a list of common problems.)

Challenge 9. Instructors tell me that my writing is too vague and general and lacks sufficient support. They say that's why my essays are so short. I don't thoroughly develop the topic I'm writing about.

STEP 2. How would I like my situation to be? (Remember to state each goal in the present tense.)

I am an effective writer, and I include enough specific information and details that instructors comment on how thorough I have been.
I earn at least a B on all of my essays and term papers.

STEP 3. What are my possible choices? (See *On Course* for a list of strategies.)

Strategy 7. Seek ideas and supporting details in our campus library.

Strategy 12. Organize my ideas and supporting details. More specifically, I will use the Question Outline explained in this strategy.

Strategy 18. Add support.

STEP 4. What's the likely outcome of each possible choice?

Our campus library seems like a great place for finding examples, experiences, explanations, and evidence to support my thesis.

This seems like an easy and effective way to organize my writing. If I give thorough answers to each question, my support should be in good shape.

Support seems to be what I'm missing, so this strategy should make a big difference in the quality of my writing.

STEP 5. Which choice(s) will I commit to doing? (Write the specific actions you will take.)

For each essay, I'll ask a librarian to help me find specific information for my topic.
I will include at least three of the following in each essay or term paper I write: Examples, Experiences, Explanations, Evidence.

STEP 6. When and how will I evaluate my reading plan?

When: I will evaluate my writing plan after I get back each essay or term paper.
How: I earn at least a B on every essay or term paper.
   None of my essays or term papers has a comment about lacking support; better yet, a comment praises my support.

STEP 1. What's my present situation? (See *On Course* for a list of common problems.)

STEP 2. How would I like my situation to be? (Remember to state each goal in the present tense.)

STEP 3. What are my possible choices? (See *On Course* for a list of strategies.)

STEP 4. What's the likely outcome of each possible choice?

STEP 5. Which choice(s) will I commit to doing? (Write the specific actions you will take.)

STEP 6. When and how will I evaluate my reading plan?

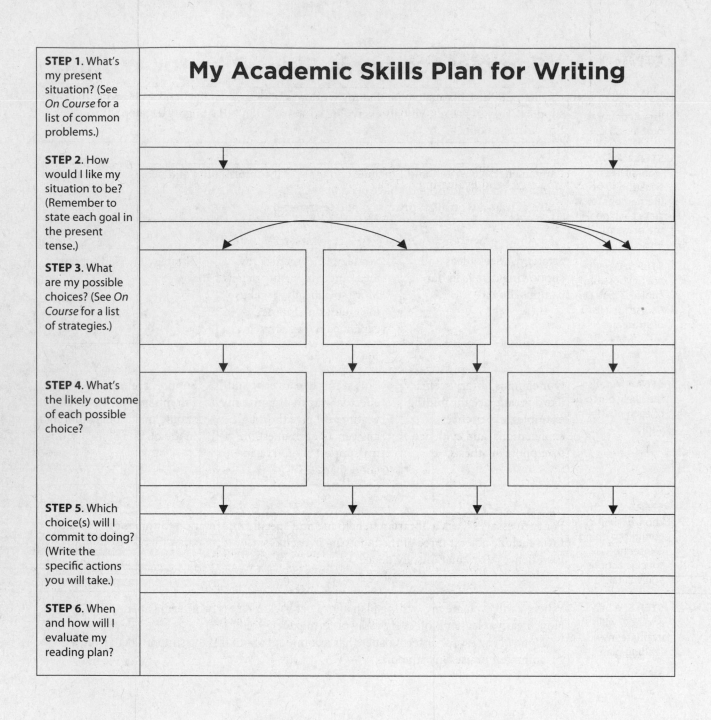

My Academic Skills Plan for Writing

Writing: Quiz Questions

(The Answer Key to Writing: Quiz Questions appears at the end of this Facilitator's Manual. Please visit the Instructor Companion Site for *On Course* at login.cengage.com for a digital version of this quiz and its answer key.)

1. Most experts recognize three components in the writing process: writing, revising, and editing.   TRUE   FALSE

2. Effective writing enhances learning because it incorporates all the elements of the CORE learning system: Collecting, Organizing, Rehearsing, and Evaluating.   TRUE   FALSE

3. A ___ states the most important idea you want to convey to your audience.

4. The two most common kinds of writing in college courses are informative and

   A. entertaining.

   B. persuasive.

   C. philosophical.

   D. personal.

5. Which of the following is NOT one of the 4Es that are supporting details as described in this chapter?

   A. Can you give EVIDENCE to support that?

   B. Can you EVALUATE your support?

   C. Can you give an EXPERIENCE to illustrate that?

   D. Can you EXPLAIN that further?

Writing: Essay Topic

Using the "One Student's Story" essays in *On Course* as models, write an essay about how you used one or more new writing strategies to overcome an academic challenge in college. First explain the academic challenge; then discuss what specific writing strategy or strategies you used; finally, identify the outcome of your efforts. Your instructor may submit your essay for possible publication in the next edition of *On Course*, where it could inspire tens of thousands of your fellow students. Additional directions for writing and submitting these essays may be found at http://oncourseworkshop.com/course-textbook/essay-contest/.

Answer Key to Quiz Questions

Chapter 1

Money Matters

Answers: 1. TRUE   2. TRUE   3. FALSE (grants do not have to be paid back, but loans do)   4. D   5. B

Understanding the Culture of Higher Education

Answers: 1. A   2. FALSE (these are features of deep culture)   3. TRUE   4. B   5. deep

Understanding the Expectations of College and University Educators

Answers: 1. TRUE   2. FALSE   3. TRUE   4. FALSE   5. TRUE

Understanding Yourself

Answers: 1. experiences   2. hard   3. soft   4. choices   5. TRUE

***On Course* at Work: Soft Skills at Work**

Answers: 1. TRUE   2. TRUE   3. FALSE   4. B   5. A

Chapter 2

Adopting a Creator Mindset

Answers: 1. A   2. B   3. D   4. D   5. TRUE

Mastering Creator Language

Answers: 1. B   2. A   3. FALSE (Creator)   4. C   5. A

Making Wise Decisions

Answers: 1. TRUE   2. FALSE (Your Inner Guide will best help you define your present situation.)
3. D   4. TRUE   5. TRUE

***On Course* at Work: Personal Responsibility at Work**

Answers: 1. TRUE   2. TRUE   3. TRUE   4. D   5. A

Believing in Yourself: Change Your Inner Conversation

Answers: 1. B   2. Critic   3. Defender   4. C   5. TRUE

Chapter 3

Creating Inner Motivation

Answers: 1. motivation 2. C 3. D 4. D 5. B

Designing a Compelling Life Plan

Answers: 1. TRUE 2. time 3. goal 4. Specific 5. C

Committing to Your Goals and Dreams

Answers: 1. commitment 2. method 3. FALSE (He sold an article to *Sports Illustrated* magazine.) 4. TRUE 5. E

On Course at Work: Self-Motivation at Work

Answers: 1. FALSE 2. FALSE 3. FALSE 4. A 5. C

Believing in Yourself: Write a Personal Affirmation

Answers: 1. FALSE 2. affirmation 3. truth 4. B 5. A

Chapter 4

Acting on Purpose

Answers: 1. URGENT 2. NOT URGENT 3. URGENT 4. NOT URGENT 5. B

Mastering Effective Self-Management

Answers: 1. FALSE (We can only manage ourselves and our own actions.) 2. C 3. A 4. B 5. TRUE

Developing Self-Discipline

Answers: 1. TRUE 2. FALSE (persistence, not creativity) 3. TRUE 4. A 5. FALSE

On Course at Work: Self-Management at Work

Answers: 1. TRUE 2. TRUE 3. FALSE 4. D 5. C

Believing in Yourself: Develop Self-Confidence

Answers: 1. TRUE 2. CAN 3. TRUE 4. C. 5. FALSE (a history of success, not *trying to be successful*)

Chapter 5

Creating a Support System

Answers: 1. TRUE 2. FALSE (Interdependence, not independence, is highly regarded.) 3. TRUE 4. C (although a group name couldn't hurt) 5. C

Strengthening Relationships with Active Listening

Answers: 1. TRUE   2. FALSE (expansion)   3. FALSE   4. TRUE   5. FALSE (100 percent responsibility)

Respecting Cultural Differences

Answers: 1. TRUE (actually 47 percent)   2. FALSE   3. B   4. microaggressions   5. A

On Course at Work: Interdependence at Work

Answers: 1. TRUE   2. TRUE   3. TRUE   4. D   5. C

Believing in Yourself: Be Assertive

Answers: 1. C   2. A   3. B   4. E (You may want to confirm that all of these services are, in fact, available at your college.)   5. Specific

Chapter 6

Recognizing When You Are Off Course

Answers: 1. B   2. TRUE   3. FALSE   4. TRUE   5. FALSE

Identifying Your Scripts

Answers: 1. D   2. TRUE   3. beliefs   4. D   5. FALSE (The opposite is true.)

Rewriting Your Outdated Scripts

Answers: 1. TRUE   2. TRUE   3. TRUE   4. TRUE   5. beliefs

On Course at Work: Self-Awareness at Work

Answers: 1. TRUE   2. TRUE   3. FALSE (the Holland Code helps you match your interests with career choices.) 4. D   5. B

Believing in Yourself: Write Your Own Rules

Answers: 1. TRUE   2. FALSE (Some of our unconscious rules are helpful.)   3. B   4. FALSE (The more classes students missed, the lower their grades were.)   5. value

Chapter 7

Developing a Learning Orientation to Life

Answers: 1. fixed   2. growth   3. B   4. FALSE (It's the other way around.)   5. B

Discovering Your Preferred Ways of Learning

Answers: 1. FALSE   2. A   3. C   4. FALSE   5. TRUE

Employing Critical Thinking

Answers: 1. TRUE   2. C   3. TRUE   4. FALSE (You are asking for a reason.)   5. TRUE

On Course at Work: Lifelong Learning at Work

Answers: 1. FALSE   2. TRUE   3. FALSE   4. the career center; the library (Answers may vary or be very specific by campus, such as the Donaghey Center for Career Excellence.)   5. A

Believing in Yourself: Develop Self-Respect

Answers: 1. how   2. TRUE   3. FALSE   4. TRUE   5. A

Chapter 8

Understanding Emotional Intelligence

Answers: 1. FALSE   2. TRUE   3. B   4. C   5. D

Reducing Stress

Answers: 1. TRUE   2. TRUE   3. TRUE   4. A   5. FALSE

Increasing Happiness

Answers: 1. TRUE   2. FALSE (Choices we make influence about 40 percent of our happiness.)   3. C   4. D   5. strawberry.

On Course at Work: Emotional Intelligence at Work

Answers: 1. TRUE   2. FALSE (emotional self-management)   3. FALSE   4. D   5. C

Believing in Yourself: Develop Self-Acceptance

Answers: 1. FALSE (It is our reputation with ourselves.)   2. TRUE   3. B   4. F   5. FALSE (We can learn higher self-esteem just as we learned lower self-esteem.)

Toolbox: Active Learning

Answers: 1. TRUE   2. A.   3. FALSE   4. D.   5. Evaluate

Toolbox: Reading

Answers: 1. TRUE   2. TRUE   3. FALSE (main idea)   4. TRUE   5. FALSE

Toolbox: Taking Notes

Answers: 1. TRUE   2. FALSE   3. TRUE   4. B   5. D

Toolbox: Organizing Study Materials

Answers: 1. TRUE   2. FALSE (The <u>C</u>ollected information needs to be <u>O</u>rganized before it is <u>R</u>ehearsed.)
3. TRUE   4. TRUE   5. TRUE

Toolbox: Rehearsing and Memorizing Study Materials

Answers: 1. TRUE   2. TRUE   3. TRUE   4. FALSE (elaborative, not collaborative)   5. FALSE

Toolbox: Taking Tests

Answers: 1. TRUE   2. FALSE   3. TRUE   4. FALSE   5. TRUE

Toolbox: Writing

Answers: 1. FALSE (also prewriting)   2. TRUE   3. thesis or main idea   4. B   5. B